Praise for

Crescent and Dove

"*Crescent and Dove* brilliantly infuses sound social science with religious interpretations of Islamic sources. The fresh analyses and insights provided by Huda and these diverse contributors are concise and convincing, adding the cultural dimension needed to comprehend the contemporary Muslim world. The contributors demonstrate a skillful and contextual knowledge of Islamic sources and challenge several traditionally held viewpoints. This book is a must-read for strategists, professionals, educators, and students of peace and nonviolence in the Muslim world."
—**Amr Abdalla,** University for Peace

"A book of tremendous importance and sublime clarity that completely upends the widespread perception of Islam as a religion of violence and intolerance. The essays in this collection should be read by all who wish to understand the role of Islam and Islamic thought in global affairs."
—**Reza Aslan,** author of *No god but God* and *Beyond Fundamentalism*

"Few topics are more important today than religion and peacebuilding. Qamar-ul Huda's groundbreaking *Crescent and Dove* is a must-read for policymakers, scholars, and students of international affairs in a world that too often fails to distinguish between the acts of a tiny minority of extremists and the religion of Islam."
—**John L. Esposito,** professor of religion and international affairs, Georgetown University

"Few books have the potential to make a dramatic and positive impact on the world, but that is the case with *Crescent and Dove*. Expanding existing theory on conflict resolution and peacemaking in Islam, this book shows how peace is made and conflicts resolved in Muslim communities throughout the world. It introduces the topics of Muslim peacemakers, religious symbols and discourse, cultural practices and influential documents that all further peaceful Muslim communities and conflict resolution between Muslims and others. The often-ignored role of Muslim women as leaders for peace and agents of change is another important contribution."
—**Ingrid Mattson,** professor of Islamic Studies, Hartford Seminary, and president of the Islamic Society of North America

"Behind explosive headlines and horrific images of violence is a quieter story of ordinary Muslims around the world drawing on the same faith to build peaceful communities. *Crescent and Dove: Peace and Conflict Resolution in Islam* tells this story. Drawing upon case studies and expanding on existing theory, Qamar-ul Huda takes readers to the largely unknown world of Islam-inspired peacebuilding. The book gives us a rare window into the existing tools and resources inherent in Islam to resolve conflict and promote cooperation. No policymaker, development leader, or civil society worker engaging Muslim societies can afford to miss this book."
—**Dalia Mogahed,** executive director, senior analyst, Center for Muslim
    Studies, GALLUP

"This comprehensive edition analyzes the principles, methods, and approaches of peacemaking and conflict resolution in Islam and offers insightful recommendations for developing efficient practical skills and knowledge for religious leaders in the field of peacebuilding. Qamar-ul Huda's well-timed work is a formative contribution to future studies as well as practical initiatives in the field."
—**Mehmet Pacaci,** affiliate professor, George Mason University

"This timely and incisive critique analyzes the intellectual heritage of Islam and the practical challenges of peacemaking, conflict resolution, mediation, and reconciliation in Muslim communities. Written by preeminent Islamic scholar Qamar-ul Huda and other experts, *Crescent and Dove* underscores the importance of Islamic peacemaking and peacebuilding initiatives at all levels in Muslim communities worldwide—initiatives by high-ranking scholars, regional and local-level politicians, imams, teachers, lawyers, activists, religious educators, artists, musicians and other civil society actors. The broad, strategic, and insightful recommendations for developing institutional capacity to prevent violent conflict and to promote sustainable peace make this a seminal work that should be required reading for agents of peace everywhere."
—**Abdul Wahab,** ambassador of the Organization of the Islamic
    Conference to the United Nations

Crescent and Dove

Crescent and Dove

Peace and Conflict Resolution in Islam

Qamar-ul Huda

Editor

UNITED STATES INSTITUTE OF PEACE PRESS
WASHINGTON, D.C.

UNITED STATES INSTITUTE OF PEACE
1200 17th Street, NW, Suite 200
Washington, DC 20036-3011
www.usip.org

First published 2010.

Printed in the United States of America.

The paper used in this publication meets the minimum requirements of American National Standards for Information Science—Permanence of Paper for Printed Library Materials, ANSI Z39.48-1984.

Library of Congress Cataloging-in-Publication Data

Crescent and dove : peace and conflict resolution in Islam / Qamar-ul Huda, editor.
    p. cm.
    "This book is the result of an international conference of Muslim scholars and practitioners who came together to address these questions, discussing contemporary Islam, its relation to violence and peacemaking, and the possibilities for reframing and reinterpreting methodologically the problems of violence and peacemaking in Muslim communities"—Introd.
    Includes bibliographical references and index.
    ISBN 978-1-60127-060-3 (pbk. : alk. paper)
    1. Peace—Religious aspects—Islam. 2. Conflict management—Religious aspects—Islam. 3. Islam and world politics. I. Huda, Qamar-ul, 1968– II. United States Institute of Peace Press.
    BP190.5.P34C74 2010
    297.2'7—dc22

                                                2010012562

For Hakim Mohammed Said,
Scholar, healer, and peacemaker

Contents

Preface

In the Name of God, the Compassionate, the Merciful

The Holy Qur'an relates the first human being was God's *Khalifah* (vice-regent) on earth (7:11; 2:29-34) into whom God blew His own Spirit (32:7-9; 15:28-34; 38:72). It also shows that all human beings are equal in respect of their origin and creation (4:1; 6:98; 49:13). These sacred passages have led the overwhelming majority of Muslims over the centuries to respect all human beings and to strive for friendly mutual coexistence with all peoples. Nothing on earth is more important than to continue this legacy and that all humanity should live harmoniously and peacefully together.

This excellent volume of essays by scholars and practitioners of Islam, edited by Dr. Qamar-ul Huda, critically analyzes the intellectual heritage of Islam with the practical challenges of peacemaking, conflict resolution, mediation, and reconciliation in Islam. In a time when religious extremist groups and zealous secularists pose serious threats to societies, these essays insightfully examine developing civil society, cultivating an ethos of pluralism, broadening political and economic systems, tapping into religious leaders for peace-building activities, encouraging critical thinking skills in educational institutions, and investing in human capital as the strongest steps toward peace-building efforts in Muslim communities.

This book also highlights real initiatives in Islamic peacemaking that are occurring in all Muslim communities every day and throughout the world. These peace-building activities include activities by high-ranking religious scholars, as exemplified in *The Amman Message* and the *A Common Word* initiatives, and profound work by regional and local-level imams, teachers, lawyers, activists, religious educators, and others in civil society. The recommendations in this volume to develop institutional capacity to prevent violent conflict from emerging and promote sustainable peace, promote economic and human development, synchronize peace-building resources, and cultivate a culture of peace-building are all extremely important steps that need to be taken in our times. The *Crescent and Dove: Peace and*

Conflict Resolution in Islam is thus a much-needed comprehensive, infor-
mative, practical-minded and well-intentioned work that could well lead
to some real and important developments for world peace and harmony in
the future, *Deo Volente*.

HRH Prince Ghazi bin Muhammad bin Talal
Amman, Jordan, 2010

Acknowledgments

This publication is the result of the efforts of many supportive people. I am first of all grateful for the contributors of the book who participated in a three-day conference on the subject of Islamic peacemaking, violence, nonviolence, religion, and conflict resolution. I am especially thankful to David Smock for being supportive and encouraging my research and fieldwork in Islamic peacemaking. Many thanks are due to Valerie Norville, Michelle Slavin, Kurt Volkan, and Brian Slattery, who meticulously helped in the publication of the manuscript. At USIP I am grateful to A. Heather Coyne, Susan Hayward, Ginny Bouvier, Steve Riskin, Renata Stuebner, Peter Weinberger, Jeff Helsing, and Linda Bishai for providing valuable feedback. I am indebted to Kiran Sharma and Jim Cornelius for diligently finding resources promptly and being patient with my endless requests for obscure materials.

There are several people whom I have met in the course of researching religious peacemaking and whose work inspired my thinking, writing, and fieldwork programming. I thank Amr Abdalla, Mohammed Abu-Nimer, Ayse Kadayifci-Orellana, John Paul Lederach, Andrea Bartoli, Ahmad Iravani, and Scott Appleby. Dr. Seyyed Hossein Nasr, Mufti Munib ur-Rehman, Hafiz Khalil, Azhar Hussein, Maulana Rashid Ahmed Thanvi, Saud Anwar, Russell Cogar, and Ahmed Mirza are inspiring figures as well.

Finally, without the persistent loving support of my wife, Rena, this project would not have been possible. My sons are a constant reminder of the importance of promoting peacemaking values in our world. This book is dedicated to Hakim Mohammed Said, a pioneer in Islamic peacemaking and a remarkable person who tried to bring comfort to those suffering.

Qamar-ul Huda

Introduction

The Peacemaking and Conflict Resolution Field and Islam

Qamar-ul Huda

What places do nonviolence and peacebuilding have in Islam? What are the challenges to mitigating violence in Muslim communities? What do Muslim religious and community leaders need in order to reform the current debate on the uses of violence and nonviolence? This book is the result of an international conference of Muslim scholars and practitioners who came together to address these questions, discussing contemporary Islam, its relation to violence and peacemaking, and the possibilities for reframing and reinterpreting methodologically the problems of violence and peacemaking in Muslim communities.

The subject of peacemaking and conflict resolution in Muslim communities is especially timely. There are two active wars in Iraq and Afghanistan, while radical Islamist groups threaten the stability of Pakistan, Egypt, Lebanon, and other states. The futility of counteracting extremism with military force is contributing to radicalization in Muslim communities; in the past ten years, the narrative of extremism has not diminished, but is flourishing among the disillusioned youth and middle class.[1] Given these challenges and others, it is vitally important to examine contemporary principles, methods, and approaches of peacemaking and conflict resolution by leading Muslim intellectuals and practitioners in the Islamic world.

More specifically, the conference explored historical examples of addressing conflict in Islam and the ways that the community of legal scholars (*ulama*) existed as an institution and asserted its political and religious authority. Muslim juridical debates among legal scholars on the subjects of war, rebellion, and resistance must be interpreted as legalistic responses to their particular social, political, and cultural contexts.[2] The arguments of the *ulama*, who developed just war theories and peacemaking engagements, must be read as commentaries on the law, not a vision for an ideal social order. Even if the *ulama* was itself influenced by the cultural, political, and social order of its time, it worked within a legal paradigm relatively unswayed by the desires of political elites and did not interfere with the law to favor its interests.

Moving beyond juridical interpretations of just war theory, the conference examined the possibilities for nonviolent interventions, peacemaking, the implementation of human rights, the reinterpretation of texts, peace education instruction, and employing successful mediation skills in an Islamic context. Several challenges arise in assessing the field of Islamic peacemaking. First, the overemphasis—by both the *ulama* and Western scholars—on the juridical and scriptural components of Islamic peacemaking practices has limited the conversation to particular legal and theological finer points. While useful to a certain degree, a legal and theological framework limits the scope of peacemaking efforts and is entirely disconnected from the field of conflict resolution. Second, scholars and practitioners need to be more self-critical of normative polemics within Islam and more deliberate with particular concepts of legal, social, political, and religious reform. Third, the agenda to correct and counteract Islamic exclusivism and radicalism has to be a serious and thoughtful endeavor, cognizant of the day-to-day cultural, social, political, and economic realities of Muslim societies.

The essays in this book capture the diversity of interpretations, concepts, and challenging situations within the field of Islamic peacemaking. The authors—both Muslim scholars and peacebuilding practitioners—offer critical perspectives that are needed to understand what works, what opportunities exist, and what areas are fertile for effective peacebuilding efforts. The essays also comment on how to engage constructively with Muslim leaders. None of the authors advocates searching for the reformers or moderate Muslim networks to counteract radicalism, or attempting to establish liberal democracies to contain, restrict, and deflate Islamists. Instead, these essays reflect the marvelous amount of scholarship and fieldwork in the discipline of peacemaking as it exists within the tradition of Islam. Historically, according to jurists, Islamic law seeks to preserve and protect life, religion, property, lineage, and intellect. These essays appreciate these values as they try to help peacemaking efforts create stable, functioning societies.[3]

Criticism of Religion

At the start of the twenty-first century, religion is associated by some with intolerance, violence, and breeding radicalism; it is regarded in some quarters as the cause for extremism and human rights violations. None of the world's religions is impervious to fomenting conflict, but Islam has often been singled out as particularly and intrinsically violent. Critics associate it with extreme intolerance and claim that it breeds radicalism. It is easy to see where the criticisms come from: With the combination of late twentieth-century fundamentalist movements, Islamist politics, al-Qaeda radicalism, Iran's theocracy, and attacks by Islamist groups against civilians across the world, it is impossible to discuss contemporary Islam without referring to the subject of violence. In 2006, Pope Benedict XVI's comments on Islam at the University of Regensburg referred to Islam as anti-rational and quoted a fourteenth-century Byzantine emperor, Manuel II Paleologus, who made derogatory references to the Prophet Muhammad and to Muslims.[4]

Many critics vociferously promote reforming Islamic thought, arguing for the urgent need to bring political, social, economic, and perhaps cultural reformation to the Arab-Muslim Middle East. Such reforms include reinterpreting religious doctrines more liberally by minimizing the importance or value of conservative, orthodox, and traditional positions. Other impulsive reforms include changing religious education, altering political systems, lessening the influence of religious law, and diluting social and cultural practices that appear to be obstacles to progress. Some policymakers advocate American idealism—the values of freedom, justice, equality, democracy, and prosperity—as an alternative system of ideas for Muslim societies. The underlying assumption is that Muslims live in a stagnant, irrational, and premodern tradition that has failed to respond to the challenges of modernity; essential values, such as progress, science, reason, freedom, and equality, have not yet set in. However, even a cursory glance at Islamic history reveals cultural and intellectual diversity; scientific and mathematical discoveries in the twelfth and thirteenth centuries; social and religious revivalist movements in the seventeenth century; nineteenth-century modernist reformation movements; pioneering work on religion, culture, and rationalism; and a massive amount of literature in twentieth-century Islamic thought on colonialism, political activism, peacemaking, governance, human rights, and democracy.[5] Islam as a civilization and faith tradition has been anything but stagnant and intellectually dormant, and, as with other civilizations, there are both intolerant and tolerant voices.

Along with ideas of reforming, reinventing, and transforming Islamic societies, unfortunately, there is much confusion about the role of religion in conflict and how conflicts are mistakenly framed in religious terms. The history of at least the past three millennia includes powerful examples of millions of people dying for the cause of someone's version of the divine, even as each of the world's religions strictly prohibits killing. The challenge is to not conflate historical events with current conflicts, or apply theological interpretations to situations that have nothing to do with religion or religious communities. On the one hand, there must be a serious debate about the political aspirations of religious groups. On the other hand, there needs to be an awareness of the many religious actors who have no particular political aspirations, yet are acutely sincere about peacebuilding, conflict prevention, and conflict resolution. In these debates, we must be honest about our level of knowledge of various religious histories and traditions. It is important to check, if not suspend, the biases we hold toward any faith-based communities and their activities, whether they be fundamentalist religious actors involved in peacemaking or progressive religious leaders involved in promoting human rights.

The world's religious traditions offer a great deal of insight into promoting peace and resolving conflicts. Religious peacemaking—commonly referred to as faith-based peacemaking—is rooted in the traditions of many faiths to affirm justice, love, reconciliation, and peaceful relations. The spiritual convictions of these religious communities inspire many of their members to work for social justice generally and involve them directly in conflict prevention, mediation, and conflict transformation work. Religious leaders and religious organizations involved in peacemaking are operating from their respective faith traditions to support personal, communal, and relational transformations.[6] Religious peacemaking involves forgiveness, recognition of pain, counseling, rehabilitation, recovery from trauma, public confessions, joint prayers, using narratives to create empathy, advocacy programs for victims, forums to explain misunderstandings, addressing the distorted image of the other in the faith tradition, and using the arts to express mutual respect. The bonds formed in interfaith peacemaking activities reveal an amazing level of openness to dialogue, allowing participants greater freedom to reconstruct broken relationships and damaged communities, reconcile conflicting parties, negotiate peace agreements, and create a common vision for peace.

The Ethics of Violence in Islam

In discussing the ethics of violence, one begins with the question of who can be attacked during war and how one distinguishes victims from combatants.[7] Such discussions have been documented in Islamic juridical discourses beginning in the ninth century, but in the past forty-five years alone, the field of Islamic peacemaking has produced a variety of theories, practices, and methodologies to use within Muslim and non-Muslim communities. At the time of Majid Khadduri's *War and Peace in the Law of Islam* (1955), scholars were obsessed with the ethics of war and the ways that Muslim legal scholars argued for and sanctioned violence. The literature then was dominated by historical juridical interpretations of war, engagement, disengagement, peaceful relations, and the rules associated with warfare. Since that time, however, the field has expanded tremendously to include scholars from conflict resolution, history, politics, sociology, anthropology, theology, and law, as well as practitioners implementing peacebuilding concepts. The broadening of the field has led to a great deal of work reframing Islamic beliefs to assert that it contains within it a long-standing tradition of peacemaking.

Glenn D. Paige, Chaiwat Satha-Anand, and Sara Gilliatt's edited book *Islam and Nonviolence* (1993) consists of six essays exploring the nonviolent dimensions of Islamic tradition and ways in which Islamic nonviolence can socially, politically, and globally transform the world to be more peaceful. Ralph Salmi, Cesar Adib Majul, and George K. Tanham's *Islam and Conflict Resolution: Theories and Practices* (1998) frames Islam against Western societies, reiterating the familiar analysis of fundamentalist movements as a threat to Islamic principles of peacemaking and civilization. Abdul Aziz Said, Nathan Funk, and Ayse Kadayifci's edited book *Peace and Conflict Resolution in Islam: Precept and Practice* (2001) analyzes several important aspects of conflict resolution, ethics, history, and politics in the Islamic tradition, highlighting Sufism as a key area containing paradigms of peacemaking. Abdul Karim Bangura's *Islamic Peace Paradigms* (2005) identifies key themes, such as dialogue, love, law, and nonviolence, to demonstrate essential modalities in promoting peace in Islamic cultures. And Mohammed Abu-Nimer's *Nonviolence and Peace Building in Islam: Theory and Practice* (2003) is a magnificent example of a Muslim scholar defining the Islamic peacemaking field within the conflict-resolution discipline. Abu-Nimer demonstrates that the fundamental principles of Islam support peacebuilding and nonviolence, and that these basic assumptions, values, and beliefs are derived from text, scripture, historical narratives, culture, and daily human experiences. He convincingly uses case studies to demonstrate how traditional dispute resolution methods in Arab-Muslim communities reveal the daily application of nonviolence and peacebuilding techniques.[8]

As the field of peacebuilding within the Islamic tradition continues to broaden, it is important to affirm unambiguously that killing any innocent being is not acceptable or legitimate. Chaiwat Satha-Anand, an important scholar and practitioner of nonviolent Islamic peacebuilding, asserts that violence is completely unacceptable in Islam and that Muslims must use nonviolent action to fight for justice and reconciliation.[9] He states that

"Islam itself is fertile soil for nonviolence because of its potential for disobedience, strong discipline, sharing and social responsibility, perseverance, and self-sacrifice, and the belief in the unity of the Muslim community and the oneness of mankind."[10] Satha-Anand disputes status-quo perspectives on Islamic just war theories, particularly the use of defensive violence, by once again reviving the nonviolent aspects of the Islamic tradition. He challenges scholars and practitioners to be critical of historical positions justifying violence and to apply an alternative framework of thinking. Policymakers, conflict resolution experts, and scholars must take seriously the work of Satha-Anand, as well as that of Said Nursi, Sakina Yakoobi, Abdul Ghaffar Khan, Shaykh 'Ali Goma'a, Hakim Mohammed Said, Dr. Seyyed Hossein Nasr, Nicolish Majid, Kabir Helminski, Din Syamsuddin, Ghazi bin Muhammad, Dr. Abdal Hakim Murad Winter, Mohammad Hashim Kamali, Shaykh Mustafa Ceric, Shaykh Al-Habib Ali al-Jifri, Yousef Sanei, and many others. In addition, even if their voices are rarely heard because they are drowned out by radical rhetoric and authoritarian systems that crush dissent, everyday Muslim leaders committed to promoting tolerance and diversity are involved in peacebuilding activities across the world.

Nonviolence in the Islamic Tradition

According to Sunni and Shiite *ulama*, basic Islamic peacemaking teachings are meant to help individuals in a society maintain healthy relationships, both with each other and with the divine. When conflicts erupt and destroy human relationships, restoring them is essential if justice is to be served. This process involves politicians, clergy, scholars, and intellectuals, who supersede those who do not have the power to institute justice. The consultation process among the authorities allows for dialogue, debate, and an exchange of views on a variety of subjects, but it is especially critical for authoritative bodies to ensure that they understand the opinions of others. Theologians, jurists, philosophers, and other scholars historically have promoted Islamic teachings of ethics to prevent, mediate, and resolve conflicts; ultimately, any level of disharmony is understood as disrupting peace. Historically, theologians stress the need for personal transformation and striving toward elevating spiritual awareness through fasting, prayer, charity, meditation, rituals, Qur'anic recitation, service, love of others, adoption of orphans, and displaying compassion and forgiveness to oneself and to others who have done harm.[11] The traditional theological thought is that once the heart and mind are gradually transformed toward peace—moving away from greed, egocentric desires, suffering, materialism, and harming others—humans then can act peacefully in the world.

The inner life thus is connected to the outer dimensions of peacemaking, at the personal, social, national, and global levels. Islamic peacemaking is founded on several principles of nonviolence and peacebuilding, including the pursuit of justice and equality; the universality and dignity of humanity; the sacredness of human life; reason, knowledge, and understanding; forgiveness; proper deeds and actions; collaborative actions and solidarity; inclusivity; and tolerance. Qur'anic verses, hadith injunctions, and narratives of the companions of the Prophet accentuate the proper ethical treatment of the elderly, orphans, prisoners, mentally challenged, neighbors, strangers, enemies, members of different religious traditions and tribes, and animals.[12] These and other principles of nonviolence and peacebuilding are integral to the faith tradition of Muslims and are crucial to Muslim peacebuilding initiatives developed by important figures such as Abdul Ghaffar Khan, Chaiwat Satha-Anand, Hakim Mohammed Said, and Jawdat Sa'id.

Part of what makes Islamic peacebuilding efforts unique are the processes by which their principles are applied. For example, Islamic efforts to create peace use a religious judge (*qadi*) to rely upon established guidelines in Islamic law (*shari'ah*). The process of mediation, arbitration, and reconciliation (*sulh*) consists of the conflicting parties agreeing on a process of resolving a dispute with a third-party mediator, who will ensure that all parties are satisfied by the outcomes. In presenting evidence of the dispute (*bayyinah*), parties use witnesses and material evidence to argue their respective positions in the case. Other customary practices of dispute resolution (*'urf*) also include the use of third-party members to reconcile a dispute (*mukhtar*). Using an intermediary to represent the party (*wasta*) has been a traditional practice to intervene in a conflict; the representative works toward a specific period of mediation (*hudna*), or truce. Conflicting parties find representatives, not necessarily lawyers, who can best present their positions as clearly as possible. The representatives then find a trusted third-party mediator who is committed to resolving the particular conflict and can guarantee that the parties receive a fair settlement. A settlement may include an agreed-upon sum of money to the victim for compensation of losses (*atwah*), which is usually tied to a public offering of forgiveness. Compensation (*ta'awruza*) is not only measured in financial terms, however; it also involves a service to the family or community and specific gestures of grief relief. For instance, *ta'lif al-qulub,* or offering peace to the heart, is a legally recognized practice of reconciliation, by which the offender periodically visits the victim's family to demonstrate remorse. These different processes allow space for conflicting parties to have their interests represented and seek the proper restoration of peace or harmony in their community.

The Essays in This Book

This book complements previous work in many ways. First, it incorporates history, theology, politics, economics, education, theory, and practice to examine the creative work that many scholars and practitioners in the field of Islamic peacemaking have done. Second, the essays combine the intellectual heritage of Islam with the practical challenges of peacemaking, conflict resolution, mediation, and reconciliation in Muslim communities. The authors—experts in their respective fields, with intricate knowledge of concepts of justice, reconciliation, dialogue, ethics, peacemaking, and conflict resolution in Islam—agree that religious peacemaking generally, and Islamic peacemaking specifically, are effective mechanisms to build peaceful communities that can foster values of coexistence, tolerance, and pluralism. They assume that Islamic peacemakers are genuinely interested in cultivating a culture of peace at all levels of society, though they are not so naïve as to think that religious leaders cannot be corrupt or do not generate obstacles to peacebuilding. Finally, though this book does not cover strategies to counter radicalism, there is strong agreement among the authors that developing civil society, cultivating an ethos of pluralism, broadening political and economic systems, tapping into religious leaders for peacebuilding activities, encouraging critical thinking skills in educational institutions, and investing in human capital are the strongest steps toward counteracting extremism.

The book is divided into two parts. Part I covers concepts of peace, Islamic conflict resolution, and peacebuilding. Part II covers peace education, nonviolent action, human rights, and peacemaking training. Part I begins with Ibrahim Kalin's excellent survey of concepts of peacebuilding in the philosophical and theological traditions of Islam. Kalin outlines the important philosophical and political debates within Islam regarding violence, nonviolence, evil, good, sin, war, peace, the status of minorities, and divergent views on establishing peace. He demonstrates how the multiple views of minorities and the legal status of Jews, Christians, Hindus, and other religious communities allowed them to make important contributions to the larger Muslim civilization. In assessing the evolution of Islamic thought regarding peace, Kalin strongly emphasizes how intellectual and cultural pluralism contributed to a profound respect and reverence for non-Muslims, creating space and time for mutual coexistence.

Asma Afsaruddin meticulously examines the early semantic use of *jihad* and its connection to political, military, and elitist perspectives. She demonstrates how, in the evolutionary growth of the expansionary dynastic state, the first generation of Muslims in the seventh-century Umayyad period ultimately used the term *jihad* to defend their dynasty's expansionary policies. Afsaruddin's essay reveals the tensions among theologians, philosophers, and military and dynastic leaders who exploited the use of *jihad* to mean martyrdom, struggling in the path of the divine, armed combat, and holy war. The necessary legal and ethical articulation of war and peace meant conflicting interpretations of key Qur'anic verses and their original intent. For military leaders and Umayyad political leaders, *jihad* was appropriated as propaganda for armed combat and the belief that *jihad* essentially meant fighting others rather than struggling with oneself. This blatant misrepresentation of the Qur'anic term had no scriptural basis, and in turn, the process of transforming the meaning of *jihad* divorced it from mainstream interpretations of the Prophet's Mecca and Medina period, ultimately causing serious tensions among scholars and believers.

Waleed El-Ansary's essay on understanding and applying accurate use of Qur'anic language as a way to counter radical self-identity highlights the importance of language in peacebuilding in Muslim communities. El-Ansary demonstrates that al-Qaeda's use of the word for participants in *jihad—mujahidun—*is based on their self-identification as righteous freedom fighters who are struggling against injustice. Referring to them as such thus legitimates their cause and reinforces their legitimate self-understanding. Seeking to counteract this abuse of language and Islamic theology, prominent Muslim scholars have preferred a new word for al-Qaeda that does not reinforce Osama bin Laden's self-definition as a religious hero and defender of the faith. Shaykh ʿAli Gomaʿa, the grand mufti of Egypt, argues that the appropriate term is *irjaf,* which has no link to Islamic theology and connotes scaremongering by bringing frightening commotion to society. This is not an issue of semantic usage; rather, this internal debate by high-ranking religious leaders shows that there is an ongoing effort to recapture religious and theological terms to delegitimize al-Qaeda's movement and simultaneously ensure that Qur'anic terms are not disparagingly abused for violent causes.

Mohammed Abu-Nimer reflects on the principles of Islamic models of conflict resolution and peacemaking and the challenges they pose to Western approaches to conflict resolution. Arguing that there are traditional cultural, religious, and indigenous approaches to resolving conflict, Abu-Nimer identifies the key principles that local leaders follow. At the same time, he shows that there are serious obstacles in Islamic peacemaking, affecting economic, social, and political development; the formation of effective intervention strategies; and the insurance that conflict reduction is sustained. Abu-Nimer's extensive fieldwork experience and straightforward assessment of problems in peacemaking reveal the gaps that exist between theory and practice, which require further investigation.

Part II begins with Zeki Saritoprak's biographical evaluation of Said Nursi, a prominent Turkish practitioner of nonviolence almost unknown in the West. Saritoprak's essay illuminates how the life of Said Nursi is a model of nonviolence for Turkish Muslims. Said Nursi's experience of the last years of the Ottoman Empire, his service in World War I, and the establishment of Turkey all contributed to his deep commitment to nonviolence. Mohandas Gandhi and Dr. Martin Luther King, Jr., are used frequently as textbook cases to study nonviolent social movements; Saritoprak's essay demonstrates how a similarly remarkable man could inspire thousands of Turkish citizens to accept nonviolence as a code for life. As the field of Islamic peacemaking lacks documentation and analysis of Muslim leaders who persistently advocated a nonviolent response to conflict, this essay raises our awareness of one such monumental figure and his immense contributions.

Waleed El-Ansary's second essay explores the issue of violence by religious actors through the prism of human development and security and the prevalent problem of economic stagnation in Muslim societies, arguing that the complex economic matrix in which religious actors operate is an important part of the problem of religious violence. He suggests that strategies to reduce violence must address economic development as well.

Reza Eslami-Somea's essay discusses current intellectual thought and trends in reform in Muslim societies, exploring how Muslim reformers have historically relied upon *shari'ah* principles for resolving societal questions of modernity. He affirms that reformers have overemphasized the role of *shari'ah* as the primary source in resolving problems such as those of gender inequality, human rights, and democracy. According to him, reformers in Muslim societies have failed to meet the challenges of modernity due to their inability to operate outside of *shari'ah* and recognize a system of universal principles of human rights and freedom. The essay contextualizes the tension between modern secular reform efforts and religious approaches to reform, indicating that real peacemaking efforts cannot take place if they are limited to one particular worldview.

Asna Husin relates the efforts of a Muslim non-governmental organization (NGO) to reform education in Aceh, an extremely poor province and conflict zone in Indonesia. In addition to difficulties in funding and retaining staff, as well as political and social chaos, the Muslim NGO also faced martial law, an ongoing military operation, and the horrendous aftermath of the 2004 tsunami. Nevertheless, the NGO persevered to complete a two-volume Islamic peacemaking textbook written by the Ulama Council of Aceh and conduct workshops to train religious schoolteachers in peacemaking. The essay both documents the harsh realities of peacemak-

ing activities and offers lessons for understanding how NGOs can overcome enormous obstacles to operate and execute an Islamic peacemaking
program.

Ayse Kadayifci-Orellana and Meena Sharify-Funk discuss Muslim
women as agents of change, documenting a rich tradition of women contributing to the field of Islamic peacemaking. The essay explores how major
Muslim women figures, often neglected in history and modern efforts in
peacemaking, have been influential in conflict prevention and resolution.
The literature in the field seriously lacks an analysis of women's contributions and approaches to conflict resolution, as well as the various practical
tools Muslim women have used in peacebuilding. Kadayifci-Orellana and
Sharify-Funk examine women NGOs in Afghanistan, Kenya, and Thailand
that creatively identified space and opportunities to counteract extremism,
mitigate electoral violence, support health services, promote human rights,
coordinate youth activities, and conduct peacebuilding training in their respective communities. The essay is a reminder of how often the larger field
of conflict resolution, and especially the field of Islamic peacemaking, does
not acknowledge the work of women.

Qamar-ul Huda analyzes the established methodological thinking and
approaches in the Islamic peacemaking literature to illustrate how scholars
have developed the field based on their particular disciplines. This analysis
demonstrates the weaknesses and strengths of methodologies in Islamic
peacemaking; however, Huda advocates the desperate need to develop
practical skills and knowledge for religious leaders to operate in the larger
field of peacebuilding. After examining numerous problems of Western
peacebuilding workshops for Muslim religious leaders, he suggests how
organizations and peace trainers can help religious leaders to be more re-
ceptive, more responsive, and ultimately transformed. Offering analysis
based on fieldwork experience, Huda suggests seven critical areas for skills
transmission workshops for religious leaders, including organizational
management skills, mediation and negotiation skills, project planning and
execution, strategic planning for intervention and conflict transformation,
and the finer art of engaging religious leaders in peacebuilding.

Contemporary Efforts at Islamic Peacemaking

Real initiatives in Islamic peacebuilding are occurring in all Muslim communities, every day and throughout the world, from Muslim minorities
in the West to majority Muslim societies in Africa, the Middle East,
and South and Southeast Asia. These peacebuilding activities include
high-ranking scholars, such as muftis and grand ayatollahs; regional and

local-level politicians; and imams, teachers, *qadis*, lawyers, activists, religious educators, artists, musicians, and others in civil society. In December 2005, the Mecca Al-Mukarramah Declaration amassed all heads of state from the Organization of Islamic Conference (OIC) to affirm "that terrorism in all its forms and manifestations is a global phenomenon that is not confined to any particular religion, race, colour, or country, and that can in no way be justified or rationalized ... we are also called upon to redouble and orchestrate international efforts to combat terrorism."[13] The conference also stated that "the Islamic civilization is an integral part of human civilization, based on the ideals of dialogue, moderation, justice, righteousness, and tolerance as noble human values that counteract bigotry, isolationism, tyranny, and exclusivism."[14]

Another example is the Second International Conference of the Assembly for Moderate Islamic Thought and Culture, sponsored by the Royal Hashemite Kingdom of Jordan in 2006. It issued a twenty-five point plan to support moderates in reforming and reviving all aspects of Islamic heritage, values, and ethical values in the global Muslim community. The assembly called for an international moderate assembly to generate a moderate movement and to coordinate activities with "all institutions and Islamic agencies, which adhere to the moderation programme."[15] Point thirteen of the plan unequivocally endorsed "affirming a committee on dialogue with leading Western thinkers and politicians."[16]

Equally important is the Muslims of Europe Conference, held in Istanbul in 2006, that addressed the issues of Muslim minorities in Europe, the rise of Islamophobia, racism, and the need to fight terrorism collectively and promote diversity and inclusivity. The twelve-point document it fostered, known as The Topkapi Declaration, reasserted its support of the European Council for Fatwa and Research to further work on engagement with society and positive integration. The fifth point of the declaration stated, "As full and dynamic citizens aware of their rights as well as their responsibilities, European Muslims have the right to criticize, dissent, and protest, as do all European citizens. This right is in accordance with the democratic processes of Europe and in accordance with their faith. Islam calls upon all Muslims to promote the common good and welfare of society as a whole and prevent what is wrong."[17]

Since 2002 the annual Doha Debates in Qatar have attracted over five hundred leading scholars, practitioners, activists, politicians, lawyers, media specialists, economists, and other professionals to a widely publicized discussion of issues such as terrorism, war, refugees, trade, education, conflict prevention, discrimination, labor rights, interfaith dialogue, and other peacemaking subjects. In November 2006, the Fiqh Council of North

America, the highest-ranking Islamic organization in the United States, issued the Thanksgiving Fatwa of Peace to demonstrate their unyielding commitment to the United States. Among the fatwa's major points were that all acts of terrorism are forbidden in Islam, it is forbidden for a Muslim to cooperate or associate with any individual or group that is involved in any act of terrorism or violence, and it is a civic and religious duty to cooperate with law enforcement authorities to protect the lives of all civilians.[18] The pronouncements of this and other high-profile organizations and conferences have their analogue in the work of many Muslim NGOs and nonprofit organizations working at peacebuilding with little recognition. These include the Wajir Peace and Development Committee in Kenya,[19] the Inter-Faith Mediation Centre in Nigeria, The Centre for Religious Dialogue in Bosnia,[20] Program Pendidikan Damai (PPD),[21] Asian Muslim Action Network (AMAN),[22] Edhi Foundation,[23] and the Institute for Inter-Faith Dialogue in Indonesia.[24]

Effective and lasting peacebuilding strategies and conflict resolution practices in Muslim communities should be constructed within an Islamic framework. Strategies must acknowledge Qur'anic evidence; other texts and narratives; the fields of jurisprudence, philosophy, and theology; and the essential foundational doctrines, creeds, beliefs, and practices of Islam. Islamic peacebuilding efforts at all levels reaffirm five basic principles. First, all of humanity has a common origin and human dignity must be recognized and respected, regardless of religion, ethnicity, or tribe. Second, the diversity among people encapsulates the richness of traditions. Third, Muslims striving to improve the world must cooperate, collaborate, and engage in dialogue with others and among themselves to foster peace. Fourth, to be actively involved with one's tradition means not to lead exclusivistic hermetic lives, but to be engaged with others in a respectful manner. And finally, practicing good deeds and striving toward justice must be present in everyday dealings with all human beings.[25] These essential principles do not contradict Western conflict resolution approaches; rather, the astounding similarities and overlapping themes among Islamic and Western peacebuilding efforts allow for more common ground in working toward ending conflict.

Notes

1.   See Al-Tayib Zain al-Abedin, ed., *Islam wa tadraf al-dini* [Islam: Refuting the Narrative of Extremism] (Cairo: Maktab al-Sharq al-Dawliya, 2009).

2.   The discourse on war and rebellion is usually categorized within the *ahkam al-bughah* literature. See Kahlid Abou El Fadl, *Rebellion and Violence in Islamic Law* (Cambridge: Cambridge University Press, 2001).

3. By focusing on approaches to peacemaking within Islamic legal thought, the authors do not mean to exclude or devalue other approaches. They readily acknowledge that there are many other disciplines with different interpretative frameworks that can make just as important—if not more important—contributions to Islamic peacemaking.

4. See Pope Benedict XVI, "Faith, Reason, and the University: Memories and Reflections," speech at the University of Regensburg, September 2006, http://www.vatican.va/. See also Organization of Islamic Conference (OIC) response, http://www.oic-oci.org/press/English/2006

5. Farhard Daftary, ed., *Intellectual Traditions in Islam* (London: I.B. Taurus Publishers, 2000); Seyyed Hossein Nasr and Oliver Leaman, ed., *History of Islamic Philosophy* (London: I.B. Taurus, 1996); Franz Rosenthal, *Muslim Intellectual and Social History* (Aldershot: Ashgate, 1990); Parviz Morewedge, ed., *Islamic Philosophical Theology* (Albany: SUNY Press, 1979); and Marshall Hodgson, *The Venture of Islam: Conscience and History in a World Civilization* (Chicago: University of Chicago Press, 1974).

6. For etymological, scriptural, and theological definitions of religious peacemaking, see John MacQuarrie, *The Concept of Peace* (London: SCM Press Ltd., 1973); Howard Zehr, *Changing Lenses* (Scottsdale, PA: Herald Press, 1995); Jacques Ellul, *Violence: Reflections from a Christian Perspective* (London: SCM Press Ltd., 1970); Scott Appleby, "Catholic Peacebuilding," *America*, vol. 189, no. 6 (2003), 1–15, www.americamagazine.com; and Joseph Bock, *Sharpening Conflict Management: Religious Leadership and the Double-Edged Sword* (Westport: Praeger Publishers, 2001).

7. See Michael Walzer, *Just and Unjust War* (New York: Basic Books, 1977), 41–42.

8. See Mohammed Abu-Nimer, *Nonviolence and Peace Building in Islam: Theory and Practice* (Gainesville, FL: University Press of Florida, 2003); Abdul Karim Bangura, *Islamic Peace Paradigms* (Dubuque, IA: Kendall Hunt, 2005); Glenn D. Paige, Chaiwat Satha-Anand, and Sara Gilliatt, eds., *Islam and Nonviolence* (Honolulu: Center for Global Nonviolence Planning Project, Matsunaga Institute for Peace, 1993); Abdul Aziz Said, Nathan Funk, and Ayse Kadayifci, eds., *Peace and Conflict Resolution in Islam: Precept and Practice* (Lanham, MD: University Press of America, 2001); Ralph Salmi, Cesar Adib Majul, and George K. Tanham, eds., *Islam and Conflict Resolution: Theories and Practices* (Lanham, MD: University Press of America, 1998).

9. Chaiwat Satha-Anand, "The Nonviolent Crescent: Eight Theses on Muslim Nonviolent Actions," in Paige, Satha-Anand, and Gilliatt, *Islam and Nonviolence*.

10. Satha-Anand, "The Nonviolent Crescent," 23.

11. See Shaykh Ali Goma'a, *Al-jihad fi'l Islam* (Cairo: Nahdet Misr, 2005); Al-Taftazani, *Nahwa, Madkhal ila l-tasawwuf al-Islami* (Cairo: Dar al-Thaqafa, 1974); and *'Ilm al-kalam wa ba'd mushkilatih* (Cairo: Maktabat al-Qahira al-Haditha, 1966); and Mahmoud Ayoub, *Islam: Faith and Practice* (Ontario: The Open Press Limited, 1989).

12. See Khalid al-Qishtayni, *Nahwa l-la'unf* [Toward Nonviolence] (Amman: Dar al-Karmil, 1984); Abdul Aziz Sachedina, "Justifications of Violence in Islamic Traditions" in J. Partout Burns, eds., *War and Its Discontents: Pacifism and Quietism in the Abrahamic Traditions* (Washington, DC: Georgetown University Press, 1996); and Iftikar H. Malik, "Islamic Discourse on Jihad, War, and Violence," *Journal of South Asian and Middle Eastern Studies*, vol. 21, no. 4 (1984), 47–78.

13. Ghazi bin Muhammad bin Talal, *True Islam and the Islamic Consensus on the Amman Message* (Amman: Hashemite Kingdom of Jordan, 2006), 103; for the complete version, see appendix 1.

14. Bin Talal, *True Islam*, 104.

15. Bin Talal, *True Islam*, 117; see points 3f and 5 in appendix 2.

16. Bin Talal, *True Islam*, 119.

17. Bin Talal, *True Islam*, 154.

18. For the complete version, see the Fiqh Council of North America, www.fiqhcouncil.org.

19. See chapter 8 of this volume.

20. Tsjeard Bouta, Ayse Kadayifci-Orellan, and Mohammed Abu-Nimer, *Faith-Based Peace-Building: Mapping and Analysis of Christian, Muslim, and Multi-faith Actors* (The Hague: Netherlands Institute of International Relations "Clingendael," 2005).

21. See chapter 9 of this volume.

22. See the Asian Muslim Action Network, www.arf-asia.org/aman.php.

23. See the Edhi Foundation, www.edhifoundation.com.

24. See the Institute for Interfaith Dialogue in Indonesia, www.interfidei.or.id/index2.php.

25. For Qur'anic verses pertaining to these themes, see 17:70, 4:1, 30:22, 10:99, 2:256, 17:107, 60:8, 31:23, 88:25–26, 42:48, 5:8, 4:135, 6:98, 11:188, 42:15, and 30:22.

Part I

Sources of Peace, Islamic Conflict Resolution, and Peacebuilding

1

Islam and Peace

A Survey of the Sources of
Peace in the Islamic Tradition

Ibrahim Kalin

The question of whether religion is a source of violence haunts the minds of many who are concerned about the issue. For critics of religion, the answer is usually in the affirmative, and it is easy to cite historical examples. Using Rene Girard's depiction of ritual sacrifices as indicators of violent proclivities in religions[1] or the exclusivist claims of different faith traditions, one can argue that religions produce violence at both social and theological levels; from the Crusades and the Inquisition in medieval Europe to *jihad* movements in Islamic history, the respective stories of Christianity and Islam can be described as nothing more than narratives of war, conflict, violence, schism, and persecution. The premeditated conclusion is unequivocal: The more religious people are, the more violent they tend to be. The solution therefore lies in secularizing the world. Religions—some more than others—need to be diminished and modernized to rid themselves of their violent essences and legacies.[2]

At the other end of the spectrum is the believer who sees religious violence as an oxymoron at best and the mutilation of his religious faith at worst. Religions do not call for violence, this believer would argue. Religious teachings are peaceful at their base, meant to reestablish the primordial harmony between heaven and earth, creator and created. When religious groups turn violent, it is because specific religious teachings and feelings have been manipulated to foment conflict for political gains. Violence is committed in the name of religion, but not condoned by it. The only valid criticism the secularist can raise against religion is that religions have not developed effective ways to protect themselves from such manipulations and abuses. In his extensive survey of modern religious violence, Mark Juergensmeyer has shown that such violence does not recognize religious and cultural boundaries and can easily find a home in the most sublime and innocuous teachings of world religions.[3] This becomes especially acute when religions fall short of inculcating a consciousness of peace and non-violence in the minds and hearts of their followers. Yet religions per se cannot be seen as sources of violence; only some bad practitioners of them can be held accountable.

Both views have strong cases and make important points about religion and violence. Both, however, are equally mistaken in resorting to a fixed definition of religion: They reduce the immense variety of religious practices to a particular tradition and, furthermore, to a particular faction or historical moment in that tradition. In speaking of Islam and violence or Hinduism and war, the usual method is to look at the sacred scriptures and compare and contrast them with historical realities that flow from their practice, or lack thereof. Discrepancies between text and history are highlighted as the breaking points in the history of that religion—the moments when the religious community did not live up to the standards of its sacred text.

Although there is some benefit to be gained from such an approach, it fails to account for the ways in which religious texts are interpreted and made part of the day-to-day experience of particular religious communities. Instead of looking at how religious texts are read, revealed, and enriched within the concrete experiences of the community, we analysts separate text from history, implicitly assuming that neither one can affect the other. This is not to deny the centrality of the scripture. In the case of Islam, the Qur'an, together with the *sunnah* of the Prophet of Islam, is and remains the main source of the Islamic worldview. The numerous interpretations that we may talk about are interpretations of the Qur'an, a single text that is variously interpreted by the Sufis, Hanbalis, Wahhabis, and modernists. That the prophetic *sunnah* is part of Islamic religious life—without it, we cannot understand a good part of the Qur'an—can be seen as confirming the significance of reading the scripture within the concrete experiences of the Muslim community: It was, in fact, how the first Muslims, who became the spiritual and moral examples of later generations, learned about the Qur'an under the guidance and tutorship of the Prophet.

Thus, Islamic history is not alien to the idea of reading religious texts primarily within the context of a living and evolving tradition. The *sunnah* was part of Islamic law from the outset; it is the origin of the tradition of transmitted religious sciences (*al-'ulum al-naqliyyah*), by which scholars looked at how previous generations of Muslims understood the Qur'an and *hadith*. Taken out of this context, Qur'anic verses become abstruse, abstract, and impenetrable for the non-Muslim, or for anyone who is unfamiliar enough with the tradition to be misled into thinking that a good part of Islamic history has come about despite the Qur'an, not because of it. Those trying to secularize Islam and those trying to apologize for it both make this mistake, and much of the current debate about Islam and violence is beset by the problems we see in the secularist and apologetic readings of the scriptural sources of Islam.

Those who consider Islam to be a religion that essentially condones violence pick certain verses from the Qur'an, link them to cases of communal and political violence in Islamic history, and conclude that Qur'anic teachings justify the unjust use of violence. The same can be done to practically any religion, but Islam has enjoyed much more fanfare than any other religion for the past thousand years or so. The apologist makes the same mistake, but in a different way, when he rejects all history as misguided, failing to see the ways in which the Qur'an—or the Bible or Rig Vedas—can easily, if not legitimately, be read to support intra- and interreligious violence. This is where the hermeneutics of the text, in the sense of both commentary on the Qur'an (*tafsir*) and the inner or esoteric meanings of the Qur'an (*ta'wil*) becomes absolutely necessary. The text itself is not violent, but it does lend itself to multiple readings that can justify peaceful or violent ends.

A second problem in considering the connection between Islam and violence is the current literature's dominant focus on the legal and juristic aspects of the issue. Questions about the use of force, conduct in war, treatment of combatants and prisoners of war, and other international law concerns are discussed mostly within a legal context, and the classical Islamic literature on the subject is called upon to provide answers. This is an important and useful exercise, but it does not address the deeper philosophical and spiritual issues that must be included in any discussion of religion and peace. This is especially true for Islam, for two main reasons.

First, legal views of peace and violence in the classical period were articulated and applied in the light of the overall teachings and aims of Islamic law (*masqasid al-shari'ah*). The *masqasid* provided a context within which the strict legality of the law was blended into the necessities and realities of communal life. Political conflicts couched in the language of juridical edicts remained as political conflicts and were never extended to a war of religions between Islam and Christianity, Judaism, Hinduism, or African religions, which Muslims encountered throughout their history. It should not be surprising that the *fatwa* of a jurist of a particular school of law allowing the use of force against a particular Christian ruler was not interpreted as an excuse to attack one's Christian or Jewish neighbors.

Second, the spiritual and ethical teachings of the Qur'an and *sunnah* underpin all Islamic principles, including, mutatis mutandis, the questions of peace and violence. The legal injunctions (*ahkam*) of the Qur'an concerning peace and war are part of a larger set of spiritual and moral principles. The ultimate goal of Islam is to create a moral and just society, in which individuals can pursue a spiritual life, and the toll of living collectively, from economic exploitation and misuse of political authority to the suppression of others, can be controlled to the greatest extent possible. Without accounting for this larger picture, it is impossible to see how Islam advocates a positive concept of peace or how its political and legal precepts, which are exploited so wildly and irrationally by both the secular and religious fundamentalists of our day, lead to creating and sustaining a just and ethical social order.

With the above discussion in mind, this essay has two interrelated goals. The first is to analyze the ways in which the Islamic tradition can be said to advocate a positive concept of peace—as contrasted with negative peace, defined conventionally as simply the absence of war and conflict. Positive peace involves the presence of certain qualities and conditions that aim to make peace a principal state of harmony and equilibrium, rather than a mere event of political settlement. This requires a close examination of the philosophical assumptions of the Islamic tradition, which have shaped Muslim societies' experiences with the peoples of other faiths and cultures. These philosophical suppositions, in turn, are naturally grounded in the ethical and spiritual teachings of Islam, and without considering their relevance to the cultural and political experience of Muslims with others, we can neither do justice to the Islamic tradition—which spans vast areas of both space and time—nor avoid the pitfalls of historical reductionism and essentialism that are so rampant in the current discussions of the subject.

The second goal is to argue that adequately analyzing peace and war in the Islamic tradition entails more than fixating on the views of some Muslim jurists in the ninth and tenth centuries as the definitive position of orthodox Islam, thus reducing the Islamic way of dealing with non-Muslims to a concept of holy war. With some exceptions,[4] the ever-growing literature of Islam and peace has been concerned predominantly with the legal aspects of declaring war (*jihad*) against Muslim and non-Muslim states, treatment the non-Muslim citizens of a Muslim state (*dhimmis*) under *shari'ah,* and expanding the territories of the Islamic state. This has obscured, to say the least, the larger context within which such legal opinions were discussed, interpreted, and changed from one century to the next and from one cultural-political era to another.

The concept of peace in the Islamic tradition should be considered in four interrelated contexts. The first is the metaphysical-spiritual context, in which peace (*salam*) as one of the names of God is seen as an essential part of God's creation and assigned a substantive value. The second is the philosophical-theological context, within which the question of evil (*sharr*) is addressed as a cosmic, ethical, and social problem. Discussions of theodicy among Muslim theologians and philosophers contain one of the most profound analyses of the questions of evil, injustice, mishap, violence, and their place in the great chain of being (below, this essay briefly shows how a proper understanding of peace in the Islamic tradition is bound to the larger questions of good and evil). The third is the political-legal context, the proper locus of classical legal and juristic discussions of war, rebellion, oppression, and political order and disorder. The current literature focuses exclusively on this area, which promises to fuel an engaging and long-standing debate in the Muslim world. The fourth is the sociocultural context, which reveals the parameters of the Muslim experience of religious and cultural diversity in communities of other faiths and cultural traditions.

All four of the contexts are interdependent and call for an even larger context, within which the questions of peace and violence can be articulated and negotiated by a multitude of scholars, philosophers, jurists, mystics, political leaders, and various Muslim communities. The Islamic tradition provides ample material for contemporary Muslim societies to deal with issues of peace, religious diversity, and social justice, all of which, needless to say, require urgent attention. The present challenge of Muslim societies is not only to deal with these issues as internal affairs, but also to contribute to fostering a global culture of peace and coexistence. Before turning to the Islamic tradition, however, a few words of definition are in order to clarify the meaning of positive peace.

Peace as a Substantive Value

Peace as a substantive and positive concept entails the presence of certain conditions that make it an enduring state of harmony, integrity, contentment, equilibrium, repose, and moderation. This can be contrasted with negative peace, which denotes the absence of conflict and discord. Even as negative peace is indispensable to prevent communal violence, border disputes, or international conflicts, substantive-positive peace calls for a comprehensive outlook to address the deeper causes of conflict, hate, strife, destruction, brutality, and violence. As Steven Lee states, it also offers a genuine measure and set of values by which peace and justice can be established beyond the short-term interests of individual, communities, or states,[5] which is critical to constructing peace as a substantive value.

Defining peace as the privation of violence and conflict turns it into a concept that is instrumental and accidental at best, and relative and irrelevant at worst. A positive-substantive notion of peace shifts the focus from preventing conflict, violence, and strife to a willingness to generate balance, justice, cooperation, dialogue, and coexistence as the primary terms of a peace discourse.[6]

Furthermore, relegating the discourse of peace to social conflict and its prevention runs the risk of neglecting the individual, who is the sine qua non of collective and communal peace. This is where the spiritual individualism of Islam, versus its social collectivism, enters the picture: The individual must be endowed with the necessary qualities to make peace an enduring reality, not only in the public sphere, but also in the private domain. The Qur'anic ideal of creating a beautiful soul—at peace with itself and the larger reality of which it is a part—brings ethics and spirituality into the heart of the discourse of positive peace. In turn, peace as a substantive value extends to the domain of both ethics and aesthetics, as it is one of the conditions that brings about peace in the soul and resists the temptations of discord, restlessness, ugliness, pettiness, and vulgarity. In Qur'anic terms, the word *ihsan* carries the meanings of virtue, beauty, goodness, comportment, proportion, comeliness, and doing what is beautiful all at once. The active participle *muhsin* denotes a person who does what is good, desired, and beautiful.[7]

In such a context, peace is not a mere state of passivity; it is being fully active against the menaces of evil, destruction, and turmoil, which may come from within or without. As R.G. Collingwood points out, peace is a "dynamic thing,"[8] requiring consciousness and vigilance, a constant state of awareness. One must engage in spiritual and intellectual *jihad* to ensure that differences within and across the collective traditions do not become grounds for violence and oppression. Furthermore, positive peace involves analyzing various forms of aggression, including individual, institutional, and structural violence.

Peace as a substantive concept is also based on justice (*adl*), for peace is predicated upon the availability of equal rights and opportunities for all to realize their goals and potentials. One of the meanings of *adl* is to be straight and equitable, that is, to be straightforward, trustworthy, and fair in one's dealings with others.[9] Such an attitude brings about a state of balance, accord, and trust, going beyond the limits of formal justice as dispensed by the judicial system. Defined in the broadest terms, justice encompasses a vast domain of relations and interactions, from taking care of one's body to international law. Like peace, justice is one of the divine names, taking on substantive importance due to its central role in Islamic theology as well as law. Peace can be conceived as an enduring state of harmony, trust, and coexistence only when coupled with and supported by justice, because it also means being secure from all that is morally evil and destructive.[10] Thus the Qur'an combines justice with *ihsan* when it commands its followers to act with "justice and good manner" (*bi'l-adl wa'l-ihsan*) (Qur'an 16:90).[11]

The Spiritual-Metaphysical Context: God as Peace

The conditions conducive to the state of peace mentioned above are primarily spiritual and have larger implications for the cosmos, the individual, and society. Three premises are directly relevant to this discussion. The first pertains to peace as a divine name (*al-salam*) (Qur'an 59:23). The Qur'anic concept of God is founded upon a robust monotheism, and God's transcendence (*tanzih*) is emphasized in both the canonical sources and the intellectual tradition. To this absolutely one and transcendent God belong "all the beautiful names" (Qur'an 7:180; 59:24), that is, the names of beauty (*jamal*), majesty (*jalal*), and perfection (*kamal*). These names prevent God from becoming an utterly unreachable and wholly other deity. Divine names represent God's face turned toward the world and are the vessels to finding God in and through His creation.

The names of beauty take precedence over the names of majesty because God says that "My mercy has encompassed everything" (Qur'an 7:156) and "God has written mercy upon Himself" (Qur'an 6:12, 54). This is also supported by a famous *hadith* of the Prophet, according to which "God is beautiful and loves beauty." In this sense, God is as much transcendent, incomparable, and beyond as He is imminent, comparable, and close (*tashbih*).[12] As the ultimate source of peace, God transcends all opposites and tensions, is the permanent state of repose and tranquility, and calls His servants to the abode of peace (*dar al-salam*) (Qur'an 10:25). "It is He who from on high has sent [sends] down inner peace and repose (*sakinah*) upon the hearts of the believers," says the Qur'an (48:4). The proper abode of peace is in people's hearts (*qulub*), which are "satisfied only by the remembrance of God (*dhikr Allah*)" (Qur'an 13:28). By linking the heart, man's center, to God's remembrance, the Qur'an establishes a strong link between theology and transcendental human experiences or spiritual psychology.

In addition to Qur'anic exegetes, the Sufis are fond of explaining the mystery of creation by referring to a sacred saying (*hadith qudsi*) attributed to the Prophet of Islam: "I was a hidden treasure. I wanted [literally, loved] to be known and created the universe [literally, creation]."[13] The key words love (*hubb, mahabbah*) and *know* (*ma'rifah*) underlie a fundamental aspect of the Sufi metaphysics of creation: Divine love and desire to be known is the reason for all existence. Ibn al-'Arabi says that God's "love for His servants is identical with the origination of their engendered existence . . . the relation of God's love to them is the same as the fact that He is with them wherever they are [Qur'an 57:4], whether in the state of their nonexistence or the state of their *wujud* . . . they are the objects of His knowledge. He witnesses them and loves them neverendingly."[14] Commenting on the above saying, Dawud b. Mahmud al-Qaysari (d. 1350), the fourteenth-century Turkish Sufi philosopher and the first university president of the newly established Ottoman state, said that "God has written love upon Himself. There is no doubt that the kind of love that is related to the manifestation of [His] perfections follows from the love of His Essence, which is the source of the love of [His Names and] Qualities that have become the reason for the unveiling of all existents and the connection of the species of spiritual and corporeal bodies."[15]

The second premise is related to what traditional philosophy calls the great chain of being (*da'irat al-wujud*). In the cosmic scale of things, the universe is the best of all possible worlds because, first, it is actual, which implies completion and plenitude over potentiality, and second, its built-in order derives its sustenance from the creator. The natural world is in a constant state of peace because, according to the Qur'an, it is *muslim* (small *m*) in that it surrenders (*taslim*) itself to the will of God and, thus, rises above all tension and discord (Qur'an 3:83; 9:53; 13:15; 41:11). In its normative depiction of natural phenomena, the Qur'an talks about stars and trees as "prostrating before God" (55:6) and says that "all that is in the heavens and on earth extols His glory" (59:24). By acknowledging God's unity and praising His name, man joins the natural world in a substantive way— underscoring the essential link between the *anthropos* and the *cosmos* in what has been called the anthropocosmic vision.[16] The thrust of this view is that the common man-versus-nature dichotomy is a false one; man and nature cannot be separated from one another. The world has been given to the children of Adam as a trust (*amanah*) and they are responsible for standing witness to God's creation, mercy, and justice on earth. Conceiving of nature in terms of harmony, measure, order, and balance is a common and persistent attitude toward the nonhuman world in Islamic thought and has profound implications for constructing peace as a principle of the cosmos.[17]

The third premise pertains to man's natural state and his place within the larger context of existence. Though the Qur'an occasionally describes the fallen nature of man in gruesome terms, presenting him as weak, forgetful, treacherous, hasty, ignorant, ungrateful, hostile, and egotistic (e.g., Qur'an 14:34; 17:11; 18:54; 22:66; 33:72; 43:15; 100:6), these qualities are eventually considered deviations from man's essential nature (*fitrah*); he has been created in the most beautiful form (*ahsan taqwim*, Qur'an 95:4), both physically and spiritually. This metaphysical optimism defines human beings as God's vicegerent on earth (*khalifat Allah fi'l-ard*), as the Qur'an says, or, to use a metaphor from Christianity, as the pontifex, the bridge between heaven and earth.[18] The *fitrah* (Qur'an 30:30), the primordial nature from which God has created all humanity, is essentially a moral and spiritual substance drawn to good and God-consciousness (*taqwa*). Its imperfections and excessiveness (*fujur*, Qur'an 91:8) are accidental qualities to be subsumed under the soul's struggle to do good (*al-birr*), through which it transcends its subliminal desires by its intelligence and moral will.

The Philosophical-Theological Context: Evil and the Best of All Possible Worlds

In the context of theology and philosophy, questions of peace and violence are treated under the rubric of good and evil (*husn/khayr* and *sharr*, or *qubuh*). War, conflict, violence, injustice, discord, and the like are seen as extensions of the general problem of evil. Muslim philosophers and theologians have been interested in theodicy from the very beginning, and for good reason, because the basic question of theodicy goes to the heart of religion. How can a just and perfect God allow evil and destruction in a world He says He has created in perfect balance, with a purpose, and for the well-being of His servants? We can rephrase the question in the present context: Why is there so much violence, turmoil, and oppression rather than peace, harmony, and justice in the world? Does evil—of which violence is as an offshoot—belong to the essential nature of things, or is it an accident that arises only as the privation of goodness?

The above questions have given rise to a long and interesting debate about evil among theologians. One particular aspect of this debate, known as the best of all possible worlds (*ahsan al-nizam*) argument,[19] deserves closer attention, as it relates to forming a positive concept of peace. The classical statement of the problem pertains to divine justice and power on one hand and Greek notions of potentiality and actuality on the other. The fundamental question is whether the world in which we live is the best that God could have created. From a moral point of view, since the world is imperfect because there is evil and injustice in it, we either have to admit that God could not create a better and more perfect world or concede that He did not create a better world by will, as part of the divine economy of creation. Obviously—similar to the Cartesian argument about the nature of God—the first alternative questions God's omnipotence (*qudrah*), whereas the second jeopardizes His wisdom and justice (*adalah*). Following another line of discussion in *kalam*, we can reformulate the question as a tension between God's nature and will. Can God go against His own nature, which is just, if He wants to—or can His will not supersede His nature? Can God contradict Himself? If we say He can, then we attribute imperfection to Him. If we say no, then we limit Him.

Even the most modest attempt to analyze the questions about the nature of God within the context of *kalam* debates will take us too far afield. What directly relates to our discussion here is how the concepts of evil, injustice, oppression, and their variations are seen as the accidental outcomes of the world of contingencies in which we live. The weaknesses and frailties of human beings contribute enormously to creating and exacerbating evil, and it is reasonable to attribute evil to ourselves rather than to the divine. This is what the Qur'an holds regarding evil and man's accountability: "Whatever good happens to you, it is from God; and whatever evil befalls you, it is from your own self [soul]" (Qur'an 4:79; 3:165).

The best-of-all-possible-worlds argument, however, shifts the focus from particular instances of individual or structural violence to the phenomenon of evil itself. In this way, we gain a deeper insight into how evil arises in the first place. We may reasonably argue that evil is part of the divine economy of creation and thus necessary. In a moral sense, it is part of divine economy because it is what tests us (Qur'an 21:36; 18:9). Without evil, there is no accountability—or freedom.[20] Mulla Sadra (d. 1649) calls it a necessity of divine providence (*al-'inayah*) and the "concomitant of the ultimate *telos* of goodness (*al-ghayah al-khayriyyah*)."[21] In an ontological sense, evil is needed because the world is imperfect by definition. The ultimate perfection belongs to God, and the world is not God. That is why God has not created "all beings as pure goodness."[22] Evil as limitation and imperfection is an outcome of the first act of separation between the divine and the nondivine, or what Muslim theologians call all that is other than God (*ma siwa' Allah*). Ultimately, however, "all is from God" (Qur'an 4:78) even if it is apart from Him. This implies that evil, as the "contrastive manifestation of the good,"[23] ceases to be evil and contributes to the greater good—which is what the best-of-all-possible-worlds argument asserts. In a rather paradoxical way, one cannot object to the existence of evil itself because it makes the world as we know it possible. But this does not absolve us of the moral duty to fight individual cases of evil, nor does it make evil an essential nature of things because it was God's decision to create the world with a meaning and purpose in the first place. Evil remains contingent and transient, and this assumption extends to the next world.[24]

The notion of evil as an ontological necessity and contingency has important implications for how we look at the world and its evil side. From a psychological point of view, accepting evil as a transient yet necessary phenomenon prevents us from becoming petty and bitter in the face of all that is blemished, wicked, imperfect, and tainted.[25] It gives us a sense of moral security against the onslaught of evil, which can and must be fought with a firm belief in the ultimate supremacy of the good. It also enables us to see the world as it is and for what it is, and strive to make it a better place in terms of moral and spiritual perfection. From a religious point of view, this underscores the relative nature of evil: Something that may appear evil to us may not be evil, and vice versa, when everything is placed within a larger framework. Thus the Qur'an says that "it may well be that you hate a thing while it is good [khayr] for you, and it may well be that you love a thing while it is bad [sharr] for you. And God knows, and you know not" (Qur'an 2:216). Mulla Sadra applies this principle to "natural evils," saying that even "death, corruption [al-fasad] and the like are necessary and needed for the order of the world [al-nizam] when they occur 'by nature and not by force or accident.'"[26]

The best-of-all-possible-worlds argument is also related to the scheme of actuality and potentiality that Muslim philosophers and theologians adopted from Aristotle. They argue that the world in which we live is one of the possibilities that the divine has brought into actuality. In this sense, the world is pure contingency (imkan), hung between existence and nonexistence. From the point of view of its actuality, however—the way it appears to us now—the world is perfect and necessary because actuality implies plenitude and perfection, whereas potentiality is privation and nonexistence.[27] The sense of perfection in this context is both ontological and cosmological. It is ontological because existence is superior to nonexistence. It is cosmological because, as stated before, the world has been created with care, order, and beauty, which the Qur'an invites its readers to look at as the signs of God—ayat Allah, or vestigia Dei, as the Scholastics called it. The perfect state of the cosmos is presented as a model for establishing a just social order. It follows that evil is a phenomenon of this world, but does not define the essential nature of things.

An important outcome of the argument is to identify evil as a rationally discernible phenomenon, a simple truism. That is to say, people know evil things when they see them manifested in front of their eyes; evil is not an abstract idea. It is a powerful position against the notion of evil as a mysterious, mythical, or even cosmological fact, over which human beings have no control. If evil can be discerned by the intellect and correct reasoning, with the help of the revelation, of course,[28] then we have a tremendous responsibility to counteract the evil that may come from within or without.

Disagreement over how much responsibility we have, however, has created diverging schools of Muslim thought. In the tenth century, Mu'tazilite theologians pushed the sovereignty of human freedom to the point of endangering God's omniscience and omnipotence. This prompted Abu'l-Hasan 'Ali b. Isma'il al-Ash'ari (d. 936), a famous Muslim scholar once a Mu'tazilite himself, to carry out his own withdrawal (*i'tizal*) and lay the foundations of Asha'rism. He and his followers believed that good and evil were ultimately determined by divine law (*al-shari'ah*), leaving no space for the independent judgment of human reason (*al-'aql*). Paradoxically, however, the moral voluntarism of the Ash'arites agrees with Mu'tazilite rationalism in underscoring the relative and contingent nature of evil: Whether determined by reason or revelation, evil is the privation of good; it does not represent the essential nature of things.

Muslim philosophers assert the same point through what we might call the ontological argument. In addition to the fact that actuality is perfection over potentiality, existence (*al-wujud*) is pure goodness (*khayr mahd, summun bonum*), and all beings that exist partake of this ontological goodness. Since God is the only necessary being (*wajib al-wujud*), this perfection, by its essence and in all regards, ultimately belongs to Him. According to Ibn Sina (d. 1037), evil has no enduring essence and appears only as the privation (*'adam*) of goodness:

> Every being that is necessary by itself is pure goodness and pure perfection. Goodness [*al-khayr*], in short, is that which everything desires and by which everything's being is completed. But evil has no essence; it is either the nonexistence of a substance or the nonexistence of the state of goodness [*salah*] for a substance. Thus existence is pure goodness, and the perfection of existence is the goodness of existence. Existence is pure goodness when it is not accompanied by nonexistence, the nonexistence of a substance, or the nonexistence of something from that substance and it is in perpetual actuality. As for the existent contingent by itself, it is not pure goodness because its essence does not necessitate its existence by itself. Thus its essence allows for nonexistence. Anything that allows for nonexistence in some respect is not free from evil and imperfection in all respects. Hence pure goodness is nothing but existence that is necessary by its own essence.[29]

Elaborating on the same idea, Mulla Sadra argues that good and evil cannot be regarded as opposites: "one is the nonexistence of the other; therefore goodness is existence or the perfection of existence and evil is the absence of existence or the nonexistence of the perfection of existence."[30] By defining good and evil in terms of existence and nonexistence, Sadra shifts the focus from a moralistic to a primarily ontological framework. Like Ibn Sina, Sadra defines goodness as the essential nature of the present world order. This leads Sadra to conclude that goodness permeates the world order at its foundation. Despite the existence of such natural evils as death and famine, "what is more and permanent is the desired goodness in nature."[31] Once evil is relativized, it is easier to defend this world as the best of all possible worlds. This is what Sadra does when he says that "the universe in its totality (*bi-kulliyatihi*) is the most perfect of all that may be and the most noble of all that can be conceived."[32]

The Political-Legal Context: Law and Its Vicissitudes

The *shari'ah* rules concerning war, peace, *jihad*, religious minorities, and the religious-political divisions of the concepts of the land of Islam (*dar al-Islam*), land of peace (*dar al-sulh*), the land of the covenant (*dar al-'ahd*), and land of war (*dar al-harb*) are an important component of the Islamic law of nations. Interpreting them contextually and historically is a significant challenge to both modern scholars of Islam and Muslims themselves. In analyzing the views of jurists on these issues from the second Islamic century onward, it is extremely common to choose specific legal rulings by certain jurists as the orthodox view of Islam, applicable to all times and places. Granted, Islamic law is based on the ultimate authority of the Qur'an and the *sunnah*, but the *shari'ah* as a legal code is structured to allow considerable freedom and leeway for Muslim scholars and communities to adjust themselves to different times and circumstances. Early generations of Muslim scholars, jurists (*fuqaha*), Qur'anic commentators (*mufassirin*), traditionalists (*muhaddithin*), and historians have used this simple fact extensively, paving the way for the rise and flourishing of various schools of law and legal opinions in Islam. The flexible, resilient nature of the *shari'ah*, however, has been grossly overlooked and understated, not only in Western scholarship, but also in the Islamic world. This has led to the oft-repeated conclusion that the teachings of the *shari'ah*—and, by derivation, Islam itself—do not contain a substantive notion of peace and a culture of coexistence.[33]

The following analysis of the legal-political aspects of traditional *shari'ah* rulings concerning war and peace is limited to three interrelated issues. The first is the Muslim community's right to defend itself against internal or external aggression and the transition of the first Muslim community from the overt pacifism of Mecca to the activism of Medina. This issue raises the question of *jihad* as an offensive versus defensive war and its relation to what is called *jus ad bellum* in the Western tradition. The second is the political context of the legal injunctions of certain jurists, namely Imam Muhammad b. Idris al-Shafi'i (d. 820) and the Hanafi jurist Muhammad b. Ahmad b. Sahl al-Sarakhsi (d. 1090), concerning the legitimacy of the territorial expansion of Muslim states on religious grounds. Some contemporary scholars have disproportionately overstated Shafi'i's justification of launching *jihad* against non-Muslim territories on the basis of their belief systems. The third issue is the treatment of religious minorities, that is, *dhimmis* living under Islamic law, and its relevance to religious diversity and cultural pluralism in the Islamic tradition.

Mecca to Medina: From Pacifism to Activism

A major concern of the Prophet of Islam in Mecca was to ensure the security and integrity of the nascent Muslim community as a religious and political unit. This concern eventually led to the historic migration of the Prophet and his followers to Medina in 622, after a decade of pressure, sanctions, persecution, torture, and a foiled attempt to kill the Prophet himself. During this period, the community's right to defend itself against Meccan polytheists was mostly exercised in what we would call today pacifist and nonviolent means of resistance. Even though the Prophet was in close contact with Meccan leaders to spread his message and protect his small yet highly dedicated group of followers, his tireless negotiations did not mitigate the Meccans' aggressive policies against the growing Muslim community. The transition from the robust pacifism of Mecca to the political activism of Medina took place when the permission to fight was given in the Qur'an (22:38–40):

> Verily, God will ward off [all evil] from those who attain to faith: [and] verily, God does not love anyone who betrays his trust and is bereft of gratitude. Permission [to fight] is given to those against whom war is being wrongfully waged—and, verily, God has indeed the power to succor them—: those who have been driven from their homelands against all right or no other reason than their saying, "Our Sustainer is God!" For, if God had not enabled people to defend themselves against one another, [all] monasteries and churches and synagogues and mosques—in [all of] which God's name is abundantly extolled—would surely have been destroyed.[34]

These and other verses (Qur'an 2:190–93) clearly define the reasons for taking up arms to defend religious freedom and set the conditions of just war (*jus ad bellum*) in self-defense. That the verse, revealed in the first year of the *hijrah*, refers to the grave wrongdoing against Muslims and their eviction from their homeland for professing the new faith confirms that the Prophet's migration was the last stage of the forceful expulsion of the Muslim community from Mecca. This was a turning point for the attitudes and tactics of the Prophet and his followers to protect themselves against the Meccans. The subsequent battles fought between the Meccans and Medinans from Badr to Khandaq until the Prophet's triumphant return to Mecca were based on the same principles of religious freedom, collective solidarity, and political unity. In addition to enunciating the conditions of just war, the above verse defines religious freedom as a universal cause for all three Abrahamic faiths. Like any other political unit, communities tied with a bond of faith have the right and, in fact, the responsibility to secure their existence and integrity against threats of persecution. This ecumenical attitude toward the religious freedom of all faith communities was a major factor in the Prophet's signing of a number of treatises with the Jews, Christians, and Zoroastrians of the Arabian Peninsula, as well as the relatively tolerant treatment of religious minorities under the *shari'ah*.[35]

The construction of *jihad* as armed struggle to expand the borders of *dar al-Islam*—and, by derivation, subsume all *dar al-harb* under Islamic dominion—is found in some of the jurists of the ninth and tenth centuries (see chapter 2). Among those, we can mention Shafi'i and Sarakhsi, who interpreted *jihad* as the duty of the Muslim ruler to fight against lands that he defined as the territory of war. Shafi'i formulated his expansionist theory of *jihad* as a religious duty, as Muslim states were engaged in prolonged military conflicts with non-Muslim territories and had become mostly successful in extending their borders. These jurists justified fighting against non-Muslims on account of their disbelief (*kufr*) rather than self-defense, but they were also adamant that *jus in bello* norms be observed: for example, avoiding excessiveness; accepting truces; and sparing the lives of noncombatants, women, and children.[36] Despite these qualifications, the views of Shafi'i and his followers represent a shift away from the Qur'anic notion of self-defense and toward armed struggle to bring about the conversion of non-Muslims. Having said that, two points need to be mentioned.

First, the views of Shafi'i and Sarakhsi do not represent the majority, let alone the orthodox, stance of jurists. The common tendency to present this particular definition of *jihad* as the mainstream position of Islam not only disregards the views of Imam Abu Hanifah (d. 767), Malik ibn Anas (d. 795), Abu Yusuf Ya'qub b. Ibrahim (d. 798), Muhammad b. al-Hasan al-Shaybani (d. 804), 'Abd al-Rahman b. 'Amr al-Awza'i (d. 774), Ibn Rushd (d. 1198), Ibn Taymiyyah (d. 1328), Ibn Qayyim al-Jawziyyah (d. 1350),[37] and others, but also ignores the historical and contextual nature of such juridical rulings. The same holds for Muslim political philosophers and theologians, who take different positions on the bifurcationist framework of *dar al-Islam* versus *dar al-harb*.[38] Moreover, the rulings were by and large the jurists' response to the de facto situation of the military conquests of Muslim states rather than their cause. Certain jurists begin to stress such reconciliatory terms as *dar al-'ahd* and *dar al-sulh* during and after the eleventh and twelfth centuries, when the Muslim states were confronted with political realities other than unabated conquest and resounding victories.

This change in tone and emphasis, however, was not a completely novel phenomenon. The concept of *dar al-sulh* can be traced back to the treaty that the Prophet had signed with the Christian population of Najran when he was in Medina.[39] This treaty, the text of which has been preserved, lays the foundations of making peace with non-Muslim communities. In addition, the policy of giving safe conduct (*aman*), that is, contractual protection to non-Muslims residing or traveling in Muslim territories, was common. Such people were known as *musta'min*, and to grant them this status was not only the prerogative of the head of state or *ulama*, but also individuals, both men and women.[40]

Second, the idea of bringing the world under the reign of *dar al-Islam* by military means and territorial expansion should be seen within the context of the geopolitical conditions of the classical Islamic world. The medieval imperial world order, of which Muslim states were a part, was based on the idea of continuously expanding one's borders because conquest (*fath*) provided economic, political, and demographic stability. In this sense, as Hitti points out, "the Islam that conquered the northern regions was not the Islamic religion but the Islamic state . . . it was Arabianism and not Muhammadanism that triumphed first."[41] When one was either conqueror or conquered, the triumphant Muslim states depended heavily on expanding their territories against both Muslim and non-Muslim rivals. The historic march of Muslim armies into territories once under non-Muslim rule was not *jihad* in the religious sense of the term, but an outcome of the power struggle to which all political establishments, Muslim or non-Muslim, were subject. Territorial expansion and military conquest did not always mean conversion. Beginning with the early history of Islam, conversion through persuasion and calling (*da'wah*) was encouraged, and a multitude of methods facilitated the conversion of individuals and masses through peaceful means. Conversion by force, which would make Islam a proselytizing religion, however, was not imposed as a policy, by either the *ulama* or the rulers. Further, conversion was not required to become part of the Muslim community and gain religious freedom, receive protection, and possess property under Islamic law. The protean concept of the *dhimmi* allowed religious minorities to maintain their traditions and resist any attempts at forceful conversion. As Islam does not have official missionaries, the agents of conversion responsible for the enormously successful and unprecedented spread of Islam were multifarious, extending from Arab traders and Sufis to Islamic communal institutions.[42] We cannot explain the en masse conversion of various ethnic, religious, and cultural communities to Islam by the military prowess of a handful of Muslim groups in Anatolia, Iran, Africa, or India.

Paradoxically, the policies of religious tolerance secured both the rights of religious minorities and the loyalties of new converts. In a manner unimaginable in the Christian kingdoms of Europe at the time, Jews, Christians, Sabeans, and Hindus had access to considerably high state posts from the time of Mu'awiyah (r. 661–80) to the dissolution of the Ottoman Empire at the beginning of the twentieth century. Jewish and Christian scientists, physicians, accountants, counselors, and statesmen were employed at Ummayad courts. St. John the Damascene (Yuhanna ed-Dimashqi) (d. 749), one of the most influential figures in the Eastern Orthodox Church and the author of the earliest anti-Islamic polemics, and his father Ibn Mansur held positions under the caliph 'Abd al-Malik (r. 685–705).[43] During the Buwayhid era in Persia, the vizier of the powerful Persian king 'Adud al-Dawlah (r. 949–82), Nasr ibn Harun, was a Christian.[44] We find similar cases in India and the Ottoman Empire, where the vertical mobility of religious minorities in state affairs was a common phenomenon. Even the *devshirme* system of the Ottomans, which has been criticized and labeled as a form of forced conversion, gave religious minorities unfettered access to the highest government positions. Three grand viziers of Suleiman the Magnificent (r. 1520–66), the most powerful Ottoman sultan, were of Christian origin: the famous Maqbul (later Maqtul), Ibrahim Pasha of Parga (d. 1536), was a Greek and an able diplomat and commander; Rustem Pasha (d. 1561) was a Bulgarian and had handled the treasury with utmost competence; and the celebrated Sokullu Mehmet Pasha (d. 1579) was a Slav from Bosnia who had served, in his youth, as an acolyte in a Serbian church.[45] Among these, the case of Sokullu is probably the most interesting, for it shows the extent to which the *devshirme* system eventually benefited Christian communities under Ottoman rule. Although Sokullu embraced Islam and became one of the most powerful men of his time, he kept close contact with his brother, who was an important religious figure in Bosnia and helped him with his status as the grand vizier.

Thus, we have to distinguish between *jihad* as just war and *jihad* as holy war,[46] which brings us to our third issue. Just war refers to a community's right to defend itself against aggression and oppression. It is defensive in nature, whereas holy war entails converting everybody else into one's religion by force, armed struggle, territorial expansion, and other means. In the first sense, *jihad* is an extension of the *jus ad bellum* tradition and can be seen as a necessity to protect justice, freedom, and order. In this regard, the position taken by the Qur'an and the Prophet concerning the use of force against oppression by Muslims and non-Muslims alike[47] is essentially a realist one, aiming at putting strict conditions on regulating war and using force. The guiding principle is that of fighting against aggression, which is "to fight in the way of God," and not to be the aggressors: "Fight [*qatilu*, literally *kill*] in the way of God against those who fight against you, but do not transgress the limits. Verily, God does not love aggressors" (Qur'an 2:190; see also 4:91; 9:36). Both classical and modern commentators have interpreted the command not to transgress (*la ta'tadu*) as avoiding war and hostilities, resorting to armed struggle only to defend one's freedom, and, once forced to fight, sparing the lives of noncombatants, especially women, children, and the elderly.[48]

Contrary to what Khadduri claims,[49] the global bifurcation of *dar al-Islam* and *dar al-harb* does not translate into a holy war or a permanent state of war between Muslims and non-Muslims. No personage illustrates this point better than Ibn Taymiyyah, whose views have been widely distorted and exploited to lend legitimacy to extremist interpretations of the classical Islamic law of nations. Even though Ibn Taymiyyah lived through the destruction wrought upon the Islamic world by the Mongols and could have been expected to take a more belligerent stance against them, he was unequivocal in stating that Muslims could wage war only against those who attacked them. For Ibn Taymiyyah, the idea of initiating unprovoked war to convert people to Islam—to engage in holy war—belies the religion itself: "If the unbeliever were to be killed unless he becomes a Muslim, such an action would constitute the greatest compulsion in religion," which would contradict the Qur'anic principle that "there is no compulsion in religion" (2:256).[50] Ibn Taymiyyah's famous student, Ibn Qayyim al-Jawziyyah, reiterates the same principle when he says that "fighting (*qital*) is permitted on account of war (*harb*), not on account of disbelief (*kufr*)."[51]

This extended meaning of *jihad* as *jus ad bellum*—that is, armed struggle in self-defense—can also be seen in the anticolonialist resistance movements of the modern period. In the eighteenth and nineteenth centuries, calls for *jihad* were issued across the Islamic world to fight against colonialism. For the anticolonialist resistance movements of this period, *jihad* functioned, first, as the religious basis for fighting against colonialism and, second, as a powerful way to mobilize people to join the resistance forces. Among others, the Baralvi family in India, Shaykh Shamil (d. 1871) in Chechenya, Shaykh 'Abd al-Qadir al-Jaza'ri (d. 1883) in Algeria, the Mahdi family in the Sudan, Ahmad 'Urabi (d. 1911) in Egypt, and the Sanusiyyah order in Libya fought against European colonial powers.[52] It was during this period of resistance that *jihad* took on a cultural tone, in the sense that the fight against colonial powers was seen as both a military and religious-cultural struggle. Despite the enormous difficulties faced by Muslim scholars, leaders, merchants, and villagers in Egypt, Africa, India, and other places, however, the calls for *jihad* against European armies did not lead to an all-out war against local non-Muslim communities. Even when the Muslim population had to bear the full brunt of colonialism, extreme care was taken not to label local non-Muslims as the enemy because of their religious and cultural affiliation with European colonial powers. When, for instance, the Sanusi call for "*jihad* against all unbelievers" worried Christians in Egypt, Muslim scholars responded by saying that *jihad* in Libya was directed at the Italian aggressors, not all Westerners or Christians.[53]

Since *jihad* as armed struggle was fought against invading European powers, it was not difficult for it to take on religious and cultural tones. Napoleon attempted to paint himself as a defender of Islam when he invaded Egypt in 1798; in a letter to local Egyptian leaders, imams, and scholars, he said that he "more than the Mamluks, serve[s] God—may He be praised and exalted—and revere[s] His Prophet Muhammad and the glorious Qur'an" and that the "French are also faithful Muslims."[54] The celebrated Egyptian historian 'Abd al-Rahman al-Jabarti (1754–1825) saw these as no more than outright lies, expected only from an infidel (*kafir*). For Jabarti and his generation, it was yet another fact confirming the necessity of launching *jihad* against the *afranj* (the French; that is, Europeans). This sense of *jihad* as anticolonialist struggle has not completely disappeared from the minds of some Muslims in the postcolonial period. Modern calls for *jihad* as holy war by such Muslim extremists as 'Abd al-Salam Faraj, who wrote the well-known *al-Faridah al-Ghai'bah* (*The Neglected Duty*)[55] presumably justifying the assassination of Anwar Sadat in 1981, and Osama bin Laden are as much the product of their strict and ahistorical reading of the classical *shari'ah* sources as the legacy of colonialism.

Treatment of Religious Minorities

Dhimmi status granted religious minorities under Muslim rule, especially Jews and Christians, some measure of economic and political protection, freedom of worship, right to own property, and, in some cases, access to high government positions. The religious-legal basis of the notion of the *dhimmi* goes back to the time of the Prophet. While the status of *dhimma* was initially given to Jews, Christians, Sabians, and Zoroastrians, its scope was later extended to include all non-Muslims living under Islam.[56] A similar course of action was followed in India when Muhammad b. al-Qasim, the first Muslim commander to set foot on Indian soil in the eighth century, compared Hindus to Jews, Christians, and Zoroastrians and declared them as part of the *ahl al-dhimmah*.[57] This decision, later sanctioned by Hanafi jurists, was a momentous event in the development of the Muslim attitude toward the religions of India and can be seen as laying the foundations of the Hindu-Muslim mode of cultural coexistence.

That the Prophet and his companions were lenient toward the People of the Book—most notably, Christians and Jews—is attested not only by the communal relationships that developed between Muslims and non-Muslims in Medina, but also recorded in a number of treatises that the Prophet signed. The Medinan Constitution (*wathiqat al-madinah*), for instance, recognizes the Jews of Banu 'Awf, Banu al-Najjar, Banu Tha'labah, and others as a distinct community with "their own religion."[58] Another treatise signed with the People of the Book of Najran reads as follows:

> They [People of the Book] shall have the protection of Allah and the promise of Muhammad, the Apostle of Allah, that they shall be secure in their lives, property, lands, creed, those absent and those present, their families, their churches, and all that they possess. No bishop or monk shall be displaced from his parish or monastery; no priest shall be forced to abandon his priestly life. No hardships or humiliation shall be imposed on them, nor shall their land be occupied by [our] army. Those who seek justice, shall have it: there will be no oppressors nor oppressed.[59]

The privileges given to *dhimmis* included things that were prohibited for Muslims, such as breeding pork and producing alcohol, which were not outlawed for Christians. The religious tax, called *jizya*, was the main economic responsibility of the *dhimmis* under *shari'ah*. Contrary to common belief, the primary goal of the *jizya* was not the humiliation of the People of the Book. While many contemporary translations of the Qur'an translate the words *wa hum al-saghirun* as "so that they will be humiliated," Ibn Qayyim al-Jawziyyah, who has written the most extensive work on the People of the Book, understands it as securing the allegiance of the People of the Book to laws pertaining to them (*ahkam al-millah*). Instead, *wa hum al-saghirun* should be understood, says Ibn Qayyim, as making all subjects of the state obey the law and, in the case of the People of the Book, pay the *jizya*.[60]

According to Abu Yusuf, one of the foremost authorities of the Hanafi school of law, the *jizya* was "48 dirhams on the wealthy, 24 on the middle class and 12 dirhams on the poor ploughman-peasant and manual worker. According to Shafi'i, the *jizya* is one dinar for the poor and four dinars for the rich."[61] It is collected once a year and may be paid in kind, that is, as "goods and similar property which is accepted according to its value."[62] Those who cannot afford to pay it are not forced to do so.[63] The exempted also include women, children, the elderly, and the sick.[64] To the best of our knowledge, the *jizya* was not a significant source of income for the state,[65] and it exempted the *dhimmis* from military service. In some cases, the *jizya* was postponed or abandoned altogether by the head of the state, as we see in India under the reigns of Akbar (r. 1556–1605), Jahangir (r. 1605–28) and Shah Jahan (1628–58).[66] The *jizya* was compensation for the protection of the *dhimmis* by the state against any type of aggression from Muslims or non-Muslims. Poll taxes were returned to the *dhimmis* when the Muslim state could not provide for the security of its non-Muslim minorities.[67] In most cases, the *jizya* was imposed not as an individual tax, like the *kharaj,* but as collective tribute on eligible *dhimmis.*[68]

While Ibn Qayyim al-Jawziyyah's famous work on the *dhimmis* contains many rulings that present a condescending view of non-Muslims and advocate policies of humiliation against them,[69] many other jurists insisted on treating the *dhimmis* with equity and justice. As people "under the protection of the Prophet," Jews, Christians, and other religious minorities were not to be forced to pay more than they could afford, nor to be intimidated and oppressed because of their religious affiliations. Advising Harun al-Rashid (r. 786–809), the famous Abbasid caliph, on the treatment of the *dhimmis,* Abu Yusuf exhorts him to "treat with leniency those under the protection of our Prophet Muhammad, and not allow that more than what is due to be taken from them or more than they are able to pay, and that nothing should be confiscated from their properties without legal justification."[70] In making this strong advice to the caliph, Abu Yusuf narrates a tradition of the Prophet in which he says that "he who robs a *dhimmi* or imposes on him more than he can bear will have me as his opponent." Another well-known case is the Prophet's order to execute a Muslim who had killed a *dhimmi.* In response to this incident, the Prophet said that "it is most appropriate that I live up fully to my [promise of] protection."[71]

These and other rules concerning the *dhimmis* show that Islam accepts the reality of the religious other in terms of a de jure reality rather than as a matter of political exigency. The underlying principle behind this attitude of accommodation is that the interests of human beings are served better in peace than in conflict. To reveal the extent of the Islamic theology of peace and cultural pluralism, we need to look at the cultural attitudes and practices of Muslim societies regarding other communities, to which we now turn.

The Sociocultural Context: Confrontation, Coexistence, and Peace

Islam does not prescribe a particular form of cultural identity, for both doctrinal and historical reasons. The absence of a central religious authority or clergy in the Islamic tradition preempts authoritarianism as a model for negotiating religious affairs in the public sphere, as attested by the multiplicity of schools of Islamic law and the notorious differences of opinion among them. However, this fact—which Muslims often state with a sense of pride—does not negate the presence of established and commonly accepted views in the Islamic tradition. To the extent that there is a set of beliefs and practices that we can consider mainstream and orthodox, it is based on the consensus of the community over generations rather than a centralized body of legal rulings. The incremental process of establishing orthodox etiquettes is not the monopoly of the *ulama*; it is shaped by a multitude of social agents, including men of letters, dervishes, saints, heretics, bards, folk singers, storytellers, political leaders, rulers, scientists, artists, traders, diplomats, philosophers, and theologians. The dissemination of religious authority on the one hand and the malleability of cultural expressions in Muslim societies on the other have challenged centralism and authoritarianism, but they have also raised questions about legitimacy and authenticity. Some, including those who are called Wahhabis, as well as some Orientalists have called this a deviation from the norms of the religion, arguing that Islamic history has been not so much Islamic as antinomian. Even if we admit that there are presumably overt discrepancies between what the *ulama* envision as a perfect *shari'ah* society and the cultural practices of Muslim societies, it is a healthy tension and functions as a mechanism of checks and balances against the strictly text-based, relatively abstract, and reductively legalistic approach of the jurists.

In creating their cultural orthopraxies, Muslim communities used the ethical universalism of the Qur'an and *sunnah*. The Qur'anic call to enjoin what is good and praised (*ma'ruf*) and forbid what is morally evil and disliked (*munkar*) is not a culture-specific injunction. It is addressed to all peoples regardless of their religious affiliations. The Prophet is considered a perfect example (*uswah hasanah*) for all humanity in his fight against all that is evil and oppressive and in defense of all that is praiseworthy and virtuous, whatever its origin might be. The notion of the middle community (*ummah wasatah*; Qur'an 2:143) supports the same ethical universalism: "And thus We willed you to be a community of the middle way, so that [with your lives] you might bear witness to the truth before all mankind, and that the Apostle might bear witness to it before you" (M. Asad's translation). This ethical-spiritual universalism aims to create an open society based on moral values, not on the received traditions of one tribe, city, or nation. This is in tandem with the fact that the Qur'an positions itself against the cultural localism and tribal parochialism of pre-Islamic Arabia—an invariable factor in the rapid spread of Islam outside the Arabic cultural zone. Once established as major cultural units, Muslim societies articulated their ethical universalism into various societal mechanisms, by which the ideal of creating a virtuous and just human habitat could be realized. The politics of gaining status and social ascendancy in the Islamic context is thus based on acquiring two universal qualities: knowledge (*ilm*) and virtue (*fadilah* and *ihsan*). Both qualities are implicit in the Qur'anic notion of God-consciousness (*taqwa*) (Qur'an 49:13), which is the ultimate criterion of nobility among people. In a broad sense, this forms the basis of an Islamic meritocracy, whereby every member of the society is urged to contribute to creating a moral and just social order.

Muslim philosophers and scientists regarded seeking knowledge and leading a virtuous life as the basis of their interest in other cultures and traditions. Historically, as the borders of the Islamic world expanded outside and beyond the Arabian Peninsula, Muslims became heir to all the major cultural traditions of the time. The Greco-Roman heritage through the Byzantine Empire and Persian culture through the Sasanids were the first two important traditions that Muslims encountered in less than a century after the Prophet's death. This was followed by Mesopotamian, Indian, black African, Central Asian, Chinese, and finally Malay-Indonesian civilizations in the fifteenth and sixteenth centuries.[72] The rapid establishment of the different cultural zones of the Islamic world went hand in hand with the rise of the numerous schools of law, Kalam, philosophy, and Sufi orders, generating a remarkable tapestry of cultural diversity within and across the *dar al-Islam*.[73] Despite occasional sectarian conflicts, such as the *mihnah* incident in the ninth century[74] or the Kadizade movement in the Ottoman Empire in the sixteenth century,[75] traditional Muslim societies succeeded in creating a stable and peaceful habitat in which both Muslim and non-Muslim members of the *ummah* contributed to cultivating a world civilization in such diverse fields as arts, sciences, trade, and architecture. The notion of cultural and religious coexistence in this milieu was not based merely on the temporary absence of conflict and confrontation between Islamic and non-Islamic elements. Its positive character was nurtured and sustained by Muslims' inclusive attitude toward other cultures and religious traditions, which makes Islamic civilization simultaneously both Islamic and Islamicate.[76]

A plethora of examples in the history of Islam illustrate the cultural ecumenism of Muslim societies, beginning with Muslim philosophers' attitudes toward pre-Islamic traditions of learning. For these early philosophers, scholars, and scientists, the search for truth occurred both within and beyond religious boundaries. Philosophers of the intellectual sciences (*ulum 'aqliyyah*) interested in Greek-Alexandrian thought as well as the scholars of transmitted sciences (*ulum naqliyyah*), specialized in such disciplines as *hadith*, Qur'anic commentary, and jurisprudence (*fiqh*), frequently referred to the Prophet's famous exhortations to "seek knowledge even if it is in China"[77] and that "wisdom is a Muslim's lost [treasure]. He takes it wherever he finds it."[78] Even as some later scholars opposed the philosophical sciences, especially their strictly Aristotelian versions, and defined knowledge (al-ʿilm) as religious science, this did not obstruct the steady development of philosophy and science in the Islamic world. Contrary to Goldziher's attempt to present the critical views of certain Hanbalite jurists on the ancient sciences (ulum al-awaʾil)—meaning Greek philosophy and science—as the orthodox Muslim position,[79] antiintellectualism remained largely confined to traditionists (al-muhaddithun), who were as much opposed to the lore of pre-Islamic times as they were to Kalam and doctrinal Sufism. For the overwhelming majority of the Muslim intelligentsia, the universality of truth was the guiding principle and ground of their quest for knowledge. No one has stated this point better than Yaʿqub b. Ishaq al-Kindi (d. 873), called the philosopher of the Arabs:

> We owe great thanks to those who have imparted to us even a small measure of truth, let alone those who have taught us more, since they have given us a share in the fruits of their reflection and simplified the complex questions bearing on the nature of reality. If they had not provided us with those premises that pave the way to truth, we would have been unable, despite our assiduous lifelong investigations, to find those true primary principles from which the conclusions of our obscure inquiries have resulted, and which have taken generation upon generation to come to light heretofore.[80]

That al-Kindi's attitude in the above quote was emblematic of his generation and later Muslim scholars is attested by Saʿid b. Ahmad al-Andalusi (d. 1070), who has divided nations (umam) according to their contribution to knowledge and science (al-ʿilm). He states this point in unequivocal terms when he says that

> We have determined that all nations, in spite of their differences and the diversities of their convictions, form tabaqatayn [two categories]. One tabaqah has cultivated science, given rise to the art of knowledge, and propagated the various aspects of scientific information; the other tabaqat did not contribute enough to science to deserve the honor of association or inclusion in the family of scientifically productive nations.[81]

Educated classes across the Islamic world shared the belief that truth transcends the contingencies of history as they studied countless schools of thought, both Islamic and pre-Islamic, producing an extensive literature on the history of ideas. The long list of scholars interested in intellectual history before and after Islam included Ibn al-Qifti (d. 1248), al-Mubashshir ibn Fatik Abu Sulayman al-Sijistani (d. c. 1000), Saʿid b. Ahmad al-Andalusi, Muhammad b. Ishaq Ibn al-Nadim (d. 1047), Abu ʿUthman ʿAmr b. Bahr al-Jahiz (d. 869), and Ibn Abi Usaybi'ah (d. 1270), as well as major writers of the *milal* tradition, such as Muhammad b. 'Abd al-Karim al-Shahrastani (d. 1153), Ahmad b. 'Ali al-Khatib al-Baghdadi (d. 1072), and Ibn Hazm al-Zahiri (d. 1064).[82] Among these works, the Egyptian *amir* Abu'l-Wafa' al-Mubashshir ibn Fatik's *Mukhtar al-hikam wa mahasin al-kilam* was noticed very early by medieval Europeans, translated into Latin and other languages, and became the first book printed by William Caxton in England in the fifteenth century, as *The Dicts and Sayings of the Philosophers*.[83] The continuity of humanity's search for truth had a normative value for most of these writers, in that their quest for knowledge was part of a larger tradition to which every seeker of knowledge belonged. When Hasan ibn Sahl was asked why he always invoked the views of those who came before him (*kalam al-awa'il*), he answered: "because it [i.e., those views] has been passed down before us; had it been unworthy and imperfect, it would have never reached us and gained [universal] approval."[84]

The concept of perennial philosophy (*al-hikmat al-khalidah*) enjoyed similar prestige due to the same notion of truth and its persistence in history. Shihab al-Din Yahya al-Suhrawardi (d. 1191), the founder of the school of Illumination (*ishraq*), made a strong case for the constancy of certain philosophical questions and the answers given to them when he said:

> Do not think that wisdom has existed only in these recent times [i.e., the pre-Islamic Persian and Greek philosophers]. No, the world is never bereft of wisdom and the person who possesses it with arguments and self-evident proofs. He is God's vice-regent on His earth, and this shall be so as long as the heavens and the earth exist.[85]

Apart from the sublime world of the intellectuals, the Islamic concept of cultural pluralism was extended to virtually all minorities living in the lands of Islam. The experience of *convivencia* among Jews, Christians, and Muslims in Andalusia was a result of the Islamic notion of cultural inclusivism.[86] While the Jews of Europe were subject to woeful vilifications and persecutions during the Middle Ages, a major Jewish intellectual tradition had developed under Muslim rule and included such prominent figures of medieval Jewish thought as Saadiah Gaon al-Fayyumi (d. 942), Solomon Ibn Gabirol (d. 1058 or 1070), Judah Halevi (d. 1141), Moses Maimonides (d. 1204), Sa'd b. Mansur Ibn Kammunah (d. 1284), Bahya Ibn Paquda (d. twelfth century), and Gersonides (Levi ben Gershom, d. 1344). This resulted in a unique interaction between medieval Jewish philosophy on the one hand and Islamic philosophy, *kalam*, and Sufism on the other.[87]

On the Indian subcontinent, a cultural syncreticism developed between Hindu and Muslim cultures. From the translation of Indian astronomical works into Arabic as early as the eighth century to Abu al-Rayhan al-Biruni's (d. 1047) historic study of India and Amir Khusraw's (d. 1325) formulation of an Islamic identity in the Indian cultural environment, a vast literature came into being, generating a unique mode of symbiosis between the two worlds at social, philosophical, and artistic levels. Perhaps the most important figure to illustrate this is Dara Shikuh (1615–59), the famous Mughal prince and son of Shah Jahan. Dara Shikuh translated and authored two important works dealing with Hinduism from an Islamic point of view. He translated the Bhagavat Gita and some fifty Upanishads into Persian as *Sirr-i Akbar* (*Great Mystery*), which he interpreted in light of the school of Advaita-Vedanta or the nondualism of Shankaracharya.[88] In making his case for the translation, Dara Shikuh says that he "read the Old and the New Testaments and the Psalms of David and other scriptures but the discourse on *tawhid* found in them was brief and in a summary form." He then turned to the Upanishads "which is undoubtedly the first heavenly Book and the fountain-head of the ocean of monotheism, and, in accordance with or rather an elucidation of the Kur'an."[89] Dara Shikuh also wrote a treatise called *Majma' al-Bahrayn,* referring to the Qur'anic verse 19:60, in which he attempted a monotheistic interpretation of Hinduism. In tandem with his universalist outlook, he defined his work as "a collection of the truth and wisdom of two Truth-knowing (*haqq-shinas*) groups," referring to Muslims and Hindus.[90] In addition to Dara Shikuh, there is the sixteenth-century Persian philosopher Mir Abu'l-Qasim Findiriski (d. c. 1640), who is reported to have met a number of Hindu mystics during his travels to India and translated and wrote a commentary on the Hindu mystical and philosophical text *Yoga-Vasishtha.*[91]

Such modes of cultural coexistence would have been impossible without the recognition of the diversity of cultures and societies as part of human existence. The Qur'an takes up this issue in several places. Working toward a common good is conditioned on the existence of different communities:

> Unto every one of you We have appointed a [different] law and way of life. And if God had so willed, He could surely have made you all one single community: but [He willed it otherwise] in order to test by means of what He has vouchsafed unto you. Vie, then, with one another in doing good works! (5:48; also 11:118).

This theme is further developed in the following verse. This time, the emphasis is on the civic responsibility of knowing one another:

> O humans! Behold, We have created you all out of a male and a female, and have made you into nations and tribes so that you might come to know one another. Verily, the noblest of you in the sight of God is the one who is most deeply conscious of Him. Behold, God is all-knowing, all-aware (49:13).

The above examples from the history of Islamic culture are neither scarce nor contrary to the norm. Even though fundamentalists—for lack of a better term—consider cases of cultural symbiosis and syncretism in the

Islamic world as deviations from an idealized and essentially ideological construct of Islam, both the Islamic intellectual tradition and Muslim societies have envisaged peace as a cross-cultural and intercommunal value.

Conclusion

A proper discussion of the Islamic concept of peace takes us beyond the minimal definition of peace as absence of conflict, and certainly beyond the limited sphere of law, be it Islamic or Western. In a broad sense, the Islamic tradition has articulated a concept of peace that extends from metaphysics and cosmology to politics and culture. We cannot understand the experience of Muslim societies with other cultures and religions without accounting for these elements. The relevance of this tradition for the present-day Muslim world requires little explanation. Today, numerous Muslim intellectuals, scholars, and leaders—from Bosnia, Turkey, and Egypt to Iran, Malaysia, and the United States—are constructing an Islamic political ethics that is compatible with the Islamic tradition and responsive to the challenges of the modern world. Questions of war and peace, communal violence, terrorism, international relations, constitutional and participatory democracy, pluralism, openness, civility, and the attitude toward the religious other are discussed from a multitude of perspectives, and the views expressed are by no means uniform and homogenous. There is, however, an emerging consensus on upholding peace as a value in itself, regardless of the political state of Muslim countries and communities across the globe. There is also a growing awareness that the Islamic tradition contains the seeds of a culture of peace. The rich heritage of traditional Islam can help contemporary Muslim societies overcome the state of spiritual and political impoverishment in which they find themselves.

However, we cannot overemphasize the significance of the consensus in the present context. Muslim communities can no longer address issues of conflict and violence without developing a proper ethics of peace. While there is legitimate ground to believe that most of the factional, ethnic, or sectarian conflicts in Muslim societies can be resolved through nonviolent means, the lack of comprehensive peacemaking approaches and practices—as supported by a network of scholars, intellectuals, leaders, activists, non-governmental organizations, and state agencies—contributes to the problem of preventing communal strife and fighting. The sense of dispossession and alienation that has plagued the Muslim masses for the last two centuries continues to fuel feelings of disappointment in the modern world. The continuing injustices in the Muslim world make the voices of wisdom and justice fade away in the present conflicts and create new forms of disillusionment and hopelessness.

Conflicts in our age have become both local and global, blurring the distinction between the two. We can no longer speak of local and national conflicts without considering their international implications, nor can we ignore the impact of global trends and relations on local issues. The Kashmir problem or the Israeli-Palestinian conflict defies conventional notions of interstate or territorial disputes. This is a particular challenge to contemporary Muslim political thought in its transition from the large political units of the empire and its constellation states to the current system of nation-states contending with the effects of globalization. It remains to be seen what the weakening of the nation-state model will bring to Muslim societies in their struggle to cope with the current challenges of economic and cultural globalization. Cultivating a culture of peace, however, is an urgent need for Muslim communities in their intercommunal relations, as well as for their relations with other societies.

Notes

1. Rene Girard, *Violence and the Sacred*, trans. Patrick Gregory (Baltimore: The Johns Hopkins University Press, 1979).

2. This is the gist of Bernard Lewis' attacks on Islamic fundamentalism in a number of highly publicized essays, including "The Roots of Muslim Rage," *Atlantic Monthly*, vol. 266, no. 3 (September 1990), 47–60, and "Islam and Liberal Democracy," *Atlantic Monthly*, vol. 271, no. 2 (February 1993), 89. Lewis considers Islamic fundamentalism—which he equates occasionally with terrorism—as arising out of the overtly religious and intolerant traditions of Islam. I have dealt with Lewis' arguments in my "Roots of Misconception: Euro-American Perceptions of Islam Before and After 9/11," in Joseph Lumbard, ed., *Islam, Fundamentalism, and the Betrayal of Tradition* (Bloomington, IN: World Wisdom, 2004), 143–87.

3. Mark Juergensmeyer, *Terror in the Mind of God: The Global Rise of Religious Violence* (Berkeley and New York: University of California Press, 2000).

4. One such exception to the rule is Richard Martin's essay, "The Religious Foundations of War, Peace, and Statecraft in Islam," in John Kelsay and James Turner Johnson, eds., *Just War and Jihad: Historical and Theoretical Perspectives on War and Peace in Western and Islamic Traditions* (New York: Greenwood Press, 1991), 91–117.

5. Steven Lee, "A Positive Concept of Peace," in Peter Caws, ed., *The Causes of Quarrel: Essays on Peace, War, and Thomas Hobbes* (Boston: Beacon Press, 1989), 183–84.

6. Gray Cox, "The Light at the End of the Tunnel and the Light in Which We May Walk: Two Concepts of Peace," in Caws, *The Causes of Quarrel*, 162–63.

7. The celebrated *hadith Jibril* confirms the same Qur'anic usage: "*Ihsan* is to worship God as if you were to see Him; even if you see Him not, he sees you." For an extensive analysis of *ihsan* as articulated in the Islamic tradition, see Sachiko Murata and William Chittick, *The Vision of Islam* (New York: Paragon House, 1994), 265–317.

8. R.G. Collingwood, *The New Leviathan* (New York: Thomas Y. Crowell, 1971), 334.

9. Ibn Mansur, *Lisan al-'Arab* (Beirut: Dar al-Kutub al-'Ilmiyyah, 1993), XIII: 457–58; and Muhammad 'Ali al-Tahanawi, *Kashshaf Istilahat al-funun* (Beirut: Dar al-Kutub al-'Ilmiyyah, 1998), 3: 288–89.

10. Muhammad Asad, *The Message of the Qur'an* (Lahore: Maktabah Jawahir al-'Ulum, n.d.), 179, commenting on the Qur'an (6:54): "And when those who believe in Our messages come unto thee, say: 'Peace be upon you. Your Sustainer has willed upon Himself the law of grace and mercy so that if any of you does a bad deed out of ignorance, and thereafter repents and lives righteously, He shall be [found] much-forgiving, a dispenser of grace.'"

11. On the basis of this verse, the tenth-century philologist Abu Hilal al-'Askari considers justice and *ihsan* as synonyms. See his *al-Furuq al-Lughawiyyah*, 194, quoted in Franz Rosenthal, "Political Justice and the Just Ruler," in Joel Kraemer and Ilai Alon, eds., *Religion and Government in the World of Islam* (Tel-Aviv: Tel-Aviv University, 1983), 97, n. 20.

12. Like other Sufis, Ghazali subscribes to the notion of what Ibn al-'Arabi would later call the possessor of the two eyes (*dhu 'l-'aynayn*), that is, seeing God with the two eyes of transcendence (*tanzih*) and imminence (*tashbih*). See Fadlou Shehadi, *Ghazali's Unique Unknowable God* (Leiden: E.J. Brill, 1964), 8–10, 51–55. For Ibn al-'Arabi's expression of the possessor of the two eyes, see William Chittick, *The Sufi Path of Knowledge* (Albany: SUNY Press, 1989), 361–62. The Mu'tazilite and Ash'arite theologians have a long history of controversy over the three major views of divine names and qualities, i.e., *tanzih*, *tashbih*, and *ta'til* (suspension). See Michel Allard, *Le problème des attributes divins dans la doctrine d'al-As'ari et des ses premiers grands disciples* (Beyrouth: Editions Del L'Impirimerie Catholique, 1965), 354–64.

13. 'Ali b. Sultan Muhammad al-Harawi al-Qari, *al-Masnu' fi Ma'rifat al-hadith al-Mawdu'* (Al-Riyad: Maktabat al-Rushd, 1404 AH), 1:141.

14. Quoted in William Chittick, *The Self-Disclosure of God: Principles of Ibn al-'Arabi's Cosmology* (Albany: SUNY Press, 1998), 22.

15. Dawud al-Qaysari, *Risalah fi Ma'rifat al-Mahabbat al-haqiqiyyah*, in his *al-Rasa'il*, ed. Mehmet Bayraktar (Kayseri: Kayseri Metropolitan Municipality, 1997), 138.

16. The term was first used by Mircea Eliade and adopted by Tu Weiming to describe the philosophical outlook of the Chinese traditions. For an application of the term to Islamic thought, see William Chittick, "The Anthropocosmic Vision in Islamic Thought" in Ted Peters, Muzaffar Iqbal, and Syed Nomanul Haq, eds., *God, Life, and the Cosmos* (Aldershot: Ashgate, 2002), 125–52.

17. See Seyyed Hossein Nasr, *Religion and the Order of Nature* (Oxford: Oxford University Press, 1996), 60–63.

18. The classical Qur'an commentaries are almost unanimous on interpreting this *khalifah* as Adam, i.e., humans in the generic sense. See Jalal al-Din al-Mahalli and Jalal al-Din al-Suyuti, *Tafsir al-Jalalayn* (Beirut: Mu'assasat al-Risalah, 1995), 6; Muhyiddin Ibn al-'Arabi, *al-Futuhat al-Makkiyyah*, ed. M. 'Abd al-Rahman al-Mar'ashli (Beirut: Dar Ihya' al-Turath al-'Arabi, 1997), 1:169.

19. Another formulation is *laysa fi 'l-imkan abda' mimma kan*, which, loosely translated, states that "there is nothing in the world of possibility more beautiful and perfect than what is in actuality." This sentence, attributed to Ghazali, has led to a long controversy in Islamic thought. For an excellent survey of this debate in Islamic theology, see Eric L. Ormsby, *Theodicy in Islamic Thought: The Dispute over al-Ghazali's "Best of All Possible Worlds"* (Princeton, NJ: Princeton University Press, 1984). See also al-Ghazali, *Ihya' 'Ulum al-Din* (Cairo: Mu'assarat al-Halabi, 1968), 4:321. The earliest formulation of the problem, however, can be traced back to Ibn Sina.

20. Plantinga's free-will defense is based on this premise. See Alvin Plantinga, "The Free Will Defense," in Max Black, ed., *Philosophy in America*, reprinted in Baruch A. Broody,

ed. *Readings in the Philosophy of Religion: An Analytical Approach* (Upper Saddle River, NJ: Prentice Hall, 1974), 187. See also Plantinga, "God, Evil, and the Metaphysics of Freedom," in Marilyn M. Adams and Robert M. Adams, eds., *The Problem of Evil* (Oxford: Oxford University Press, 1990), 83–109.

21. Mulla Sadra, *al-Hikmat al-Muta'aliyah fi 'l-Asfar al-'Aqliyyah al-Arba'ah* (Beirut: Dar Ihya' al-Turath al-'Arabi, 1981), II:3, 72.

22. Sadra, *Asfar,* 78.

23. Frithjof Schuon, *In the Face of the Absolute* (Bloomington, IN: World Wisdom Books, 1989), 39.

24. This is the main reason that a good number of Sufis, philosophers, and some theologians believe that hell is temporary, whereas paradise is eternal. For the debate between the Mu'tazilites and the Ash'arites on this issue, see Sa'd al-Din al-Taftazani, *Sharh al-Maqasid* (Beirut: 'Alam al-Kutub, 1989), 5:131–40.

25. See Qur'an (41:49–50): "Man never tires of asking for the good [things of life]; and if evil fortune touches him, he abandons all hope, giving himself up to despair. Yet whenever We let him taste some of Our grace after hardship has visited him, he is sure to say, "This is but my due!"—and, "I do not think that the Last Hour will ever come: but if [it should come, and] I should indeed be brought back unto my Sustainer, then, behold, the ultimate good awaits me with Him" (M. Asad's translation).

26. Sadra, *Asfar,* II:3, 92–3; see also 77.

27. See Plotinus, *The Enneads,* V, IX, 5, 248, and Sadra, *Asfar,* I:3, 343–44. Baqillani considers the potential (*bi'l-quwwah*) as nonexistent. See his *Kitab al-Tawhid,* 34–44, quoted in Franz Rosenthal, *Knowledge Triumphant: The Concept of Knowledge in Medieval Islam* (Leiden: E.J. Brill, 1970), 216.

28. As the leader of the skeptics (*imam al-mushakkikin*), Fakhr al-Din al-Razi disagrees. His objection, however, clarifies another aspect of the discussion of theodicy in Islam. As al-Razi points out, there is no dispute that some actions are good while others are bad. The question is "whether this is because of an attribute that belongs [essentially] to the action itself or this is not the case and it is solely as an injunction of the *shari'ah* [that actions and things are good or bad]." Al-Razi hastens to add that the Mu'tazilites opt for the first view and "our path"—that is, the Asha'rites—believe in the second. See Fakhr al-Din al-Razi, *al-Arba'in fi Usul al-Din* (Cairo: Maktabat al-Kulliyat al-Azhariyyah, 1986), 1:346. For a defense of the same Ash'arite position, see Taftazani, *Sharh al-Maqasid,* 4:282, where it is asserted that human reason is in no place to judge what is good (*al-husn*) and what is evil (*al-qubh*). For Sabziwari's defense of the Mu'tazilites, the philosophers, and the Imamiyyah on the rationality of good and evil, see his gloss on Sadra's *Asfar,* II:3, 83–84.

29. Ibn Sina, *Kitab al-Najat,* ed. Majid Fakhry (Beirut: Dar al-Ufuq al-Jadidah, 1985), 265; see also Ibn Sina, *al-Mubahathat,* ed. Muhsin Bidarfar (Qom: Intisharat-i Bidar, 1413 AH), 301.

30. Sadra, *Asfar,* II:1, 113.

31. Sadra, *Asfar,* II:3, 76. The intrinsic goodness of things in their natural or ontological state has given rise to a number of popular formulations of the problem, the most celebrated one being Merkez Efendi, the famous Ottoman scholar. When asked if he would change anything were he to have the center of the world at his hands, he replied that he would leave everything as it is; hence the term *merkez* (center).

32. Sadra, *Asfar,* III:2, 114; see also II:2, 114; III:1, 256; and III:2, 106–34. Sadra employs two arguments to defend the best-of-all-possible-worlds argument, which he calls the ontological (*inni*) and causal (*limmi*) methods (*manhaj*).

33. This is what Tibi claims in his essentialist generalizations and oversimplifications about the Islamic pathos of peace and war. Cf. Bassam Tibi, "War and Peace in Islam," in Terry Nardin, ed. *The Ethics of War and Peace: Religious and Secular Perspectives* (Princeton: Princeton University Press, 1996), 128–45.

34. Muhammad Asad, *The Message of Qur'an: Translation and Transliteration,* 2nd edition (Watsonville, CA: The Book Foundation, 2008).

35. Concerning the Zoroastrians and Sabeans and their being part of the People of the Book, Abu Yusuf narrates a number of traditions of the Prophet to show that they should be treated with justice and equality as are the other *dhimmis*. The inclusion of the Zoroastrians among the *dhimmis* is inferred from the fact that the Prophet had collected *jizyah* from the Majus of Hajar. See A. Ben Shemesh, trans., *Taxation in Islam: Abu Yusuf's Kitab al-kharaj* (Leiden: E.J. Brill, 1969), 88–89.

36. Some of these stipulations can be followed from Shaybani's *Siyar*; see Majid Khadduri, *The Islamic Law of Nations: Shaybani's Siyar* (Baltimore: The John Hopkins University Press, 1966), 75–94; also Muhammad Hamidullah, *The Muslim Conduct of State* (Lahore: S. Ashraf, 1961), 205–8.

37. See the definition of *sulh* in the *Encyclopedia of Islam*, 2nd ed., P.J. Bearman, Th. Bianquis, C.E. Bosworth, and W.P. Heinrichs, eds. (Leiden: E.J. Brill, 1960–2005) 9–845a.

38. As a representative text of the Ash'arite *kalam*, see Sa'd al-Din al-Taftazani, *Sharh al-Maqasid*, 5:232–320, where the long discussion of the imamate contains no references to *jihad* as conquering non-Muslim territories. See also Ibn Khaldun, *Muqaddimah*, trans. Franz Rosenthal, ed. N.J. Dawood (Princeton: Princeton University Press, 1969), 158–60, and Fakhr al-Din al-Razi, *al-Arbain fi Usul al-Din*, 2: 255–70. The Muslim philosophers, especially Abu Nasr al-Farabi, define *jihad* as just war and stress the virtues of the city (*madinah*) or the human habitat. See Joel L. Kraemer, "The *Jihad* of the *Falasifa*," *Jerusalem Studies in Arabic and Islam*, vol. 10 (1987), 293, 312. Butterworth holds the same view about al-Farabi's notion of warfare in his "Al-Farabi's Statecraft: War and the Well-Ordered Regime," in James Turner Johnson and John Kelsay, eds., *Cross, Crescent, and Sword: The Justification and Limitation of War in Western and Islamic Tradition* (New York: Greenwood Press, 1990), 79–100.

39. See *dar al-sulh* in *Encyclopedia of Islam*, 2:131a.

40. Shaybani, *Siyar*, 158–94; also *aman* in *Encyclopedia of Islam*, 1:429a.

41. Philip K. Hitti, *History of the Arabs* (New York: St. Martin's Press, 1970), 145. Dozy makes a similar point when he says that "the holy war is never imposed except only when the enemies of Islam are the aggressors. Otherwise, if we take into account the injunctions of the Qur'an, it is nothing but an interpretation of some theologians." R. Dozy, *Essai sur l'histoire de l'Islamisme* (Leiden: Brill, 1879), 152.

42. See Richard Bulliet, "Conversion to Islam and the Emergence of a Muslim Society in Iran," in Nehemia Levtzion, ed. *Conversion to Islam* (New York: Holmes and Meier Publishers, Inc., 1979), 30–51. See also the introduction by the editor, 9.

43. See Daniel J. Sahas, *John of Damascus on Islam: The "Heresy of the Ishmaelites"* (Leiden: E.J. Brill, 1972).

44. T.W. Arnold, *The Preaching of Islam* (Delhi: Renaissance Publishing House, 1984; originally published in 1913), 63–64.

45. See Lord Kinross, *The Ottoman Centuries: The Rise and Fall of the Turkish Empire* (New York: Morrow Quill, 1977), 259.

46. Abdulaziz A. Sachedina, "The Development of Jihad in Islamic Revelation and History," in *Cross, Crescent, and Sword*, 36.

47. On the question of rebellion and irregular warfare (*ahkam al-bughat*) in Islamic law, see Khaled Abou el Fadl, *Rebellion and Violence in Islamic Law* (Cambridge: Cambridge University Press, 2001). For a shorter synoptic account, see el Fadl, "*Ahkam al-Bughat*: Irregular Warfare and the Law of Rebellion in Islam," in *Cross, Crescent, and Sword*, 149–76.

48. Imam Shawkani, *Fath al-Qadir*, ed. Sulayman 'Abd Allah al-Ashqar (Kuwait: Shirkat Dhat Salasil 1988); Muhamad Asad, *The Message*, 41; Shaykh Muhammad al-Ghazali, *A Thematic Commentary on the Qur'an*, trans. A. Shamis (Herndon, VA: International Institute of Islamic Thought, 2000), 18–19.

49. In his *War and Peace in the Law of Islam* (Baltimore: The Johns Hopkins University Press, 1955), Majid Khadduri goes so far as to translate *jihad* as warfare (p. 55) and permanent war (p. 62), and claims that "the universalism of Islam, in its all-embracing creed, is imposed on the believers as a continuous process of warfare, psychological and political, if not strictly military" (p. 64). This belligerent view of *jihad* will be hard to justify in the light of both the legal and cultural traditions of Islam.

50. Ibn Taymiyyah, "Qa'idah fi Qital al-Kuffar," quoted in Majid Khadduri, *Islamic Law of Nations*, 59.

51. Ibn Qayyim al-Jawziyyah, *Ahkam ahl al-Dhimmah*, 3rd ed., Subhi al-Salih, ed. (Beirut: Dar al-'Ilm li'l-Malayin, 1983), 1:17.

52. See John Voll, "Renewal and Reform," in John Esposito, ed., *The Oxford History of Islam* (Oxford: Oxford University Press, 2000).

53. Rudolph Peters, *Islam and Colonialism: The Doctrine of Jihad in Modern History* (The Hague: Mouton Publishers, 1979), 86. Peters' work presents an excellent survey of how *jihad* was reformulated as anticolonialist resistance in the modern period. See also Allan Christelow, *Muslim Law Courts and the French Colonial State in Algeria* (Princeton: Princeton University Press, 1985), for the struggle of Muslim jurists to continue the tradition of Islamic law under the French colonial system.

54. Sheik Al-Jabarti, *Napoleon in Egypt: Al-Jabarti's Chronicle of the French Occupation*, trans. Shmuel Moreh (Princeton: Markus Wiener Publishers, 1997), 26.

55. Faraj's treatise has been translated by Johannes J.G. Jansen as *The Neglected Duty: The Creed of Sadat's Assassins and Islamic Resurgence in the Middle East* (New York: Macmillan Publishing Company, 1986), 160–230.

56. There is a consensus on this point among Hanafi and Maliki schools of law as well as some Hanbali scholars. For references in Arabic, see Yohanan Friedmann, *Tolerance and Coercion in Islam: Interfaith Relations in the Muslim Tradition* (Cambridge: Cambridge University Press, 2003), 85–86. For the inclusion of Zoroastrians among the People of the Book, see Friedmann, *Tolerance and Coercion*, 72–76. Shafi'i considers the Sabeans, a community mentioned in the Qur'an, as a Christian group. See Ibn Qayyim al-Jawziyyah, *Ahkam Ahl al-Dhimmah*, 1:92.

57. The incident is recorded in Baladhuri's *Futuh al-Buldan*. See Friedmann, *Tolerance and Coercion*, 85.

58. The text of the Madinan treatise is preserved in Ibn Hisham's *Sirah*. It is also published in Muhammad Hamidullah, *Documents sur la Diplomatie a l'Epoque du Prophete et des Khalifes Orthodoxes* (Paris: G.P. Masionneuve, 1935), 9–14. For an English translation, see Khadduri, *War and Peace*, 206–9.

59. Quoted in Khadduri, *War and Peace*, 179. The original text of the Najran treatise is quoted in Abu Yusuf, *Kitab al-kharaj*, and Baladhuri, *Futuh al-buldan* (Cairo: Maktabat al-Tijariyyah al-Kubra, 1959).

60. Ibn Qayyim al-Jawziyyah, *Ahkam Ahl al-Dhimmah*, 1, 24.

61. Ibid., 1, 26.

62. Abu Yusuf, *Kitab al-Kharaj*, 84. See also Shaybani, *Siyar*, in Khadduri, *War and Peace*, 143.

63. Ibn Qayyim, *Ahkam Ahl al-Dhimmah*, 1: 32ff.

64. Ibid., 42, 49.

65. This is not to deny that there were examples to the contrary. When one of the governors of 'Umar b. 'Abd al-'Aziz asked permission to "collect huge amounts of *jizyah* owed by Jews, Chrsitans and Majus of al-Hirah before they accepted Islam," 'Umar b. 'Abd al-'Aziz responded by saying that "God has sent the Prophet Muhammad to invite people to Islam and not as a tax collector." This letter is quoted in 'Abu Yusuf, *Kitab al-Kharaj*, 90.

66. See Aziz Ahmad, *Studies in Islamic Culture in the Indian Environment* (Oxford: Oxford University Press, 1964), 80–81.

67. Abu Yusuf mentions the case of Abu 'Ubaydah returning the *jizyah* to the *dhimmis* of Hims when he was not able to provide protection for them against the Roman emperor Heraclius. See the letter by Abu 'Ubaydah mentioned by Abu Yusuf, *Kitab al-Kharaj*, 150.

68. See Khadduri, *War and Peace*, 188–89.

69. These include some restrictive rulings on what the People of the Book could wear and what religious symbols they could display. See A.S. Tritton, *The Caliphs and Their Non-Muslim Subjects* (London: Oxford University Press, 1930), chapters 7 and 8. As Tritton notes, however, such rulings were not implemented strictly and displayed considerable variety across the Islamic world. A case in point, which Tritton mentions (p. 121), is Salah al-Din al-Ayyubi who had some Christian officers working for him without following any strict dress code.

70. Khadduri, *War and Peace*, 85.

71. Quoted in Friedmann, *Tolerance and Coercion*, 40.

72. The major and minor religions that the Islamic world encountered throughout its history make a long list: the religious traditions of the pre-Islamic (*jahiliyyah*) Arabs; Mazdeans in Mesopotamia, Iran, and Transoxania; several Christian sects, such as Nestorians in Mesopotamia and Iran; Monophysites in Syria, Egypt, and Armenia, Orthodox Melkites in Syria; Orthodox Latins in North Africa; Jews in various places; Samaritans in Palestine; Mandaeans in south Mesopotamia; Harranians in north Mesopotamia; Manicheans in Mesopotamia and Egypt; Buddhists and Hindus in Sind and the Panjab; tribal religions in Africa; and pre-Islamic Turkic tribes. See J. Waardenburg, "World Religions as Seen in the Light of Islam," in A.T. Welch and P. Cachia, eds., *Islam: Past Influence and Present Challenge* (Edinburgh: Edinburgh University Press, 1979), 248–49. See also Waardenburg, *Muslims and Others: Relations in Context* (Berlin and New York: Walter de Gruyter, 2003).

73. The six cultural zones of the Islamic world comprise Arabic, Persian, Turkish/Turkic, Indian, Malay-Indonesian, and African spheres of culture in which the expression of Islam as a religious and cultural identity has been more heterogeneous and complex than the Christian, Hindu, or Chinese worlds have been. For a discussion of these zones, see S.H. Nasr, *The Heart of Islam* (San Francisco: Harper Collins, 2003), 87–100.

74. See for details, M. Hinds, "Mihna," in *Encyclopaedia of Islam*, 7:26.

75. See Semiramis Cavusoglu, "The Kadizadeli Movement: An Attempt at Seri'at-Minded Reform in the Ottoman Empire," unpublished dissertation, History Department, Princeton University, 1990. See also Madeline C. Zilfi, "Vaizan and Ulema in the Kadizadeli Era," Proceedings of the Tenth Congress of the Turkish Historical Society, Ankara, 1994, 2493–2500.

76. Marshall Hodgson's suggestion of the term *Islamicate* to express the hybrid and multi-faceted nature of Islamic civilization is not completely without justification, as many previously non-Islamic elements were incorporated into Islamic civilization in a relatively short period of time. See Hodgson, *The Venture of Islam* (Chicago: University of Chicago Press, 1974).

77. See Al-Rabi' b. Habib al-Basari, *Musnad al-Imam al-Rabi'*, Bab fi al-'Ilm wa talabih wa Fadlih. This is also narrated by Abu Bakr Aamad b. 'Amr al-Bazzar in his *al-Bahr al-Zukhkhar*, also known as *Musnad al-Bazzar* (Beirut: Mu'assasat 'Ulum al-Qur'an, 1409 AH), 1:175, where he claims that there is no foundation (*asl*) for this *hadith*.

78. Abu 'Isa Muhammad Tirmidhi, *Sunan al-Tirmidhi*, Kitab al-'Ilm 'an Rasul Allah, Bab ma Ja'a fi Fadl al-Fiqh 'ala al-'Ibadah; Ibn Majah, *Sunan Ibn Majah*, Kitab al-Zuhd, Bab al-hikmah. This *hadith* has been transmitted in many *hadith* collections with some variations.

79. Ignaz Goldziher, "The Attitude of Orthodox Islam Toward the 'Ancient Sciences,'" in M.L. Swartz, trans. and ed., *Studies on Islam* (New York: Oxford University Press, 1981), 185–215. For an important criticism of Goldziher's conceptualization, see Dimitri Gutas, *Greek Thought, Arabic Culture* (London: Routledge, 1998), 166–71.

80. Ya'qub b. Ishaq al-Kindi, *Rasa'il*, 1:97, quoted in Majid Fakhry, *A History of Islamic Philosophy* (New York: Columbia University Press, 1983), 70.

81. Sa'ib b. Ahmad al-Andalusi, *Science in the Medieval World: Book of the Categories of Nations* (*Tabaqat al-Umam*), trans. S.I. Salem and A. Kumar (Austin: University of Texas Press, 1991), 6.

82. See Franz Rosenthal, *The Classical Heritage in Islam* (London: Routledge, 1975), 25–51.

83. The Arabic text of *al-Mukhtar* has been edited by A. Badawi (Beirut: The Arab Institute for Research and Publishing, 1980, 2nd ed.). The original English translation is by Curt F. Buhler (London: Oxford University Press, 1941).

84. Quoted in Abu Sulayman al-Sijistani, *Muntakhab Siwan al-hikmah*, ed. D.M. Dunlop (The Hague: Mouton Publishers, 1979), 3.

85. Shihab al-Din Yahya b. Habash al-Suhrawardi, *Hikmat al-Ishraq* [*The Philosophy of Illumination*], trans. and ed. John Walbridge and Hossein Ziai (Provo, UT: Brigham Young University Press, 1999), 2.

86. For Andalusia, see Anwar Chejne, *Muslim Spain: Its History and Culture* (Minneapolis: University of Minnesota Press, 1974), and Salma Khadra Jayyusi and Manuela Marin, eds., *The Legacy of Muslim Spain* (Leiden: E.J. Brill, 1992). For the concept of *convivencia* and the Jewish contributions to Andalusian civilization, see V.B. Mann, T.F. Glick, and J.D. Dodds, eds., *Convivencia: Jews, Muslims, and Christians in Medieval Spain* (New York: The Jewish Museum, 1992).

87. See, among others, Arthur Hyman, "Jewish Philosophy in the Islamic World," in S.H. Nasr and Oliver Leaman, eds., *History of Islamic Philosophy* (London: Routledge, 1996), 677–95, and Paul B. Fenton, "Judaism and Sufism," in *History of Islamic Philosophy*, 755–68.

88. See Aziz, *Studies*, 191–96; Annemarie Schimmel, *Islam in the Indian Subcontinent* (Leiden: E.J. Brill, 1980), 99–100.

89. From the introduction to *Sirr-i Akbar*, quoted in *Majmau'l-bahrain or the Mingling of the Two Oceans by Prince Muhammad Dara Shikuh*, trans. M. Mahfuz-ul-Haq (Calcutta: The Asiatic Society, 1929), 13.

90. *Majmau'l-bahrain*, 38.

91. Fathullaj Mujtabai, *Hindu Muslim Cultural Relations* (New Delhi, National Book Bureau, 1978), 82; Edward G. Browne, *A Literary History of Persia* (New York: Charles Scribner's Sons, 1906), 4:257–58.

2

Recovering the Early Semantic Purview of *Jihad* and Martyrdom

Challenging Statist-Military Perspectives

Asma Afsaruddin

This chapter deals with the changing semantic significations and ethical-legal implications of the critical Arabic term *jihad*, from its Qur'anic provenance to its contested meanings through the first three centuries of Islam. Linked to *jihad* is the social-legal concept of martyrdom, which appears to have taken root by the second century of Islam (eighth century of the Common Era). The early plurality of meanings associated with *jihad* finds reflection in the early conceptualizations of martyrdom; both would then in tandem become considerably circumscribed in meaning. These transformations are further discussed against their appropriate historical background as may be reconstructed from the sources at our disposal, allowing us to map these semantic transformations in their proper contexts. The paper concludes with a consideration of the implications of our historical critical study for contemporary perspectives on violence and peacebuilding within the Islamic context.

By the early third century of the Islamic era (the ninth century of the Common Era), *jihad* as primarily armed combat had become the accepted meaning in influential circles, particularly in the administrative and juridical ones. This occurred even though the term *jihad* in Qur'anic usage is clearly a polysemous word and, as even a cursory reading of some of the related literature reveals, was understood as such by early religious authorities and scholars. Exegetical glosses from the early period on the full Qur'anic phrase *al-jihad fi sabil Allah* (translated as "striving" or "struggling in the path of God") explain it as referring to a wide array of activities other than military defense of Islam, such as embarking on the pursuit of knowledge and earning one's livelihood by licit means, as will be seen later. Concomitantly, extra-Qur'anic literature (primarily exegesis and *hadith*, which refers to the statements attributed to the Prophet Muhammad) records various perspectives on martyrdom (*shahada*, a term that does not occur in the Qur'an in this sense) that reflect the polyvalence of the term *jihad*. As we shall see later, an individual who met death while struggling in any licit and noble pursuit during one's mundane existence on earth could be regarded as a martyr (*shahid*, plural *shuhada'*).

The different legal and ethical articulations of war and peace that have emerged in Islamic thought testify to the different—and conflicting—ways of reading and interpreting some of the key Qur'anic verses dealing with this topic. Some of these variant ways of understanding the sacred text will be outlined below. A comprehensive understanding of the Qur'anic treatment of the term *jihad* and other related terms is also a necessary prelude to our discussion of the development of the concept of martyrdom, which appears to be a later, extra-Qur'anic one.

The Qur'anic Discourse

The specific Qur'anic terms that have a bearing on our topic are *jihad*, *qital*, and *harb*. *Jihad* is a much broader term; its basic Qur'anic signification is "struggle," "striving," or "exertion." The lexeme *jihad* is frequently conjoined to the phrase *fi sabil Allah* (literally, "in the path of God"). The full locution in Arabic, *al-jihad fi sabil Allah*, consequently means "struggling or striving for the sake of God." This translation points to the polysemy of the term *jihad* and the potentially different meanings that may be ascribed to it in different contexts, since the phrase "in the path of/for the sake of God" allows for human striving to be accomplished in multiple ways. *Qital* is the term that specifically refers to fighting or armed combat and is a component of *jihad* in specific situations. *Harb* is the Arabic word for war in general. The Qur'an employs this last term four times, to refer to illegitimate wars fought by those who wish to spread corruption on earth (5:64); to the thick of battle between believers and nonbelievers (8:57, 47:4); and, in one instance, to the possibility of war waged by God and His prophet against those who would continue to practice usury (2:279).[1] This term is never conjoined to the phrase "in the path of God" and has no bearing on the concept of *jihad*.

At the semantic level, the facile translation of *jihad* into English as holy war, as is common in some scholarly and nonscholarly discourses, constitutes a misrepresentation and misunderstanding of the term's Qur'anic usage. According to the Qur'anic worldview, human beings should be engaged constantly in the basic moral endeavor of enjoining what is right and forbidding what is wrong (e.g., Qur'an 3:104, 110, 114; 7:157; 9:71, 11). The "struggle" implicit in the application of this precept is *jihad*, properly and plainly speaking, and the endeavor is both individual and collective. The means for carrying out this struggle vary according to circumstances, and the Qur'an often refers to those who "strive with their wealth and their selves" (*jahadu bi-amwalihim wa-anfusihim*; see, e.g., Qur'an 8:72). The term "holy war" further implies a battle waged in the name of God to effect the forcible conversion of nonbelievers, and often a total, no-holds-barred war intended to annihilate the enemy,[2] both of which objectives are doctrinally unacceptable in Islam. Qur'an 2:256 states categorically that "there is no compulsion in religion," while another verse (10:99) asks, "As for you, will you force men to become believers?" With regard to righteous conduct during war (*jus in bello*), the Qur'an prohibits initiation of aggression against the enemy (2:190) and resorting to unjust behavior prompted by anger and desire for revenge (5:8).[3] There is no scriptural warrant, therefore, for waging war (or employing other means) to compel non-Muslims to accept Islam.

The counsel and examples of prominent early Muslim leaders further establish the imperative to behave in a humane manner while engaged in fighting and to grant immunity to noncombatants. Thus, according to the well-known historian al-Tabari, Abu Bakr had advised his general Usama b. Zayd, before the expedition to Mut'a in 11/632, "not to kill women, children, and the elderly," nor to mutilate or commit treacherous actions. Usama was further advised not to cut down fruit trees or burn houses and cornfields and to refrain from killing livestock. He was also instructed that, when he and his army encountered hermits in their monasteries, they were not to molest them or destroy their monasteries.[4] Almost all classical legal manuals refer to this report in their sections on international law and relations (*siyar*; see further below).

As we will see a little later, a number of medieval jurists came perilously close to endorsing a form of holy war, but stopped short of it because of the Qur'anic constraints on the forcible conversion of non-Muslims and its proscription against unethical conduct during the waging of war. But such jurists did broaden the semantic and legal purview of *jihad* to sanction its launching as a preemptive and expansionist war fought to extend the territorial realm of Islam, undergirded by the hope that this would pave the way eventually for non-Muslim inhabitants to enter the fold of Islam, as will be discussed below.

Reading the Qur'an in Context

Many of the Qur'anic rulings pertaining to both nonviolent and violent struggle against wrongdoing and to uphold good cannot be properly understood without relating them to specific events in the life of the Prophet. A significant number of Qur'anic verses are traditionally understood to have been revealed in connection with certain episodes in Muhammad's life. Knowledge of the "occasions of revelation" (*asbab al-nuzul*), as obtained from the biography of the Prophet and the exegetical literature, is indispensable for contextualizing key verses that may at first sight appear to be at odds with one another.[5] A specific chronology of events thus needs to be mapped out so that the progression in the Qur'anic ethics of warfare may be understood against its historical backdrop, to which we proceed next.

The Meccan Period

According to sources, from the onset of the revelations to Muhammad in circa 610 CE until his emigration to Medina from Mecca in 622 during the period known as the Meccan period, the Muslims were not given permission in the Qur'an to physically retaliate against their persecutors, the pagan Meccans. Verses revealed in this period counsel the Muslims rather to steadfastly endure the hostility of the Meccans. While recognizing the right to self-defense for those who are wronged, in this early period, the Qur'an maintained that to bear patiently the wrongdoing of others and to forgive those who cause harm is the superior course of action in resisting evil. Four significant verses (42:40–43) reveal this highly significant, nonmilitant dimension of struggling against wrongdoing (and, therefore, *jihad*) in this early phase of Muhammad's prophetic career:

> The requital of evil is an evil similar to it: hence, whoever pardons and makes peace, his reward rests with God—for indeed, He does not love evil-doers. Yet surely, as for those who defend themselves after having been wronged—no blame whatever attaches to them: blame attaches but to those who oppress people and behave outrageously on earth, offending against all right; for them is grievous suffering in store! But if one is patient in adversity and forgives, this is indeed the best resolution of affairs.

In Qur'anic discourse, patience is thus a component and a manifestation of the *jihad* of the righteous; quietist and activist resistance to wrongdoing are equally valorized. For example, one Qur'anic verse (16:110) thus states, "As for those who after persecution fled their homes and strove actively (*jahadu*) and were patient (*sabaru*) to the last, your Lord will be forgiving and merciful to them on the day when every soul will come pleading for itself." Another (47:31) states, "We shall put you to the test until We know the active strivers (*al-mujahidun*) and the quietly forbearing (*al-sabirin*) among you." Quietist, nonviolent struggle is not the same as passivity, however, which, when displayed in the face of grave oppression and injustice, is clearly earmarked as immoral in the Qur'anic view. "Those who are passive" (*al-Qa'idun*) earn divine rebuke in the Qur'an (4:95).

The active inculcation of patience is frequently insisted upon in the Qur'an, for which generous posthumous rewards are promised. For instance, Qur'an 39:10 states that "those who are patient will be given their reward without measure," and Qur'an 25:75 states, "They will be awarded the high place [in heaven] for what they bore in patience ... abiding there forever." This high Qur'anic estimation of the moral attribute of patience is reflected in a statement found in the *Sahihayn* ("the two 'sound' *hadith* compilations") of al-Bukhari (d. 870) and Muslim (d. 875), attributed to the Prophet Muhammad, which states that humans have not been given anything better or more abundant than patience.[6]

The verses quoted above underscore the nonviolent dimension of *jihad* during the Meccan period, which lasted thirteen years compared to the Medinan period of ten years. The Qur'anic verses that were revealed during this period and dictated the conduct of the Prophet and his Companions are thus of extremely important consideration in any discussion on the permissibility of engaging in armed combat within the Islamic context. As these early verses show, the Muslims were allowed to engage in self-defense but without resorting to fighting in the early period. For the most part, this meant resisting the Meccan establishment by first secret and then active public propagation of the faith, through manumission of slaves who had converted to Islam, and, for some, by emigration to Abyssinia-Ethiopia, the Christian king of which was sympathetic to the early Muslims, and later, to Medina.[7]

Both Muslim and non-Muslim scholars, medieval and modern, have tended to downplay the critical Meccan phase in the development of the Qur'anic doctrine of *jihad*. It is, however, practically impossible to contextualize the Qur'anic discourse on the various meanings of *jihad* without taking the Meccan phase into consideration. The introduction of the military aspect of *jihad* in the Medinan period can then be appropriately and better understood as a last-resort option, resorted to when attempts at negotiations and peaceful proselytization among the Meccans had failed during the first thirteen years of the propagation of Islam.

The Medinan Period

In 622 CE, which corresponds to the first year of the Islamic calendar, the Prophet received divine permission to emigrate to Medina, along with his loyal followers. There he set up the first Muslim polity, combining the functions of prophecy and temporal rule in one office. The Medinan verses, accordingly, have increasingly more to do with organization of the polity, communitarian issues, ethics, and defense of the Muslims against Meccan hostilities. A specific Qur'anic verse (22:39–40) permitting fighting was revealed in Medina, although its precise date cannot be determined. The verse states:

> Permission [to fight] is given to those against whom war is being wrongfully waged, and indeed, God has the power to help them: those who have been driven from their homes against all right for no other reason than their saying, "Our Provider is God!" For, if God had not enabled people to defend themselves against one another, monasteries, churches, synagogues, and mosques—in all of which God's name is abundantly glorified—would surely have been destroyed.

Another verse (2:217) states:

> They ask you concerning fighting in the prohibited months.[8] Answer them: "To fight therein is a serious offense. But to restrain men from following the cause of God, to deny God, to violate the sanctity of the sacred mosque, to expel its people from its environs is with God a greater wrong than fighting in the forbidden month. [For] disorder and oppression are worse than killing.

Until the outbreak of full-fledged war a little later in the same year, the Qur'an, in this and other verses previously cited, referred to the reasons— *jus ad bellum*—that justify recourse to fighting. In verses 42:40–43, in which self-defense is allowed but not through violent means, the reasons are the wrongful conduct of the enemy and their oppressive and immoral behavior on earth. In verses 22:39–40 quoted above, a more explicit reason is given: wrongful expulsion of the Muslims from their homes for no other reason than their avowal of belief in one God. Furthermore, the Qur'an asserts, if people were not allowed to defend themselves against aggressive wrongdoers, all the houses of worship—it is worthy of note here that Islam is not the only religion indicated—would be destroyed and thus the word of God extinguished. The verse thus implies that Muslims may resort to defensive combat even on behalf of non-Muslim believers who are the objects of the hostility of nonbelievers. In the final verse cited (2:217), the Qur'an acknowledges the enormity of fighting during the prohibited months, but at the same time, asserts the higher moral imperative of maintaining order and challenging wrongdoing. Therefore, when both just cause and righteous intention exist, war in self-defense against an intractable enemy may become obligatory.

> Fighting (*al-qital*) is prescribed for you, while you dislike it. But it is possible that you dislike a thing which is good for you, and that you love a thing which is bad for you. God knows and you know not (2:216).

The Qur'an further asserts that it is the duty of Muslims to defend those who are oppressed and who cry out to them for help (4:75), except against a people with whom the Muslims have concluded a treaty (8:72).

With regard to initiation of hostilities and conduct during war (*jus in bello*), the Qur'an has specific injunctions. Verse 2:190, which reads, "Fight in the cause of God those who fight you, but do not commit aggression, for God loves not aggressors," forbids Muslims from initiating hostilities. Recourse to armed combat must be in response to a prior act of aggression by the opposite side. The Qur'an further counsels (5:8), "Let not rancor towards others cause you to incline to wrong and depart from justice. Be just; that is closer to piety." This verse may be understood to complement 2:190 in spirit and intent, warning against excesses that may result from an unprincipled desire to punish and exact revenge.

During the month of Ramadan in the third year of the Islamic calendar (624 CE), full-fledged hostilities broke out between the Muslims and the pagan Meccans in what became known as the Battle of Badr. In this battle, a small army of Muslims decisively routed a much larger and more experienced Meccan army. Two years later, the Battle of Uhud was fought, in which the Muslims suffered severe reverses, followed by the battle of Khandaq in 627. Apart from these three major battles, a number of other minor campaigns were fought until the Prophet's death in 632. Some of the most trenchant verses exhorting the Muslims to fight were revealed on the occasions of these military campaigns. One such verse is 9:5, which has been termed the sword verse (*ayat al-sayf*). It states:

> And when the sacred months are over, slay the polytheists wherever you find them, and take them captive, and besiege them, and lie in wait for them at every conceivable place.

Another verse (9:29), often conjoined to the above, runs:

> Fight against those who—despite having been given revelation before—do not believe in God nor in the Last Day, and do not consider forbidden that which God and His messenger have forbidden, and do not follow the religion of the truth, until they pay the *jizya* with willing hand, having been subdued.

The first of the sword verses (9:5), with its internal reference to the polytheists who may be fought after the end of the sacred months, would circumscribe its applicability to only the pagan Arabs of Muhammad's time; this is, in fact, how many medieval scholars, such as al-Shafi'i[9] and al-Tabari,[10] understood the verse. The second of the sword verses is seemingly directed in general at the People of the Book—that is, Jews and Christians—but again, a careful reading of the verse clearly indicates that it does not refer to all the People of the Book, but only those from among them who do not, in contravention of their own laws, believe in God and the Last Day and do not forbid wrongdoing. This understanding is borne out by comparing verse 9:29 to verses 3:113–15, for example, which state:

> They are not all the same. Among the People of the Book are a contingent who stand [in prayer] reciting the verses of God at all times of the night while they prostrate. These are they who believe in God and the Last Day and enjoin what is right and forbid what is wrong. They hasten to [perform] good deeds and they are among the righteous. And whatever they do of good will not be rejected [by God] and God knows best the God-fearing.

The Qur'an, in another verse (2:193), makes unambiguously clear that, when hostile behavior on the part of the foes of Islam ceases, then the reason for engaging them in war also lapses. This verse states:

> And fight them on until there is no chaos (*fitna*) and religion is only for God, but if they cease, let there be no hostility except to those who practice oppression.

The harshness of the two sword verses is thus considerably mitigated, and their general applicability significantly restricted, by juxtaposing with them conciliatory verses, such as the ones cited above, and other such verses. Among other such verses is the one that has been characterized as the peace verse (8:61):

> If they incline toward peace, incline you toward it, and trust in God. Indeed, He alone is all-hearing, all-knowing.

And

> Slay them wherever you catch them, and turn them out from where they have turned you out; for persecution is worse than slaughter. But if they cease, God is Oft-forgiving, Most Merciful (2:191–92).

> God does not forbid you from being kind and equitable to those who have neither made war on you on account of your religion nor driven you from your homes. God loves those who are equitable (60:8).

These verses make warring against those who oppose the propagation of the message of Islam, and consequently resort to persecution of Muslims, contingent upon their continuing hostility. Should they desist from

such hostile persecution and sue for peace instead, the Muslims are commanded to accede to their request. The Qur'an (60:8) further makes clear
that non-Muslims of goodwill and peaceableness cannot be the targets of
war simply on account of their different religious backgrounds.[11]

Jihad and Its Multiple Implications

The scholarly literature from the first three centuries of Islam reveals
that there were competing definitions of how best to strive in the path
of God, engendered by the polyvalence of the term *jihad*. Recent rigor-
ous research has established that there was a clear divergence of opinion
regarding the nature of *jihad* and its imposition as a religious duty on the
believer, through the first century of Islam and into the second half of the
second century. In an excellent article on early, competing conceptions of
jihad, two distinguished historians of Islamic thought—Roy Mottahedeh
and Ridwan al-Sayyid—have pointed out that, during the Umayyad period (661–750), there were multiple and conflicting perspectives on this
subject held by jurists from Syria and elsewhere.[12] The Kufan jurist Sufyan
al-Thawri (d. 778) was of the opinion that *jihad* was primarily defensive,
and that only defensive *jihad* could be considered obligatory on the individual. Jurists from the Hijaz (from the province of western Arabia that
includes Mecca and Medina) tended to place greater emphasis on religious
practices such as prayer and mosque attendance and did not consider *jihad*
obligatory for all. Thus the Medinan scholar 'Abdallah ibn 'Umar, son of
the second caliph 'Umar ibn al-Khattab, is on record as having challenged
those who had wished to elevate combative *jihad* to the level of a religious
obligation. In this highly significant report, a certain Yazid b. Bishr al-
Saksaki relates that he traveled to Medina and visited 'Abd Allah b. 'Umar
there. An Iraqi man came to Ibn 'Umar and reproached him thus: "What
is the matter with you that you perform the *hajj* and *'umra* but have abandoned fighting in the path of God (*al-ghazu fi sabil allah*)?" To which Ibn
'Umar responded, "Fie on you! Faith is founded on five pillars: that you
worship God, perform the prayer, give *zakat*, perform the pilgrimage, and
fast during Ramadan. This is according to what the Messenger of God,
peace and blessings be upon him, have told us. After that *jihad* is all right
(*thumma al-jihad hasan*)."[13] This report is a resounding reprimand to those
who harbor an excessive regard for military *jihad* as a religious obligation.
It contains a firm reminder that the essential duties for a Muslim remain
the five pillars; combative *jihad*, if one should choose to engage in it, is a
voluntary act, which by its very nature cannot displace any one of the five
pillars as a fundamental obligation for the faithful.

In contrast to Hijazi and Iraqi scholars, Syrian jurists such as al-Awza'i (d. 773) often held the view that even aggressive war could be considered obligatory. No doubt this last group was influenced by the fact that the Syrian Umayyads during his time were engaged in border warfare with the Byzantines, and there was a perceived need to justify these hostilities on a theological and legal basis.[14] It would not be an exaggeration to state that to express support for expansionist war at this time (the Umayyad period) was to proclaim one's support for the existing government and its policies. Anxieties about serving under the worldly Umayyad and later the 'Abbasid rulers are preserved in some reports in the early literature. For example, the early *hadith* work known as the *Musannaf* of 'Abd al-Razzaq records the displeasure of pious Muslims at the military adventurism of their perceived unscrupulous rulers. One report specifically warns the pious not to join in the military campaigns of those "who fight seeking [the gains of] the world," for then they would forfeit their "portion in the hereafter."[15]

By the early Abbasid period—roughly the mid-to-late eighth-century CE, second century of Islam—the military aspect of *jihad* began to receive greater emphasis in certain official and juridical circles. *Jihad* from this period on would progressively be conflated with *qital* (fighting), collapsing the distinction that the Qur'an maintains between the two. As jurists and religious scholars of all stripes became consolidated as a scholarly class and accrued to themselves commensurate religious authority by the tenth century, they arrogated to themselves the right to authoritatively define *jihad* and circumscribe the range of activities prescribed by it. With the powerful theory of abrogation (*naskh*) at their disposal, some of the jurists effectively rendered null and void the positive injunctions contained in the Qur'anic verses that explicitly permitted the conclusion of truces with foes and counseled peaceful coexistence, particularly with the People of the Book. One of the most important verses that a number of these scholars declared to have been abrogated or superseded by the so-called sword verse (9:73)[16] is 2:256, which forbids compulsion in religion.[17] In the process of politicizing *jihad*, the daring abrogation of this critical Qur'anic verse (2:256) was by no means accepted by all. Two celebrated Qur'an commentators, Muhammad Jarir al-Tabari (d. 923)[18] and Ibn Kathir (d. 1373),[19] resolutely maintained that this verse had not been abrogated and its injunction remained valid for all time. It is significant that al-Tabari's juridical work *Ikhtilaf al-fuqaha'* (*The Differences of the Jurists*) does not list Qur'an (9:5) as an abrogating verse, revealing that even as late as the tenth century, there was by no means a juristic consensus on its status.[20]

Our discussion so far makes clear that the monovalent and aggressive understanding of *jihad* promoted by some scholars within the context of international law undermined the rich diversity of meanings associated with the term in Qur'anic and early *hadith* discourse. Accordingly, martyrdom also progressively came to be understood almost exclusively in a statist-military sense, and a hortatory literary genre, called *fada'il al-jihad* in Arabic, developed around the often greatly exaggerated merits of falling on the battlefield in defending the realms of Islam.

The jurist al-Shafi'i (d. 820) is said to have been the first to permit *jihad* to be launched against non-Muslims as offensive warfare, although he qualified non-Muslims as referring only to pagan Arabs and not to non-Arab non-Muslims, as mentioned above. He further divided the world into the abode of Islam (*dar al-Islam*) and the abode of war (*dar al-harb*), referring to non-Muslim territories, while recognizing a third possibility: the abode of treaty (*dar al-'ahd*) or abode of reconciliation (*dar al-sulh*), referring to non-Islamic states that could enter into a peace treaty with the Islamic state by rendering an annual tribute.[21] In the absence of actual hostilities, the Shafi'i school of thought posited a state of cold war between the abodes of Islam and war, which required constant vigilance against the latter.[22] Political theorists after al-Shafi'i would enshrine this concept in their writings by averring that one of the duties of the caliph was to launch *jihad* at least once a year, although others were of the opinion that this duty could be fulfilled simply by being in an adequate state of military preparedness to forestall enemy attacks.[23]

Al-Shafi'i's perspectives on *jihad* were, in many ways, a marked departure from earlier juristic thinking, and reflect a certain hardening of attitudes toward non-Islamic states by his time (late eighth and early ninth century). This is quite evident when his views are compared with those of jurists from the earlier Hanafi school of law, eponymously founded by Abu Hanifa (d. 767). Hanafi jurists, for example, did not subscribe to a third abode of treaty, as devised by al-Shafi'i, but were of the opinion that the inhabitants of a territory that had concluded a truce with Muslims and paid tribute to the latter became part of the abode of Islam and were entitled to the protection of the Islamic government.[24] The Hanafis also adhered to the position that nonbelievers could only be fought if they resorted to armed conflict, and not simply on account of their disbelief.[25] This remained a principle of contention between later Shafi'i and Hanafi jurists.

It is worth emphasizing that the concepts of *dar al-Islam* and *dar al-harb* have no basis in the Qur'an or *sunnah*. The invention of these terms and the resulting aggrandizement of the military aspect of *jihad* were based, rather, on ad hoc juristic interpretations, particularly of verses 9:5 and 9:29, largely in deference to realpolitik in the Abbasid period. As an imperial state in control of a vast and diverse political realm, the Abbasids had to develop a sophisticated law of nations, termed in Arabic *siyar* (lit. motions, travels). From the vantage point of realpolitik, *jihad* could be understood as defensive or offensive fighting with the primary purpose of guaranteeing the legitimate security needs of the polity. Thus, during the Umayyad period (661–750), the constant border skirmishes with the hostile Byzantines predisposed Syrian and Iraqi jurists in particular to endorse the concept of an offensive *jihad* (in opposition to Medinan and Meccan jurists living far away from the metropole) as an effective military strategy against an intractable enemy. It should not come as a surprise to us that, on account of the sensibilities of the day, politically expedient considerations had to be couched in religious rhetoric and morally legitimized, a proclivity that is not exactly unknown to us today.[26]

Patience (*Sabr*) as an Aspect of *Jihad*

To recover the full semantic and historical trajectory of the Qur'anic term *jihad* and the duties understood to be inherent in it in the early period of Islam—and, therefore, to resurrect the multiple significations of martyrdom embedded in it—we have to go back to the sources that record early, variegated points of view. The more belligerent interpretation of *jihad* that had become ascendant by the ninth century did not efface the earlier multiplicity of views on the term's signification. Some sources lead one to the belief that by this century, the belligerent faction (hawks, to use present-day jargon) had basically won and the nonmilitant faction (doves) had receded to the sidelines at best, or at worst, been completely superseded. Yet a careful scrutiny of alternative sources at our disposal—alternative, that is, to standard juristic, exegetical, and *hadith* literature—establishes that the supposedly superseded nonmilitant views of the quietists continued to be preserved and disseminated in works that emanated from dissenting, pietistic circles.[27] This trend became even more strongly manifested in Sufism in later centuries, but one of my purposes in this paper is to show that these alternate opinions are not to be merely dismissed or marginalized as Sufi, for they predate the rise of institutionalized Sufism.

The literature of dissent arising in these circles constitutes in part a genre called *fada'il al-sabr*, or the excellences or virtues of patience. It is a genre that is meant to be in competition with the well-known genre of *fada'il al-jihad*, which praises the excellences or merits of armed combat.[28] In a conscious, vaunting fashion, the *fada'il al-sabr* extols the Qur'anic virtue of patience, which was an important aspect of *jihad*, as we have seen. Together, these two genres represent countervailing and competing definitions of how best to struggle for the sake of God. A ninth-century work, for instance, on the merits of patience by Ibn Abi al-Dunya (d. 894), called *al-Sabr wa-'l-thawab 'alayhi* (*Patience and the Rewards for It*) records the following report on the authority of 'Isma Abi Hukayma, who related that:

> The Messenger of God, peace and blessings be upon him, wept and we asked him, "What has caused you to weep, O Messenger of God?" He replied, "I reflected on the last of my community and the tribulations they will face. But the patient from among them who arrives will be given the reward of two martyrs (*shahidayn*)."[29]

This report clearly contests those reports that assign the highest merit to military martyrs and trumps them by allocating the reward of two such martyrs to the patient individual. Reports such as this contradict Reuven Firestone's statement in his monograph on *jihad* to the effect that there is virtually no evidence of dissenting traditions challenging the militaristic interpretation of *jihad* in the medieval period.[30] Careful scrutiny of these *fada'il al-sabr* reports has the potential to yield invaluable insights that considerably nuance and transform our current state of knowledge concerning early, multiple perspectives on how best to strive in the path of God.[31]

The Excellences of Patience

The understanding of *jihad* as primarily armed combat took perhaps about a century to develop. The reasons for proposing this thesis are as follows. The Qur'an, the earliest document we possess for the Muslim community, attests to multiple meanings of the locution *al-jihad fi sabil Allah* (striving or struggling in the path of God). Furthermore, as previously mentioned, the Qur'an does not have a single word for *martyr* or *martyrdom*, two concepts that are intrinsically linked to the concept of *jihad* as armed combat against the enemies of Islam. One of the Qur'anic verses (3:169, 47:4, cf. 2:154) that has been construed to refer to the special status of the military martyr runs thus: "Do not think that those who were slain in the path of God are dead. They are alive and well provided for by their Lord." Some of the exegetical and *hadith* works, however, make clear that the phrase "slain in the path of God" was not understood to be restricted to those fallen in battle, but could be glossed in several ways, as discussed below. The common Arabic word for martyr is *shahid*. It is telling that nowhere in the Qur'an is this word used for a martyr; rather it is only used, interchangeably with *shahid*, to refer to a legal or eye witness.[32] Only in later extra-Qur'anic tradition does this word acquire the meaning of "one who bears witness for the faith," particularly by laying down his life. Extraneous, particularly Christian, influence may be suspected here. Muslim encounters with Levantine Christians in the late seventh century very likely contributed to this development. Arthur Jeffrey points to the probable influence of the cognate Syriac word for martyr-witness, *sahedo*, on the Arabic *shahid* and the latter's subsequent acquisition of the secondary and derivative meaning of *martyr*.[33] The fact that we encounter the term *shahid* in the sense of martyr-witness only in the *hadith* literature already implies the later development of this strand of meaning.

Militant versus Nonmilitant Struggle: A Contest of Piety

Many of the *fada'il al-sabr* reports contained in Ibn Abi al-Dunya's work referred to above testify in fact to a competitive discourse on piety that emphasizes the primacy of the Qur'anic virtues of patience and forbearance over other traits and activities, including *jihad*, understood exclusively as armed combat in this context. One such laudatory report is attributed to a certain Abu 'Imran al-Juni, who stated, "After faith, the believer (*'abd*) has not been given anything more meritorious (*afdal*) than patience with the exception of gratitude, but it [patience] is the more meritorious of the two and the fastest of the two to reap recompense (*thawab*) [for the believer]."[34] A similar report attributed to the eighth century scholar Sufyan b. 'Uyayna (d. 813) says, "The believers (*al-'ibad*) have not been given anything better or more meritorious than patience, by means of which they enter heaven."[35]

These reports are clearly at loggerheads with other, probably more frequently quoted, reports claiming that falling on the battlefield brings swift and immeasurable heavenly rewards to the martyr. One of the best-known reports on the issue of compensation for the *shahid* is recorded by Muslim and Ibn Maja (d. 886) in their two authoritative *hadith* collections, which state that all the sins of the martyr will be forgiven except for his debt.[36] Another report in an early collection of *hadith* by 'Abd al-Razzaq al-San'ani (d. 826) is attributed to the famous eighth-century preacher and scholar al-Hasan al-Basri (d. 728); he relates that the Prophet had stated, "Embarking upon the path of God or returning from it is better than all the world and what it contains. Indeed, when one of you stands within the battle ranks, then that is better than the worship of a man for sixty years."[37] 'Abd al-Razzaq records another report in which a certain Abu Mijlaz relates that he was passing by a Qur'an reciter, who said that "God has favored those who strive with their wealth and their selves by conferring on them a rank above those who are sedentary" (4:95). At this point, Abu Mijlaz interrupted the reciter by saying, "Stop. It has reached me that it is seventy ranks, and between each two levels, [a distance of] seventy years is reserved for the emaciated charge horse." Abu Mijlaz's impromptu exegesis is, first of all, evidence that *jihad* has come to be understood by the eighth century to primarily indicate armed combat, undermining the term's Qur'anic polysemy. It is also indicative of how high *jihad* in the sense of armed combat had risen as a religiously mandated activity in the estimation of a significant number of influential people, expressed in terms of generous divine recompense in the hereafter.

Interestingly, a report found in praise of patience invokes language very similar to that of Abu Mijlaz's report in praise of *jihad*. Considered together, these two reports suggest that there were efforts made to counter this kind of excessive glorification of the merits of military activity. This *hadith* is recorded by Ibn Abi al-Dunya in his work on *sabr*, and is attributed to the fourth caliph, 'Ali b. Abi Talib (d. 661). 'Ali relates:

> The Messenger of God, peace and blessings be upon him, said, "Patience is of three kinds: patience during tribulations, patience in obedience to God, and patience in avoiding sin. Whoever has patience during a tribulation until he averts it by the seemliness of his forbearance, God will ordain for him three hundred levels [of recompense]; the distance between each level would equal that between the sky and the earth. And whoever has patience in obedience to God, God writes down for him six hundred levels; the distance between each level would equal that between the boundaries of the earth till the edge of the divine throne. And whoever has patience in avoiding sin, God prescribes for him nine hundred levels; the distance between each level is twice the distance between the boundaries of the earth up to the edge of the divine throne."[38]

The shared idiom of these two reports in terms of how many levels or ranks the armed combatant and the patient quietist would earn or rise to in the hereafter suggests the vaunting nature of these reports and their conscious positing of opposed hierarchies of moral excellence.

Another report is attributed to al-Hasan al-Basri and is recorded by 'Abd al-Razzaq in his *Musannaf*. In this report, al-Hasan says, "There is nothing more arduous or exacting (*ajhad*) for a man than the money which he spends honestly or for a right cause and the prayer that he says deep in the middle of the night."[39] Al-Hasan's use of the Arabic superlative *ajhad*, related etymologically to the term *jihad*, stresses the greater moral excellence of basic, nonmilitant, personal acts of piety.

Reports such as these highlight the general signification of *jihad* as striving to better oneself morally and spiritually. Therefore, the emphasis is on nonmilitant acts of courage: charity, prayer, or speaking the truth even at the cost of imperiling one's life or facing other negative consequences. This meaning is consistent with the famous prophetic *hadith* that describes the various means of carrying out *jihad*: by the hand, by the tongue, and by intent (that is, silently with the heart).[40] Another perhaps equally well-known *hadith* quotes the Prophet as remarking on his return from a military campaign, "We have returned from the lesser *jihad* (physical, external struggle) to the greater *jihad* (spiritual, internal struggle)."[41] This latter *hadith* underscores the two principal modes of carrying out *jihad* and a hierarchical ordering of their merits, with the internal, spiritual struggle trumping the external, physical one. This *hadith* is not to be found in the early collections, but its advocacy of the superiority of the spiritual struggle is reflected in another prophetic statement found in the relatively early *hadith* works of Ahmad ibn Hanbal (d. 855) and al-Tirmidhi (d. 892), which states, "One who strives against his own self is a *mujahid*, that is, carries out *jihad*."[42] Another *hadith* recorded by Muslims similarly emphasizes the internal, spiritual aspect of striving for God; it affirms, "Whoever strives (*jahada*) with his heart is a believer."[43]

Competing Definitions of *Shahid*

Verbal jousts over which specific actions are to be considered the most morally excellent remain a predominant theme in the *hadith* and ethical literature and reflect the medieval Muslim's concern to identify and rank the moral valences of specific deeds. That there was a sizeable contingent of people who challenged the growing prevalence of the idea of *jihad* as primarily armed combat and the consequent romanticization of the concept of military martyrdom is often clear from the content of many of the early *akhbar* or reports that are labeled in Arabic *mawquf* (roughly, arrested or truncated). As a technical term, it identifies these reports as being attributable to a Companion of Muhammad rather than directly to the Prophet himself (with a corresponding diminution in its probative value). For instance, the *Musannaf* of 'Abd al-Razzaq, which was compiled earlier than al-Bukhari's authoritative *hadith* collection, contains a number of Companion reports that relate competing definitions of *shahid*. A few examples will suffice. One report attributed to the Companion Abu Hurayra states that the *shahid* is one who, were he to die in his bed, would enter heaven.[44] The explanatory note that follows states that it refers to someone who dies in his bed and is without sin (*la dhanb lahu*). Another report, also recorded by 'Abd al-Razzaq and related by Masruq b. al-Ajda', declares that there are four types of *shahada* or martyrdom for Muslims: the plague, parturition or delivery of a child, drowning, and a stomach ailment.[45] Significantly, there is no mention of martyrdom being earned on account of dying on the battlefield in this early report. An expanded version of this report, however, originating with the Companion Abu Hurayra, quotes the Prophet as adding to this list of those who achieve martyrdom, "one who is killed in the way of God (*man qutila fi sabil Allah*)."[46] It is this expanded version containing the all five definitions of a *shahid* that is recorded later in the *Sahih* of al-Bukhari.[47]

Another early eighth-century *hadith* work records multiple significations of the term *shahid*. The *Muwatta'* of Malik b. Anas (d. 795), the eponymous founder of the Sunni Maliki school of law, records that the Prophet identified seven kinds of martyrs in addition to those who died from fighting on the battlefield. Thus, "he who dies as a victim of an epidemic is a martyr; he who dies from drowning is a martyr; he who dies from pleurisy is a martyr; he who dies from diarrhoea is a martyr; he who dies by [being burned in] fire is a martyr; he who dies by being struck by a dilapidated wall falling is a martyr; and the woman who dies in childbed is a martyr."[48] This report and the one cited above assigns martyrdom to the believer who suffers a painful death from a variety of debilitating illnesses, from a difficult labor in the case of women, or from falling victim to an unfortunate accident, such as being crushed to death by a falling wall, in addition to falling on the battlefield. These are some of the fullest reports we have, which point to a wide spectrum of meanings assigned to martyrdom in the early centuries of Islam.

Privileging Nonviolence

The multiple, nonviolent significations of the phrase *fi sabil Allah*, particularly in the early period, is clear from a noteworthy report recorded in 'Abd al-Razzaq's *Musannaf*, which relates that a number of the Companions were sitting with the Prophet when a man from the tribe of Quraysh, apparently a pagan and of muscular build, came into view. Some of those gathered exclaimed, "How strong this man looks! If only he would expend his strength in the way of God!" The Prophet asked, "Do you think only someone who is killed [in battle] is engaged in the way of God?" He continued, "Whoever goes out in the world seeking licit work to support his family, he is on the path of God; whoever goes out in the world seeking licit work to support himself, he is on the path of God. Whoever goes out seeking worldly increase (*al-takathur*) has embarked, however, on the way of the devil (*fa-huwa fi sabil al-shaytan*)."[49] This report contains a clear rebuttal of those who would understand striving in the way of God in primarily military terms. This range of meanings is to be expected, since the quotidian struggle of the individual to live his or her life in the way of God (*fi sabil Allah*) infuses even the most humdrum of licit activities with moral and spiritual significance and, thus, divine approbation. The report also emphasizes the importance of personal intention in determining the moral worth of an individual's act. Since the meritorious nature of an individual's striving for the sake of God is contingent upon purity of intent, one may understand this report as counseling caution against accepting at face value ostentatious pietism or assuming that what appears to be a pious activity to humans will be deemed as such by God, who alone knows the true intention of the individual.

Other reports proclaim that those practicing the virtues of veracity and patience and evincing compassion for the disadvantaged are equivalent in moral status to the military martyrs and strive equally hard in the path of God. A report recorded by Ibn Abi al-Dunya, attributed to 'Abd al-'Aziz b. Abi Rawwad (d. 775), a pious *mawla* (a non-Arab Muslim convert) of Khurasanian descent, relates, "A statement affirming the truth (*al-qawl bi'l-haqq*) and patience in abiding by it is equivalent to the deeds of the martyrs."[50] Three of the most authoritative Sunni *hadith* compilers—al-Bukhari, Muslim, and al-Tirmidhi—report that the Prophet declared that "the one who helps widows and the poor are like fighters in the path of God."[51]

These noncombative significations continued to circulate through the late Middle Ages and were added to by later scholars. Thus the eleventh-century Andalusian jurist and theologian Ibn Hazm (d. 1064 CE) affirmed a general higher moral valuation of the defense of Islam through non-militant, verbal, and scholarly means, by a hierarchical ordering of actions that qualify as meritorious struggle in the path of God. *Jihad* is best exercised, he affirms, through, first, the invitation of people to God by means of the tongue; second, the defense of Islam through sound judgment and carefully considered opinions; and third, armed combat, in this order of importance. With regard to the third type of *jihad*, Ibn Hazm states that this is its least important aspect. When we look at the Prophet himself, he says, we realize that the majority of his actions fall into the first two categories, and although he was the most courageous of all human beings, he engaged in little physical combat.[52] This hierarchy clearly challenges the mainly juridical understanding of *jihad* as primarily military activity and affirms the more meritorious struggle of the learned scholar in explaining and defending Islam through reasoned argument and the marshaling of rational proofs.

The eleventh-century Andalusian scholar Ibn 'Abd al-Barr (d. 1070), in his treatise on the excellences of knowledge, records a *hadith* from the Prophet related by his Companion Abu Hurayra, which declared, "The prophets are two ranks higher in excellence than the scholars while the scholars are a rank above the martyrs in excellence."[53] In this report, scholarship clearly ranks higher than armed combat as meritorious activity. One who failed to see that the pursuit of knowledge constituted *jihad* might be suspected of being deficient in knowledge and insight, another report recorded by Ibn 'Abd al-Barr declares.[54] When Ibn 'Abbas, a close Companion of the Prophet famous for his knowledge of Qur'anic exegesis, was queried regarding what constituted *jihad*, he replied that the best act of *jihad* was the establishment of a mosque in which the religious precepts, the prophetic *sunnah*, and jurisprudence were taught and studied.[55]

Al-Tirmidhi (d. 892) records the following report in his authoritative collection of *hadith*: "Whoever departs in the pursuit of knowledge is in the path of God (*fi sabil Allah*) until he returns."[56] Accordingly, one who died while engaged in the pursuit and dissemination of knowledge was considered a martyr. Thus a report emanating from the two Companions Abu Hurayra and Abu Dharr quotes the Prophet as saying, "When death overtakes the seeker of knowledge while he is so engaged, then he dies a martyr."[57] The high moral valence assigned to knowledge in the Qur'an, which is the ultimate criterion distinguishing the believer from the unbeliever,[58] is unambiguously signaled in this report. But more important, within the competing discourses regarding the purview of martyrdom, it is a valuable proof-text that undermines an exclusive militant understanding of it and underscores instead the self-sacrifice and effort inherent in intellectual and rational pursuits.

Conclusion: Implications for Understanding Violence and Peacebuilding in the Islamic Milieu Today

One of the purposes of this article was to survey the Qur'anic significations of the term *jihad* and contrapose to them juridical and other discourses that developed over time. Another was to trace the extra-Qur'anic development of the concepts of martyr and martyrdom in tandem with these changing conceptualizations of *jihad*. Our scrutiny of diverse sources reveals the existence of a rich and variegated discourse, in which these concepts were broadened and streamlined, sometimes underscoring Qur'anic perspectives and at other times undermining them. Our sources point to contestations in the early period of the semantic and exegetical parameters of these terms that yielded a broad spectrum of meanings in changing historical circumstances. By the ninth century, as we have noted, a more circumscribed understanding of *jihad* as primarily military activity emerged among certain religious scholars, primarily jurists, which superimposed itself on the earlier, multifaceted understanding of the concept. Reports that record dissenting views, however, continued to circulate through the early medieval period, ameliorating and challenging establishment militaristic perspectives on *jihad* and martyrdom. These early reports remain for us today important as historical and literary artifacts of intense dialectics of piety involving various groups who struggled to articulate a vision of the just social order desired by God for humankind and the best means to implement it.

The struggle to achieve a just social order has acquired greater urgency among Muslims today in the post-September 11 milieu. The lament is frequently (and rightly) heard today that the term *jihad* has been "hijacked" by Muslim extremists and its broad spectrum of ethical and spiritual meanings basically jettisoned to focus on its combative aspects only. We saw the process of circumscription start roughly in the late eighth century, as certain jurists annexed the term *jihad* to concerns of state security and to the defense of a *pax Islamica* with non-Muslim lands in a perceived adversarial world order. These juridical views are particularly encoded in *siyar* works, which deal with the law of nations. In this process, as we saw, *jihad* essentially became reduced to *qital*. But the jurists viewed the taking of life, when morally justified, as an act of enormity, which, in the context of war, had to be strictly circumscribed by considerations of ethical and moral conduct during fighting. They based their rulings about just conduct during battle on specific Qur'anic verses (as mentioned above), the *sunnah* of the Prophet, and the praxis of the early, particularly Rashidun caliphs. As noted above, Abu Bakr's instructions concerning restrained and honorable conduct during fighting undergird *jus in bello* discussions among Muslim scholars. These commands that explicitly grant immunity to noncombatants and categorically forbid excessive and brutal actions of violence have continued to be repeated in legal manuals and treatises on warfare and remain the basis for essential rules of conduct during war.[59]

Battles fought for worldly reasons have been dubbed *jihad* by some Muslims, often due to political motivations, which have been challenged by other Muslims. Evidence to this end may be found in early *hadith* literature, such as the *Musannaf* of 'Abd al-Razzaq, as previously mentioned. *Jus ad bellum* considerations of this sort are to be found not so much in the legal corpus, but in early *hadith* and ethical literature, which sometimes documents the dissent of the pious laity, who occasionally did not see eye to eye with a number of the jurists. As the conditional combative aspect of *jihad*, it is *qital*, rather than *jihad*, that is a much broader concept, the appropriate equivalent of the Christian concept of just war.

Although the classical jurists reductively conflated *jihad* with *qital*, they were on the whole careful to uphold norms of humane conduct during and after the execution of war, as we have noted, making exceptions only for extreme emergencies. In contrast to this enduring legal tradition, the militants of today have departed entirely from the classical tradition and have dangerously—even nihilistically—distorted *jihad* to make it the equivalent of *hirabah* (brigandage). *Hirabah* was the term coined by the premodern jurists to refer to illegitimate violence, whether on the basis of intent, conduct during its commission, or both, and its perpetration by extra-state rogue elements.[60] In today's parlance, *hirabah* is the equivalent of terrorism in its scorched-earth policy and disregard for the sanctity of civilian life. Rogue militants in the Muslim world today dress up *hirabah* as *jihad*. Unfortunately, when we apply the latter term to their violent activities, we too become complicit to a certain degree in granting them legitimacy (see chapter 3).

The discussion above points to the rich possibilities for extrapolating legal and ethical norms of just peacemaking today from the historical polysemy of the term *jihad* and the variegated praxis that the concept has engendered through time. Much valuable work has been done already in highlighting core values within Islamic thought that are consistent with an emerging universal lexicon of peace and social justice.[61] But further work needs to be done in crafting coherent and sophisticated schemas of peacemaking and peacebuilding from these core values within Islam, which will complement schemas evolving from other religious as well as secular traditions today.

Notes

1. These are the only instances in which the word *harb* is employed in the Qur'an, and, therefore, hardly a common Qur'anic usage, as Reuven Firestone maintains in his book, *Jihad: The Origin of Holy War in Islam* (Oxford: Oxford University Press, 1999), 140, n. 23.

2. For various definitions of holy war, see, e.g., Roland Herbert Bainton, *Christian Attitudes toward War and Peace: A Historical Survey and Critical Reevaluation* (New York: Abingdon Press, 1960), 158; the collection of essays in *The Holy War*, ed. T. P. Murphy (Columbus, OH: Ohio State University Press, 1976); *Cross, Crescent, and Sword: The Justification and Limitation of War in Western and Islamic Tradition*, ed. James Turner Johnson and John Kelsay (New York: Greenwood Press, 1990); and Walter Wink, *Engaging the Powers: Discernment and Resistance in a World of Dominion* (Minneapolis: Fortress Press, 1992), 212–13.

3. The later juridical literature developed these Qur'anic notions further and enumerated a list of proscribed actions during combat, including killing noncombatants and chopping down trees; see Khaled Abou el Fadl, "The Rules of Killing at War: an Inquiry into Classical Sources," *Muslim World*, vol. 89, no. 2 (1999), 144–57.

4. Al-Tabari, *Tarikh al-rusul wa 'l-muluk* (Cairo: n. pub., 1905), 3:213–14.

5. These traditional sources were used by the editors of the standard 1924 Cairo edition of the Qur'an to determine a chronology of Qur'anic verses and chapters that is widely accepted. For a useful account of Qur'anic chronology, see Hanna Kassis, *A Concordance of the Qur'an* (Berkeley: University of California Press, 1983), xxxv–xxxix.

6. See A. J. Wensinck, *Concordance et indices de la tradition musulmane* (Leiden: E. J. Brill, 1936–1969), 3:242.

7. For traditional accounts of these events, see the highly accessible rendering into English of the Prophet's biography by Martin Lings, *The Life of Muhammad* (Cambridge: Islamic Texts Society, 1995).

8. These were four specific months deemed sacred in the pre-Islamic period during which fighting was prohibited.

9. Al-Shafi'i, *al-Risala*, ed. Ahmad Shakir (n.p., 1891), 430–32.

10. Al-Tabari, *Jami' al-bayan 'an ta'wil ay al-Qur'an* (Beirut: Dar al-kutub al-'ilmiyya, 1995), 3:18, where he cites a *hadith* to this effect related by the Companion al-Dahhak.

11. See further Sohail Hashmi, "Interpreting the Islamic Ethics of War and Peace," in Terry Nardin, ed., *The Ethics of War and Peace* (Princeton: Princeton University Press, 1996), 146–66.

12. Roy Mottahedeh and Ridwan al-Sayyid, "The Idea of the Jihad in Islam before the Crusades," in *The Crusades from the Perspective of Byzantium and the Muslim World*, ed. Angeliki E. Laiou and Roy Parviz Mottahedeh (Washington, DC: Dumbarton Oaks Research Library and Collection, 2001), 23–29.

13. Ibn Abi Shayba, *al-Kitab al-musannaf fi 'l-ahadith wa-'l-athar*, ed. Muhammad 'Abd al-Salam Shaahiin (Beirut: Dar al-kutub al-'ilmiyya, 1995), 4:237.

14. Mottahedeh and al-Sayyid, "Idea of the Jihad," 25–27.

15. Abd al-Razzaq al-San'ani, *Al-Musannaf*, ed. Habib al-Rahman al-A'zami (Beirut: al-Maktab al-islami, 1970–72), 5:189.

16. This verse states: "Strive against the unbelievers and the hypocrites and be stern with them; their refuge is Gehenna, a wretched destiny;" see Ibn al-'Arabi, *al-Nasikh wa'l-mansukh fi al-Qur'an al-karim* (Beirut: Dar al-kutub al-'ilmiyya, 1997), 61; Ibn al-Jawzi, *Nawasikh al-Qur'an* (Beirut: Dar al-kutub al-'ilmiyya, n.d.), 94.

17. Al-Jawzi, *Nawasikh al-Qur'an*, 93.

18. Al-Tabari, *Jami' al-bayan*, 3:25.

19. Ibn Kathir, *Tafsir al-Qur'an al-'azim* (Riadh: Dar Tiba, 1998), 1:416–17.

20. Al-Tabari, *Ikhtilaf al-fuqaha'* (Cairo: n.p., 1933), 1–21.

21. Al-Shafi'i, *Kitab al-umm* (Bulaq: Maktaba al-kubra al-amiriyya, 1903), 4:103–4.

22. Al-Shafi'i, *al-Risala*, ed. Ahmad Shakir (n.p., 1891), 430–32.

23. Majid Khadduri, *War and Peace in the Law of Islam* (Baltimore: Johns Hopkins University, 1955), 64–65; see also the eleventh century Shafi'i jurist and political theorist al-Mawardi's (d. 1058) famous treatise, *The Ordinances of Government*, trans. Wafaa H. Wahba (Reading, UK: Garnet, 1996), 16–17.

24. See Majid Khadduri, *The Islamic Law of Nations: Shaybani's Siyar*, trans. and ed. Majid Khadduri (Baltimore: Johns Hopkins University, 1966), 12–13; Khadduri, *War and Peace*, 145.

25. As did the Hanafi jurist Ahmad al-Tahawi (d. 933) in his *Kitab al-Mukhtasar*, ed. Abu al-Wafa al-Afghani (Hyderabad: Lajnat ihya' al-ma'arif al-nu'maniyya, 1950), 281, cited in Khadduri, *Islamic Law*, 58.

26. The author therefore questions, for example, Reuven Firestone's recent affirmation of *jihad* as holy war on the basis of his broad definition of it as any "religious justification for engaging in war fought for religious purposes"; see his book, *Jihad*, 15. I maintain that it is necessary for us to interrogate ostensible religious purposes and the rhetoric of religious

triumphalism in the invocation of *jihad* as aggressive military activity by certain Muslim exegetes and jurists. Such a line of inquiry would be revealing of more mundane and politically expedient motivations for expanding the semantic and legal purview of *jihad* to include expansionist war fought for political and secular ends clothed in religious garb.

27. See, e.g., Muhammad al-Qurtubi, *Jami Ahkam al-Qur'an* (Cairo: Dar al-kutub al-misriyya, 1935), 2:348.

28. The *fada'il* literature is a prolific one in the medieval period. Works of praise were composed about many meritorious activities and religious duties, in addition to prominent people and places. For a brief introduction to this genre, see Asma Afsaruddin, *Excellence and Precedence: Medieval Islamic Discourse on Legitimate Leadership* (Leiden: E.J. Brill, 2002), 26–35, and the references cited therein.

29. See Ibn Abi al-Dunya, *Al-Sabr wa-'l-thawab 'alayhi*, ed. Muhammad Khayr Ramadan Yusuf (Beirut: Dar Ibn Hazm, 1997), 85.

30. See Firestone, *Jihad*, 100.

31. The author's monograph in progress, *Striving in the Path of God: Jihad and Martyrdom in Islamic Thought and Praxis* (Oxford: Oxford University Press, forthcoming) discusses these literatures further.

32. It should be pointed out that the Qur'an uses the term *shahid* as an eyewitness for both God and humans; in relation to God, see Qur'an (3:98; 6:19; 41:53, etc.).

33. Arthur Jeffrey, *The Foreign Vocabulary of the Qur'an* (Baroda: Oriental Institute, 1938), 187; Keith Lewinstein, "The Reevaluation of Martyrdom in Early Islam," in *Sacrificing the Self: Perspectives on Martyrdom and Religion*, ed. Margaret Cormack (Oxford: Oxford University Press, 2002), 78–79. This relationship obviously needs to be better studied and documented, which is presently beyond the purview of this chapter. See further on this topic the useful article by A. J. Wensinck, "The Oriental Doctrine of the Martyrs," in his *Semietische Studiën uit de nalatenschap* (Leiden: A.W. Sitjhoff, 1941), 91–113, which establishes striking parallels between Christian and post-Qur'anic Muslim concepts of martyrdom, and the article by Etan Kohlberg "Shahid," in the *Encyclopaedia of Islam*, ed. C.E. Bosworth, E. van Donzel, W.P. Heinrichs, and G. Lecomte (Leiden: E.J. Brill, 1997), 9:104.

34. Ibn Abi 'l-Dunya, *Sabr*, 85.

35. Ibid., 51.

36. See Wensinck, *Concordance*, 2:165.

37. 'Abd al-Razzaq, *Musannaf*, 5:259, 9:543.

38. Ibn Abi 'l-Dunya, *Sabr*, 31.

39. 'Abd al-Razzaq, *Musannaf*, 11:105.

40. This is a *hadith* reported by Muslims and included by al-Nawawi in his *Forty Hadith*, trans. Ezzeddin Ibrahim and Denys Johnson-Davies (Cambridge: Islamic Texts Society, 1997), 110.

41. This *hadith*, which appears to have emanated from Sufi circles, is recorded by al-Ghazali, *Ihya' 'ulum al-din* [*The Book of Invocation*], trans. Kojiro Nakamura as *Ghazali on Prayer* (Tokyo: University of Tokyo, 1973), 167. For further attestations of this *hadith*, see further John Renard, "*Al-Jihad al-Akbar*: Notes on a Theme in Islamic Spirituality," *Muslim World*, vol. 78, no. 3–4 (1988): 225–42.

42. Wensinck, *Concordance*, 1:389.

43. Ibid., 5:455.

44. 'Abd al-Razzaq, *Musannaf*, 5:268.

45. Ibid., 5:271

46. Ibid., 5:270–71.

47. Al-Bukhari, *Sahih*, ed. Qasim al-Shamma'i al-Rifa'i (Beirut: Dar al-qalam, n.d.), 2:420–21.

48. Malik b. Anas, *Al-Muwatta'*, ed. Bashshar 'Awad Ma'ruf and Mahmud Muhammad Khalil (Beirut: Mu'assasat al-Risala, 1994), 1:366–67.

49. 'Abd al-Razzaq, *Musannaf*, 5:272.

50. Ibid., 116.

51. Wensinck, *Concordance*, 1:389.

52. Ibn Hazm, *Kitab al-Fisal fi al-milal wa-'l-ahwa' wa-'l-nihal* (Cairo: al-Matba'a al-adabiyya, 1321), 4:135.

53. Ibn 'Abd al-Barr, *Jami' bayan al-'ilm wa-fadlihi*, ed. 'Abd al-Hamid Muhammad al-Sa'dani (Beirut: Dar al-kutub al-'ilmiyya, 2000), 18.

54. Ibid., 49. This report is attributed to Abu al-Darda'; also cited by Ibn Qayyim al-Jawziyya, *Fadl al-'ilm wa-l-'ulama'*, ed. Salih Ahmad al-Shami (Beirut: al-Maktab al-islami, 2001), 101.

55. Ibid.

56. Cited by Ibn Qayyim al-Jawziyya, *Fadl al-'ilm*, 99.

57. Al-Barr, *Jami' bayan al-'ilm*, 49; Ibn Qayyim al-Jawziyya, *Fadl al-'ilm*, 100.

58. Thus the Qur'an (39:9) asks, "Are those who know and those who do not know to be reckoned the same?" The Qur'an further describes knowledge as a great bounty from God bestowed upon His prophets and their followers through time (2:151–52; 4:113; 5:110; 12:22; 28:14, etc.).

59. See further my discussion of this in *Striving in the Path of God*, chapter 8.

60. The classic study of this phenomenon is Khaled Abou El Fadl, *Rebellion and Violence in Islamic Law* (Cambridge: Cambridge University Press, 2001).

61. See, e.g., Mohammed Abu-Nimer, *Nonviolence and Peacebuilding in Islam: Theory and Practice* (Gainesville: University Press of Florida, 2003).

3

Revisiting the Qur'anic Basis for the Use of War Language

Waleed El-Ansary

In discussing peacebuilding activities in Muslim countries—or any-where—one needs to pay attention to how civil-society members and government officials use language.[1] The specific words that Muslim re-ligious authorities use in referring to peacebuilding, conflict resolution, and justice are usually grounded in religious texts, theology, practical ethics, and history. Since religious authorities are trained in Qur'anic syntax, gram-mar, and classical Arabic, the way words are used or misused could pose problems in theological interpretations. This is significant for policymakers because the way language is used or misused by extremists reveals their levels of self-understanding, self-posturing, and ability to use language to their advantage. For example, the al-Qaeda leadership have consistently defined themselves as *mujahidun*—literally, participants in *jihad*—since before the horrendous attacks of September 11, 2001. This misuse of the term, legally, theologically, and politically, has been the cause of much de-bate among Muslim religious leaders. This essay discusses the arguments within Muslim scholarship over the language of peace and reconciliation, examining how these arguments have addressed specifically the ways in which terrorists such as Osama bin Laden exploit Qur'anic language to serve their causes. The debates on language reflect critical efforts by grand muftis, qadis, and many others who are profoundly disgusted at the distor-tion of sacred texts to push back against those who justify terrorism.

Recently federal agencies, including the State Department, the Department of Homeland Security, and the National Counterterrorism Center, have all heeded the advice of analysts such as Douglas Streusand not to employ terms that bin Laden and al-Qaeda members use to describe themselves, particularly terms based on *jihad*.[2] Since *jihad* is broadly defined as "striving or making effort" for the sake of God, Streusand argues that "describing [our enemies] . . . as *jihadis* or *mujahidun* not only validates their claim to legitimacy, but also implies that we consider Islam itself our enemy."[3] He suggests that the best term for warfare, which does not meet the standards of *jihad* in the Islamic legal tradition, is *hirabah*; he adds that "another potentially useful word is *irhab*, the Arabic word for terrorism," and that "*irhabi* is the literal translation of 'terrorist.' "[4] Although contemporary Arab analysts often employ the latter terms in exactly this way, these are mistaken translations and a strategic error, according to Shaykh 'Ali Goma'a, the grand mufti of Egypt.[5] As we shall see, the correct translation of *terrorist* is *irjafi* rather than *irhabi*. Bin Laden himself uses the difference between the classical and modern meanings of *irhab* to validate his claim to legitimacy on one hand and support his argument that the war on terror is a war against Islam on the other. The classical usages and meanings of the root from which *irhabi* derives, *rahiba*, are overwhelmingly positive, for the Qur'an employs this root to refer to the fear of God ("the beginning of wisdom" in the Abrahamic traditions) or holding God in awe:

> O Children of Israel, remember My favor wherewith I favored you; and fulfill my covenant, and I shall fulfill your covenant; and have awe of Me (*irhabuni*) (Qur'an 2:40).[6]

The Qur'an also employs the root to refer to those who fear God, that is, monks or *ruhban* (singular *rahib*), the institutional form of which is *rahbaniyyah*:

> Then We sent Our Messengers to follow in their footsteps, and We sent Jesus the Son of Mary and We gave him the Gospel and placed mercy and kindness in the hearts of those who follow Him. But [as for] monasticism (*rahbaniyyah*), they invented it—We had not prescribed it for them—only seeking God's beatitude. Yet they did not observe it with due observance. So We gave those of them who believed their reward; but many of them are immoral (Qur'an 57:27).

Finally, the Qur'an employs the root to refer to an aggressor's fear of retaliation, which deters initiating an attack:

> Make ready for them whatever force you can and of horses tethered that thereby you may awe (*turhibuna*) the enemy of God and your enemy, and others besides them, whom you know not: God knows them. And whatever thing you expend in the way of God shall be repaid to you in full, and you will not be wronged (Qur'an 8:60).[7]

Although English translations of *turhibuna* often emphasize striking fear into the enemy, the term connotes deterrence based on self-defense with an aim toward peace, as classical Qur'anic commentaries point out. Classical Qur'anic scholar al-Tabari (d. 923) explains the meaning of this verse as "scaring the enemies of God and your enemies with your preparation (*bi i'dadikum*)."[8] A contemporary scholar, Muhammad Asad, translates *turhibuna* as "deter."[9] Considering the implications of these different appearances of the root *r–h–b* in the Qur'an, the term *irhabi* has the classical connotation of a God-fearing, peace-loving, attack-deterring monk.

Bin Laden accordingly embraces the term *irhabi*, exploiting the difference between classical and modern usages to argue for the possibility of commendable rather than reprehensible terrorism. This distinction makes little sense in English, but it makes perfect sense in parsing the difference between classical and modern Arabic. In response to questions from followers on the moral status of terrorism, bin Laden argues that

> terrorism (*irhab*) can be commendable and it can be reprehensible. Terrifying an innocent person and terrorizing him is objectionable and unjust, also unjustly terrorizing people is not right. Whereas, terrorizing oppressors and criminals and thieves and robbers is necessary for the safety of people and for the protection of their property. There is no doubt in this. Every state and every civilization and culture has to resort to terrorism under certain circumstances for the purpose of abolishing tyranny and corruption. Every country in the world has its own security system and its own security forces, its own police and its own army. They are all designed to terrorize whoever even contemplates to attack that country or its citizens. The terrorism we practice is of the commendable kind for it is directed at the tyrants and the aggressors and the enemies of Allah.[10]

There are currently dozens of competing definitions of terrorism in Arabic because of complications in agreeing on a basis for determining when the use of violence is legitimate.[11] Bin Laden exploits such complications by making a false analogy, focusing on "terrorizing oppressors and criminals and thieves and robbers" or those who commit crimes against others, not crimes against themselves. The United States is accordingly a terrorist target for what is perceived as a "Crusader-Zionist" foreign policy that threatens "the safety of [our] people and protection of their property," according to bin Laden—not its domestic policy, which is irrelevant to his self-proclaimed "tit-for-tat" strategy based upon "reciprocity."[12] In short, past United States foreign policy determines whether terrorism is commendable or reprehensible, whether there are spiritual payoffs or penalties for retaliatory attacks. For analysts such as Michael Scheuer, former chief of the Central Intelligence Agency's (CIA) Bin Laden Issue Station, it follows that there is thus a foreign policy trigger point, at which terrorism can be considered commendable.[13]

Streusand therefore rightly argues that U.S. officials should not dignify such extremists by calling them *mujahidun*. Bin Laden's argument completely violates Islamic legal requirements for *jihad* and the murder of innocent civilians inflicts an injustice for which no strategic results could ever compensate.[14] Yet the same argument applies to the term *irhabi*, and Streusand's first suggestion for translating *terrorism* into Arabic as *hirabah* is problematic because of linguistic, legal, and practical concerns, according to Shaykh Goma'a.[15] Linguistically, he points out that the Qur'anic verse employing the verbal form of this term refers to "those who wage war (*yuharibuna*) against God and His Messenger."[16] *Hirabah* shares the same root as *harb*, or war, which may be just or unjust and generally connotes fighting between two legal entities (*tarafayn*)—unlike terrorism, from a linguistic point of view. The term *muharib*, or one who engages in *hirabah*, can mean combatant, fighter, or warrior, with neutral connotations. Furthermore, *hirabah* implies a sense of hand-to-hand combat far more courageous than the terrorist attacks on September 11, though *muharib* can involve deceit and betrayal, a striking behind the back.

Grand Mufti Goma'a maintains that, from an Islamic legal perspective, *hirabah* also generally connotes brigandage or armed highway robbery, not attacks within a city, as occurred on September 11. Furthermore, dissociating *hirabah* from a money-taking motive altogether to include bin Laden, who is all too willing to spend his money maximizing American casualties, is too much of a stretch, according to Goma'a.[17] Although Sherman Jackson ably points out that several later Maliki jurists adopted such a position, it is still a minority view.[18] And because combat associated with brigandage is more courageous than striking from behind, Goma'a links the legal argument on brigandage to the aforementioned linguistic argument in mutually reinforcing terms. He also points out that, since *hirabah* may involve theft rather than murder, the legal sanction is highly variable. The related Qur'anic verse prescribes a fourfold hierarchy of punishments: "execution, or crucifixion, or the cutting off of hands and feet from opposite sides, or exile from the land." Accordingly, legal scholars debate the circumstances under which the various penalties should apply. Should execution or crucifixion be reserved for highway robbery that involves murder, cutting off of hands and feet from opposite sides to highway robbery that does not involve murder, and exile to obstruction of highways involving neither robbery nor murder? A term for terrorism with less ambiguity in punishment would be preferable.

Finally, from a practical point of view, Goma'a points out bin Laden's claim that his Muslim critics are actually "waging war against God and His Messenger," not the members of al-Qaeda. Therefore, the term offers extremists a very easy opportunity to turn the tables on their critics and exploit the term to their benefit.

Thus, the grand mufti suggests an alternative term: *irjaf*.[19] This word, which denotes subversion and scaremongering to bring quaking and commotion to society, is derived from the root *rajafa*, which means to quake, tremble, be in violent motion, convulse, or shake. The Qur'an applies derivatives of this term to the natural, supernatural, and social orders, referring to earthquakes, the Day of Judgment, and those who bring commotion to society, respectively. For example, the Qur'an states:

> So the earthquake (*rajfa*) took them unawares, and they lay prostrate in their homes in the morning (7:78).[20]

Another Qur'anic application of the root to the Day of Judgment occurs as follows:

> One day the earth and the mountains will be in violent commotion (*tarjufu*). And the mountains will be as a heap of sand poured out and flowing down (73:14).[21]

A social application, most relevant for the purposes of this discussion, occurs only once:

> Now; if the hypocrites do not give over, and those in whose hearts there is sickness and they that make commotion (*murjifun*) in the city, We shall assuredly urge thee against them and then they will be thy neighbors there only a little (33:60).[22]

In the context of this verse, al-Qurtubi, the renowned thirteenth-century Qur'anic commentator and Maliki jurist, explains the meaning of *irjaf* with respect to "shaking of the hearts (*tahrik al-qulub*)," noting the root's corresponding application to "the shaking of the earth (*rajafat al-ard*)."[23] Within an Islamic context, connecting this metaphor of creating commotion on earth (*murjifun*) with that of shaking hearts (*tahrik al-qulub*) connotes that those who do wrong are in fact acting against the wishes of the divine. Also, many other commentators, such as al-Shawkani, the towering intellectual figure of early nineteenth-century Yemen, note linguistically that one of the names of the ocean is *al-rajjaf* because of the commotion its powerful waves create.[24] And al-Haqqi, the eighteenth-century commentator, explains that *irjaf* may be executed "either by action or by word (*ama bi'l fa'ili aw bi'l qawli*)," suggesting different forms of terrorism; intense social divisions caused through erroneous interpretations of verses of the Qur'an to justify violence can be considered forms of *irjaf*.

Goma'a thus maintains that the term *murjifun* (singular, *murjif*), as well as the equivalent rendering *irjafiyyun* (singular, *irjafi*), is a far better translation of terrorists than *muharibun* or the equivalent rendering *hirabiyyun*. Of course, there are multiple ways to bring about such intense commotion to society, but all of these fall under *irjaf*, his recommended translation of the word terrorism. From a linguistic perspective, he points out that the term unambiguously connotes the cowardice, deceit, and betrayal associated with terrorism in striking from the back, unlike *hirabah*. The grand mufti's discussion of the usage of *murjifun* not only deflates bin Laden's pompous and grandiose ideology, but reduces him from monk to criminal. Moreover, *irjaf* is clearly distinguished from conventional warfare, *harb*, since the *murjifun* (or *irjafiyyun*) do not constitute a legal entity, whereas their target does.[25] The legal sanction for *irjaf* is also much clearer than *hirabah*, for the punishment—execution—is unambiguous. Finally, from a practical point of view, it is far more difficult for bin Laden and al-Qaeda members to argue that they do not cause commotion within cities, and that their critics attempting to prevent such violence do. The term *irjaf* thereby effectively eliminates the possibility of extremists turning the tables on their critics.

With respect to important precedents for the use of the term *murjifun*—and, by extension, *irjafiyyun*—Goma'a cites the Khawarij, a violent sect that emerged in the late seventh century, assassinated 'Ali ibn Abi Talib, the fourth of the "rightly guided caliphs," and massacred many Muslims. He also cites the twelfth-century Ibn Tumart of the Maghrib, known as al-Zalam al-Qattal, or the Unjust Slaughterer, for his violent purges and massacres; he claimed to be the Mahdi, destined to reform Islam.

Analysts such as Streusand raise a crucial and profound point in arguing that it is a strategic error for U.S. officials to use terms that extremists use to describe themselves, such as *mujahidun*. But if that is the case, *irhabiyyun* should not be used either, as bin Laden and extremists embrace it based on the divergence between classical and modern meanings of the term. And although *hirabah* is clearly less problematic than *irhab* as a translation of the word terrorism, it is not satisfactory either. It lacks linguistic and legal precision, inviting extremists to apply the same charge to their critics. From this point of view, *irjaf* is the optimal translation of terrorism. It is unambiguously negative, legally precise, and prevents bin Laden and other extremists from using it to claim their causes as legitimate.

Those who object that *irjaf* is not now well-known enough to serve its purpose fail to realize, first, that Muslims clearly recognize its extremely negative connotation even if they do not know all its meanings; second, that *irhab* itself had a much better connotation when it was first employed; and third, that there is a natural progression or series of phases in the attempt to describe new (or newly recurring) phenomena. Given the centrality of the Qur'an in Arabic culture, and that *irjaf* is the best Qur'anic term for terrorism, it can initially supplement the term *irhab* before ultimately supplanting it. Only a strategic minority need first employ the term for it to be effective. Rather than being like a silver bullet, the usage of the term *irjaf* is more analogous to a gas that expands naturally, suffocating the necessary intellectual conditions for justifying violent forms of extremism as it spreads. The correct use of Qur'anic terminology could be a powerful linguistic weapon in the ongoing intellectual battle for the minds of would-be terrorists. In the future, one would hope for more collaboration with leading scholars in the Islamic world on such matters, particularly in Egypt, given its status as the intellectual capital of the Arab world. How can we wage a battle for hearts and minds unless we understand how those hearts and minds receive our message?

Notes

1.   The author gratefully acknowledges the help of Shaykh 'Ali Goma'a, the Grand Mufti of Egypt, in granting personal interviews on the subject of this chapter, as well as the Ammerdown Center in Bath, England, for sponsoring a conference entitled "The Use of Language in the 'War' Against Terrorism" in June 2007, which was the occasion for this chapter's earliest draft. The author also wishes to thank Joseph Lumbard for reviewing earlier versions of the paper.

2.   The State Department publicly announced this policy on April 24, 2008.

3.   Douglas Streusand, *National Post*, Issues & Comment section, May 26, 2007. Available online with commentary at Dave Sim's Blog & Mail, http://davesim.blogspot.com/ 2007/05/dave-sims-blogandmail-258-may-27th-2007.html (accessed November 19, 2009). See also Douglas Streusand and Harry Tunnell, "Choosing Words Carefully: Language to Help Fight Islamic Terrorism," National Defense University, Center for Strategic Communications, 2006. Available online at the U.S. Army Professional Writing Collection, http://www.army.mil/professionalwriting/volumes/ volume4/july_2006/7_06_4.html (accessed November 19, 2009).

4.   Streusand, *National Post*.

5.   See, e.g., Shaykh 'Ali Goma'a, *Samāt al-'Asr* (Cairo: Dar al-Farūq, 2006), 131–32, a volume consisting of articles in his weekly column in *al-Ahrām*, the most popular newspaper in Egypt.

6.   See also Qur'an (7:54) and (16:31). All translations are the Aal al-Bayt rendering, available at Al Tafsir (Mirror), www.altafsir.com (accessed November 19, 2009), unless otherwise noted.

7.   Slightly modified from the Aal al-Bayt translation.

8.   For the complete *tafsir* of al-Tabari as well as other major commentators, see www. altafsir.com.

9.   Asad's translation of this verse reads: "Hence, make ready against them whatever force and war mounts you are able to muster, so that you might deter (*turhibuna*) thereby the enemies of God, who are your enemies as well, and others besides them of whom you may be unaware, [but] of whom God is aware; and whatever you may expend in God's cause shall be repaid to you in full, and you shall not be wronged."

10. See transcripts of responses to questions from followers from the *Frontline* special, "Hunting Bin Laden," at www.pbs.org/wgbh/pages/frontline/shows/binladen/who/interview.html (accessed November 19, 2009). For a useful collection and translation of twenty-four of bin Laden's statements, see Bruce Lawrence, ed., *Messages to the World: The Statements of Osama bin Laden* (New York: Verso, 2005).

11. See, e.g., Alex P. Schmid and Albert J. Jongman, *Political Terrorism: A New Guide to Actors, Authors, Concepts, Data Bases, Theories, and Literature* (New Brunswick, NJ: Transaction Publishers, 2005).

12. Tit-for-tat is merely the strategy of starting with cooperation, and thereafter doing what the other player did on the previous move. For further analysis of Osama bin Laden's strategic deviation from Islamic heritage using game theory, as well as its implications for our strategic response, see Waleed El-Ansary, "The Economics of Terrorism: How bin Laden Is Changing the Rules of the Game," in Joseph Lumbard, ed., *Islam, Fundamentalism, and the Betrayal of Tradition: Essays by Western Muslim Scholars* (Bloomington, IN: World Wisdom Books, 2004), 191–235.

13. Michael Scheuer, *Through Our Enemies' Eyes: Osama bin Laden, Radical Islam, and the Future of America* (Dulles, VA: Potomac Books, 2006).

14. For a critical evaluation of bin Laden's understanding of the Qur'an, see, e.g., Rosalind Gwynne, "Usamah bin Ladin, the Qur'an, and *Jihad*," *Religion*, vol. 36, no. 2 (2006), 61–90, and David Dakake, "The Myth of a Militant Islam," in Lumbard, ed., *Islam*, 3–37. Islam is not a religion in which the ends justify the means, and no Muslim is allowed to return one injustice with another injustice. Bin Laden therefore argues for the need to "go beyond" traditional Islamic views and applauds the terrorists who executed the September 11 attacks for doing so. Seen in this light, he is not an authentic product of Islamic thought, but attempting to bypass the rules of just war by arguing that the old rulings of Islamic law are no longer adequate and that new rulings are necessary based on *ijtihad*. In Islam, according to bin Laden, this is a creative but disciplined effort to freshen views on old issues or derive legal rulings for new situations, including warfare, from the accepted juridical sources of Islam. An ethical judgment, such as *ijtihad*, however, is not just one religious judgment among many, to be weighed against other judgments—political, economic, or social—in deciding how to act. It is itself an all-things-considered judgment based on spiritual principles, taking all other factors into account. In short, bin Laden's Machiavellian strategy, which is ruthless and immoral, combines elements of Islamic and secular views in a spiritually lethal, syncretistic manner, and is the product of a completely erroneous *ijtihad* that he is not qualified to attempt in the first place. The spiritual and intellectual qualifications necessary for proper *ijtihad* are so enormous that there is a debate over whether anyone today has the qualifications to perform it, particularly since it requires in-depth knowledge of the Islamic intellectual heritage as well as the transmitted sciences. And regardless of whether or not contemporary Muslims believe the gate of *ijtihad* is closed to them, the overwhelming majority of them reject bin Laden's *ijtihad* and Machiavellian tactics, even if many of them also criticize U.S. foreign policy in the Middle East.

15. The following analysis is based on a series of the author's interviews with Shaykh Goma'a in June 2007.

16. Yusuf 'Ali translates this verse as follows: "The punishment of those who wage war against Allah and His Messenger, and strive with might and main for mischief through the land is: execution, or crucifixion, or the cutting off of hands and feet from opposite sides, or exile from the land: that is their disgrace in this world, and a heavy punishment is theirs in the Hereafter" (5:33).

17. The Grand Mufti is obviously well aware of variations in the interpretation of *hirabah*. For an interesting survey of such views and an argument that *hirabah* is terrorism, see Sherman Jackson, "Domestic Terrorism in the Islamic Legal Tradition," *Muslim World*, vol. 91, no. 3–4 (2001), 293–310.

18. As Ibn Rushd points out, "They [Islamic legal scholars] agreed that *hirabah* is a show of armed force and the obstruction of the highways outside the city. They disagreed about the brigands inside the city." Indeed, Abu Hanifa and al-Shafi'i argued that *hirabah* cannot occur there. Ibn Rushd, *The Distinguished Jurist's Primer*, vol. 2 (Reading, UK: Garnet Publishing, 2000), 547. For some later Maliki views, see Jackson, "Domestic Terrorism," 293–310.

19. This argument is also largely based on the author's interviews of Shaykh Goma'a, although part of it is present in Alī Goma'a, *Samāt al-'Asr*, 131–32.

20. See also Qur'an (7:91) and (29:37).

21. See also Qur'an (79:6).

22. Arberry's translation. Some other translations of this term include "scare-mongering," "those who stir up sedition," "alarmists," and other types of subversion to bring commotion to society. Goma'a points out that the term's meaning is not limited to these instances, and that, because the Qur'an is intended for all places and times, the full range of meanings must be employed.

23. See www.altafsir.com for the complete *tafsir* of al-Qurtubi and the following commentators.

24. See, e.g., Seyyed Hossein Nasr, *Science and Civilization in Islam* (Chicago: Kazi Publications, 1996).

25. It is important to note that scholars believe that *irjaf* occurs within a city, as the verse makes explicit, and therefore applies to New York or Baghdad. This differentiates it from *hirabah*, which has the connotation of occurring outside a city.

4

An Islamic Model of Conflict Resolution

Principles and Challenges

Mohammed Abu-Nimer

T he field of conflict resolution and peacebuilding has grown significantly in the last three decades, especially among American
and European governments, non-governmental organizations
(NGOs), and academic institutions. As hundreds of undergraduate, graduate, and even doctorate programs have been launched, offering degrees to
mostly young graduates or second-career students, conflict resolution as
a study and practice has become increasingly professionalized. The field's
roots, however, still lie in the conceptualization of interest-based negotiation practices, communication skills, and recently, frameworks for postconflict peacebuilding—that is, conflict transformation, reconciliation, and
dialogue theories.[1]

In the early 1990s, when the field was mainly based on Western conflict
resolution approaches and cultural values, a few scholars and practitioners
began questioning the applicability of these skills and concepts in a non-
white, non–Anglo Saxon-American context.[2] They urged mediators, facilitators, and negotiators to take cultural differences more seriously when
using American conflict resolution techniques in the Middle East or other
non-Western cultural contexts. The debate in the conflict resolution field
continues as to whether generic models of conflict resolution and peacemaking can apply across cultures. In developing his human needs theory,
Burton has argued vehemently that cultural differences are not significant.[3]
On the other side of the debate, Zartman has edited a special volume

exploring African models of conflict resolution, attempting to highlight culture's crucial role in shaping the ways in which Africans resolve conflicts.[4]

In the context of this debate, Muslim and non-Muslim scholars and practitioners have explored the relevance of Western conflict resolution processes, values, and frameworks for Muslim cultural and religious settings.[5] Other works have sought to develop the field of Islamic peacebuilding and conflict resolution, and a few academic courses are offered, mostly in Western universities and institutes, focusing on the topic.[6] To define and develop the concept of Islamic conflict resolution, many of these efforts focus on two primary sources: the theological foundations of the faith—the Qur'an and *hadith*—and the Muslim historical and cultural practices of conflict resolution. The traditional dispute resolution processes employed by Muslim elders in many societies involve a clear, step-by-step process of mediation (*wasatah*), arbitration (*tahkim*), and reconciliation (*sulh*), derived from the above texts, historical examples, and episodes from the life of the Prophet himself. Many anthropologists and conflict resolution scholars have examined these processes, from tracing broadly the religious roots and values behind them to isolating their details, such as which verbal and nonverbal gestures may be inappropriate during a negotiation.[7] Several conclusions can be drawn from their research and experience.

First, as Western conflict resolution processes are based on Western cultural values and norms, they cannot be applied automatically to Muslim cultural contexts. Muslim culture and Islam have a different set of values and norms that can come into play in conflict resolution practices. Second, the Western values of individualism and negotiating for tangible, concrete outcomes can be at odds with Muslim conceptions of conflict resolution, in which collectivist and intangible outcomes—related to public image as well as psychological and social issues—are often central. Third, when a negotiation uses a third party, the Western model's assumption of that party's neutrality, in a Muslim context, can result in promoting the status quo and preserving asymmetric power relations. Muslims expect the third party in a negotiation to take a stand, articulating certain values of justice and peace. Fourth, Western conflict resolution models are based on legalistic and contractual cultural values, often requiring disputants to use semilegal frameworks to legitimize their processes and agreements. In addition to using legal systems, Muslim conflict resolution processes use social, cultural, and religious values as the basis for any mediation. Fifth, under Western models, the legitimacy and credibility of a third party to a negotiation are based on formalized professional training, certification, education, and legal expertise. Within a Muslim cultural context, the legitimacy of conflict resolution processes and third-party intervention stems from a negotiator's religious, social, and cultural rank. Age, gender, class, or tribal affiliation are often more important than legal training or other formal education credentials. These differences between Western and Muslim models of conflict resolution arise from a differing set of principles regarding what the ideal outcome of a peacebuilding effort might be—ideals, in the Muslim case, developed over centuries of Islamic thought, belief, and commentary, but drawing heavily from the Qur'an and *hadith*.[8] Awareness of these principles can help Westerners be more effective in their peacebuilding efforts in Muslim societies. That said, even as the principles of traditional dispute resolution techniques are derived from sacred texts and historical examples, the extent to which leaders are able and willing to translate these principles and integrate them into their actual daily procedures of dispute resolution lies at the heart of the problem.

Challenges in Applying Islamic Conflict Resolution Models

The majority of ongoing violent conflicts in the world are taking place in Muslim countries or involve Islamic groups. Thus, focusing on conflict resolution and peacemaking from an Islamic perspective could be an appropriate step in attempting to reduce the violence and destruction brought by these conflicts. However, we must be careful not to reduce what are complex situations to simple cases of religious conflict. Doing so would imply that the ongoing tensions among Israel and its neighbors can be boiled down to a straightforward conflict between Jewish and Muslim values, or that the U.S. war in Iraq can be understood as a result of friction between Christian and Muslim values. Clearly, in neither case is this correct. Examining how Islamic values can be turned to nonviolence thus requires, first, a certain amount of self-reflection for non-Muslims. How can Jewish and Christian values also be brought to bear? How can these conflicts of values be assessed in the context of the asymmetric power dynamics between the Muslim and Western worlds, militarily and socioeconomically, both historically and in the present?

The historical relationship between most Muslim societies and Europe and the United States is characterized by collective memories of colonial and imperial policies aimed at suppressing the rights and identities of locals. Suspicion of any foreign plan or agenda quickly and easily brings back these memories of victimhood and exploitation, as well as the need to protect cultural and religious identities. That it is often Muslim Americans and Muslim European scholars and practitioners who have taken up the task of exploring the roots of Islamic peace and conflict resolution does not necessarily help. Due to these scholars' multicultural and bilingual affiliations and characteristics, they are usually associated with being for-eigners or holding U.S. or European agendas. Such an image injures their credibility and capacity to successfully implement conflict resolution ap-proaches, which themselves run the risk of being far too abstract to address cultural differences meaningfully, let alone help the people who have actu-ally experienced violent conflict firsthand.

Internal problems in the Muslim world also present enormous obstacles to successfully resolving conflicts. The current regimes of several Muslim countries have survived by relying on the state security apparatus, promot-ing values of tribal and clannish loyalty, disregarding public accountability, creating authoritarian and hierarchical social and cultural arrangements, excluding women from public leadership, and promoting ethnic and sec-tarian policies of exclusion.[9] If peacebuilding efforts grow serious, such regimes may see them as a threat to their power. Moreover, Islamic educa-tional systems, in most cases, have been shaped by the policies established by the ruling elites. They lack critical education curricula; commerce and economics are the typical areas of study for students. Due to either lack of economic resources or deliberate political policies, many Muslim coun-tries invest relatively little in their educational systems. Finally and perhaps most unfortunately, religious institutions have been coopted and shaped to serve ruling elites in many Muslim societies. Their religious leaders are of-ten viewed as echoing the ruling corrupt leadership and contribute to per-petuating the regimes' systems of social and political control. Their formal training continues to follow religious *madrasa* systems, which have been in place for centuries without any major revisions or reforms.[10]

The problems of making implicit or explicit assertions about the con-nection between Islam and violence—to say nothing of the realities of the Muslim world—create extremely difficult terrain for any study or ar-ticulation of Islamic sources of peace and nonviolence. Without consider-ing this, scholars and practitioners cannot effectively reach out to Muslim communities. However, this terrain can be navigated; Islamic principles of peacebuilding can be isolated and elaborated upon, in the hopes of work-ing toward peace among Muslims and between Muslims and the rest of the world.

Islamic Principles and Values of Peacebuilding

Muslim and non-Muslim scholars and writers often emphasize the peace-ful nature and message of Islam, identifying among its values and princi-ples ideas such as unity, supreme love of the creator, and accountability for all actions. They point to the innumerable verses in the Qur'an commanding believers to be righteous and above passion in their dealings with their fellow beings. Love, kindness, affection, forgiveness, and mercy are recommended as virtues of the true faithful.[11] Other Islamic values also directly relate to peacebuilding and development, such as justice (*adl*), benevolence (*ihsan*), compassion (*rahmah*),[12] and wisdom (*hikmah*). Using the Islamic values of service (*amal*), faith (*yakeen*), and love (*muhabat*), Abdul Ghaffar Khan[13] argues that the connection between Islam and peacebuilding is more obvious and stronger than the religion's stereotypical link to violence. Also, Islam emphasizes social justice, brotherhood, equality of mankind—including the abolition of slavery as well as racial and ethnic barriers—tolerance, submission to God, and recognition of the rights of others. These values are repeatedly stated in both the Qur'an and the Prophet's tradition. Below, the values and principles in Islam that relate directly to peacebuilding are emphasized.

Social Justice

Among Islam's goals is to establish a just society. In Islam, acting for the cause of God is synonymous with pursuing justice (*adl*), which the Qur'an enjoins Muslims to do (5:8, 57:25, 16:90, 4:58, 42:15). It is a Muslim's duty to work for justice and reject oppression and injustice on both the interpersonal and structural levels, as several Qur'anic verses have strong messages concerning social justice and responsibility.[14] The Islamic conception of justice is an absolute value, not relative. It is essential to be consistent with justice; that is to say, justice for all is an absolute value and not reserved for the Muslim community. It is a duty to be pursued among believers and for believers to love those who are non-Muslims too.[15] The early caliphates, particularly that of Umar Ibn Khattab, were known for their strong pursuit of justice. The pursuit of justice and peacebuilding is directly linked because there is a correlation among the act of preserving the common good, serving others, protecting the weak, preserving human dignity, and ensuring that peace is established and sustained in human affairs.

The link between peacebuilding and justice is never far from the surface in Islam. Justice and peace are interconnected and interdependent.[16] As peace is the product of order and justice, the pursuit of justice is part of striving for peace, an obligation for both the ruling elite and mass faithful. But more than that, it is a natural obligation of all humanity.[17] Furthermore, within the pursuit of justice is a consistent message to resist and correct conditions of injustice, which can be accomplished through activism, third-party mediation, and divine intervention. The Prophet has called Muslims to mobilize and be steadfast against injustice, even if the injustice is originated by a Muslim.[18] Thus, Islamic conflict resolution processes and frameworks emphasize justice. Both the aggrieved parties and mediators are expected to pursue it as a means to end conflict.

Social Empowerment through Doing Good (Khayr and Ihsan)

As a religion, Islam spread on the bases of helping and empowering the weak and the underdog, and it continues to be characterized as a religion of dynamism and activism. Struggling against oppression (*zulm*), assisting the poor, and pursuing equality among all humans are core religious values emphasized throughout the Qur'an and *hadith*. As the Qur'an (17:24–26) states, "one should do good (*ihsan*, which carries the connotations of grace, beneficence, kindness) not only to one's parents and relations, but also to orphans, the needy, the helpless, and the neighbor." The Prophet himself reinforces this by saying that "a true Muslim is one who does no mischief to any other Muslims, but the true *mu'min* [man of genuine faith who is superior to a formal Muslim in merit] is one who does no mischief to his neighbors" and of whom they have no fear.[19] Good deeds are associated with the straight path (*sirat el mustaqim*) and with all the virtue of the Prophet.[20]

Social and economic empowerment are so important in Islam that they are even equated with worshipping God.[21] Almsgiving (*zakat*) and charity (*sadaqah*) are central virtues for doing good in life and helping others, particularly the needy. The funds collected through *zakat* and *sadaqah* are intended for the poor; there are stipulations of fixed shares of inheritance for women and children and a host of regulations regarding the just treatment of debtors, widows, orphans (Qur'an 90:13–16), and slaves (Qur'an 24:33).[22] Where *zakat* is one of the five pillars of Islam, necessary to the practice of the faith, *sadaqah* is a good deed that every Muslim must carry out within his limits. It is prescribed in at least twenty-five Qur'anic verses, all of which encourage Muslims to take more responsibility for the social injustices that exist in their communities.[23] The Prophet's compassion for the underprivileged who suffered from personal misfortune or from social and economic injustices was not the result of Qur'anic teaching only, but was born from his own experience.[24] The Qur'an supported such compassion: "Therefore treat not the orphan with harshness, nor repulse the petitioner [unheard]" (93:9–10). Thus, Muslims are to give charity and assist those who are poor and in need for help. Caring for and helping the underprivileged is a central mechanism for social empowerment and maintaining a sense of community, and extends to larger, political actions. Abolishing slavery was a clear example of the ethical standpoints and principles that guided Muslims in dealing with oppression, poverty, and human suffering.

On the interpersonal level, Muslims are expected to preserve good relationships with others: "No Muslim can become a *mu'min* [genuine believer] unless he likes for all others [not only Muslims] what he likes for him and he makes friends with them for God's sake."[25] Verse (16:90) states that "God commands you to treat [everyone] justly, generously and with kindness." Verse (28:77) counsels, "Be good and kind to others even as God is to you." Doing good extends beyond the interpersonal to a group or community level. A nation cannot survive according to Islam without making fair and adequate arrangements for the sustenance and welfare of all the poor, underprivileged, and destitute members of the community. The ultimate goal is to eliminate their suffering and poverty. In conflict resolution terms, for Muslims, a peacebuilding process should bring about justice and good deeds, which ultimately lead to positive and fulfilling interactions and behavior with other Muslims and non-Muslims.

Universality and Dignity of Humans

Through the Qur'an and *hadith*, Islam delivers a firm and clear message of universal humanity—the belief that all humans have common origins—and this commonness calls for equal rights and treatment as well as aspirations toward solidarity among all people. According to Islam, human beings are the most dignified and exalted of all creatures. They have the potential to learn, discover, and know, the ability to decide which actions to take, and to bear the consequences of all actions. In the Islamic tradition, human beings are entrusted to be God's vice-regent on earth. Thus, protecting human life and respecting human dignity are sacred in Islam. The honor that God bestowed on humans is also stressed: "We have honored the sons of Adam; provided them with transport on land and sea; given them for sustenance things good and pure; and conferred on them special favors, above a great part of Our Creation" (Qur'an 17:70). Thus, the work, worship, and life of a person should aim to preserve, protect, and foster human dignity. Islamic scholars have cited several Qur'anic verses to establish the importance of human dignity and pride.[26] It is considered a good deed to intervene or act to protect a person's basic dignity and pride, because man, as one of God's creations, deserves respect and protection. As Fahmi Howeidy argues, "In Islam every person has human sacredness and is under protection and sacrosanct until he himself violates his sanctuary. He removes with his own hands such a protection blanket by committing a crime that removes part of his immunity. With this dignity, Islam protects its enemies, as well as its children and elders. According to Islamic sources, God blessed humanity with dignity and this blessing is the basis for all human relationships."[27]

The Islamic value of universal human dignity is one of the essential foundations of its approach to conflict resolution. Elder Muslim mediators and arbitrators often have utilized social and cultural techniques to preserve the human dignity of both the victim and the offender, including *sulha*, a traditional ritual based on public ceremony to restore honor and dignity to victims. In many cases, successfully resolving a conflict depends on the capacity of these traditional mediators to restore the victims' social and cultural dignity in public.

Equality

Islamic teaching instructs Muslims to push beyond simply reaching a settlement in a specific dispute; it aspires to create one human family. Islam grants no privilege based on race, ethnicity, or tribal association. For many scholars, the only two criteria in demonstrating oneself as a believer are faith (*iman*) and good deeds (*aml-e-salih*). There is no difference whatsoever between people except in their devotion to Allah, since the divine is the common creator of all humans.[28]

A saying of the Prophet acknowledges the origin of and universal equality among humans: "You are all from Adam and Adam is made of dust." Ibn Taymiya (1263–1328), a well-known Muslim scholar, argued in these terms: "The desire to be above other people is injustice because all people are of the same species. A man's desire to put himself higher and reduce the others lower is unjust."[29] Traditional mediators and arbitrators often cite such sayings in calling for brotherhood and harmony, and in a conflict resolution process, the principle requires the third party to treat its disputants equally throughout the entire intervention.

Sacredness of Human Life

Peacebuilding and development approaches assume that human life is valuable and must be saved and protected, and that resources should be utilized to preserve life and prevent violence. The Qur'an clearly upholds the sacredness of human life: As verse 5:32 reads, "and if any one saved a life, It would be as if he saved the life of the whole people." Verse 6:15 enjoins the reader to "not take a life which Allah has forbidden save in the course of justice." A person's life is an integral part of the great cosmic purpose. Consequently, what the individual does matters profoundly, and even destroying and wasting resources that serve human life is prohibited. When Muslims in the early period launched an armed conflict, their rulers instructed them to avoid destruction and restrict their wars. The first caliphate of Abu Bakr, upon dispatching his army to the Syrian borders, stated these famous words:

Stop, O people, that I may give you ten rules for your guidance in the battlefield. Do not commit treachery or deviate from the right path. You must not mutilate dead bodies. Neither kill a child, nor a woman or an aged man. Bring no harm to the trees, nor burn them with fire, especially those which are fruitful. Slay not any of the enemy's flock, save for your food. You are likely to pass by people who have devoted their lives to monastic services, leave them alone.[30]

In a similar context, the fourth caliph, Ali, reacted to his people's pressure to go to war by saying, "if I order you to march on them on warm days, you say 'this is the fire of summer. Give us time until the heat is over.' If I ask you to march on them in winter, you say' this is the bite of the frost. Give us the time until the cold is over.' All this and you fleeing from the heat and the cold, but, by God, you are more in flight from the sword."[31] In this context, Ali was challenging those who wanted to use war to resolve conflict; by emphasizing their propensity to fight, he showed that they were not close to the divine and must do more to protect lives, avoid violence, and be patient in times of conflict.

Due to the sacredness of human life, nonviolent intervention becomes a primary tool for Muslims to resolve their conflicts. If violence is unavoidable, the same principle limits the type of force that can be used in fighting. Beyond any doubt, the strict conditions on how to treat innocent people prohibit excessive force as a means to resolve any conflict.

A Quest for Peace

Peace in Islam is reflected in the word *Islam* itself: In Arabic, it is triliteral with *salam,* the word for peace, indicating that making peace is one of the essential ideas of the religion. A Muslim, according to the Qur'an, is he who has made peace through complete submission to God and doing good for his fellow man.[32] The centrality of peace is reflected in Muslims' daily greetings to each other, *as salam alaikum,* which translates to "peace be on you."[33]

In Islam, peace is a state of physical, mental, spiritual, political, and social harmony—living at peace with God through submission to Him and with fellow human beings by avoiding mischief on earth. Peace also has social and personal dimensions. The religion obligates its believers to seek peace in all aspects of their lives, for the ideal society that the religion seeks to create is not only just, but peaceful.[34] The Qur'an instructs Muslims to not use violence to settle their differences, but instead rely on arbitration or even simple forbearance.[35] Many Qur'anic verses stress the principle of peace. Verse 5:64 states that "whenever they kindle the fire of war, God extinguishes it. They strive to create disorder on earth and God loves not those who create disorder." Treating everyone—without exception—with tolerance and kindness is also emphasized: "God commands you to treat [everyone] justly, generously and with kindness" (Qur'an 16:90); "Repel evil [not with evil] but something that is better (*ahsan*)—that is, with forgiveness and amnesty." In supporting nonviolence in Islam, Jawdat Said, a famous Syrian reformist religious writer, calls attention to a famous *hadith* widely quoted in Islamic literature and, as he describes it, often hung as a calligraphic adornment in people's homes: "Whenever violence enters into something it disgraces it, and whenever 'gentle-civility' enters into something it graces it. Truly, God bestows on account of gentle conduct what he does not bestow on account of violent conduct."

The quest for peace is also clear in the Prophet's tradition and life. During his Meccan period (610–22), he showed no inclination toward the use of force in any form, even for self-defense. He conducted nonviolent resistance through all his instructions and teaching during that period, in which Muslims were a minority. The Prophet's teachings focused on the value of patience and steadfastness in facing oppression; for thirteen years, he fully adopted nonviolent methods, relying on his spiritual preaching in dealing with aggression and confrontation.

That said, the injunction against violence is not absolute. Scholars agree that certain conditions permit the use of force, though there has been a massive amount of writing and lively debates, by Muslims and non-Muslims alike, regarding what Islamic teachings do and do not allow. Much of this debate has centered on the changing meanings of the term *jihad,* which, in the Qur'an, refers to striving and self-exertion, but in later Muslim thought was broadened to include holy war in order to justify offensive wars (see chapter 2 of this volume). Despite the unfortunate militant connotations the term has acquired, particularly in the Western media,[36] many studies conclude that *jihad* does not mean the constant use of the sword to resolve problems with non-Muslim enemies or among Muslims. On the contrary, *jihad* has been interpreted as striving and struggling to live according to principles of faith. The Qur'an states that "there is no compulsion in religion" (2:256). In addition to the previous verses, which indicate the possibility of peaceful and nonviolent *jihad,* different sects in Islam have emphasized that there are several levels of *jihad,* and that *jihad* in the sense of struggling with oneself is the most difficult to achieve.[37] The portrayal of Muslim militants fighting for religious reasons is a challenge to the accepted definition mentioned above; however, in general, as Saiyidain argues, while "there are circumstances in which Islam contemplates the possibility of war—for instance, to avert worse disasters like the denial of freedom to human conscience ... the essential thing in life is peace. It is towards the achievement of peace that all human efforts must be sincerely diverted."[38] Shunning violence and aggression in all its forms has been a primary focus of Islamic values and tradition.

Peacemaking

Open communication and face-to-face discussion of conflicts are considered in peacebuilding as more conducive to building good relationships than avoidance or violence. They reduce the cost of an ongoing conflict and address all parties' grievances. When a third party is part of a peacebuilding intervention, it is mainly to facilitate communication, reduce tension, and assist in rebuilding relationships. Such interaction is necessary to engage the conflicting parties in truly building peace. Islam encourages such a process through active intervention, particularly among Muslims themselves. A particular verse (49:9–10)—subject to misinterpretation—states that

> if two parties among the believer fall into a quarrel, make you peace between them. But, if one of them transgresses beyond bounds against the other, then fight against the one that transgresses until it complies with the command of Allah. But, when it so complies, then make peace between them with justice and be fair. For God loves those who are fair. The believers are but a single brotherhood; so make peace between your brothers and fear Allah that you may receive mercy.

Scholars searching for a legitimate basis for the use of violence have pointed out these verses to diminish pacifists. But the verses do not so much advocate violence as support the concept of mediation and third-party intervention to resolve disputes fairly and justly. In addition, they reflect a core Islamic value of shunning aggression. As the Qur'an (5:2) points out, Muslims should not be involved in violence at all and should settle conflicts peacefully.[39]

Peacemaking was one of the Prophet's central qualities while living in Mecca, even before his prophecy. Being known as the Faithful (al-Ameen) allowed him to mediate and arbitrate in many disputes among various tribes. During that period, his creative methods of peacemaking and advocating justice were highly praised by believers and nonbelievers. Islamic conflict resolution methods can easily rely on these classic cases of intervention.

Forgiveness (Afu)

While justice ought to be pursued and evil fought, forgiveness nevertheless remains a higher virtue (Qur'an 42:40, 24:43). Believers are urged to forgive even when they are angry (Qur'an 42:37). As the Prophet said, "God fills with peace and faith the heart of one who swallows his anger, even though he is in a position to give vent to it." The Prophet himself, when he entered Mecca with his Muslim followers, set an example of great forgiving attitude toward Meccans who fought him, saying that "there is no censure from me today on you [for what has happened is done with]; may God who is the greatest amongst forgivers forgive you."[40] The

Prophet always prayed when he was persecuted during the Meccan period, saying—in an echo of Jesus when he was persecuted—"forgive them Lord, for they know not what they do."[41] According to another story about him, some of his followers asked that he invoke the wrath of God upon the Meccans because of their persecution of early Muslims. He replied, "I have not been sent to curse anyone but to be a source of beneficence (rahmah) to all."[42] A saying in Islamic ethics similarly runs that "the most gracious act of forgiving an enemy is his who has the power to take revenge."[43] Thus in the Qur'an, Muslims are instructed to "repel evil [not with evil] but with something that is better (ahsan)—that is, with forgiveness and amnesty" (41:34).[44] Conflict resolution processes according to the above principles have a greater chance of resulting in forgiveness and reconciliation among disputants rather than temporary settlement.

Deeds, Actions, Individual Responsibility, and Choice

Islam emphasizes deeds over mere talk. An individual is responsible for his own actions; no one else can guide him, nor can he bear responsibility for others' actions.[45] According to Islam, a person has three major levels of responsibilities by which God judges him: responsibility toward Allah, to be fulfilled through performing religious duties faithfully; responsibility to oneself by living in harmony with oneself; and responsibility toward living in harmony and peace with other people.

The idea of doing good deeds thus extends to social action, and Muslims are encouraged and pushed to improve their communal life, support each other, abolish poverty, and help the needy. The sense of individual choice and call for involvement with society can even apply to the political governing system, in which the ruler expects his followers to take full responsibility and stop injustice if it is committed. Abu Bakr, the first caliph after the Prophet, told the people: "I am no better than you. I am just like any one of you. If you see that I am pursuing a proper course, then follow me; and if you see me err, then set me straight."[46] Arising from individuals' responsibilities to their communities and vice versa, Islamic conflict resolution models promote outcomes with actions and concrete steps, rather than declarations or abstract statements, to ensure the implementation of an agreement.

Patience (Sabr)

Muslims are encouraged to be patient and to suspend their judgment of others, whether they are Muslims or non-Muslims. Patience is a virtue of believers who can endure immense challenges and still maintain strong belief in God. The story of Job (Ayoub) is held in high regard for his belief and patience, despite his experience of numerous tragedies. Such a value is very appropriate to peacebuilding and nonviolent resistance, as such initiatives often produce few immediate effects and are considered a long-term investment in the community. Those carrying out an intervention also need a great deal of patience to carry out initiatives for peace and development in the community and engage in sustainable dialogue processes.

Collaborative Actions and Solidarity

Peacebuilding approaches assume that collaborative and joint efforts to resolve a problem are more productive than competitive efforts by individuals only. This comports with Islamic beliefs. A well-known *hadith* stating that "God's hand is with the *jama'a* [group]" is often utilized to motivate disputants to work together and reach an agreement. The *hadith* also comments on reducing the costs to individuals if they stand alone in a conflict. Unfortunately, it has been used to create unity and mobilize support against an enemy. But it can also be used to motivate people to avoid political and social splits or rivalries (*fitna*) and turn them to collective actions in a social or economic development context.

Solidarity among Muslims is, perhaps obviously, a central value too, as the well-known traditional saying "help your brother [Muslims] whether he is an aggressor or a victim of aggression" suggests. When Muslims asked the Prophet how they could assist their brother when he was the aggressor, he replied, "By doing your best to stop him from aggression"[47]—a clear message to avoid the use of violence and prevent aggression by Muslims against both other Muslims and non-Muslims. This kind of solidarity is the opposite of tribal solidarity (*assabiyyah*), assisting members of the same clan against outsiders regardless of the conditions. While *assabiyyah* remains a strong norm among Arab and non-Arab Muslims, essential teachings have attempted to abolish it based on the principles, discussed above, of the equality of all humankind. Similarly, in the cooperation and collaboration that accompany conflict resolution processes, parties shift from competing and adversarial views to shared and mutual understanding.

Ummah

The concept of *ummah* has been a basis for collective action since the time of the Prophet. During Islam's early period in Mecca, the Prophet utilized values of collaboration and collectivism to mobilize his followers and to respond nonviolently to the accusation and force of those who did not follow his prophecy. Against the suggestion that *ummah* has vanished due to the rise of nation states and multiple political regimes in the Muslim world, Farid Esack argues that "the notion of Ummah has not only survived but continues to give Muslims a deep sense of belonging." He stresses that "the universal community under God has always been a significant element in Muslim discourse against tribalism and racism."[48] It has even been expanded to include God-believing non-Muslims, as scholars stress that the People of the Book, as recipients of the divine revelation, were recognized as part of the *ummah,* based on the Qur'anic verse (23:52): "Surely this, your community (*ummah*), is a single community." The charter of Medina—the first constitution the Prophet created—is further proof of such an inclusive and religiously diverse community.[49] The Prophet instructed his followers on many occasions on the importance of unity and solidarity among the believers and Muslims, comparing their relationship to the organs of the body that communicate pain if one part is ill, or to a building solidified by the strength of its various parts. He instructed Muslims to avoid causes of dissension: "Do not entertain envy or spite in your hearts; do not terrorize your fellow men; do not backbite them; do not increase prices against one another; Servants of God, for every Muslim is a brother to another Muslim. He should never wrong his brother, never leave him in a lurch at the time of need, never seek to humiliate him." Then the Prophet pointed to his heart and said: "Righteousness resides here."[50] Islamic conflict resolution is based on communal and collective solidarity, often seen in the public rituals for reconciliation (*sulha*). In addition, most interventions—whether mediation or arbitration—are not restricted to the individual disputants, but tend to involve additional people from the community and extended family.

Inclusivity and Participatory Process

Participatory forums and inclusive procedures are more productive and effective than authoritarian, hierarchical, and exclusionary decision-making approaches. Thus, peacebuilding strategies are based on either assisting parties in joint interest–based negotiation or bringing in a third party to facilitate such a process, rather than using imposition and competition. The Muslim tradition of mutual consultation (*shura*) and its governing process fit into this mold. Under *shura,* through public and private consultation, a leader should seek active advice and input from his followers before making a decision. *Shura* has been widely discussed and explained by Islamic scholars, particularly those who support the notion that democracy is not necessarily contradictory to Islam. For these scholars, there are number of key points. First, *shura* is not a mere consultation by the rulers only, but an inclusive process in which all *ummah* are asked for input into the decision-making process. Second, it involves all matters of concern to the *ummah.* Third, the people of the *shura* represent all segments of society—parties and religious groups, both Muslim and non-Muslim. They are different from people who use *ijtihad* to practice jurisprudence. Fourth, freedom of expression is the core of *shura*. If freedom of expression of all people is not guaranteed or practiced, then *shura* is understood to not be practiced.[51] These principles in Islamic tradition and religion encourage the involvement and responsibility of the people rather than passivity or acceptance of oppression. It is a Muslim's duty to resist the *zulm* and work against it. A saying of the Prophet instructs: "Best of the *jihad* is a word of truth (*haq*) to an oppressing sultan." Another opines that "if people saw the oppressor and did not warn or consult him, God is about to punish them." Conflict resolution processes that build on this value can foster sustainable agreements, particularly at the community and public policy levels, as communities feel ownership over the process and outcome.

Pluralism and Diversity

Pluralism and diversity are core values in the Islamic tradition, at least among People of the Book. The Qur'an supports diversity and tolerance of differences based on gender (see verses 49:13, 53:45), skin color language (30:23), different beliefs (64:2), different ranks (6:165), and different social grouping and communities (2:213, 10:19, 7:38, 13:30, 16:63, 29:18, 35:42, 41:42, 64:18). It asserts that differences are inherent in human life. Ethnic, tribal, and national differences have no effect on closeness to God; the extent and degree of faith is the sole criterion by which those groups are judged. Tolerance of non-Muslim believers is repeatedly emphasized in both the Qur'an and *hadith*. Muslims are asked to remember that there is no difference in the treatment of people of different religions except in their faith and deeds (Qur'an 2:62, 3:113–14, 5:68). That said, Islam is less tolerant of nonbelievers. Throughout history, those who were cast as *kufar* (*kafir* is singular for infidel) were persecuted and punished by rulers and followers.

In peacebuilding, diversity and tolerance of differences are core principles of practice. Islamic conflict resolution processes and models are based on this assumption to bring people to the realization that they are different, and such differences are not a basis for discrimination or biases, but an aspect of common strength. Thus it is harmful and unjust to deprive people of their rights because of their national, racial, religious, or other category affiliation. These values have been made integral parts of Islam since its inception.

Conclusion

The above discussion identifies the important Islamic assumptions, principles, and values that constitute the basic elements of an Islamic peacebuilding and conflict resolution approach to all types and levels of conflicts, from interpersonal and family tensions to disputes among countries and nations. Such an approach ought to incorporate and be guided by several major objectives: increasing solidarity among members of the community, bridging the gap of social and economic injustice, relieving the suffering of people and sparing human lives, empowering people through participation and inclusivity, avoiding violations of the Islamic faith and ensuring freedom of worship, promoting equality among all members of the community, and utilizing and encouraging the values of diversity and tolerance. Initiatives for peacebuilding in an Islamic community would greatly benefit if the above principles were integrated as a part of planning, implementation, and evaluation.

The challenges facing conflict resolution and peacebuilding exercises in today's Muslim communities are vast. Many Muslim countries are marked by authoritarianism, poor education systems, and coopted religious leaders. Nevertheless, the ideals of conflict resolution ideals have been transmitted to Muslims young and old through their cultural and religious beliefs and practices as well as other socialization agents, and Muslims are frustrated by the lack of current mechanisms to apply those values and principles in their communities. By listening to that frustration and framing peacebuilding exercises to not only respect Muslim values, but address the realities of many Muslims' lives, those interested in resolving conflicts in the Muslim world can move closer to achieving their goals.

Notes

1. See Ronald Fisher, *Interactive Conflict Resolution* (Syracuse: Syracuse University Press, 1997), and John Paul Lederach, *Peace Building in Divided Societies* (Syracuse: Syracuse University Press, 1997).

2. Kevin Avruch, Peter Black, and Joseph Scimecca, eds., *Conflict Resolution: Cross-Cultural Perspectives* (New York: Greenwood Press, 1991).

3. J.W. Burton, *Conflict Resolution and Prevention* (New York: St. Martin's Press, 1990).

4. William Zartman, ed., *Traditional Cures for Modern Conflicts: African Conflict Medicine* (Boulder, CO: Lynne Rienner, 2000).

5. Mohammed Abu-Nimer, "Conflict Resolution in an Islamic Context," *Peace and Change*, vol. 21, no. 1 (1996), 22–40; Abdul Aziz Said, Ayse Kadayifci, and Nathan Funk, *Peace and Conflict Resolution in Islam: Precept and Practice* (Lanham, MD: University Press of America, 2001); Paul Salem, *Bitter Legacy: Ideology and Politics in the Arab World* (Syracuse: Syracuse University Press, 1994).

6. See Said, Kadayifci, and Funk, *Peace and Conflict Resolution*; Abu-Nimer, "Conflict Resolution"; Abdulaziz Sachedina, "Justification for Violence in Islam," in *War and Its Discontents: Pacifism and Quietism in the Abrahamic Traditions,* ed. J.P. Burn (Washington, DC: Georgetown University Press, 1996); Jawdat Said, "Peace—Or Nonviolence—in History and with the Prophets," unpublished paper, Forum on Islam and Peace in the 21st Century, American University, Washington, DC, 1997; Karim Crow, "Nurturing an Islamic Peace Discourse," unpublished paper, Center for Global Peace, American University, Washington, D.C., 1997;

Khalid Kishtainy, "Violent and Nonviolent Struggle in Arab History," in *Arab Nonviolent Political Struggle in the Middle East*, ed. Ralph E. Crow, P. Grant, and Saad E. Ibrahim (Boulder: Lynne Rienner Publications, 1990). See also American University International Peace and Conflict Resolution (IPCR) Master Program; Eastern Mennonite University, Summer Peace Building; Kroc Institute, Notre Dame University.

7.   See Mohammed Abu-Nimer, *Nonviolence and Peacebuilding in Islam: Theory and Practice* (Gainesville: University Press of Florida, 2003); Cathy Witty, *Mediation and Society: Conflict Management in Lebanon* (New York: Academic Press, 1980); Nizar Hamzeh, "The Role of Hizbullah in Conflict Management Within Lebanon's Shia Community," in *Conflict Resolution in the Arab World: Selected Essays*, ed. Paul Salem (Beirut: American University of Beirut, 1997), 93–121; George Irani, "Ritual of Reconciliation: Arab-Islamic Perspective," unpublished manuscript, U.S. Institute of Peace, 1998.

8.   This study relies on two sources: Ali Abdullah Yusuf, *The Meaning of the Holy Qur'an* (Beltsville, MD: Amana Publications, 1989), and the more common writings of the early Muslim period usually referred to as the first Caliphate-constitutional period. For resources see Abu-Nimer, *Nonviolence and Peace Building*.

9.   Many studies analyze the political and sociocultural conditions and realities of the Muslim states. For more details on many Arab regimes, see Abu-Nimer, *Nonviolence and Peace Building*.

10.   See Amr Abdullah, *Islamic Madrasah System in Bangladesh* (Washington, DC: Salam Institute, 2005).

11.   Razi Ahmad, "Islam, Nonviolence, and Global Transformation," in *Islam and Nonviolence*, ed. Glenn Paige, Chaiwat Satha-Anand, and Sarah Gilliatt (Honolulu: Center for Global Nonviolence Planning Project, Matsunaga Institute for Peace, University of Hawaii, 1993), 27–53.

12.   "He who does not show compassion to his fellow men is undeserving of God's compassion." Tirmidhi, 34, *al-Adab al-Mufrad*, ch. 53, 47–48, cited in Khwaja Ghulam Saiyidain, *Islam, the Religion of Peace* (New Delhi: Har-Anand, 1994).

13.   Abdul Ghaffar Khan is a famous Muslim leader who created a nonviolent social and political movement to fight the British colonial forces for independence.

14.   See Qur'an (16:90), "Allah commands justice, the doing of good, and liberality to kith and kin, and he forbids all shameful deeds, and injustice and rebellion"; Qur'an (4:58), "Allah doth command you to render back your trusts to those to whom they are due; And when ye judge between man and man, that ye judge with justice: verily how excellent which giveth you!"; Qur'an (4:135), "Ye who believe! Stand out firmly for justice, as witnesses to Allah, even as against yourselves, or your parents, or your kin, whether it be [against] rich or poor: for Allah can best protect both. . . . Follow not the lusts [of your hearts], lest ye swerve, and if ye distort [justice] or decline to do justice, verily Allah is well-acquainted with all that ye do." See Yusuf, *Meaning*.

15.   Howeidy cites Zamakshari: "And in this—pursuing justice with enemies—there is a great warning that if justice is a duty to be applied when dealing with the infidels who are the enemy of God, if it had such a powerful characteristic then what its duty among the believers who are God's supportive and favorites?" see Fahmi Howeidi, *Islam and Democracy* (Cairo: Cairo Center for Translation and Publication, 1993), 55.

16.   The notion that peace cannot be achieved without justice is echoed by many peace-building researchers and activists; see Lederach, *Peace Building*; Heidi Burgess and Guy Burgess, "Justice without Violence: A Theoretical Framework," in *Justice without Violence*, ed. Paul Wehr, Heidi Burgess, and Guy Burgess (Boulder: Lynne Rienner, 1994).

17. John Kelsay, *Islam and War: A Study in Comparative Ethics* (Louisville: John Knox Press, 1993). See also Qur'an (4:58), "God does command you to render back your trust to those whom they are due. And when you judge between people, that you judge with justice. Indeed, how excellent is the teaching that He gives you. For verily God hears and sees all things"; and Qur'an (60:8), "God loves those who are Just."

18. An example of a *hadith*: "Oh, Ye who believe, be steadfast in service of God's truth and bear witness for justice and let not hatred of a people seduce you so that you deal with them unjustly. Act justly for that is what piety demands. He who supports a tyrant or oppressor knowing he is a tyrant casts himself outside the pale of Islam." Based on this *hadith* and others, Saiyidain argues that refusal to support wrongdoing by one's country is a proof of patriotism or an act of virtue.

19. Saiyidain, *Islam*, 33.

20. See Qur'an (3:104), "And these may spring from you a nation who invites to goodness and enjoin right conduct and forbid indecency. Such are they who are successful; and Qur'an (2:62), "Those who believe [in the Prophet of Islam] and those who are Jews and Christians and the Sabeans [that is who belongs to any religious group who believe in God and the Last Day of Judgment] and whose deeds are good, shall have their reward with their Lord. On them there shall be no fear nor shall they grieve.

21. Saiyidain, *Islam*, 153.

22. *Zakah* is also encouraged and described in detail with its rewards in Qur'an (2:262–72).

23. See Qur'an (2:177), "It is not righteousness that ye turn your faces towards east or west; but it is righteousness to believe in Allah and the last day, and the book, and the messengers; to spend your substance, out of love for him, for your kin, for orphans, for the needy, for wayfarer, for those who ask, for the ransom of slaves; to be steadfast in prayer, and practice charity, to fulfill the contract that ye have made, and to be firm and patient in pain (or suffering) and adversity"; and Qur'an (93:7–9), "People are responsible and have obligations to those who are underprivileged in their community. Islam repeatedly stresses such principles. Did He not find thee and orphan and provided for thee shelter (and care). And He found thee wondering and gave thee guidance and He found thee in need and made thee independent [in financial sense]."

24. Saiyidain, *Islam*, 98.

25. Tradition in Tirmidhi: book 39, ch. 19, and book 45, ch. 98. Also in *Sunan Ibn Majah*, Musnad Ahmad, cited in Saiyidain, *Islam*, 161.

26. See Qur'an (95:4), "We have indeed created man in the best of moulds"; Qur'an (7:11), "It is We Who created you and gave you shape; then We bade the angels bow down to Adam, and they bowed down; not so Iblis; he refused to be of those who bow down; and Qur'an (2:30), "Behold, thy Lord said to the angels: I will create a vice-regent on earth."

27. Howeidy, *Islam and Democracy*.

28. See Qur'an (49:13), "Oh mankind! We created you from a single [pair] of a male and female, and made you into nations and tribes, that ye may know each other (not that ye may despise each other). Verily the most honored of you in the sight of Allah is (he who is) the most righteous of you. And Allah has full knowledge and is well-acquainted (with all things)."

29. Al-Sharif al-Radhay, *Nahj al-Blagha*, vol. 1, cited in Kishtainy, "Violent and Nonviolent Struggle," 12.

30. *Sahih Muslim*, vol. 3, trans. Abdul Hamid Siddiqi (Lahore: Sh. Muhammad Ashraf, 1976–1979), 838, cited in Satha-Anand, "Core Values for Peacemaking in Islam: The Prophet's Practice as Paradigm," in *Building Peace in the Middle East: Challenges for States and Civil Society*, ed. Elise Boulding (Boulder: Lynne Rienner, 1993), 11. Also in Tabari Mohammad b. Jarir, *Kitab Al-Umam wal-Muluk*, vol. 3 (Cairo: Dar-ul-Ma'arif, 1969), 226–27.

31. Al-Sharif al-Radhay, *Nahj al-Balagha*, vol. 1, cited in Kishtainy, "Violent and Nonviolent Struggle."

32. See Qur'an (2:112), "Nay, whoever submits himself entirely to God, and is the doer of good to others, he has his reward from His Lord."

33. The Qur'an (25:63, 10:10) states: "And the servants of Allah most gracious are those who walk the earth in humility and when others address them, they say 'peace! ... enjoy in paradise: "They shall hear therein no vain or sinful talk, but only the saying, Peace, Peace" (Qur'an 56:26).

34. Kelsay, *Islam and War*.

35. Qur'an (8:46), "And Obey Allah and His Messenger; And fall into no disputes, lest ye lose heart and your power depart; and be patient and persevering: for Allah is with those who patiently persevere."

36. The association of Muslims with *jihad* and violence has become very strong, particularly in Western media. Such mischaracterization is reflected in the popular term "the people of the sword." Some argue that the self-fulfilling prophecy of *jihad* has become a phenomenon of our times. Not only are Muslim activists—violent and nonviolent alike—suffering misperceptions and misrepresentation, but the religion and its followers also sustain labeling and stereotyping as a result. There is much emphasis and domination of such stereotypes and generalizations among writers who study Islam in general and political Islam in particular. Esposito captures such misperceptions when he states that "a combination of ignorance, stereotyping, history, and experience, as well as religio-cultural chauvinism, too often blind even best-intentioned when dealing with the Arab and Muslim World." See John Esposito, *The Islamic Threat* (Oxford: Oxford University Press, 1992).

37. Several *hadith* support such interpretations. Muslim groups such as Sufism, Ismailism, and Ahmaddiyya emphasize the spiritual rather than the physical *jihad*. Others suggest that *da'awa*, or calling—the spread of Islam through preaching and persuasion—is the major form of *jihad* for a Muslim.

38. Saiyidain, *Islam*.

39. See Qur'an (5:2), "And let not the hatred of some people in [once] shutting you out of the sacred mosque lead you to transgression [and hostility on your part]. Help one another in righteousness and piety. But help ye not one other in sin and rancor"; and Qur'an (49:10), "The believers are but a single brotherhood: so make peace and reconciliation between your two (contending) brothers."

40. Based on Ibn Sad, *Al-Tabaqa Al Kubra*, cited in Saiyidain, *Islam*, 107.

41. Ibn Majah, *Sunan* (Delhi: Faruqi Press, n.d.), 22–23, cited in Saiyidain, *Islam*, 166.

42. Based on Ibn Sad, *Al-Tabaqa Al Kubra*, cited in Saiyidain, *Islam*, 93.

43. Saiyidain, *Islam*, 93.

44. For similar verses on forgiveness with better actions or *ahsan*, see Qu'ran (4:148, 13:22, 7:199, and 28:54).

45. See Qur'an (19:96), "On those who believe and work deeds of righteousness, will [Allah] Most Gracious bestow love"; Qur'an (17:7), "If you do good, it will be for your own self; if you do evil, it will react on you"; and Qur'an (16:97), "Whoever acts righteously, man or woman, and has the faith, verily We will give such a person a good life and give his reward in the hereafter also, according to the best of their actions."

46. That said, Al-Ash'ari and Din ibn Jama'a (d. 1333) forbade uprisings against tyrants. The duty of Muslims is obedience, no matter how unjust the ruler; see Henry Thompson, *World Religion in War and Peace* (Jefferson, NC: McFarland & Company Publishers, 1988).

47. Imam Bukhari, *al-Adab al Nabawi*, 66; Tjrid al-Bukhari, *Kitab al-Mazalim*, 22:1–2, cited in Saiyidain, *Islam*, 159.

48. Farid Esack examines the Islamic theology of liberation based on the experience of Muslims in South Africa in fighting against apartheid. Esack describes an astonishing account of the utilization of Islamic beliefs and values in mobilizing Muslims to resist and fight the South African system, particularly by building community coalitions with non-Muslims. Such experiences affirm the great potential to construct coalitions across religious boundaries and identities in resisting war, violence, and injustice.

49. The notion of the *ummah* as a diverse religious and individual community appears particularly in the Medinan period—the Qur'an mentions it forty-seven times—versus only nine times in the Meccan period.

50. Al-Mattaqi (Ala-ud-Din Ali), *Kanz-ul-Ummal*, vol. 1, 134–35, cited in Saiyidain, *Islam*, 158.

51. Tawfiq Al-Shadi, *Fiqh Al-Shura Walestisharah* [*The Jurisprudence of Consultation and Shura*] (Cairo: Dar al-Wafa, 1992), 293, cited in Howeidy, *Islam and Democracy*.

PART II

PEACE EDUCATION, NONVIOLENT ACTION, HUMAN RIGHTS, AND PEACEMAKING TRAINING

5

Bediüzzaman Said Nursi's Paradigm of Islamic Nonviolence

Zeki Saritoprak

Among twentieth-century figures of nonviolence, Mohandas Gandhi, Nelson Mandela, and Dr. Martin Luther King, Jr., are three towering icons. They exemplify exceptional dedication to social change through nonviolent action and are used as textbook cases for students of peacemaking around the world. Even in Muslim countries, they are studied as people who struggled for justice and peace—against colonialism, against apartheid, and for civil rights, respectively. Likewise, Bediüzzaman Said Nursi was known among some of his contemporaries as a "Gandhi of Turks."[1] But Muslim students rarely have the opportunity to ask the vital question of which Muslim figures are examples of nonviolence.

As a university professor, I presented the same question to my American classroom, composed primarily of middle-class Catholic students. I was sure that my students would generate a tremendous amount of conversation, but there was complete silence and a real sense of confusion. Having attended university and seminaries in Egypt, Turkey, and the United States, I had not realized my own students and colleagues in North America could not identify a single nonviolent Muslim figure. Some could not or would not believe that nonviolence is an essential ethical practice prescribed by Islamic religious teachings. For the first time, I recognized that the Islamic ethics of nonviolence was a foreign concept to American students, educators, and media, as well as to the larger population. Jewish, Christian, Buddhist, Hindu, Confucian, perhaps even Baha'i teachings of peace were easily cited or promoted on college campuses, but I found my-self talking about one of the most widely practiced religions in the world as if it were an unknown phenomenon.

In truth, Muslim nonviolent leaders are not unusual or exceptional; like other nonviolent leaders, they struggled to defeat colonialism, overthrew brutal dictators, raised dissent, and were viewed as authorities who natu-rally contested injustice. They practiced essential basic ethical practices of love, compassion, and nonviolence toward all. One such figure was Bediüz-zaman Said Nursi, a Turkish Islamic scholar who, in the early half of the twentieth century, was the symbol for being deeply committed to tradition, religious ethics, piety, devotion, and loving his religion. He advocated non-violence, promoted interfaith cooperation, and sought to understand oth-ers while not losing himself in materialism. At that time, Turkey's Kemalist secularists were in power and aggressively hostile to tradition and religion, as they believed that both would hinder Turkey's modernization efforts. Thus, Nursi paid dearly for his commitment to nonviolent action and for his teachings of loving all and hating none; the authorities imprisoned and tortured him regularly. Yet his nonviolent teachings live on: Today, there are hundreds of thousands of practitioners of nonviolence because of Said Nursi and his remarkable legacy. His contribution to Islamic nonviolence and peacemaking is studied in many study groups, where students simulate his nonviolent exercises to follow his model.

This essay is intended to inform those who are unaware of Bediüzza-man Said Nursi and of the vast field of the Islamic ethics of nonviolence. By focusing on a single Muslim peacemaker, it does not mean to ignore, neglect, or dismiss the hundreds of nonviolent Muslims that were Nursi's contemporaries; rather, this essay aims to illustrate the creative thinking and acting by one of the most influential Muslim peacemakers in the twentieth century and show how his writings still serve as a base for much discussion and emulation.

Bediüzzaman Said Nursi was born in 1876 in the small village of Nurs, in the province of Bitlis in Eastern Anatolia in modern-day Turkey. He was one of seven children of a middle-class farmer family known for their piety and generosity. He died a peaceful death on March 23, 1960, in the city of Urfa in southeastern Turkey, believed to be the birthplace of the prophet Abraham. His life since the days of his adolescence was recorded and is well-known in Turkish society, for Nursi experienced a variety of life-changing events in different parts of the world, from Eastern Anatolia to Siberia, from Western Europe to Syria, during war and after conflict, and in economically challenging times.

In his youth, Nursi experienced the variety of the Ottoman school sys-tem in Eastern Anatolia studying classical Islamic sciences, but learning modern sciences as well. He complained that the *madrasa* schooling system of his time was insufficient in emphasizing the study of religious over modern sciences, but in thinking that, he also offered a new approach, promoting studies of both religious and modern sciences. He went to Istanbul, the capital of the Ottoman Empire, and met with the Ottoman sultan, Abdulhamid II; there, he asked for the sultan's support for his idea of establishing a university with multiple campuses that would teach both sciences. Abdulhamid himself was sympathetic to this idea, but his aides were not. Nursi later met with the next Ottoman sultan, Reşad, who supported the project financially. Nursi then established the foundations of his university in Eastern Anatolia, teaching religious sciences to his students—and training them to use weapons for defense. Foretelling the onset of World War I, he said, "Be prepared. A big calamity and disaster is approaching."[2] Some Ottoman military officers who visited his school asked, "Is this a military barracks or *madrasa*?" The government took Nursi's weapons due to concern about the so-called event of Bitlis, a local revolt. Nursi had not supported the revolt and even tried to minimize its damage. While teaching and educating his students two months after this incident, however, World War I broke out,[3] and Nursi and his students needed to participate to defend Bitlis, his hometown.

Nursi (later the commander of a unit) and his students volunteered as soldiers to protect their city. Being an advocate of nonviolence, Nursi was not at ease with war, but the city, needing defense against foreign occupation, forced him to action. He understood that the war required spiritual as well as physical training, and therefore, he taught his students Islamic sciences even during the fighting. It is believed that he dictated his famous commentary on the Qur'an at the front line while mostly on his horse. At the time, his actions may have appeared out of line, but in the war against the occupying Russian forces, Turkish soldiers testified that their spiritual strength gave them the means to survive the worst conditions.

There is no evidence or anecdote of Nursi killing anyone during the war, though Nursi's biographers recount how Nursi successfully protected Armenian children that were captured during fighting between Armenians and Turks. In response to Nursi's peacemaking behavior toward Armenian children, the Armenians chose not to kill Muslim children.[4] Eventually, Nursi was wounded and taken to a Russian prison in Siberia, where his outspoken nature was also evident. When the chief of staff of the Russian army, Nikolai Nikolaevich Yudenich (1862–1933) approached the prisoners, Nursi refused to stand up because of his faith convictions. Nursi was nearly executed for this stance, but he refused to apologize to the general. When the general saw how Nursi intensely prayed before his sentence was carried out, he pardoned Nursi and apologized to him.[5]

The effect of World War I on Said Nursi is evident in his writings. On one occasion, when he addressed his experience in Siberia, Nursi referred to a Qur'anic verse which says, "A day which makes even children old" (73:17). Nursi would say that even though he was not too old, anyone who experienced the war would be considered old even if they were young.[6] Later in his life he criticized both World War I and World War II; these wars, he said, were not fought for justice, truth, and religion, but for stubbornness, nationalism, and increasing the advantage of certain powerful nations over weaker nations. To Nursi, the oppression caused by these two wars was so horrible that one could not find a comparable moment in all of human history. "In a place that housed one-thousand innocent children, women, elders, the ill," Nursi wrote, "they attacked such a place with the excuse that there were one or two enemy soldiers in hiding and annihilated them with bombs. Also, they ally themselves with the most vicious oppressors of bourgeoisie, and the most extreme anarchists of socialists and communists who shed the blood of thousands, perhaps millions, of innocents."[7] To express the misguidance of the perpetrators of these wars, he refers to a Qur'anic verse—"surely, humans are extreme wrongdoers and ignorant" (14:34)—and uses another verse to call for a response: "Do not incline towards those who oppress, or else fire will touch you" (11:113). In such a tumultuous time, Nursi asked his students not to associate themselves with the oppressors, or else they would share in the oppression. He said, "To be pleased with oppression is oppression."[8]

He struggled against the British occupation of Istanbul in 1919, and although he carried a pistol and dagger, he never used either of them. On one occasion, according to his biographers, the British army attempted to seize him at a home. Reciting a Qur'anic verse—"We have put a barrier before them and a barrier behind them and covered them over so they cannot see" (36:8)—Nursi mysteriously escaped without the soldiers ever noticing. This occasion would have been the most probable place to use his weapons against his opponents, but his escape allowed him to leave peacefully.

There is no doubt that the Qur'an was the main source for Nursi's approach to living a nonviolent life. Probably the most frequently used verse in this regard was "no one bears the burden of others" (6:164), which constituted the foundation of Nursi's understanding of nonviolence. Drawing upon this verse, Nursi accepted what can be called the principle of the individuality of a crime, suggesting that the neighbors and relatives of a criminal could not be punished for the criminal's action. In other words, the blame for the crime of an individual was limited to the individual only. Thus, he strongly opposed both World War I and World War II because those involved in the wars were not distinguishing between combatants and the innocent.[9] Nursi referred to this Qur'anic verse over and over again to his students and the administrators of the Turkish republic. He called it the absolute justice of Islam, which comes from the Qur'anic verse that says that killing one human being is equated to the killing of all humanity (5:32). Based on this verse, Nursi argued, "In the sight of the mercy of God, right is right. There is no difference between a small right and a big right. A small right cannot be nullified for the big right. Without the consent of an individual, his life and his rights cannot be sacrificed for the entire community."[10] For Nursi, it would be wrong to incline to relative justice when absolute justice was possible. More broadly, he argued that "the time of hatred and animosity has passed. The two world wars have shown how animosity is ugly, and how it can be destructive and wrong. It is proven that there was not any benefit in hatred." He added, "The thing which is most deserving of love is love itself; and the thing most deserving of hatred, is hatred itself."[11] He formulated the philosophy of his teachings in a very simple principle—"love love and hate hatred"[12]—that everyone could understand, yet it captured the philosophy that all human beings make errors, and we should be disgusted by the errors but not by those who commit them.[13]

Another Qur'anic verse that Nursi took to heart states: "Call to the way of your Lord with wisdom and beautiful discourse and debate with them in the best way" (16:124). Nursi considered persuasion to be the most important aspect of his teaching. He believed that this was the way to be followed in a civilized world. On one occasion, he said, "the way to defeat civilized people is the way of persuasion, and not the way of force, which is applied to those people who don't understand words."[14] Nursi carefully distinguished between the person and the attributes that that person might manifest. "A person," he said, "is loved not for his person-hood, but for his character." Here Nursi elaborated on some negative characteristics of Muslims that are not Islamic and do not deserve to be loved, and some positive characteristics of non-Muslims that deserve to be loved. He said, "It is not necessary that every attribute of every Muslim is Muslim; as it is not necessary that every attribute of every non-Muslim is non-Muslim."[15] In addition to arguing generally for tolerance, in focusing on the importance of a person's characteristics rather than merely religious affiliation, Nursi was significantly criticizing both Muslims' and non-Muslims' lack of deep understanding of their traditions and how easily they were being absorbed by the changing times.

Supporting his idea of character, Nursi gives some examples of negative characteristics and how they can be destructive. "Through self-centricity and egotism," Nursi wrote, "a person would like to destroy everything he can, even the entire world when seen as an obstacle for his desire and greed." Islam, however, had proven that it could plant good attributes even in the wildest societies: "Yes, the Arabs whose hardness of heart caused them to bury their female children alive, through Islam their hearts were cleaned and waxed to the extent that they became so sensitive toward creatures that it prevented them from stepping on even ants."[16] According to Nursi, this was a great revolution—and in our modern day, there is a need for a similar purification of character, a hearkening to the time that Islamic civilization historically demonstrated tolerance, pluralism, and respect for other traditions.

Nursi insisted to his followers that they absolutely respect others and treat them as if they were their own brothers or sisters in the family. As human beings are created on a higher order than other creatures, so their capacity for both destruction and creativity is greater. "If respect and compassion were taken out from hearts," Nursi argued, "reason and intellect would make human beings such horrible and cruel monsters to the extent that they would not be able to be ruled by politics anymore."[17] To demonstrate the point, one could refer to the story of the two sons of Adam, Cain and Abel: "When each of them made an offering, and when it was accepted from one and not from the other, the one whose offering was not accepted said to his brother, 'I will kill you.' His brother said, 'God only accepts from those who are pious. If you stretch your hands to kill me, I will never stretch my hand to kill you, because I fear God, the Lord of the universe" (5:27).

Nursi elaborated on similar Qur'anic verses, particularly in his *Treatise on Brotherhood*. He draws this entire treatise from similar verses, such as "believers are brothers, make peace between your brothers" (49:10) and "respond with what is the most beautiful, then you will see that the one with whom you have enmity becomes a passionate friend of yours" (41:34).[18] Nursi emphasized the importance of brotherhood as one of the five essential principles of Islamic civilization. True brotherhood recognizes the ties of the nation, the religion, and professions, and rejects aspects that divide the community, such as racism and nationalist chauvinism. Nursi believed that Western civilization failed to embrace this universal principle due to its emphasis on individualism, and the two world wars were examples of this: They were fought largely due to the interests of individual states and their aggressive natures. He quoted from the famous fourteenth-century Iranian poet, Hafiz Shirazi, who wrote, "The world is not a possession worthy of quarrelling over"; also, "two phrases explain the comfort and the peace of the two worlds: deal with your friends generously (*muruwwat*) and deal with your enemies in a peaceful (*mudarat*) way."[19]

Nursi further elaborated on the ugliness of hatred, stating, "In the life of believers, partisanship, stubbornness, jealously, which cause hypocrisy, and division, ill feelings and hatred … are ugly, unacceptable, harmful, wrong, and poison for the life of humanity."[20] His treatise was intended for a Muslim audience, but he focused on creating fellowship among all people. "Your creator is the same," he argued. "You worship the same God. You receive your subsistence from the same compassionate divine being." This powerful message of peace, brotherhood, and love relates directly to the senseless sectarian violence occurring in Iraq, Afghanistan, and Pakistan between Sunnis and Shi'ites. Nursi's single treatise on brotherhood is powerful enough that it could be a critical aid in peacemaking in these countries, which would benefit from training in tolerance, respect, and dismantling inner cycles of conflict.

In 1955, Turkey, Iraq, Pakistan, Iran, and the United Kingdom adopted the Central Treaty Organization (CENTO) to commit to peacebuilding efforts and create coalitions against aggression. Nursi believed this organization could enact the principle of brotherhood on a larger scale. In a letter to the prime minister and president of Turkey, he wrote, "Your agreement with Iraq and Pakistan, God willing, will prevent the danger of nationalism. Instead of the friendship of four or five million nationalists, this agreement will bring to the country the friendship of four hundred million Muslims around the world [the population of Muslims in the world at the time], and eight hundred million Christians and adherents of other religions who are deeply in need of global peace. I wanted to share these feelings because I had a conviction from the depth of my heart."[21] When he spoke of unity among Muslims in a famous article—"The Voice of Truth," published in the newspaper *Volkan* on March 27, 1909—he presented love as the foundation of this unity: "Hatred should be only directed to ignorance, poverty, and hypocrisy," he said. In addition, he addressed the non-Muslim population: "Let non-Muslims be confident that our unity will attack these three vices. Our relationship with non-Muslims will be in the way of persuasion. That is because we know them as civilized people and it is our duty as Muslims to present Islam as a beloved and highly valuable religion. We know them as a people of conscience."[22]

Nursi understood nonviolence as an integral part of being a Muslim in the modern period. "Yes, sword and weapons were used to progress Islam and to break and destroy the rigidity and stubbornness of enemies, as well as to stop their attacks," he acknowledged, but argued further that "human coexistence is the future for civilization; instead of the sword, economic development and spiritual words of truthfulness will defeat enemies."[23] By disconnecting from the use of force of the past he was breaking away from many of his contemporaries who stressed violence. Regarding the relationship between Turks and Armenians, Nursi warned those who wanted to use force: "To me those who use the sword now will have the same sword turn and touch their orphans. Today, victory is not through the sword. The sword should exist, but it should be in the hands of reason. Also there are reasons for friendship. That is because they are our neighbors and neighbors are friends of neighbors."[24]

Throughout Nursi's writings—his magnum opus is the 6,000-page *Risale-i Nur*, in which he developed the principles of the implementation of nonviolent actions of love, tolerance, and the use of reason—there is a profound focus on responding to evil with kindness, to working for peace regardless of the obstacles and oppressive conditions. He firmly believed that responding to evil with evil would create a vicious cycle and increase the spread of evil. He said, "If you want to defeat your opponents [or oppressors], respond to their evil actions with kindness. If you respond to their bad actions with bad responses, this will increase evil. Even if they are apparently defeated, they will keep hatred alive in their hearts toward you. If you respond with good deeds against their bad deeds, they will repent and become your friends."[25]

Here, Nursi referred to Qur'anic verses that reminded him of several important characteristics of believers. One verse says that believers are those who do not bear false witness and those who do not respond profanely to abuse (25:72). Another verse says, "If you forgive and exonerate their mistakes, surely God is the most forgiving and the most compassionate" (64:4). Clearly the driving impetus for Nursi's love for others was scripturally based; while this may appear as a fundamentalist reading of religion, actually within the Islamic tradition, Nursi followed the importance of emulating the prophetic model to further his spirituality and love for the divine.

Despite all his negative experiences in war, Nursi's *Damascus Sermon*, which was revised in 1950, was very hopeful about the future of peace in the world: "God willing, through the power of Islam, the goodness of civilization will overcome its badness and thus will purify the earth and secure global peace."[26] In the sermon, Nursi made his famous contribution of positive action (*musbet hareket*) as the principle of his understanding of nonviolence.[27] He reflected upon years of mistreatment and injustice, yet still advocated peacemaking activities:

> I have never accepted oppression or humiliation since my childhood and never obeyed it. This has been proven by many events in my life. For example, in Russia I did not stand up for the chief of staff of the Russian army when I was a prisoner of war. I also did not care about the threat of execution in the martial law court. However, for

thirty years [in 1960], I have dedicated myself to positive action and not negative action. In order not to get involved in the duty of God, I have decided to accept all of what is done to me with patience and pleasure—this is what earlier martyrs had experienced. The most important matter in this time is the spiritual *jihad*.[28]

Nursi's understanding of *jihad* seems to differ greatly from that of many of his contemporaries. He said, "Spiritual *jihad* is the *jihad* of this century." One of the reasons that Nursi focused on spiritual *jihad* was that any violence in society would violate the rights of innocent people; violence had to be prevented with kindness, generosity, and love. Transgression was not allowed even during war: When nations or individuals retaliated, then they fell into a cycle of violence and hatred. Nursi's understanding of *jihad* involved preventive action through communication and open dialogue. Thus, his own greatest *jihad* was his writings, sermons, and teachings, especially those that brought nonpracticing Muslims back to the faith. According to Nursi, the best way to help people was to strengthen their faith, improving their ethical behavior and also benefiting them in the hereafter. In a letter to his students, he mentioned that he did not listen to the radio or listen to the news during World War II because he was involved in a larger spiritual cause of struggling to reach paradise. In one statement he wrote, "If one had funds equivalent to the budget of Germany and the United Kingdom, he would not hesitate to spend it on gaining his afterlife [the eternal abode of peace]."[29] Nursi's method of positive action can be considered a new way of nonviolence. Normally when we speak of nonviolence practice, we speak of hunger strikes, picketing, vigils, sit-ins, blockades, and other types of demonstrations. Nursi's nonviolent practice does not include any of the above-mentioned methods. He dedicated himself and asked his students to dedicate their time to helping people with their spiritual life as well as their earthly life. On one occasion, when the government asked him not to distribute his work, Nursi responded, "Yes, as it is a duty to provide tickets for travelers for their journey, providing a certificate and light for those traveling toward eternity on such a way that is full of darkness is such a duty that no other duties can be more important than that. To deny such a duty is only possible if one can deny the existence of death."[30] In other words, Nursi was affirming that as people need tickets to go from one location to another, there is a longer trip than all the worldly trips, and that is the trip to the afterlife. It is his job to provide tickets for those traveling toward the afterlife through strengthening their faith.

According to Nursi, acting in an ethical and positive way—taming anger and revenge—would protect the lives of others. There are several examples of Nursi responding to intolerance without anger, but with love. On one occasion in 1958, Nursi intended to visit Ankara. Government officers

heard of his visit and attempted to prevent his entrance into the city. However, about one thousand people were waiting for Nursi on the road. The
slightest provocation would set off riots against security forces. Calling the
chief of security, Nursi said, "I thank you for what you have done. It is really
torture for me to have people kissing my hand." He continued to say, "We
are protecting the public order and the security of the country by ensuring
that every heart is spiritually resilient; this protects them from doing wrong
things against society. You intervene after the crimes are committed. That
is the difference between you and us." Following these exchanges, Nursi
continued, "I have spent eleven months in Eskişehir Prison, nine months
and ten days in Denizli Prison, and twenty months in Afyon Prison. All
the prisoners are reformed. They have abandoned their old criminal lives
and they are now moral human beings." Nursi continued by discussing his
experience in Denizli Prison: "There was a man who was charged with the
killing of four people. After reading the *Risale-i Nur* and following my
model of nonviolence he was completely rehabilitated. One day he came to
me with a small insect in his hand, and he said 'O teacher, am I allowed
to kill this insect? Is it a sin to do so?'" Nursi asked the officer, "Is the country much better off with the man's reformed life?"[31]

Nursi died in March 1960, but his message continued through his students, followers, and admirers. A Turkish prosecutor in the city of Afyon
in 1948 stated that Nursi had approximately 500,000 students around the
country. His obituary in *The New York Times* stated that his teachings had
over one million followers by early 1960. Today, the message of Nursi is
carried out by many in a powerful, charismatic, organized way, most notably by Fethullah Gülen, who benefited from the writings of Nursi as well
as the legacy of the Ottomans. Gülen has inspired millions to work in a variety of social services, including the establishment of schools, educational
institutions, charities, media outlets, and youth groups around the world
for both Muslims and non-Muslims alike.[32] Gülen through these efforts
has been contributing in a greater scale to global peace efforts.[33] In the
summer of 2004, I visited Macedonia in Eastern Europe. During my visit,
I had a chance to visit a school established by admirers of Gülen. I was
told that during the civil war between the various peoples of the former
Yugoslavia, the school became a haven for peace. Those who were fighting
each other sent their children there for safety. While their parents were out
fighting each other, the students were learning together in peace.

Nursi's nonviolent model already has made an outstanding contribution
to the larger world. One can argue that Nursi's entire life was based on the
Qur'anic verse: "Peace is better" (4:128).

Notes

1. From a December 24, 1948, letter by Colonel Halit Akmansu, one of the Turkish commanders in the Turkish independence war. See Necmeddin Şahiner, *Son Şahitler,* vol. 2 (Istanbul: Nesil, 1981), 145.

2. Bediüzzaman Said Nursi, *Tarihçe-i Hayat,* in *Risale-i Nur,* vol. 2 (Istanbul: Nesil, 1996), 2134; see also Necmeddin Şahiner, *Bediüzzaman Said Nursi* (Istanbul: Yeni Asya Yayinevi, 1979), 156.

3. Nursi, *Şualar,* in *Risale-i Nur,* vol. 1, 1091.

4. I find it interesting that in the West there are no historical narratives of Turkish and Kurdish Muslims during World War I who were compassionate toward the Armenian population. While the military operations against the Armenians and other ethnic groups is a contested issue in modern-day Turkey, today students are taught of hundreds of cases in which Turkish Muslims, for example, helped prevent crimes, protected civilians and orphans, gave food to refugees, or established clinics.

5. Necmeddin Şahiner, *Bediüzzaman Said Nursi* (Istanbul: Yeni Asya Yayinevi, 1979), 174.

6. Nursi, *Lem'alar,* in *Risale-i Nur,* vol. 1, 708.

7. Nursi, *Kastamonu Lahikasi,* in *Risale-i Nur,* vol. 2, 1649.

8. Ibid.

9. For further examples, see Thomas Michel, "Muslim-Christian Dialogue and Cooperation in the Thought of Bediüzzaman Said Nursi," Society of Jesus, http://www.sjweb.info/documents/dialogo/muslimchristiancoop.doc (accessed January 27, 2010).

10. Nursi, *Mektubat,* in *Risale-i Nur,* vol. 1, 370. For an English version of the source, see Bediüzzaman Said Nursi, *Letters 1928–1932,* trans. Şukran Vahide (Istanbul: Sözler Neşriyat, 1997), 74–75.

11. Nursi, *Hutbe-i Şamiye,* in *Risale-i Nur,* vol. 2, 1968.

12. Nursi, *Divan-i Harbi Orfi,* in *Risale-i Nur,* vol. 2, 1930.

13. In Islamic seminary ethics courses, it is common to spend a great deal of time reflecting on and studying the differences between sin and sinner and how to respond appropriately to these ethical dilemmas.

14. The term *civilized people* should not be taken literally. Nursi was referring to people who become irrational and zealous of their causes to a point that they sacrifice their culture of etiquette.

15. Bediüzzaman Said Nursi, *Munazarat* (Istanbul: Yeni Asya Nesriyat, 1996), 70–71.

16. Nursi, *Muhakamat,* in *Risale-i Nur,* vol. 2, 2032.

17. Nursi, *Şuâlar,* 888.

18. Another similar verse states "Those who swallow their anger and forgive people, surely God forgives those who do beautiful things" (3:134).

19. Nursi, *Mektubat,* 472.

20. Ibid., 469.

21. Nursi, *Enirdağ Lahikasi,* in *Risale-i Nur,* vol. 2, 1904.

22. With slight change of translation from Bediüzzaman Said Nursi, *The Damascus Sermon*, trans. Şükran Vahide (Istanbul: Sözler Neşriyat, 1996), 81.

23. Nursi, *The Damascus Sermon*, 37–38.

24. Nursi, *Manazarat*, 68.

25. Nursi, *Mektubat*, 471.

26. Nursi, *Hutbe-i Şamiye*, 1965.

27. For details on positive action, see Zeki Saritoprak, "An Islamic Approach to Peace and Nonviolence: A Turkish Experience," *Muslim World*, vol. 95, no. 3 (July 2005), 413–27.

28. Nursi, *Emirdağ Lahikasi*, 1912.

29. At this time, England and Germany were among the wealthiest nations in the world, viewed as having the greatest ability to influence world affairs.

30. Nursi, *Lem'alar*, 675.

31. This story was recounted by Said Özdemir (b. 1930), a student of Nursi who was with him on the trip to Ankara. The event happened in the city of Konya. See M. Said Özdemir, "Islam ve Şiddet: Risale-i Nur Perspektifi" [Islam and Violence: The Risale-i Nur Perspective], in *Çok Kültürlü Bir Dünyada Imanli Anlamli ve Bariş Içinde Yaşama Pratiği: Risale-i Nur Yaklaşimi* [*Bringing Faith, Meaning, and Peace to Life in a Multicultural World: The Risale-i Nur's Approach*] (Istanbul: Nesil, 2004), 135–204.

32. For more on Fethullah Gülen, see his books, *Pearls of Wisdom* (Fairfax, VA: The Fountain, 2000); *The Messenger of God: Muhammad* (Somerset, NJ: The Light, 2005); *Essays, Perspectives, Opinions of M. Fethullah Gülen* (Somerset, NJ: The Light, 2004). See also www.rumiforum.org.

33. For Gülen's contribution to global peace, see Zeki Saritoprak, "Gülen and His Global Contribution to Peace Building," *Today's Zaman*, October 31, 2007.

6

Economics and the Clash of Civilizations

Reexamining Religion and Violence

Waleed El-Ansary

R eligion and economics are connected in ways that have profound implications for the current debate about religion, conflict, and peace. Unfortunately, much of the literature on the latter is based on a too-abstract view of the former. Such analyses can lead one to over-emphasize the role of religion in conflict and underemphasize its role in peace. The tension between Francis Fukuyama's end of history, with the triumph of Western democratic capitalism, and Samuel Huntington's clash of civilizations, in which none is able to triumph over the others, depends fundamentally on competing theories of modernization and the effects of economic industrialization on other aspects of culture.[1] But such theories do not receive serious treatment from either thinker, and Huntington's definition of civilization even fails to "take into account the existence of major differences of substance and quality between pre-modern classic civilizations and modern industrial civilizations."[2]

This essay clarifies the interconnections among religion, conflict, and peace from an Islamic economic perspective, highlighting their implications for development strategies seeking to change the intellectual and socioeconomic conditions that result in violent forms of extremism. It first examines the interconnections among religion, economics, and civilization from an Islamic point of view. It then draws the implications of this for the interconnections among religion, conflict, and peace, arguing that trade-offs among Schumacher's three objectives of work—to provide necessities, enrich ourselves, and enrich our community—can affect clashes within (as opposed to between) civilizations, and that conventional economic development programs based on these trade-offs can backfire by fomenting extremist combinations of secular and religious thought. Finally, it examines the implications of this for contemporary development strategies in the Islamic world, exploring how Islam and Islamic civilization can be central to accord and dialogue among civilizations.

Traditional Objectives of Human Work: Interconnections among Religion, Economics, and Civilization

If man is created for a higher purpose, as Islam and other religions assert, then what are the objectives of work? Brian Keeble points out that it would be inconceivable that work would necessarily entail conflict between spiritual and other needs:

> [Otherwise] we would have to face an awkward question: how it ever came about that, in order to sustain his earthly existence, man should be obliged to follow a course of physical action that seems a direct denial of his deepest nature, as if by some ghastly mistake of his Creator it is man's destiny to follow a direction that leads him away from the very thing it is his nature to be? If we are to avoid such a dilemma, we must conclude that in some way work is, or should be, profoundly natural and not something that must be avoided or banished as being beneath our dignity.[3]

If work is not only supposed to help keep us alive, but also help us strive toward perfection, then we can derive three purposes of human work, as Schumacher points out:

> First, to provide necessary and useful goods and services.
> Second, to enable every one of us to use and thereby perfect our gifts like good stewards.
> Third, to do so in service to, and in cooperation with, others, so as to liberate ourselves from our . . . egocentricity.[4]

In Islam, all three objectives are forms of *jihad,* applicable to both what man does (*amal*) and what he makes (*sun'*).[5] Unfortunately, the meaning of *jihad* has been obscured by the erroneous Western image of Islam as the religion of the sword (see chapter 2). Although *jihad* in its outer meaning relates to the defense of the Islamic world from invasion by non-Islamic forces, it was upon returning from the Battle of Badr, which threatened the existence of the Islamic community, that the Prophet of Islam said, "You have returned from the lesser *jihad* to the greater *jihad*"[6]—the struggle to integrate the whole of life around a sacred center, which has corresponding doctrines in all major religious traditions.[7] Within Christianity, the inner struggle is indicated by Christ's statement, "Think not that I come to send peace on earth; I came not to send peace, but a sword."[8] The word *jihad* "is derived from the root *jhd*, whose primary meaning is 'to strive' or 'to exert oneself.'"[9]

Applied to Islamic economics, the Qur'an suggests that to struggle for a living is tantamount to defending the faith.[10] The Prophet stressed this before the aforementioned Battle of Badr, when a young man with a strong physique was running to his shop through the area where the Prophet was marshalling his men. Someone remarked that he wished the youth would use his body and health to run in the way of God by enlisting to defend the faith. The Prophet responded, "If this young man runs with the intention of not depending on others and refraining from begging, he is in the way of God. If he strives for the livelihood of his weak parents or weak children, he is in the way of God. If he tries to show his health out of pride, he is in the way of the devil."[11] According to this view, every aspect of life is sacred. Nothing is outside of the Absolute and no aspect of life is profane, for everything is attached to God; what might appear to be the most mundane of activities has religious significance. All three of Schumacher's objectives of work thus can be related to various Islamic sciences. Islamic law clarifies the first objective "to provide necessary and useful goods and services" by defining what such goods and services are. Similarly, Islamic metaphysics and the cosmological sciences are central to the second objective of work, "to enable every one of us to use and thereby perfect our gifts like good stewards," because what man makes—or man's art—should communicate a spiritual truth and presence analogous to nature, or God's art. "The ethical aspect of work in this case embraces also the aesthetic"[12]—"every man is a special kind of artist" in this perspective; the artist is not "a special kind of man."[13] Finally, the third objective to perfect our gifts "in service to, and in cooperation with, others, so as to liberate ourselves from our . . . egocentricity" is intimately related to the esoteric dimension of Islam, or Sufism, dealing with intention.[14]

Thus, the three objectives of work and related Islamic sciences address questions of what to produce, how to produce it, and how to conduct exchange. Moreover, these sciences may be said to fall loosely within the three dimensions of *islam, iman,* and *ihsan,* articulated in the renowned *hadith* of Gabriel defining, first, right action, which is the subject of Islamic law; second, right thought, which is the subject of Islamic theology, philosophy, and sciences of nature; and third, right intention, which is the subject of Islamic mysticism.[15] Of course, the three dimensions and three objectives are not reducible to a strict one-to-one correspondence. Islamic law also has implications for the division of labor in the second objective because of the legal concept of *fard kifa'i*,[16] which includes community obligations, such as building orphanages and hospitals. If no community members fulfill such material needs, each member of the community is spiritually accountable. Similarly, some members of the community must practice each profession to fulfill the material needs of society, making the division of labor not only a right, but a legal duty.[17]

Similarly, the Islamic approach to the making of things in the second objective has always been closely wed to the spiritual practices of Islam, for the necessary condition in this approach is consciousness of one's contingency and complete dependence on the Absolute, or "spiritual poverty" (*faqr*).[18] As Yusuf Ibish points out,

> The Damascene weavers, for example, preceded their work by hours if not days of spiritual preparation: prayers, meditation and contemplation were an integral part of the creative process, at the end of which beautiful design would emerge: outwardly inspiring designs reflecting inwardly the realized harmony with the source of all inspiration. One could say the same for the calligraphers: purity of soul and nobility of character were regarded as indispensable conditions for the accomplishment of this, the sacred art of Islam *par excellence*.[19]

Because greed eliminates the spiritual vision necessary to execute the art that results from this inner *jihad*, Sufism affects Islamic production processes, not just exchange processes.[20] With the above interlocking relationships among economic and religious realms in mind, one can say that Islamic law has more implications for the first objective than it does for the others. Similarly, Islamic metaphysics and cosmological sciences have a special connection to the second objective, because the theoretical sciences provide the axioms for the productive sciences.

The intersection of all three dimensions, however, founded on the Qur'an and *hadith*, is not only necessary to create Islamic civilization, but constitutes the essence of Islam. Likewise, the application of all three dimensions to economics constitutes the essence of Islamic economics and is crucial to Islamic civilization. Islamic metaphysics and sciences of nature transform everything in the productive sciences, from architecture and urban planning to the art of dress and personal living space. The same applies to the practical sciences dealing with everything from the spiritual significance of social organization to the treatment of the environment. The links among work, spiritual education, and sacred ambiance, forged by the Islamic theoretical sciences, is thus crucial to understanding the interconnections among religion, economics, and civilization from the Islamic point of view.[21] Unfortunately, much of the contemporary literature on Islamic economics tends to ignore these crucial connections, reducing

Islamic economics to the first dimension on Islamic law, with all that this implies for the meaning of the discipline and its differences from conventional, or neoclassical, economics.[22] Civilization as traditionally understood is thus intimately connected with revelation in that metaphysics and the traditional sciences of nature are related to the inner meaning of revelation.[23] Analogous arguments apply to all major religious traditions and civilizations.[24]

Thus, the question of whether or not modern production processes fulfill the three objectives is crucial to determining whether or not religious approaches to the study of man and nature have anything to say about such processes, and therefore, the extent of the interconnections among religion, economics, and civilization. The same applies to the legitimacy of the three objectives as criteria of work to begin with. Clearly, all economists recognize the first objective of work to provide necessary and useful goods and services. But some recognize the other objectives to various degrees, acknowledging that different types of work have different effects. Adam Smith acknowledged the second objective to some extent, arguing that an extremely high division of labor employing few of man's faculties could have serious social costs by reducing certain human capabilities. He states:

> The understandings of the greater part of men are necessarily formed by their ordinary employments. The man whose life is spent in performing a few simple operations . . . has no occasion to exert his understanding . . . . He naturally loses, therefore, the habit of such exertion and generally becomes as stupid and ignorant as it is possible for a human creature to become . . . but in every improved and civilised society this is the state into which the labouring poor, that is, the great body of the people, must necessarily fall, unless government takes some pains to prevent it.[25]

But other figures, such as James Mill, the father of John Stuart Mill, opposed this view, denying the existence of such harmful effects and arguing that all types of work were homogeneous in terms of the second objective.[26] He also denied the possibility of the third objective to liberate ourselves from our egocentricity based on psychological hedonism, leaving only the first objective applicable to economics. More recently, some neoclassical economists have adopted a syncretic position, assuming that all types of work are homogeneous on one hand while asserting the legitimacy of all three objectives on the other.[27] From an Islamic point of view, however, if industrial production processes do not fulfill all three objectives, then any trade-offs among them can only exist in the short or medium terms, not the long term, as Islam requires that all three objectives are satisfied. This tension between the Western economic view and the Islamic religious view of work has serious implications for economic development and peace-making activities, to which we now turn.

Implications for the Interconnections among Religion, Conflict, and Peace

A Huntington-style clash of civilizations certainly follows from the assumption that industrial production processes are not spiritually neutral, but the causal chain is fundamentally different from that of Huntington's argument. Trade-offs between the first objective of work on one hand and the second and third objectives of work on the other can clearly lead to power asymmetries between civilizations, enhancing both the desire and the ability of an industrial civilization to clash with nonindustrial civilizations based on strictly economic interests. For their part, nonindustrial civilizations' attempts to avoid subjugation through industrialization break the link between work and a spiritual education within these civilizations, providing the intellectual conditions for violent forms of religious extremism through lethal combinations of religious and secular thought. This is consistent with Huntington's suggestion that modernization ultimately leads to non-Westernization, after initial effects in the opposite direction, but the analysis is fundamentally different: The resulting clash of civilizations is ultimately driven by economic interests, rather than any differences in the religious cores of civilizations themselves. The same economic interests can have the reverse effect on clash within a civilization, reducing its probability if costs and benefits make economic cooperation more attractive than conflict—as we see in the European Union—reinforcing Huntington's conclusion while undermining his analysis.

This does not imply that Fukuyama's analysis is correct. On the contrary, it is much more deeply flawed when viewed through an Islamic lens. Although modernization greatly weakens the religious core of civilizations, the differences among civilizations do not disappear. Moreover, increased conflict follows when the loss of the three objectives of work weakens—not strengthens—the spiritual core of civilizations, as the civilizations decay, deviate, and move toward what René Guénon calls "uniformity without unity."[28] Thus, an Islamic economic lens shows that Huntington is right in predicting increased conflict, but wrong in attributing that to a strengthening of civilizations. And Fukuyama is correct in predicting increasing uniformity between civilizations, but wrong in predicting extreme uniformity as well as less conflict. Lacking the central distinction between traditional and deviant manifestations of religion in civilizations based on the three objectives of work, both Huntington and Fukuyama ultimately overemphasize the role of religion in conflict and underemphasize its role in peace from this point of view. Table 6.1 illustrates these various possibilities.

Table 6.1 Civilizational Differences and Conflicts

		Degree of conflict	
		High	Low
Civilizational differences	Strong	Huntington (pessimist)	Traditional (all three objectives)
	Weak	Nietzsche, violent extremists	Fukuyama (optimist)

The framework suggests that Huntington and Fukuyama must either argue that industrial production processes ultimately fulfill all three objectives of work or maintain that the three objectives are not legitimate criteria of work to begin with. The traditional quadrant in this table presupposes the fulfillment of all three objectives of work in nonindustrial civilizations, while the extremist quadrant presupposes trade-offs among the objectives with modernization, leading to conflict among civilizations. These two quadrants may be viewed as complementary because they deal with different periods of time, whereas the other quadrants of Huntington and Fukuyama are mutually exclusive. The framework does not imply that fulfilling all three objectives is sufficient to completely eliminating conflict among civilizations, but it clearly implies that it is a necessary condition.

The preceding economic analysis and presuppositions highlight certain facts that Huntington's clash of civilizations thesis obscures, in particular the tremendous military and economic inequality between Western and other civilizations, especially Islamic civilization, and the fact that opposition to the influence of Western economic interests within other civilizations should not be confused with opposition to Western civilization as such. The same applies to the possibility that Western economic interests can employ the clash of civilizations thesis as a camouflage to dominate other civilizations on the pretext that those civilizations are its enemies, choosing from within them forces that are on their side against other forces within that civilization.

Thus, the question of whether or not industrial production processes fulfill the three objectives of work is crucial to determining the interconnections among religion, conflict, and peace, as well as the extent of the interconnections among religion, economics, and civilization. An enormous literature challenges the systematic deskilling of work in modern production processes and its consequences for civilization.[29] With respect to the second objective, Ugo Pagano points out that competitive industrial markets necessarily and systematically deskill work for "efficiency gains."[30] Humanistic economists, such as Mark Lutz and Kenneth Lux, argue that such costs are a "negative externality," like pollution, that must be prevented.[31] And Rama Coomaraswamy concludes, "Only when an individual's body and soul can participate in his work—something never possible in a factory—can the medieval principle that *laborare est orare* fully apply."[32]

Michael Novak maintains that Christian principles are fully consistent with democratic industrial capitalism and even uniquely created it.[33] Unfortunately, he does not write anything on the Christian approach to the productive sciences in his magnum opus, *The Spirit of Democratic Capitalism,* to support his claim. Perhaps this is due to his interest in the practical rather than productive sciences, for according to him, his "favorite book was Aristotle's *Nicomachean Ethics* and the *Commentary* of St. Thomas Aquinas on it."[34] Perhaps confusingly, Schumacher employs Aquinas' views on the productive sciences to demonstrate the opposite view, that industrial capitalism is anti-Christian (he explains modern neurosis accordingly).[35] Frithjof Schuon confirms this view, noting that the only premodern use of machines was for toys rather than for production.[36] He dismisses the common objection that "there have always been machines and that the nineteenth century merely introduced more perfect machines," maintaining that:

> this argument contains a radical error. It arises from a lack of any feeling for "dimensions" or, to put it in another way, from an inability to distinguish between qualitative and eminent differences and those which are quantitative or accidental.[37]

Breaking the link between work and a spiritual education in industrial development programs now carries the unintended consequence of dangerous combinations of secular and religious thought in religious fundamentalism,[38] for "there are many ways of being modern."[39] As Ghazi bin Muhammad points out:

> The rise of secularism has paradoxically contributed, by way of militant and ignorant reaction, to the rise of fundamentalism. For the banners of fundamentalism invariably contain slogans against atheism and secularism, and draw many simple believers to them on that account. Now it may well be asked how is this leading to "disequilibrium and upheaval" among traditional religious culture, if secularism only leads to "more religion"? The answer is that the religious fundamentalism which is waxing in the modern world is vastly and qualitatively different from the traditional religion which is waning, and that the difference between them is, precisely, that fundamentalism is opposed to all traditional "religious culture" as such (and therefore, in the end, bound to damage and impoverish religion as such).[40]

From this point of view, modernist economic development solutions substitute one problem with worse environmental and political ones. Both Huntington and Fukuyama have failed to properly identify the interconnections among religion, economics, and civilization, with all that this implies for the interconnections among religion, conflict, and peace. This analysis is consistent with other historical and empirical critiques of Huntington's thesis. Sato points out that industrialization

> caused gaps in national strength, between those countries which had succeeded in industrializing and those others which had not, that gradually widened .... Thus when it comes to the clash of civilizations, the most violent conflicts are those between a (pre-modern) classic civilization and a modern industrial civilization, as was the case with the Opium Wars. In this sense, and contrary to Huntington's assertion, it was during the period often called the "Age of Imperialism," from the mid-nineteenth century into the twentieth century, that the clash of civilizations reached its highest peak. Whatever the level of violence, the outcome of a clash between a modern industrial civilization and a classic civilization is clear from the beginning. As a result, most regions within the sphere of classic civilizations where the process of industrialization could not be launched soon enough fell victim to the drive by the Western powers (as well as the late industrializing states like Russia and Japan) for colonization.[41]

Obviously, conflict among colonial powers for territory in other civilizations, and therefore clash within Western civilization, is complementary to clash among civilizations: Both clashes within and among civilizations go together with modernization.[42]

Moreover, Huntington's suggestion that the core clash between the Western and the Islamic worlds over political values is inconsistent with the 1995–2001 World Values Survey public opinion data from seventy countries on attitudes toward democracy, political and religious leadership, and gender and sexuality. A remarkable study of these data by Pippa Norris and Ronald Inglehart shows that "surprisingly similar attitudes toward democracy are found in the West and the Islamic world."[43] The data show that the core clash among the Western and Islamic worlds is over gender equality and sexual liberalization rather than democracy, or *eros* rather than *demos*. Whether the aforementioned economic interests that generate conflict within and among civilizations have asymmetric effects in the future, reducing them in the former and increasing in the latter, remains to be seen. We now turn to economic development solutions seeking to minimize the possibility of such a conflict.

Implications for Economic Development Strategies in the Islamic World and Civilizational Dialogue

The above analysis suggests the crucial importance of the spiritual significance of production processes in Islamic civilization. Unfortunately, Muslim economists have not translated this into a development strategy.[44] Although they frequently claim that an Islamic economy differs from industrial capitalism, socialism, or some combination of the two, they have not addressed this difference in terms of the central issue, leaving the literature open to ridicule by Timur Kuran and others.[45] As Schumacher states, "the implicit assumption is that you can have a technological transplant; that technology is ideologically neutral; that you can acquire the hardware without the software that lies behind it, has made the hardware possible, and keeps it moving."[46] If all civilizations had industrialized in this way, we would not be here discussing the issue today. Even if Muslims wanted to blindly imitate (*taqlid*) modern Western economic development, there is not enough capital to provide sufficient employment using capital-intensive industrial technologies.[47]

In short, an authentic Islamic theory of exchange and development must point in a completely different direction, based on a different approach to technology. Without it, Islamic economics is fatally incomplete. This current lacuna is perplexing in light of the contemporary literature on the Islamic natural and productive sciences on one hand and the classical literature on the Islamic productive sciences and economic institutions on the other.[48]

Accordingly, the first step in an Islamic development program must be recovering the Islamic intellectual heritage, shaping education accordingly, and bringing forth science and technology for peacemaking purposes.[49] Education is the greatest resource: It can shape supply and demand according to Islamic principles.[50] This is particularly urgent given that "only a minority in any civilization consciously and actively participates in the spirit of the tradition, the majority remaining more or less fallow, open, that is, to receive influences of no matter what kind."[51] On the one hand, the contemporary Islamic educational system must integrate the findings of modern science into higher orders of knowledge based on the traditional sciences of nature. On the other hand, contemporary Islamic productive sciences must integrate neutral technologies into the making of things based on traditional metaphysical principles. In terms of trade-offs, or the lack thereof, between the three objectives of work, there are four possible assessments of a particular technology or production process: no trade-offs, fulfilling both spiritual and material objectives; trade-offs that fulfill only material objectives; trade-offs that fulfill only spiritual objectives; and no trade-offs, fulfilling neither spiritual nor material objectives.

The first combination is ideal from the Islamic point of view, whereas the second combination runs against Islamic values (but not egoistic preferences), trading spiritual for material objectives. As previously discussed, it is unsustainable; it ultimately collapses to the fourth combination, which loses all objectives. The third combination is also internally inconsistent, as fulfilling material needs is a spiritual duty. An authentic Islamic economic system might therefore accept some modern technologies and production processes while rejecting others, seeking to restore the traditional connections among technology, the crafts, and ultimately art.[52] An appropriate Islamic development proposal could start with several of Jean-Louis Michon's recommendations regarding schools of traditional arts, educating the general public on the meaning and symbolism of Islamic design.[53] Such a school would be open for children from the age of twelve who have obtained their primary education; the period of studies would extend over seven years, which Michon distributes as follows:

(a) First year (orientation) allows access by the pupils to all the different workshops, which gives them a general initiation into artistic activities and facilitates the placement of each pupil in the branch corresponding best to his taste and ability.

(b) Three years of training in the chosen craft. After completion and passing the practical and general/theoretical examinations, a diploma of "skilled craftsman" in the specific branch is granted, the pupil may then leave the school and establish himself as an independent craftsman if he so wishes.

(c) Three years of specialization in the already chosen craft, with practical training in the other crafts pertaining either to the same category of techniques (e.g., incrustations, which may be either in wood or metal; engraving and sculpture, which may be in stone, wood, or plaster) or to the same family of materials (e.g., pottery and tile mosaics; weaving of wool, silk and cotton; using different techniques on leather, wood, metal, and the like).[54]

Completion of these final three years and passing the terminal examinations leads to the diploma for a master in traditional art. While this is only one part of one proposal, it is a crucial beginning stage for any authentic Islamic approach to economic development.

However, the ruling elites of the Islamic world, with the possible exceptions of Iran, Jordan, and Morocco, have yet to take an authentic Islamic education, technology, and development strategy seriously. Indeed, many people tend to think that whoever has the power has the truth, and, in light of the colonial experience, the Islamic world should follow the West. As Schuon explains:

> For youth the final humiliation is to be weak and thus open to colonization; weakness is then often seen as synonymous with tradition, as if no question of truth need arise either in the evaluation of Western strength or in the interpretation of traditional values. What gives strength, they think, is true, even if it leads down to hell[55] ... people have in all ages imitated those who were strongest; before having strength people want to

have at least the appearance of strength, and the ugly things of the modern world have become synonymous with power and independence. The essence of artistic beauty is spiritual, whereas material strength is "worldly," and, since the worldly regard strength as synonymous with intelligence, the beauty of the tradition becomes synonymous not merely with weakness, but also with stupidity, illusion and the ridiculous; being ashamed of weakness is almost always accompanied by hatred of what is looked on as the cause of this apparent inferiority—in this case, tradition, contemplation, truth.[56]

Because "the conquered imitate the conquerors," as Ibn Khaldun also suggested, secular thought in the colonial era created an educational domino effect that any Islamic development policy must correct.[57] Victor Danner confirms this assessment of the issue in his brilliant final chapter of *The Islamic Tradition*.[58] Such a scenario would have been unimaginable if there were only scholarly debates between Muslim and Western thinkers instead of the military conquest of the Islamic world and the imposition of colonial educational institutions spreading secular thought.[59] Economists such as Thomas Schelling have written extensively about such domino effects quickly shifting equilibrium over time, or the ways in which the so-called micromotives of a few can trigger enormous shifts in macrolevel behavior, although economists generally apply this to other contexts.[60] To combat the inferiority complex preventing the existence and application of authentic Islamic development policies, it is important to recall Schumacher's crucial point:

There has never been a time, in any society in any part of the world, without its sages and teachers to challenge materialism and plead for a different order of priorities. The languages have differed, the symbols have varied, yet the message has always been the same: "Seek ye *first* the kingdom of God, and all these things [the material things which you also need] shall be *added* unto you." They shall be added, we are told, here on earth where we need them, not simply in an after-life beyond our imagination. Today, however, this message reaches us not solely from the sages and saints but from the actual course of physical events. It speaks to us in the language of terrorism, genocide, breakdown, pollution, exhaustion. We live, it seems, in a unique period of convergence. It is becoming apparent that there is not only a promise but also a threat in those astonishing words about the kingdom of God—the threat that "unless you seek first the kingdom, these other things, which you also need, will cease to be available to you."[61]

Conclusion

Confusion over the interconnections among religion, economics, and civilization has had devastating consequences for the analysis of the interconnections among religion, conflict, and peace. Islamic economic analysis of these interconnections, based on a spiritual hierarchy, implies that all three traditional objectives of work must be fulfilled in all civilizations to avoid clash within and among civilizations. From this point of view, an Islamic theology of development must inform economic development programs in the Islamic world; as other chapters in this volume argue, the West also must recognize the role that it has played in past conflict (see chapters 4 and 5). Finally, although, as Seyyed Hossein Nasr writes, "there are numerous factors today which oppose dialogue and understanding between civilizations and even within civilizations," Islam and Islamic civilization can play a central role in encouraging such dialogue, for

> Islam is the last major religion of this cycle of human history, and the Qur'an speaks explicitly of the veracity of religions sent to mankind before Islam. As for Islamic civilization occupying the middle belt of the world, by geography as well as by its historical experience, it is suited in every way to carry out civilizational dialogue with various civilizations and to be itself a bridge between East and West, reflecting the light of that blessed olive tree to which the Qur'an refers as being neither of the East nor of the West, as it is also the message of surrender to the Lord Who is the Lord of all the East and all the West.[62]

Notes

1. See Francis Fukuyama, *The End of History and the Last Man* (New York: Free Press, 2006), and Samuel Huntington, *The Clash of Civilizations and the Remaking of World Order* (New York: Touchstone, 1997).

2. Seizaburo Sato, "The Clash of Civilizations: A View from Japan," *Asia Pacific Review* (October 1997). Available online at Okamoto International Affairs Research Institute, Clash of Civilizations and Its Critiques, http://sbpark.com/inn60.html (accessed November 22, 2009).

3. Brian Keeble, *Art: For Whom and For What?* (Ipswich, UK: Golgonooza Press, 1998), 75.

4. E.F. Schumacher, *Good Work* (New York: Harper & Row, 1979), 3–4. Regarding striving for perfection, he cites the Biblical injunction: "Be ye therefore perfect, even as your Father which is in heaven is perfect" (Matthew 5:48) He also cites: "Whichever gift each of you has received, use it in service to one another, like good stewards dispensing the grace of God in its varied forms."

5. As S.H. Nasr points out in an essay on Islamic work ethics, "Work carried out in accordance with the *shari'ah* is a form of *jihad* and inseparable from the religious and spiritual significance associated with it." Seyyed Hossein Nasr, *Traditional Islam in the Modern World* (London and New York: KPT, 1987), 35.

6. Muslim scholars view many sayings of the Prophet as commentaries on the Qur'an, suggesting a hierarchy of texts. Moreover, Muslim scholars classify statements of the Prophet hierarchically according to the reliability of the chain of transmission. See, e.g., Muhammad Zubayr Siddiqi, *Hadith Literature: Its Origin, Development and Special Features* (Cambridge: Islamic Texts Society, 1993).

7. See, e.g., the chapter on holy war in Whitall Perry, *A Treasury of Traditional Wisdom* (Cambridge: Quinta Essentia, 1971), 391–412. For correspondences among Indo-European

traditions with applications to the economic realm, see Georges Dumézil, *The Destiny of the Warrior*, trans. Alf Hiltebeitel (Chicago: University of Chicago Press, 1969).

8.   Matthew (10:34).

9.   Nasr, *Traditional Islam*, 28. The Qur'an employs the word *jihad* or one of its variations thirty times, two of which refer to actions taken by non-Muslims against Muslims to force them to worship something other than God. The other twenty-eight times refer to struggle for the sake of God (*jihad fi sabilillah*), implicitly or explicitly. For a brief introduction to the Qur'anic usage of the term, see, e.g., Louay Fatoohi, *Jihad in the Qur'an* (Kuala Lumpur: A.S. Noordeen, 2002).

10.   See, e.g., Muhammad Abdul-Rauf, *A Muslim's Reflections on Democratic Capitalism* (Washington, DC: American Enterprise Institute, 1984), 5.

11.   Al-Ghazzali, *Ihya' 'Ulum al-Din*, vol. 2 (New Delhi: Kitab Bhavan, 1982), 54.

12.   Nasr, *Traditional Islam*, 43. He also notes that *husn*, the root of *ihsan* in Arabic, means both beauty and goodness, whereas *qubh* means both ugliness and evil.

13.   According to the famous quote of Ananda Coomaraswamy, "The artist is not a special kind of man, but every man is a special kind of artist." See his *Transformation of Nature in Art* (New York: Dover, 1956).

14.   See, e.g., Yusuf Ibish, "Economic Institutions," in R.B. Serjeant, ed., *The Islamic City: Selected Papers from the Colloquium Held at the Middle East Centre, Faculty of Oriental Studies in Cambridge, United Kingdom* (Paris: UNESCO, 1980), and "Traditional Guilds in the Ottoman Empire: An Evaluation of their Spiritual Role and Social Function," Islamic World Report, 1999.

15.   For an in-depth treatment of each dimension and corresponding Islamic sciences, see William Chittick and Sachiko Murata, *The Vision of Islam* (Albany, NY: SUNY Press, 1994). The Prophetic saying is narrated by 'Umar as follows:

> One day when we were sitting with the Messenger of God there came unto us a man whose clothes were of exceeding whiteness and whose hair was of exceeding blackness, nor were there any signs of travel upon him, although none of us knew him. He sat down knee unto knee opposite the Prophet, upon whose thighs he placed the palm of his hands, saying: "O Muhammad, tell me what is the surrender (*islam*)." The Messenger of God answered him saying: "The surrender is to testify that there is no god but God and that Muhammad God's Messenger, to perform the prayer, bestow the alms, fast Ramadan, and make, if thou canst, the pilgrimage to the Holy House." He said, "Thou hast spoken truly," and we were amazed that having questioned him he should corroborate him. Then he said, "Tell me what is faith (*iman*)." He answered, "To believe in God and His angels and His books and His messengers and the Last Day, and to believe that no good or evil cometh but by His Providence." "Thou hast spoken truly," he said, and then: "Tell me what is virtue (*ihsan*)." He replied, "To worship God as if thou sawest Him, for if thou seest Him not, yet seeth He thee." "Thou hast spoken truly," he said, and then: "Tell me of the Hour." He answered, "The questioned thereof knoweth no better than the questioner." He said, "Then tell me of its signs." He answered, "That the slave-girl shall give birth to her mistress; and that those who were but barefoot naked needy herdsmen shall build buildings ever higher and higher." Then the stranger went away, and I stayed a while after he had gone; and the Prophet said to me: "O 'Umar, knowest thou the questioner, who he was?' I said: "God and His Messenger know best." He said, "It was Gabriel. He came unto you to teach you your religion (*din*)."

Martin Lings in *Muhammad: His Life Based on the Earliest Sources* (Rochester, VT: Inner Traditions International, 1983), 330–31.

16. This is in contrast to individual duties (*fard 'ayni*), such as prayer.

17. Nasir al-Din Tusi clarifies this point in his classic work on Islamic ethics:

> It is said that when Adam (peace be upon him!) came into the world and sought sustenance, he had to perform a thousand tasks until bread was baked, the thousand and first being to cool the bread, which he then ate. The same idea is to be found expressed by the Philosophers in the following way: a thousand hardworking individuals are required before one morsel can be put into the mouth.
>
> Now, since the work of Man pivots on mutual aid, while cooperation is realized by men undertaking each other's important tasks fairly and equally, it follows that the diversity of crafts, which proceeds from the diversity of purposes, demands [a measure of] organization; for if the whole species were to betake themselves in a body to one craft, there would be a return of the situation against which we have just been on guard. For this reason, Divine Wisdom has required that there should be a disparity of aspirations and opinions, so that each desires a different occupation, some noble and other base, in the practice of which they are cheerful and contented.

Nasir al-Din Tusi, *The Nasirean Ethics*, trans. G.M. Wickens (London: G. Allen and Unwin, 1964), 189. This is one reason why monopoly (*al-ihtikar*) is a form of injustice (*zulm*), according to the *hadith* that "only the sinner monopolizes things," and why craftsmen often collectively donated goods to those in need.

18. For the man who has acquired *faqr*, its immediate consequence is "detachment with regard to all manifested things, for the being knows from then on that these things, like himself, are nothing, and that they have no importance whatsoever compared with the absolute Reality." This detachment implies "indifference with regard to the fruits of action … which enables the being to escape from the unending chain of consequence which follows from this action." René Guénon, "*Al-Faqr* or 'Spiritual Poverty,'" *Studies in Comparative Religion* (Winter 1973), 16–20, http://kataragama.org/al-faqr.htm (accessed February 10, 2010).

19. Ibish, "Traditional Guilds," 6.

20. This also explains the fact that, though traditional craftsmen generally had adequate incomes, they did not amass significant wealth: "It is indeed interesting to note that, among those who had become large landowners [in Egypt] in the 19th century—perhaps the most significant sign of affluence at the time—we have not found a single shaykh of a guild." Gabriel Baer, *Egyptian Guilds in Modern Times* (Jerusalem: Israel Oriental Society, 1964), 74. But it is significant that if a particular *shaykh* or master craftsman happened to amass wealth, it was frequently donated to Islamic educational or religious institutions, such as a *madrasa* or a *zawiyah*.

21. This linkage does not mean that books articulating Islamic metaphysics and the sciences of nature are necessary before Islamic art can be produced. This is because of the importance of the oral tradition in Islam; metaphysics and the spiritual significance of nature do not have to be articulated in books to be inwardly realized. Many Islamic guilds trace their spiritual lineage back to 'Ali, the cousin of the Prophet, or to the Prophet himself.

22. For a detailed treatment of this issue, see Waleed El-Ansary, "The Spiritual Significance of *Jihad* in the Islamic Approach to Markets and the Environment," dissertation, Department of Human Sciences, George Washington University, Washington, DC, 2006.

23. See, e.g., Seyyed Hossein Nasr, *Science and Civilization in Islam* (New York: Barnes & Noble Books, 1992).

24. See Seyyed Hossein Nasr, "Civilizational Dialog and the Islamic World," http://www.islamonline.net/english/Contemporary/2004/08/article01c.shtml (accessed November 22, 2009).

25. Adam Smith as cited in E.F. Schumacher, *This I Believe* (Foxhole, Dartington: Green Books, 1997), 99–100.

26. For an excellent survey of classical and neoclassical approaches to work in the history of economic thought, see Ugo Pagano, *Work and Welfare in Economic Theory* (Oxford: Basil Blackwell, 1985).

27. Some economists adopt this position implicitly by acknowledging the validity of religious beliefs on one hand and employing the neoclassical approach to work as forgone leisure on the other. On the latter point, see, e.g., Pagano, *Work and Welfare,* 111–15.

28. René Guénon maintains that unity implies qualitative differences that are spiritually integrated, whereas uniformity implies a quantitative aggregate involving division and conflict with no lasting basis for integration. See René Guénon, *The Reign of Quantity and the Signs of the Times* (Ghent: Sophia Perennis et Universalis, 2001). This is consistent with McIntyre's argument that philosophical ethics is ultimately reducible to the way of Aristotle and the way of Nietzsche.

29. See, e.g., E.F. Schumacher, *Small Is Beautiful: Economics as if People Mattered* (New York: Harper & Row, 1989); Neil Postman, *Technopoly: The Surrender of Culture to Technology* (New York: Vintage Books, 1992); Pagano, *Work and Welfare*; and Waleed El-Ansary, "The Traditionalist Critique of Industrial Capitalism," *Sophia*, vol. 12, no. 1 (Summer 2006).

30. See Pagano, *Work and Welfare,* especially chapter 1. For a useful survey of neoclassical counterarguments and the corresponding rebuttal, see Louis Putterman, *Division of Labor and Welfare: An Introduction to Economic Systems* (Oxford: Oxford University Press, 1990), chapter 4. Some of the literature on workers' self-management is perhaps closest to the Islamic perspective, though the former rarely proposes religious solutions or critiques the secular sciences' nature. In any case, one cannot justify the deskilling of work in efficiency terms if it renders preferences internally consistent, since efficiency would have no coherent goal as its basis. See El-Ansary, "Spiritual Significance."

31. See Mark Lutz and Kenneth Lux, *The Challenge of Humanistic Economics* (Menlo Park, CA: The Benjamin/Cummings Publishing Company, 1979), chapter 8.

32. Rama Coomaraswamy, "Traditional Economics and Liberation Theology," in Seyyed Hossein Nasr, ed., *In Quest of the Sacred* (Oakton, VA: The Foundation for Traditional Studies, 1987). Roger Sworder also provides a remarkable overview of the traditional critique of industrial production processes in "The Desacralization of Work," in Harry Oldmeadow, ed., *The Betrayal of Tradition: Essays on the Spiritual Crisis of Modernity* (Bloomington, IN: World Wisdom, 2005), 183–216.

33. See Michael Novak, *The Spirit of Democratic Capitalism* (New York: Simon and Schuster, 1982).

34. Novak, *Democratic Capitalism,* 24. For an important Muslim response to Novak from a critical point of view that does not enter the debate over production processes, see, e.g., Muhammad Abdul Rauf, *A Muslim's Reflections on Democratic Capitalism* (Washington, DC: American Enterprise Institute, 1984).

35. As Schumacher observes, "A great part of the modern neurosis may be due to this very fact: the lack of dignifying work in industrial society; for the human being, defined by Thomas Aquinas as a being with brains and hands, enjoys nothing more than to be creatively, usefully, productively engaged with both his hands and his brains." E.F. Schumacher, *Small Is Beautiful*, 122. Schumacher's lectures on art in *Not by Bread Alone: Lectures by E.F. Schumacher* (Bloomington, IN: World Wisdom Books, forthcoming) also definitively reject Novak's thesis, as do the works of Eric Gill and A.K. Coomaraswamy.

36. He states:

> Attempts which, in antiquity and in the Middle Ages, came nearest to mechanical inventions were those that served chiefly for amusement and were regarded as curiosities and thus as things which became legitimate by very reason of their exceptional character. The ancients were not like feckless children who handle anything within reach, but on the contrary like men of ripe judgment who avoid certain orders of possibilities the disasterous consequences of which they foresee.

Frithjof Schuon, *Castes and Races* (Middlesex: Perennial Books, 1982), 22, fn. 10. According to this argument, "machines kill not only the soul of the worker, but the soul as such," and so also the soul of the capitalist; also "the crafts by their human and spiritual quality prevent this gross alternative" (Schuon, *Castes and Races*, 20). Obviously, changing the pattern of ownership from the individual to the collectivity does nothing to correct such problems.

37. Schuon, *Castes and Races*, 21–22.

38. We examine this issue in Waleed El-Ansary, "The Economics of Terrorism: How Bin Laden Is Changing the Rules of the Game," in Joseph Lumbard, ed., *Islam, Fundamentalism, and the Betrayal of Tradition: Essays by Western Muslim Scholars* (Bloomington, IN: World Wisdom Books, 2004).

39. John Gray, *Al Qaeda and What It Means to Be Modern* (New York: The New Press), 2.

40. Ghazi bin Muhammad, *The Sacred Origin of Sports and Culture* (Louisville, KY: Fons Vitae, 1998), 36–37. He provides a concise but penetrating analysis of these issues in the section, "What Is Culture?"

41. Sato, "The Clash of Civilizations: A View from Japan."

42. Other empirical studies of conflicts between 1950 and 1992 show that "traditional realist influences such as contiguity, alliances, and relative power, and liberal influences of joint democracy and interdependence, provide a much better account of interstate conflict [than Huntington's thesis]." Bruce M. Russett, John R. Oneal, and Michaelene Cox, "Clash of Civilizations, or Realism and Liberalism Déjà Vu? Some Evidence," *Journal of Peace Research*, vol. 37, no. 5 (September 2000), 583. Also see Manus I. Midlarsky, "Democracy and Islam: Implications for Civilizational Conflict and the Democratic Peace," *International Studies Quarterly*, vol. 42, no. 3 (1998), 485–511.

43. Pippa Norris and Ronald Inglehart, "Islam and the West: Testing the 'Clash of Civilizations' Thesis," John F. Kennedy School of Government, Harvard University, April 2002, http://www.hks.harvard.edu/fs/pnorris/Acrobat/Clash%20of%20Civilization.pdf.

44. For a critical review of the literature, see, e.g., Seyyed Vali Nasr, *Islamization of Knowledge: A Critical Overview*, International Institute of Islamic Thought Occasional Paper 17 (Islamabad: International Institute of Islamic Thought, 1992), and his "Whither Islamic Economics?" *Islamic Quarterly*, vol. 30, no. 4 (1986), 211–20. For an earlier survey of the literature, see Muhammad Nejatullah Siddiqi, *Muslim Economic Thinking: A Survey of Contemporary Literature* (Leicester: The Islamic Foundation, 1981). For a more recent study of

the Islamic economic thought of six Muslim thinkers, see Mohamed Aslam Haneef, *Contemporary Islamic Economic Thought: A Selected Comparative Analysis* (Kuala Lumpur: Ikraq, 1995). Even Muhammad Baqir al-Sadr, the renowned Muslim philosopher and author of *Iqtisaduna* (Our Economics), does not discuss Islamic production processes. See Muhammad Baqir al-Sadr, *Iqtisaduna* (Tehran: World Organization for Islamic Services, 1994).

45. See, e.g., Timur Kuran, *Islam and Mammon: The Economic Predicaments of Islamism* (Princeton, NJ: Princeton University Press, 2004).

46. Schumacher, *This I Believe*, 99.

47. See, e.g., part 3 of Schumacher, *Small Is Beautiful*.

48. In addition to the relevant works previously cited in this chapter, see the monumental compilation of volumes in Ali Goma'a, ed., *Takshif al-Turath al-Islami al-Iqtisadi [Revealing the Islamic Economic Heritage]* (Cairo: International Institute of Islamic Thought, 1997).

49. The modern world "has been shaped by its metaphysics, which has shaped its education, which in turn has brought forth its science and technology." Schumacher, *Small Is Beautiful*, 120.

50. Schumacher, *Small Is Beautiful*, 59.

51. Schuon, *Castes and Races*, 58.

52. Burckhardt suggests how to integrate traditional and contemporary technologies to accomplish this as follows:

> Here is the criterion which allows us to know whether the introduction of a certain mechanical tool will destroy the authenticity of a traditional art; all that confers form on objects must be reserved to manual work. Thus, for example, one may admit that a woodcarver might cut his cedar planks with a mechanical saw, but not that he might carve their ornamentation with a countersink punch. Also, it is relatively indifferent, in the art of the rug, whether a certain color be obtained by chemical dye or plant dye, provided that it has the desired tone and stability, leaving aside the very particular charm which dwells in the slight variation of hue proper to plant dyes. For a final example, we will mention the case of the potter who uses, without prejudice to his work, a kiln of modern construction.

Jean-Louis Michon, "Titus Burckhardt and the Sense of Beauty," *Sophia*, vol. 5, no. 2 (1999), 130.

53. See, e.g., Jean-Louis Michon, "Education in the Traditional Arts and Crafts and the Cultural Heritage of Islam," in Seyyed Hossein Nasr, ed., *Philosophy, Literature, and Fine Arts* (Jeddah: King Abdulaziz University, 1982), 49–62.

54. Ibid., 57.

55. Schuon, *Castes and Races*, 58.

56. Ibid., 79.

57. Ibn Khaldun was the renowned fourteenth century Muslim scholar famous for the *Muqaddimah*, an introduction to his book of universal history. For an excellent survey and critical analysis of various views on the withering of the Islamic scientific tradition, see Muzaffar Iqbal, *Islam and Science*, especially chapter 5.

58. He states that

> the governing classes (in the Muslim world) took to Western culture and its attractions with enthusiasm. They were the ones whose sons were educated in Western schools and who set the cultural pace for everyone else in society. The Western-

educated minority became the partisans of Westernization: they began to dress like Westerners, to talk with Western ideas, to yearn for Western ways of life. The intoxicating effects of Western civilization now began working on the minds of the Westernized minority in the Islamic world. They clamored for the demolition of Islamic civilization in the name of progress, which was identified with Western civilization.

Victor Danner, *The Islamic Tradition: An Introduction* (Amity, NY: Amity House, 1988). The final chapter, "The Contemporary Muslim World," provides an exceptional analysis of several arguments discussed in the present chapter.

59. Although we recognize that modern military technology is currently necessary for defense, this does not mean that industrial technology should be deployed throughout the economy, though it is exceedingly difficult to separate such applications.

60. Thomas C. Schelling, *Micromotives and Macrobehavior* (New York: Norton, 1978).

61. Schumacher, *Small Is Beautiful*, 248–49.

62. See Nasr, "Civilizational Dialog."

7

Human Rights
and Islamic Reform

Reza Eslami-Somea

S ome Muslim scholars have vigorously argued that traditional religious thought in Islam is not merely traditional, but immutable, and
many faithful Muslims turn to traditional religious ideas to deal with
both individual difficulties and current social questions. This line of thinking assumes that the historical framework from which traditional Muslim
thought arose is applicable to our modern lives without serious qualifica-
tion. This assumption should not go unchallenged. One needs to pause to
reflect whether a historical position on law, philosophy, or theology can
respond to the questions of the modern era. Sociological, economic, and
political circumstances in every community may change, rapidly or progressively. Every society faces new and unprecedented questions and problems that need contemporary solutions. Applying the historical *shari'ah* as
a unified body of law without considering a society's contemporary needs
would create severe problems and hardships and lead to ambiguity in both
public life and the legal system.[1] The conflict between *shari'ah* and modern
human rights standards is particularly serious in the area of international
law regarding discrimination against women and religious minorities.[2]

Early Muslim jurists developed their discourses on *shari'ah* from two
fundamental sources of Islam: the Qur'an and *sunnah* (the Prophet's traditions and patterns of behavior).[3] *Shari'ah* took shape as a comprehensive
legal and ethical system by the mid-third century of Islamic history.[4] But
jurists engaged in these discourses never claimed that the laws were to
be divine. As a normative tradition, it was rather a process of human interpretation of, and legal deviation from, the scriptures within historical
time.[5] In other words, *shari'ah* is not the whole of Islam, but an analysis of

127

its fundamental sources as understood in a particular historical, legal, and theological context. Thus, it should be possible for contemporary Muslim jurists to undertake a similar process of interpretation and application of the sources in the present historical context, and to develop an alternative Islamic legal discourse, such as a human rights law, which is very much appropriate for today. Only then would Islamic law offer adequate solutions to resolve the problems and hardships facing Muslim societies in the modern era.[6]

Religious reformers have long been concerned about the inability of *shari'ah* to cope with the needs of contemporary Muslim societies or offer suitable solutions;[7] the movement for the reconstruction of *shari'ah* has been present almost since the construction of *shari'ah* itself. In the establishment of Muslim nation-states, modern technologies of communication, and cross-cultural dialogues, the concept of religious reformism has been greatly elaborated upon, as Muslim reformers and traditional jurists have debated how to advance a more rational discourse on this issue.[8]

Some demanded the establishment of a *shari'ah* state and the total application of *shari'ah* to public as well as private life. Ibn Taymiyya, a thirteenth-century scholar, maintained that the state and religion should be inseparable, and that the establishment of *shari'ah* as a model of the state was the only answer to the problems of Muslim societies.[9] Ideas on the *shari'ah* state and Islamic resurgence, as An-Na'im puts it, "had a significant impact through their acceptance and propagation by the eighteenth-century movements of Muhammed ibn Abd al-Wahab in Arabia and Shah Wali Allah in India."[10] Recent proponents of applying *shari'ah*, such as Maulana Mawdudi, were influenced by Ibn Taymiyya's ideas as well.[11]

Contemporary Muslim scholars have critiqued their own societies in lagging behind in science and technology compared to Western states. They have stressed the need to reconstruct religious thought for the Islamic *ummah*—the broader community—and have proposed several theories and methods by which to remedy the shortcomings and problems of religious society.[12] These theories reflect a variety of opinions among Islamic thinkers and differ only in how they identify the problems of society.[13] But due to the fundamental social changes that the modern world has brought, a profound question confronts all religious thought and Muslim reformists more acutely: whether and how the idea of change can be reconciled with the concept of the eternal, which religious scholars advocate. A Muslim reformist must explain why, if Islam is of divine origin, there should be any need to change it—and what, if anything, is subject to revision.[14]

Muslim thinkers have taken a range of stances on the question of change in Islam. Some emphasize the evolution of *shari'ah* itself as evidence that change can occur. Others focus their attention on institutions, economic systems, political reform, or cultural barriers. Some have eagerly sought to change almost everything, omitting whatever they deem inappropriate and including whatever seems convenient.[15] Some thinkers have argued for the "reawakening and unity of Muslims," for going "back to roots,"[16] and for "try[ing] the neglected sources."[17] Still others, aware that the problems of Islamic reform are not only legal, and that a few changes in *shari'ah* would not bring forth solutions, have hoped to free religion from tribal impurities to lead society toward a dynamic culture, progress, and social justice.[18] They have concentrated on reconstructing Islamic philosophy to reformulate even basic concepts of reform.[19]

Along with Islamic reformism, modernism emerged in the wake of the political and cultural subjugation of Muslim societies to Western colonialism in the nineteenth century, and in response to social, economic, and political dysfunctions produced by modernization in the twentieth century.[20] In many ways, it was the Islamic equivalent of *la theologie nouvelle*, which sought to reform Catholicism in Europe and to bring the church into contact with the modern world.[21] According to Vali-Reza Nasr, "modernism initiated the criticism of traditional Islam and opened the door to the possibility of interpreting the religion based on a worldview alien to it."[22]

The modernist movement argued that Islam must be reconstructed to meet the challenges of modernity and sought solutions within the paradigms of philosophy, theology, sociology, and politics. In practice, the modernists separated Islam as a religion from Islam as a civilization or cultural system, declaring their loyalty to the first and dismissing the second under the assumption that Islamic civilization and culture had been weakened by colonialism.[23] Since the Constitutional Revolution (1906–11), religious thinkers and modernists in Iran also have attempted to reevaluate the validity of Islamic tradition and both reformulate and redefine certain religious doctrines and institutions in terms of the prevailing ideas of the time.[24]

However, opposition from the *ulama* and religious conservatives prevented Islamic modernism, as a movement of religious reform, from institutionalizing principles of change in religious thought and institutions in Muslim societies.[25] The *ulama*, whose education and orientation not only restricted them to traditional roles, but prevented them from even perceiving the problems, adhered to *shari'ah* as it was constructed and received. They saw *shari'ah*, first, as closely intertwined with all aspects of life, and second, as a comprehensive system containing all the solutions to man's and society's problems.[26] Autocratic governments also confronted the reformists, whose views they claimed endangered *shari'ah* as well as people's unity and national security.[27] As a result, religious reformists—and reformists in general—have attained little success or impact on their societies.

This essay argues that the religious reform movements failed at least in part because they were too focused on religion itself and on preserving society within the confines of religious traditions. Reform proposals lacked an epistemological understanding of fundamental concepts of institutional change; the proposals failed to deal effectively with the theoretical aspects of social and political difficulties in Muslim societies. One should not think of reforming society unless one completely has a grasp of the principles of change and their effect on individuals, communities, and institu-tions, as well as on the larger nation. The reformists, who were primarily religious leaders, could not distinguish between religion and religious knowledge, between eternal religion and the changing nature of religious knowledge, and more important, the demands of modernity. They looked for a solution from inside the religion, relying heavily on the limitations of their training in law, jurisprudence, and Qur'anic studies to formulate changes. They expected the religion, especially *shari'ah,* to answer all society's questions and be the source of reformation. That there were presuppositions and extrareligious issues to consider was absent from their theories. Without altering the traditional assumptions about *shari'ah* and its applicability to current times, the reconstruction of religion had to be ineffective.

It is crucial for religious reformers to examine religious sources within a historical context. Epistemologically, the reformer needs to consider every presupposition and the extrareligious issues that impinge on his or her thought. A modern reformist, then, should undertake, as the early Muslim jurists did, a process of understanding, interpreting, and applying the sources within the context of the present to develop alternative religious knowledge in any areas, such as human rights law. Only in this way can the religious thinker appreciate the impact of time enough to make the religion more compatible with modern life.

The Expansion and Contraction of Religious Knowledge

The theory of the expansion and contraction of religious knowledge was recently asserted by Dr. Abdolkarim Soroush of Iran.[28] Originally inspired by epistemological studies, it considers the problems of Muslim societies from different perspectives, trying to reconcile change with immutability—that is, modernity with religion—which is the main point of modern religious reformism. However, the theory's unique characteristics lead to different conclusions from those of other religious reform efforts.[29]

Soroush positions himself within a broader project of Islamic reform-ism in the modern world. He accepts the inevitably changing character of the modern world, but his solution does not aim at the reconstruction of Islam. For Soroush, "Islam is unchanging. Any attempt to reconstruct Islam is both futile and illusory. It is not Islam that must change, but the human understanding of Islam."[30] The religion is divinely sent and ab-solutely tied to its origins. Nevertheless, to be understood, it is bound to pass through the channel of human cognitive faculties operating in the complex setting of human social relations.[31] Thus, one cannot attribute sa-credness and completeness to any interpretation of the religion; sacredness and absoluteness reside in the message, not in the human interpretation of it. According to Soroush, no understanding of religion can ever be sacred and ultimate, as every understanding is contingent upon the pursuit of a methodical, rational, and justifiable inquiry,[32] which always takes place within the broader context of human inquiry concerning the world of be-ing in general. Inquiry of faith is not isolated from discovering meaning of the universe.

Likewise, no text stands alone; every text needs to be placed with a context. "It is theory-laden, its interpretation is in flux," Soroush argues, "and presuppositions are here as actively at work as elsewhere in the field of understanding. Religious texts are no exception."[33] Therefore, any interpre-tation is subject to expansion and contraction according to prior assump-tions or inquiry. Because presuppositions are time-bound, they can, and do, change. Religious knowledge—or the science of religion, which is the product of understanding and comprehending—should exhibit continu-ous change as well.[34]

Further, according to Soroush, scholarly interpretations are affected by the intellectual worldview they operate in and their comprehension of other human sciences.[35] Religious knowledge and interpretation is in a continuous dialogue with other branches of human knowledge, changing and reforming over time.[36] Man-made science and knowledge should not replace religion, but the body of knowledge amassed by the human in-tellect should be a guide to refining and developing man's understanding of religion. Every religious scholar ought constantly to consult the text and the tradition in a reflective and self-critical manner, being constantly aware of the framework they take for granted as they try to make sense of religious texts. If needed, they must amend this framework to keep it rationally viable.[37]

Soroush rightly notes that one must not confine the scope of religion to the body of legal texts.[38] For at least a century, *shari'ah* has been em-phasized as the single definitive source for religious knowledge, but it is a small part of religious knowledge. Since its inception, it was subject to change, just like any other humanly constructed body of knowledge. The same holds true for the interpretation of religious texts, theology, and the rational methodology of jurisprudence.[39]

If the theory of expansion and contraction attempts to define a research program for religious reformism, then Muslim scholars need to revise their understanding of religion in the light of the many profound questions that modernity poses.[40] Soroush's reformist thinking is mainly concerned with justice, human rights, democracy, reasoning, minority rights, and freedom for all. The theory does not opt for the Islamization of knowledge or scientification of religion; it opts for accepting the humanization of religion, in the sense that it is affected—as are humans themselves—by factors both profane and sacred. This is the basic foundation on which the theory of expansion and contraction stands.[41]

Soroush's theory does not discuss overtly how it relates to the social sciences, but its principles and conclusions may be applied in any domain, including human rights law[42]—and viewed through the lens of human rights, the interpretative and implementation processes of *shari'ah* need to change. Even if such changes were to lead ultimately to a totally different *shari'ah* or legal system in Muslim society, however, the structure of the system could still be religiously acceptable. This is, indeed, what Muslim societies faced with mounting difficulties need.[43]

Conservative and Reformist Responses to Human Rights: The Debate within Islam

Islamic reformism has been active in the human rights domain, as the concept of rights has preoccupied contemporary Muslim thinkers. They highlight the theoretical and practical problems and shortcomings of *shari'ah* in this area, but, naturally, have sought Islamic solutions by rendering *shari'ah*-sanctioned rights more compatible with modern standards and values.[44] Conservative jurists and conservatives generally have challenged this effort. They deny that modern human rights theory can be universally applied in Islamic societies, on the grounds that it is derived from the evolution of Christianity and Western liberal theories, and thus, is not acceptable or applicable to other societies with different religious and cultural values and traditions.[45] Human values and the dignity of all humankind are honored in all religions and cultures,[46] but as the understandings of these values differ from culture to culture, conservatives (with the support of politicians in some cases) have argued that the idea of cultural relativity[47]—that is, that some values translate across cultures with relative ease—compromises the spirit of *shari'ah*.[48] Some Muslim jurists have argued that *shari'ah* laws are God-given and divine, suited to both the social and economic conditions of society and the physical and emotional differences between genders within the family.[49] Others emphasize general principles, such as human honor and the equality of genders in human dignity, in Islamic sources, concluding that *shari'ah* laws respect and guarantee human rights and freedoms in the public and private spheres of human life.[50] Some even conceive of *shari'ah* as affording more inclusive guarantees and protections for human rights than international human rights standards provide. Maulana Mawdudi, an Islamist and non-legally trained scholar, claims that *shari'ah* invented human rights and that international human rights law seeks to codify rules that *shari'ah* introduced in the seventh century.[51] Having presented his ideas on human rights, Mawdudi asserts that

> this is a brief sketch of those rights which 1,400 years ago Islam gave to man . . . . It refreshes and strengthens our faith in Islam when we realize that even in this modern age, which makes such loud claims of progress and enlightenment, the world has not been able to produce more just and equitable laws than those given 1,400 years ago.[52]

In attempting to redefine and Islamize the concept of human rights, conservatives ignore the structural aspects and critical points in the human rights debate—such as the equality of all human beings before the law[53]—or wrongly understand and interpret modern concepts of human rights and liberty. On the equality of human beings, Mawdudi stated that "Islam not only recognizes the principle of absolute equality between men irrespective of color, race, or nationality, it makes it an important reality."[54] He does not mention gender or religion.[55] Similarly, in classifying the most important human rights and civil liberties, Wafi simply limits the definition of civil liberty as the right to "conclude contracts, shoulder civil obligations, and to dispose freely of property."[56] This approach, as An-Na'im states, "is both simplistic and misleading,"[57] emphasizing the positive aspects of *shari'ah* and overlooking the controversial negative aspects. To be fair, certain Muslim feminists commit the same error, selecting certain verses of the Qur'an favoring the status of women while overlooking other verses and many traditions in *sunnah*, "failing to take into account the ways in which the parts they select have been interpreted by *shari'ah* jurists."[58] To undertake any reform in *shari'ah*, reformists need to be clear on what *shari'ah* is, rather that what it can or ought to be.[59]

Islamic conservatives have also grappled with human rights declarations, but they do so by subordinating international human rights provisions to Islamic laws and subjecting them to *shari'ah* qualifications. They reject the universality of human rights and, in most respects, fall far below the human rights standards guaranteed under the International Bill of Rights.[60] The conservative arguments are mostly derived from Islamic governments' political considerations, however, and clearly contrast with demands for democracy and human rights in Muslim states.[61]

For reformists, modern human rights theory does not contradict any specific religion or culture; rather, it underlines basic rights, values, and standards for all human beings, in every tradition. They believe that, under modern conditions, as Bielefeldt puts it, "a normative consensus across cultural and religious boundaries" is needed, and call upon Muslim societies to engage in cross-cultural dialogue on fundamental human rights and freedoms.[62] Tibi states that "in order to embrace human rights as entitlements, Muslims need to embrace cultural modernity."[63] He also notes a basic conflict between cultural modernity and premodern doctrines. An element of this conflict is the incompatibility of Islamic restrictions on the individual with the notion of individual freedom in cultural modernity.[64]

Aware that the existing normative framework of *shari'ah* contradicts international human rights standards, reformists took up the challenge. They emphasized the deficiencies of *shari'ah* in the field of human rights, and sought solutions within religion itself by reevaluating *shari'ah* laws and offering new interpretations of Islamic sources. They hoped that this could result in a change in the political and legal edifice, and the reconciliation of a religious human rights framework with modern human rights theory. They also stressed the original meaning of *shari'ah* as a path or guide, rather than a detailed legal code. Al-Ashmawy contends that *shari'ah* does not form a comprehensive legal system; rather, it consists mainly of general religious and ethical principles, such as respect between genders and tolerance toward minorities.[65] Mahmasani also states that particular legal instructions in *shari'ah* "often dominated the general principles, and, with repeated imitation, took a rigid and formalistic taint alien to the original substance."[66]

Taking their cues from the great social and political changes in modern societies, Islamic reformists demanded the recognition of human rights as an entitlement of all human beings. They considered human dignity to be an essential part of Qur'anic teaching and emphasized, in their promotion of human rights, the role of *ijtihad*[67] in changing *shari'ah* laws.[68] They emphasized the nation, citizens, and human rights rather than the religious community and duties of individuals, which helped constitutional movements in the Middle East at the turn of the twentieth century in their struggle against despotic rule. Shaikh Muhammad Abduh, a prominent reformer of the late nineteenth century, advocated constitutionalism and argued that human rights "must be translated into rights provisions of national constitutions in order to afford individuals effective legal guarantees for the rights involved."[69] The Tunisian scholar Mohammed Talbi demands full recognition of freedom of religion and conscience beyond the *shari'ah* concept of limited tolerance. He also argues against *shari'ah* corporal punishments, as the ultimate goals underlying these punishments are justice and equality. He states that, "were it possible for us today to ensure a life of justice and equality in a different way, this would certainly be a way pointing in the same direction as the Qur'an does."[70] Some reformers, advocating a progressive reading of the Qur'an, *sunnah*, and early Islamic history, argue that the early jurists misinterpreted Islamic sources. In discussing women's rights, Fazlur Rahman states that "women's inferior status written into Islamic law . . . is by and large the result of prevailing social conditions rather than of the moral teachings of the Qur'an."[71]

The advocacy of democracy and civil liberties has become part of the campaigns of independent non-governmental organizations (NGOs) defending human rights throughout the Middle East and North Africa.[72] Many reformists reject the use of any religious platform, arguing for democratic government as the only legitimate government. Soroush opposes the formulation of an official Islamic political ideology that reduces religion to a political platform.[73] He does not identify democracy with a particular Western culture, but rather "considers democracy a form of government that is compatible with multiple political cultures, including Islamic ones."[74] For Soroush, unlike a *shari'ah* model of government, a democratic government does not compromise people's extrareligious rights. This study relates to his idea that democracy is the only form of government that guarantees human rights. In his view, Muslims and non-Muslims should enjoy equal rights, for both belong to the greater human family, in which faith cannot serve as a basis for rights.[75] Professor Abdullahi Ahmed An-Na'im moves these ideas forward, providing an Islamic solution to the question of human rights in *shari'ah*.

An-Na'im's Reform Methodology: Moving Outside Islam

Mahmoud Mohammed Taha, the leader of the Republican Brotherhood in Sudan, was executed in 1985 for his opposition to what he believed to be arbitrary and distorted applications of *shari'ah* in Sudan. He proposed another reform methodology that provided an alternative and modern conception of Islamic public law.[76] Taha's teachings were subsequently elaborated by Professor Abdullahi Ahmed An-Na'im, a scholar and disciple of Taha.[77] An-Na'im's position is based on the idea that Islamic sources point to two levels of the message of Islam: the Meccan (610–22 AD) and subsequent Medinan periods (622–32 AD).

The message of the Meccan period was described as the eternal and fundamental message of Islam, emphasizing the basic values of justice as well as the equality and inherent dignity of all human beings, regardless of gender, race, religion, or any innate characteristics.[78]After this earlier message was violently rejected, the message of the Medinan period was revealed and implemented. Practically speaking, the Medinan period consisted of an established community that abided by a rule of law and was governed by consensus building.[79] An Na'aim argues that the public law of *shari'ah* was developed more according to the Medinan period than the Meccan period, as in the first century of Islam, in the hope of establishing a comprehensive legal system, the founding jurists undertook a process of abrogation (*naskh*) of certain scriptural texts to reconcile the duplication and inconsistencies that arose.[80] Taha, however, believed that *naskh* could not be permanent, since otherwise "there would be no point in having revealed the earlier texts."[81] He maintained that *naskh* was an essentially logical and necessary process of implementing the appropriate texts and postponing the implementation of others until the right circumstances for their implementation should arise.[82] As Medinan conditions no longer existed, Taha posited, Muslims should return to the original message of the Mecca period, and the basis of *shari'ah* should be gradually moved accordingly, from the texts of the Medinan to the earlier Meccan period.[83] Such an evolutionary principle of interpretation would reverse *naskh*, thereby enshrining those texts which were abrogated in the past into current law and abrogating texts which have been enacted as *shari'ah*.[84] The new body of law would be the modern *shari'ah*.

An-Na'im examines Taha's theory within the domain of public law, constitutional order, criminal justice, international relations, and human rights, seeking to reconcile the modern version of *shari'ah* with international human rights standards. His reform methodology appears to be a practical and practicable model, offering an Islamic rationale for religious reform in the public domain, harmonizing the public law aspects of *shari'ah* with international human rights concepts,[85] and formulating a modern idea of Islamic public law that deals with the real hardships of Muslim societies.[86] The theory is a very important contribution to reformist efforts in the modern era. But it, too, seeks a solution from inside the religious tradition and therefore neglects extrareligious issues and values as they are defined in Soroush's theory. It hardly challenges the theology of religion in this respect, and modifies only the methodology in constructing the same *shari'ah* that has always existed.[87] Moreover, in applying the theory to criminal justice, An-Na'im confines the theory to non-*hudud* punishments,[88] with the exception of apostasy.[89] Although he demands clear and restrictive definitions for applying *hudud* punishments,[90] he seems "committed to the proposition that public law in Muslim countries should be based on Islam."[91] The theory, therefore, fails to be comprehensive and deviates from its goal of shifting away from the Medinan-period texts to Meccan-period texts. The subject of *hudud* punishments is both contentious in Islamic juristic discourses and incompatible with the international human rights standards with which An-Na'im attempts to reconcile *shari'ah*. *Hudud* punishments are severe and have been questioned by the international human rights community, and excluding them from the main theory does not solve the criminal justice problems in Muslim societies.[92]

Also, as the theory confines itself only to public law, other areas in *shari'ah*, such as family law, need to be examined.[93] In practice, most Muslim countries, facing the theoretical and practical problems of *shari'ah* laws on the one hand and the legally undetermined views of reformists on the other, have adopted a pragmatic solution in their legal systems.[94] They have reaffirmed *shari'ah* laws in the private sphere with some reforms in family law to improve women's family and public rights.[95] However, they have distanced themselves from *shari'ah* criminal law. Nowadays only a few Muslim countries apply *hudud* punishments.[96] Joseph Schact writes that "there is a strong tendency [in Muslim countries] to restrict the applicability of *hadd* punishment as much as possible."[97] Certain human rights and freedoms are also mentioned in the constitutions of most Muslim states, which guarantee some basic human rights standards, such as the equality of all citizens before the law. But these rights are not fully observed.[98] In fact, the notions of constitutionalism and democratic structure of government, as Bielefeldt notes, "are still missing or poorly developed in many Muslim countries."[99]

Many legal scholars welcome the reforms mentioned above. There appears to be increasing demand for democratic political reforms, constitutionalism, and international human rights standards in the legal system.[100] However, due to fundamental and explicit Qur'anic injunctions and their authoritative traditional interpretations, the efficiency of these modifications and adjustments remains limited. This constrains reform efforts to pragmatic solutions to specific problems in Islamic law, solutions that are temporary, short-term remedies. They do not address conceptual and theoretical problems, nor do they provide structural support for major legal reforms. The fundamental reform in legal structures, principles, and standards that is needed to properly enforce universal norms and standards of human rights law cannot be achieved within the current parameters of legal systems. The contradictions between *shari'ah* as it is currently under-stood and universal human rights norms cannot be avoided. Any claim about *shari'ah* consistency with modern human rights law would be, legally speaking, problematic in theory and practice.

On the other hand, a solution that takes in extrareligious considerations must still win the support of Muslims. Merely denying *shari'ah* laws in human rights, or promoting universal human rights laws, would not have legitimacy among scholars and the faithful. The denial of *shari'ah* standards from a secular perspective only brings friction to a tradition, because as An-Na'im notes, "secularism is not an Islamic response to the challenges facing Muslim societies."[101] Politically, some conservatives believe that promoting international human rights is really only a tool for Western powers to intervene in Muslim countries' internal affairs and weaken their religious and cultural beliefs.[102] From an Islamic perspective, any reform must be both sufficient and legitimate within the tradition: sufficient in that it could provide solutions for human rights problems with *shari'ah* and legitimate in that it is based on Islamic sources and criteria.[103] The interpretations of the scriptural imperatives of Islam must be considered as valid and appropriate for application today in Muslim societies.[104]

An extrareligious set of reforms in legal systems and human rights law that also has legitimacy within Islam could only be achieved through broader religious and cultural initiatives based on cross-cultural founda-tions and work among members of societies with different beliefs and backgrounds.[105] Cultural reform would establish the appropriate grounds to address *shari'ah* restrictions and deficiencies in private and public sub-jects, as well as the possibility of a new interpretation of religious sources that is more compatible with human rights. Only religious dialogue among people of different convictions—especially scholars and intellectuals—could lead to a different and modern outcome that Muslims could re-gard as acceptable and legitimate.[106] It may result in a different outlook on political structure and on people's demand for constitutional democracy and guarantees of fundamental rights and freedoms. It also provides a fo-rum to promote the equality of all human beings, not only in dignity and honor, but in rights and liberties as well. That is what makes the Muslim community a pluralistic society where people are considered equal citizens, enjoying basic rights and freedoms. The key to this, as An-Na'im states, is "to convince Muslims that the other person with whom they must identify and accept as their equal in human dignity and rights includes all other human beings, regardless of gender and religion."[107]

Reformists need to begin by directing their energy toward democratiz-ing political structures, implementing fundamental human rights, and protecting freedoms for all, not by modifying *shari'ah*. The problems facing reformists are structural, historical, political, and economic, not just religious. Contemporary Muslim scholars must also discuss the legal foundations of international human rights and their parallels in local cultures. In addition, NGOs could highlight those *shari'ah* laws that legitimize human rights violations—the laws that authorities invoke to deny or restrict individuals' rights and freedoms.

Traditional mechanisms of reform within the framework of *shari'ah* are limited and inadequate for achieving the necessary degree of change. They are limited by the restrictions of *shari'ah* principles and, as An-Na'im notes, "will create extremely serious problems in practice."[108] Any approach to human rights must first seek to establish and demonstrate how basic human rights derive from, and are directly attributable to, fundamental characteristics of the human personality, rather than Western cultural values. This approach should locate the objective foundations of human rights in reason, human dignity, and natural law. From this perspective, human rights are not grounded in religious sources and are not a religious matter; they are extrareligious, comprising values that deal with all human beings equally, whether they are believers or not.

Such an argument relates to both An-Na'im's and Soroush's theories. An-Na'im's reform methodology holds that pragmatic solutions and traditional reform techniques within the limits of *shari'ah* would only generate theoretical and practical problems. Scholars should then "call for the establishment of a new principle of interpretation"[109] to make *shari'ah* more compatible with international human rights norms and standards. This argument coincides with Soroush's theory that any interpretation of *shari'ah* is bound by the presuppositions in the scholar's intellectual worldview— and therefore extrareligious factors should be considered as well.

Historically, practical problems have almost always been the cause and motive behind reformist movements; the direction of religious reformism has mostly been from the inside toward the outside, from legal deficiencies toward the realities of the time, toward a harmony between religion and the modern world. A dialogue between what is internal and external to religion could result in the compatibility of *shari'ah* principles with international human rights standards. Such a dialogue cannot take place within *shari'ah* to create a modern version of *shari'ah*, for it does not relate to *shari'ah* at all; it is a rational argument, providing the intellectual foundations for Islamic thought in the field of human rights.

Notions such as justice, freedom, and human rights are generally defined on rational and intellectual grounds and cannot be determined by religious criteria and qualifications alone. Fundamental human rights are intended to develop and fully realize the human personality, which is thought to be the foundation of human dignity, with all the responsibilities that this implies. This distinguishes humankind from all other creatures. The human intellect and will are indispensable, and liberty is their most eminent characteristic, the very foundation of human dignity and responsibility. Human rights are derived from, and are directly attributed to, the fundamental characteristics of human personality.[110] However, human rights are also political and legal standards. As a political means of recognizing human dignity in a legally binding structure, they have to do with political justice, establishing the normative criteria as "genuinely modern safeguards to facilitate human life with dignity. To provide such safeguards is the purpose of human rights."[111]

The role of extrareligious issues in interpreting religious sources must be rethought because it may contribute toward understanding what is internal and what is external to religion.[112] In the Islamic context, it could render *shari'ah* principles more compatible with modern realities. Every religion has, in one way or another, contributed to the idea of rights, raising the value of mankind and merit of human honor and dignity.[113] Any religious society can prepare its own laws and legal system based on these general principles as well as its collective rationale, wisdom, and human nature in its own historical context.[114] Human rights law requires an adequate intellectual framework as well. Muslim scholars should acknowledge human rights as individual entitlements, promoting the idea of equality of all individuals before the law, regardless of gender, religion, or any other trait, for human rights can be applied only in a society where the concept of the individual has been introduced and is well situated in its cultural patterns—in other words, a civil and plural society that is truly democratic, regardless of religion.

Notes

1. Abdullahi Ahmed An-Na'im, *Toward an Islamic Reformation* (Syracuse: Syracuse University Press, 1996), 1–2. Muhammed S. al-Ashmawi also states that the application of *shari'ah* is not desirable because this would only contribute to establishing totalitarian regimes. See Bassam Tibi, "Islamic Law/Shari'a, Human Rights, Universal Morality, and International Relations," *Human Rights Quarterly,* vol. 16, no. 2 (1994), 279.

2. See Ishtiaq Ahmad, "Abdullahi An-Na'im on Constitutional and Human Rights Issues," in Tore Lindholm and Kari Vogt, eds., *Islamic Law Reform and Human Rights, Challenges and Rejoinders* (Oslo: Nordic Human Rights, 1993), 65.

3. In the Shi'ite school of Islam, *sunnah* also includes the traditions and sayings of the Prophet's twelve successors, known as *imams*. See Hassan S. Amin, *Islamic Law and Its Implications for Modern World* (Glasgow: Billing & Sons, 1989), 31–41; William Montgomery Watt, *Islamic Philosophy and Theology* (Edinburgh: Edinburgh University Press, 1985), 122–28.

4.   A. Ahmed An-Na'im, "Human Rights in the Muslim World: Socio-Political Conditions and Scriptural Imperatives: A Preliminary Inquiry," *Harvard Human Rights Journal*, vol. 3 (1990), 17–19; An-Na'im, *Toward an Islamic Reformation*, 29–31; Joseph Schacht, *An Introduction to Islamic Law* (Oxford: Clarendon, 1964), 28–68; Noel James Coulson, *A History of Islamic Law* (Edinburgh: Edinburgh University Press, 1964), 9–74; Fazlur Rahman, *Islam*, 2nd ed. (Chicago: University of Chicago Press, 1979), 53–59, 79.

5.   An-Na'im, "Human Rights in the Muslim World," 21; An-Naim, *Toward an Islamic Reformation*, 185. See also D. Brown, *Rethinking Tradition in Modern Islamic Thought* (Cambridge: Cambridge University Press, 1996).

6.   Sayeed argues that the response of sociopolitical Islam to modern necessities, and Western challenges in particular, "could be more effective if there were a systematic effort on the part of Muslim societies to reinterpret their values and traditions, and reorganize their political and economic institutions." Khalid Bin Sayeed, *Western Dominance and Political Islam, Challenge and Response* (New York: Oxford University Press, 1995), 1. See also An-Na'im, "Human Rights in the Muslim World," 17, and An-Naim, *Toward an Islamic Reformation*, 297–99.

7.   See generally Mohammed Arkoun, "The Concept of 'Islamic Reformism,'" in Tore Lindholm and Kari Vogt, eds., *Islamic Law Reform and Human Rights* (Oslo: Nordic Human Rights, 1993), 11–24.

8.   See Mohammed Arkoun, "The Concept of 'Islamic Reformism,'" in *Islamic Law Reform*; Vali-Reza Nasr, "Religious Modernism in the Arab World, India, and Iran: The Perils and Prospects of a Discourse," *The Muslim World*, vol. 83 (1993), 20–47; Seyyed Hossein Nasr, "Present Tendencies, Future Trends," in Marjorie Kelly, ed., *Islam, the Religious and Political Life of a World Community* (Westport, CT: Praeger, 1984).

9.   Ibn Taymiyya, *Al-Siyasa al-Shar'iyya fi Islah al-Ra'iy wa al-Ra'iyya*, ed. Muhammad Mubarak (Beirut: 1966). Translated by Omar Farrukh as *Ibn Taimyya on Public and Private Law in Islam*, in An-Na'im, *Toward an Islamic Reformation*, (Syracuse: Syracuse University Press, 1996), 36.

10. An-Na'im, *Toward an Islamic Reformation*, 37–38. See also John L. Esposito, *Islam and Politics*, 2nd ed. (Syracuse: Syracuse University Press, 1991), 33–36, and Rahman, *Islam*, 196–206.

11. Ishtiaq Ahmed, *The Concept of an Islamic State: Analysis of the Ideological Controversy in Pakistan* (New York: St. Martin's Press, 1987). See also Muhammad Asad, *Principles of State and Government in Islam* (Berkeley: University of California Press, 1961), 14–29. For the ideas of Hassan al-Turabi of Sudan, see John L. Esposito, "Sudan's Islamic Experiment," *The Muslim World*, vol. 76 (1986), 181; Khalid Duran, "The Centrifugal Forces of Religion in Sudanese Politics," *Orient*, vol. 26 (1985), 572, and An-Na'im, *Toward an Islamic Reformation*, 39–42.

12. An-Na'im notes that Islamic resurgence, in fact, seeks "to provide the Muslims with adequate answers from within their own tradition to the social, political, and economic problems facing Muslim societies." An Na'im, *Toward an Islamic Reformation*, 4. A prime champion revivalist in this spirit was Imam Abu Hamed Mohammed al-Ghazzali (1074–1128 AC), a great Islamic scholar and the author of *Kitab al-Ihya al-Ulum al-Din* (Reviving of Religious Knowledge). William M. Watt, *The Faith and Practice of al-Ghazali* (Chicago: Kazi, 1982). Ibn Taymiyya may also be considered a Muslim reformer for having challenged the rigidity of *taqlid* (the imitation and following of the jurists of a school of Islamic jurisprudence). He tried to restore *shari'ah* to its proper place and influence by advocating a

strict model of an Islamic state ruled by *shari'ah,* discussed below. See K.C. Wheare, *Modern Constitutions* (London: Oxford University Press, 1966), 139.

13. See generally John O. Voll, *Islam: Continuity and Change in the Modern World* (Boulder, CO: Westview Press, 1982); Aziz Ahmad, *Islamic Modernism in India and Pakistan, 1857–1964* (Oxford: Oxford University Press, 1967); and Edward Mortimer, *Faith and Power: The Politics of Islam* (New York: Vintage Books, 1982).

14. From the Islamic reformists' point of view, it seems that surrendering to the flux of change leaves little room for tradition and, thus, for religion; blind insistence on the fixity of a body of tradition and denial of the radical transformations that have actually occurred in the human mode of life would render religious life in today's changing world virtually impossible. Thus, Muslim reformists have espoused a wide range of opinions on a variety of subjects. See generally Bassam Tibi, *The Crisis of Modern Islam: A Pre-Industrial Culture in the Scientific-Technological Age,* trans. Judith von Sivers (Salt Lake City: University of Utah Press, 1988), and Nasr, "Present Tendencies, Future Trends," 94. Hourani writes of Abduh that "the key to his defense of Islam, indeed to all his thought about it, was a certain conception of true religion: a distinction between what was essential and unchanging in it and what was inessential and could be changed without damage." Albert Hourani, *Arabic Thought in the Liberal Age, 1798–1939,* 2nd ed. (New York: Cambridge University Press, 1983).

15. For them, the main measure of convenience has been to assess whether adding a new element or omitting a conventional one would add to the socioeconomic strength and viability of the religion. One can, therefore, see radical elements of socialism (the hope for social justice) or mild positivism (presenting religion as scientific) in the writings of such thinkers. Apparently, the presumption is that, to be viable, religion must have a say on every subject. In this vein, books have been written to show how the Qur'an and Islamic sayings have anticipated, for example, the Laplacian theory of the expansion of the universe, the human conquest of space, the importance of vitamins, and the hazards of microbial infections. There has also been emphasis on the formulation of Islamic psychology, sociology, economics, and other disciplines. See Hossein Kamaly, "The Theory of Expansion and Contraction of *Shari'a:* A Research Program for Islamic Revivalism (an Iranian Perspective)," unpublished paper, February 1995. For ideas and thoughts of Sayyid Qutb, Ali Abd al-Raziq, and Tariq al-Bishri, see Leonard Binder, *Islamic Liberalism: A Critique of Development Ideologies* (Chicago: University of Chicago Press, 1988), 128, 170, and 243, respectively. In the political domain, see also Ali Abd al-Raziq, *Al-Islam wa Usul al-Hukumah* [*Islam and the Foundations of Government*] (Beirut: Dar Makhahat al-Haya, 1966).

16. S. Jamal al-Din Asadabadi (Afghani) (1837–97) and Mohammed Abduh. They also emphasized the need to incorporate modern philosophical and scientific disciplines to show that Islam is not inconsistent with modernity. See Rahman, *Islam,* 216–17; An-Na'im, *Toward an Islamic Reformation,* 61. See also Nikki Keddie, *Jamal al-Din al-Afghani: A Political Biography* (Berkeley: University of California Press, 1972).

17. Other proposals include "find a brave inspired leader," "return to, or strict application of, Qur'an and *Sunna,*" and "the reaffirmation of the authenticity and uniqueness of the Qur'anic experience." See An Na'im, *Toward an Islamic Reformation,* 46–47, and John O. Voll, "Renewal and Reform in Islamic History: *Tajdid* and *Islah,*" in John L. Esposito, ed., *Voices of Resurgent Islam* (New York: Oxford University Press, 1983), 32–47.

18. Dr. Ali Shariati (1933–77). See generally Majid Khadduri, *Political Trends in the Arab World* (Baltimore: Johns Hopkins University Press, 1970), 64–65; Aharon Layish, "The Contribution of the Modernists to the Secularization of Islamic Law," *Middle Eastern*

Studies, vol. 14 (1978), 263; Fazlur Rahman, "Islamic Modernism: Its Scope, Methods, and Alternatives," *International Journal of Middle East Studies*, vol. 1 (1970), 319, 324–26.

19. Mohammed Iqbal (1877–1938) wrote his famous book, *The Reconstruction of Religious Thought in Islam* (Lahore: Institute of Islamic Culture, 1986). See also Rahman, *Islam*, 231, and Sayeed, *Western Dominance and Political Islam*, 156.

20. See generally Tibi, *Crisis of Modern Islam*; Mohammed Arkoun, *Pour une critique de la raison islamique* (Paris: Maisonneuve et Larose, 1984); Fazlur Rahman, *Islam and Modernity: Transformation of an Intellectual Tradition* (Chicago: University of Chicago Press, 1982); Hourani, *Arabic Thought*; Malcolm Kerr, *Islamic Reform* (Oxford: Oxford University Press, 1966); Hamid Enayat, *Modern Islamic Political Thought* (Austin: University of Texas Press, 1982).

21. L. Praamsma, *The Church in the Twentieth Century*, vol. 7 (St. Catherine, Ontario: Paideia Press, 1981).

22. Vali-Reza Nasr, "Religious Modernism," 36. See also Michael Walzer, *The Revolution of Saints: A Study in the Origins of Radical Politics* (Cambridge: Harvard University Press, 1965), 9–10.

23. For detailed accounts of characteristics and specifications of Islamic modernism, reformism, and revivalism, see Jacques Waardenburg, "Islam as a Vehicle of Protest," in Ernest Gellner, ed., *Islamic Dilemmas: Reformers, Nationalists, and Industrialization* (Berlin: Mouton Publishers, 1985), 22–49; Esposito, *Islam and Politics*, 32–59; Fazlur Rahman, "Revival and Reform in Islam," in P.M. Holt, Ann K.S. Lambton, and Bernard Lewis, eds., *The Cambridge History of Islam, Islamic Society, and Civilization*, vol. 2B (Cambridge: Cambridge University Press, reprint 1982), 632–56; Iqbal, *The Reconstruction of Religious Thought*; H.A.R. Gibb, *Modern Trends in Islam* (Chicago: University of Chicago Press, 1947); Charles C. Adams, *Islam and Modernism in Egypt* (New York: Russell and Russell, 1968); and Said Amir Arjomand, *The Shadow of God and the Hidden Imam: Religion, Political Order, and Social Change in Shi'ite Iran from the Beginning to 1890* (Chicago: University of Chicago Press, 1984). See also Munawir Sjad Zali, *Islam and Governmental System: Teachings, History, and the Reflections* (Jakarta: INIS, 1991), 31–143.

24. On the emergence of religious modernism in contemporary Iran and the work of Muslim reformists such as Ali Shariati (1933–77), Mahdi Bazargan (1907–95), and Murtadha Mutahhari (1920–79), see Mehrzad Boroujerdi, *The Iranian Intellectuals and the West: The Tormented Triumph of Nativism* (Syracuse: Syracuse University Press, 1996); Nasr, "Religious Modernism"; Yann Richard, "Shari'at Sangilaji: A Reformist Theologian of the Reza Shah Period," in Said Amir Arjomand, ed., *Authority and Political Culture in Shi'ism* (Albany: State University of New York Press, 1988), 159–77; Mangol Bayat-Philip, "Tradition and Change in Iranian Socio-Religious Thought," in Michael E. Bonine and Nikki R. Keddie, eds., *Modern Iran: The Dialectics of Continuity and Change* (Albany: SUNY Press, 1981); H.E. Chehabi, *Iranian Politics and Religious Modernism: The Liberation Movement of Iran under the Shah and Khomeini* (London: I.B. Tauris, 1990); W. Millward, "Aspects of Modernism in Shi'a Iran," *Studia Islamica*, vol. 37 (1973); Nikki R. Keddie, *Roots of Revolution* (New Haven, CT: Yale University Press, 1981); Said Amir Arjomand, *The Turban for the Crown* (Oxford: Oxford University Press, 1988); Ervand Abrahamian, *Iran between Two Revolutions* (Princeton, NJ: Princeton University Press, 1982); Shahrough Akhavi, *Religion and Politics in Contemporary Iran* (Albany: SUNY Press, 1980).

25. For some *ulama*, modernism threatens to break the universal sovereignty of religion and the monopoly of faith over absolute truth. It also could lead to secularism, advocating

privatization of faith and secularizing of society and culture. See Vali-Reza Nasr, "Religious Modernism," 34–35, 41–43.

26. See generally Hamid Enayat, *Modern Islamic Political Thought*; Mohammed Arkoun, *Pour une critique de la raison islamique*; Daryush Shayegan, *Qu'est ce qu'une revolution religieuse* (Paris: Les presses d'aujourd'hui, 1982); and Abdallah Larouni, *The Crisis of the Arab Intellectual: The Traditionalism or Historicism*, trans. Diamid Cammell (Berkeley: University of California Press, 1976).

27. Ann Elizabeth Mayer, "Universal Versus Islamic Human Rights: A Clash of Cultures or a Clash with a Construct?" *Michigan Journal of International Law*, vol. 15 (1994), 315–16, 319; Esposito, *Voices of Resurgent Islam*; E. Mayer, "Islamic Rights or Human Rights: An Iranian Dilemma," *Iranian Studies*, vol. 29 (1996), 280–82; and Fred Halliday, "Relativism and Universalism in Human Rights: The Case of the Islamic Middle East," *Political Studies*, vol. 43 (1995), 154.

28. This theory first appeared in 1988 in an Iranian periodical called *Keyhan Farhanghi* and sparked a controversy in Iranian intellectual circles. Abdolkarim Soroush, a leading moderate revisionist thinker of the Muslim world and prominent Iranian religious intellectual, was attacked by the conservative clergy, who accused him of skepticism and of corrupting the minds of the uninitiated. His theory was published in 1990. For a summary of this controversial debate, see Mehrzad Boroujerdi, "The Encounter of Post-Revolutionary Thought in Iran with Hegel, Heidegger, and Popper," in Serif Mardin, ed., *Cultural Transitions in the Middle East* (New York: E.J. Brill, 1994), 248–55.

29. See Abdolkarim Soroush, *Qabz va Bast-i Tiorik-i Shari'at* [The Theory of Expansion and Contraction of Religious Knowledge] (Tehran: Serat, 1990), 47–52.

30. Soroush, *Qabz va Bast*, 99. See also Abdolkarim Soroush, *Reason, Freedom, and Democracy in Islam: The Essential Writings of Abdulkarim Soroush*, ed. Mahmoud Sadri and Ahmad Sadri (Oxford: Oxford University Press, 2000); Hossein Kamaly, "The Theory of Expansion and Contraction"; Abdulkarim Soroush, "Evolution and Devolution of Religious Knowledge," lecture delivered at McGill University, Montreal, April 1995; Valla Vakili, *Debating Religion and Politics in Iran: The Political Thought of Abdulkarim Soroush* (New York: Council of Foreign Relations, 1996), 9–10; Mehrzad Boroujerdi, *The Iranian Intellectuals and the West: The Tormented Triumph of Nativism* (Syracuse: Syracuse University Press, 1996); and Forough Jahanbakhsh, *Islam, Democracy and Religious Modernism in Iran (1953–1997): From Bazargan to Soroush*, Ph.D. thesis, McGill University, 1997, 248.

31. Kamaly, "The Theory of Expansion and Contraction"; Soroush, *Qabz va Bast*, 243.

32. Kamaly, "The Theory of Expansion and Contraction"; Soroush, *Qabz va Bast*, 249; Abdolkarim Soroush, "Qabz va Bast dar Mizan-i Naqd va Bahs" [The Theory of Expansion and Contraction at the Level of Critique and Discussion], *Kiyan*, vol. 1, no. 2 (1991), 5.

33. Soroush, "Evolution and Devolution." See also Boroujerdi, "The Encounter of Post-Revolutionary Thought," 248–55.

34. Soroush argues that, since it is only through those presuppositions that one can hear the voice of revelation, religion is silent. Moreover, the interpretation of the text is social by nature and depends on the community of experts. It entails right and wrong, certain and dubious ideas. A wrong interpretation is as important as a right one, from the evolutionary point of view. See Soroush, "Evolution and Devolution"; Vakili, *Debating Religion and Politics*, 10–11; and Jahanbakhsh, *Islam, Democracy, and Religious Modernism*, 249–51.

35. Vakili, *Debating Religion and Politics*, 11.

36. The preceding arguments, as Soroush points out, can be briefly outlined as follows:
   1. Religion, or revelation for that matter, is silent.
   2. The science of religion is relative, that is, relative to presuppositions.
   3. The science of religion is age-bound, because the presuppositions themselves are time-bound.
   4. Revealed religion, itself, may be true and free of contradictions, but science of religion is not necessarily so.
   5. Religion may be perfect or comprehensive, but not the science of religion.
   6. It is understood that religion is divine; but the interpretation of religion is a human endeavor. See Soroush, *Qabz va Bast*, 278; Hossein Kamaly, "Theory of Expansion and Contraction," 98; and Jahanbakhsh, *Islam, Democracy, and Religious Modernism*, 249–50.

37. See Kamaly, "Theory of Expansion and Contraction," and Vakili, *Debating Religion and Politics*, 9–12.

38. Vakili, *Debating Religion and Politics*.

39. Abdolkarim Soroush also notes that what is eternal is the religion itself, not our understanding of it. Every man's religion is his understanding of the truth about religion, just as every man's science is his understanding of the truth about nature. See Soroush, *Qabz va Bast*, 346; Kamaly, "Theory of Expansion and Contraction."

40. Kamaly, "Theory of Expansion and Contraction."

41. Ibid.

42. Soroush champions democracy, pluralism, and human rights. He argues for reform in key social and political areas, and dismisses any attempts to formulate an official Islamic political ideology, for no single understanding of Islam is ever complete or final. See Vakili, *Debating Religion and Politics*, 7. See also Ziba Mir-Hosseini, *Islam and Gender: The Religious Debate in Contemporary Iran* (Princeton, NJ: Princeton University Press, 1999), 217–46.

43. Vakili, *Debating Religion and Politics in Iran*, 12.

44. Ahmad, "Abdullahi An-Na'im on Constitutional and Human Rights Issues," 62–63; Ann E. Mayer, *Islam and Human Rights, Tradition and Politics* (Boulder, CO: Westview Press, 1991), 52–57; John L. Esposito, *The Islamic Threat: Myth or Reality?* (New York: Oxford University Press, 1992).

45. See al-Sadiq al-Mahdi, "Islam—Society and Change," in *Voices of Resurgent Islam*, 231–32; Reza Afshari, "An Essay on Islamic Cultural Relativism in the Discourse of Human Rights," *Human Rights Quarterly*, vol. 16 (1994), 246–47, 249; Roger M. Savory, "Islam and Democracy: The Case of the Islamic Republic of Iran" in C.E. Bosworth, Charles Issawi, and R. Savory, eds., *The Islamic World from Classical to Modern Time, Essays in Honor of Bernard Lewis* (Princeton, NJ: Darwin Press, 1989), 826–27; Mayer, "Universal versus Islamic Human Rights," 319. Also generally Ahmed Farrag, "Human Rights and Liberties in Islam," in Jan Berting, Peter R. Baehr, J. Herman Burgers, Cees Flinterman, Barbara de Klerk, Rob Kroes, Cornelius A. van Minnen, and Koo VanderWal, eds., *Human Rights in a Pluralist World: Individuals and Collectivities* (Westport, CT: Meckler, 1990), 141.

46. Abdullahi Ahmed An-Na'im, ed., "Towards a Cross-Cultural Approach to Defining International Standards of Human Rights: The Meaning of Cruel, Inhuman or Degrading Treatment or Punishment," in *Human Rights in Cross-Cultural Perspectives, A Quest for Consensus* (Philadelphia: University of Pennsylvania Press, 1992), 4.

47. Bassam Tibi observes that the "legal notion within 'Islamic intellectual tradition' differs considerably from the European one" and that international law lacks "a substantive cultural consensus" needed for an international legal order. See Tibi, *Islam and the Cultural Accommodation of Social Change* (Boulder, CO: Westview Press, 1991), 61. It should be noted that Tibi, generally a secular scholar, does not primarily advocate cultural relativism, but mainly cultural pluralism within the emerging global civilization. See Afshari, "An Essay on Islamic Cultural Relativism," 249–50.

48. Ayatollah Mohammad Yazdi, then head of the Judiciary of Iran, said on March 10, 1995, during a Friday prayer service: "Who says that human rights devised by the West should be applied to the whole world? ... Some nations have their own cultures, some nations have their own religions, you cannot describe as human rights violations the issues which concern their religion and culture ... Islamic human rights differ from the Declaration of Human Rights. Islam has its own rules and regulations." See Mayer, *Islam and Human Rights, Tradition and Politics*, 294. In 1983, Iran's UN Ambassador, Sa'id Raja'i Khorasani, also proclaimed that the UDHR, "which represented a secular understanding of the Judeo-Christian tradition, could not be implemented by Muslims and did not accord with the system of values recognized by the Islamic Republic of Iran." Mayer, "Universal Versus Islamic Human Rights," 315–16.

49. Abul-A'la Mawdudi, *Human Rights in Islam*, 2nd ed., trans. Khurshid Ahmad (London: Islamic Foundation, 1986), 19, 23, 32; Muhammad Zafrullah Khan, *Islam and Human Rights*, 4th ed. (UK: Islamic International Publications, 1989), 36–59.

50. See J. Adams, "Mawdudi and the Islamic State" in *Voices of Resurgent Islam*, 99–133; Amyn B. Sajoo, "Islam and Human Rights: Congruence or Dichotomy?" *Temple International and Comparative Law Journal*, vol. 4 (1990), 25; A.K. Brohi, "Islam and Human Rights," *PLD Lahore*, vol. 28 (1976), 148–60; and A.K. Brohi, "The Nature of Islamic Law and the Concept of Human Rights," in International Commission of Jurists, Kuwait University, and Union of Arab Lawyers, *Human Rights in Islam, Report of a Seminar Held in Kuwait, December 1980* (International Commission of Jurists, 1982), 43–60.

51. Mawdudi, *Human Rights in Islam*, 9. On Mawdudi's views in this respect, see also An-Na'im, *Toward an Islamic Reformation*, 38–39; Heiner Bielefeldt, "Muslim Voices in Human Rights Debate," *Human Rights Quarterly*, vol. 17 (1995), 603, 614; Riffat Hassan, "On Human Rights and the Qur'anic Perspective," in Arlene Swidler, ed., *Human Rights in Religious Traditions* (New York: Pilgrim Press, 1982), 63. Also Sultanhussein Tabandeh, *A Muslim Commentary on the Universal Declaration of Human Rights* (London: F.T. Goulding, 1970), 1, 85; Farrag, "Human Rights and Liberties in Islam," 141; and Khan, *Islam and Human Rights*, 49.

52. Mawdudi, *Human Rights in Islam*.

53. See Hassan, "On Human Rights and the Qur'anic Perspective," 63.

54. Mawdudi, *Human Rights in Islam*, 21.

55. In contrast, article 2 of the Universal Declaration of Human Rights reads: "Everyone is entitled to all rights and freedoms set forth in this Declaration, without distinction of any kind, such as race, color, sex, language, religion, political or other opinion, national or social origins, property, birth or other status." The Universal Declaration of Human Rights (the UDHR), G. A. Res. 217A (III), U. N. GAOR Res. 71, UN Doc. A/810 (1948); See also Bielefeldt, "Muslim Voices," 603.

56. Ali abdel Wahid Wafi, "Human Rights in Islam," *Islamic Quarterly*, vol. 11 (1967), 64, 69.

57. An-Na'im, "Human Rights in the Muslim World," 22.

58. Ibid, 40.

59. Ibid.

60. Mayer, "Universal versus Islamic Human Rights," 324–25, 327–47; Mayer, *Islam and Human Rights, Tradition and Politics,* 24–27, 73, 76–77; Bielefeldt, "Muslim Voices in Human Rights Debate," 604–6; and Tibi, "Islamic Law, Human Rights, Universal Morality," 290–91.

61. The 1990 Cairo Declaration on Human Rights departs significantly from the Universal Declaration of Human Rights through the use of religious language and expressly links individual rights to *shari'ah.* See M.H.A. Reisman, "Some Reflections on Human Rights and Clerical Claims to Political Power," *Yale Journal of International Law,* vol. 19 (1994), 517.

62. Bielefeldt, "Muslim Voices," 606. See also S. Aldeeb Abu-Sahlieh, "Muslims and Human Rights: Challenges and Perspectives," in W. Schmale, ed., *Human Rights and Cultural Diversity* (Goldbach: Keip, 1993); and H. Patrick Glenn, *Legal Traditions of the World, Sustainable Diversity in Law* (Oxford: Oxford University Press, 2000), 193–96.

63. Tibi, "Islamic Law, Human Rights, Universal Morality," 298. Stressing cultural pluralism, Tibi notes that "we must place human rights in our globalized yet fragmented world." He adds that while there is a need for unity on human rights standards on an international level, implementing these rights takes place in a multicultural context that has to be accounted for (282–84). See also Tibi, "The Iranian Revolution and the Arabs: The Quest for Islamic Identity and Search for an Islamic System of Government," *Arab Studies Quarterly,* vol. 8 (1986), 37–42; R.J. Vincent, *Human Rights and International Relations* (Cambridge: Cambridge University Press, 1986), 99–105.

64. Tibi, "Islamic Law, Human Rights, Universal Morality," 290–91. See also Dale Eickelman, "Inside the Islamic Reformation," *Wilson Quarterly,* vol. 22 (1998), 80–89; Michael Fischer and Mehdi Abedi, *Debating Muslims: Cultural Dialogue in Post-Modernity and Tradition* (Madison, WI: University of Wisconsin Press, 1990); and J. Cooper, Ronald L. Netter, and Mohammed Mahmoud, eds., *Islam and Modernity: Muslim Intellectuals Respond* (London: I.B. Tauris, 1998).

65. Muhammad Said al-Ashmawy, *L'islamisme contre l'Islam,* trans. Richard Jacquemond (Paris: Éditions la découverte, 1989), 7; and Bielefeldt, "Muslim Voices," 607.

66. Subhi Mahmasani, "Adaptation of Islamic Jurisprudence to Modern Social Needs," in John J. Donohue and John L. Esposito, eds., *Islam in Transition: Muslim Perspectives* (New York: Oxford University Press, 1982), 183. See also Mohammed Talbi, "Religious Liberty: A Muslim Perspective," in *Conscience and Liberty,* vol. 31 (1991); Bielefeldt, "Muslim Voices," 609; and An-Na'im, *Toward an Islamic Reformation,* 99.

67. In brief, *ijtihad* (independent legal reasoning leading to new judgment) is the endeavor of an Islamic scholar to find solutions for today's problems by studying the original sources and considering the basic principles. Also An-Na'im "Human Rights in the Muslim World," 48.

68. Patrick Bannerman, *Islam in Perspective: A Guide to Islamic Society, Politics, and Law* (London: Routledge, 1988), 46; Hassan, "On Human Rights and the Qur'anic Perspective," 63; Kevin Dwyer, *Arab Voices: The Human Rights Debate in the Middle East* (Berkeley: University of California Press, 1991), 44–45; An-Na'im, *Toward an Islamic Reformation,* 50–51. See also Abdulaziz Sachedina, *The Islamic Roots of Democratic Pluralism* (New York: Oxford University Press, 2001), 15–21, 81–83; S. Aldeeb Abu-Sahlieh, "Introduction à la lecture

juridique du Coran," *Revue de droit international et de droit compare,* vol. 65 (1988), 76; R. Arhaldez, "La loi musulmane à la lumière des sciences coraniques," *Archives de philosophie du droit,* vol. 83 (1993); Mohammed Talbi and Maurice Bucaille, *Réflexions sur le Coran* (Paris: Seghers, 1989); and Glenn, *Legal Traditions,* 177–78.

69. Mayer, *Islam and Human Rights,* 50–51; See also Ali Rahnema, *Pioneers of Islamic Revival* (London: Zed, 1994).

70. Bielefeldt, "Muslim Voices," 609–10. See Sachedina, *Islamic Roots of Democratic Pluralism,* 83–91; Amor Abdelfattah, Néji Baccouche, and Mohammed Talbi, eds., *Études sur la tolérance: anglais, français, arabe* (Tunis: Académie tunisienne des sciences, des lettres et des arts [Beit al-Hikma], 1995).

71. Fazlur Rahman, "Status of Women in the Qur'an," in Guity Nashat, ed., *Women and Revolution in Iran* (Boulder, CO: Westview Press, 1983), 37. See also Barbara Freyer Stowasser, "The Status of Women in Early Islam," in Freda Hussain, ed., *Muslim Women* (London: Croom Helm, 1984), 15–18; Alya Baffoun, "Women and Social Change in the Muslim Arab World," in Azizah al-Hirbi, ed., *Women and Islam* (Oxford: Pergamon Press, 1982); and Haleh Afshar, "Islam and Feminism: An Analysis of Political Strategies," in Mai Yamani, ed., *Feminism and Islam: Legal and Liberty Perspectives* (London, Ithaca: Cornell, 1996), 197–216.

72. Mayer, "Universal versus Islamic Human Rights," 364–71, 377–79.

73. Denying the possibility of ruling by one official religious ideology, he maintains that religious states must be democratic. See Vakili, *Debating Religion and Politics,* 7.

74. Vakili, *Debating Religion and Politics,* 21, 42. See also Soroush, *Reason, Freedom, and Democracy.*

75. Soroush holds that a non-Muslim is not required to renounce his faith to enjoy equal human rights in a Muslim society. Vakili, *Debating Religion and Politics,* 25. For his ideas on religious government and the clerical establishment, see also Jahanbakhsh, *Islam, Democracy and Religious Modernism,* 251–74.

76. His main book is *The Second Message of Islam,* trans. Abdullahi An-Na'im (Syracuse: Syracuse University Press, 1987).

77. An-Na'im's reform methodology is discussed mainly in *Toward an Islamic Reformation.*

78. See Qur'an (17:70, 49:13).

79. Qur'an, chapters 4 and 6. Ustadh Taha argues that "the Meccan and Medinese texts [of the Qur'an] differ, not because of the time and place of revelation, but essentially because of the audience to which they are addressed." In other words, the shift was in response to the dictates of the time. See Mahmoud M. Taha, *The Second Message of Islam,* trans. by A.A. An-Na'im (Syracuse: Syracuse University Press, 1987), 125.

80. See An-Na'im, *Toward an Islamic Reformation,* 49, and An-Na'im "Human Rights in the Muslim World," 47.

81. An-Na'im, *Toward an Islamic Reformation,* 56.

82. Ibid.

83. Taha, *The Second Message of Islam.*

84. An-Na'im, *Toward an Islamic Reformation,* 56.

85. Tibi, "Islamic Law, Human Rights, Universal Morality," 286.

86. An-Na'im, "Human Rights in the Muslim World," 21.

87. Reza Afshari, "An Essay on Islamic Cultural Relativism," 263–65; Ann Elizabeth Mayer, "Current Muslim Thinking on Human Rights," in A. Ahmed An-Na'im and Francis M. Deng, eds., *Human Rights in Africa: Cross-Cultural Perspectives* (Washington, DC: Brookings Institution, 1990).

88. Offenses for which a specific punishment is strictly applied without allowing discretion to either official or private body or person.

89. He believes, the Qur'an does not prescribe any punishment for apostasy in this life; but Muslim jurists have classified apostasy as a *hadd* (singular of *hudud*) punishment by death, as prescribed in *sunna*. See An-Na'im, *Toward an Islamic Reformation*, 109, 113–15.

90. An-Na'im, *Toward an Islamic Reformation*, 115.

91. Ann Elizabeth Mayer, "A Critique of An-Na'im's Assessment of Islamic Criminal Justice," in "Islam and Human Rights: Different Issues, Different Contexts; Lessons from Comparisons," in *Islamic Law Reform and Human Rights* (Oslo: Nordic Human Rights, 1993), 37.

92. Ann E. Mayer, "A Critique of An-Na'im's Assessment," 37–52; Afshari, "An Essay on Islamic Cultural Relativism," 263–65.

93. For more critical views on An-Na'im's work, see Arkoun, "The Concept of Islamic Reformation," 18–21, and Ahmad, "Abdullahi An-Na'im on Constitutional and Human Rights Issues," 68–74. For An-Na'im's response to these critics, see A. Ahmed An-Na'im, "Toward an Islamic Reformation: Responses and Reflections," in *Islamic Law Reform and Human Rights*, 97–116.

94. Bielefeldt, "Muslim Voices," 610–14; Schacht, *An Introduction to Islamic Law*, 76–77.

95. Such reforms have restricted certain practices, such as child marriage, polygamy, and the husband's right to repudiate his wife unilaterally. See Bielefeldt, "Muslim Voices," and Schacht, *An Introduction to Islamic Law*, 161–68. The 1917 Ottoman law of family rights was an early reform in this area. See James Norman D. Anderson, *Law Reform in the Muslim World* (London: Athlone, 1976), 49, 118–23. Muhammad Abduh, grand mufti of Egypt in late nineteenth-century Egypt, also advocated restrictions on polygamy. See Esposito, *Islam and Politics*, 51; and Bielefeldt, "Muslim Voices," 611.

96. Muhammad Makki Naciri, "Judicial Aspects of Religious Liberty in Morocco," in *Conscience and Liberty* (1991), 73–75; Al-Ashmawy, *L'islamisme contre l'Islam*, 50; A. Ahmed An-Na'im, "Religious Liberty in Egypt: Under the Shadow of the Islamic *Dhimma* System," and Khalid Duran, "Religious Liberty and Human Rights in Sudan," both in Leonard Swidler, ed., *Religious Liberty and Human Rights in Nations and in Religions* (Philadelphia: Ecumenical, 1986), 43–59 and 74, respectively; and Aly A. Mansour, "*Hudud* Crimes," in M.C. Bassiouni, ed., *The Islamic Criminal Justice System* (New York: Oceana Publications, 1982), 199. *Hudud* punishments are now applied in few countries—Iran, Sudan, Pakistan, and Afghanistan.

97. Schacht, *Introduction to Islamic Law*, 176.

98. The constitutions of Syria, Turkey, Iran, Persian Gulf States, and Iraq are some examples in this respect. See Amin, *Islamic Law and Its Implications*, 58–67.

99. Bielefeldt, "Muslim Voices," 614.

100. Mayer, *Islam and Human Rights, Tradition and Politics*, 52, 204.

101. An-Na'im, *Toward an Islamic Reformation*, 48. See also Muhammad Nuwayhi, "A Revolution in Religious Thought," in John J. Donohue and John L. Esposito, eds., *Islam in Transition: Muslim Perspectives* (New York: Oxford University Press, 1982), 160–68.

102. Sayeed, *Western Dominance and Political Islam*, 5–49; Mohammed Arkoun, *Rethinking Islam: Common Questions, Uncommon Answers*, trans. and ed. Robert D. Lee (Boulder, CO: Westview Press, 1994), 24–26, 106–13.

103. An-Na'im, "Human Rights in the Muslim World," 46.

104. Ibid., 51.

105. Vincent, *Human Rights and International Relations*, 99–105.

106. Tibi, "Islamic Law, Human Rights, Universal Morality," 296–98. Also generally Tibi, *The Crisis of Modern Islam*; Arkoun, *Pour une critique de la raison islamique*; and Voll, *Islam: Continuity and Change in the Modern World*.

107. An-Na'im, *Toward an Islamic Reformation*, 180.

108. Ibid., 34. See also An-Na'im, "Human Rights in the Muslim World," 46; Taha, *The Second Message of Islam*; A. Ahmed An-Na'im, "The Rights of Women and International Law in the Muslim Context," *Whittier Law Review*, vol. 9 (1987), 491; A. Ahmed An-Na'im, "Islamic Law, International Relations, and Human Rights: Challenge and Response," *Cornell International Law Journal*, vol. 20 (1987), 17.

109. An-Na'im, *Toward an Islamic Reformation*.

110. Michael Freeman, "The Philosophical Foundations of Human Rights," *Human Rights Quarterly*, vol. 16 (1994), 491–514; Walter Kasper, "The Theological Foundations of Human Rights," *Catholic Lawyer*, vol. 34 (1991), 253–69; Michael Perry, "Is the Idea of Human Rights Ineliminably Religious?" *University of Richmond Law Review*, vol. 27 (1993), 1027; J. Donnelly, *Universal Human Rights in Theory and Practice* (London: Cornell University Press, 1989), 16–19; and Rhoda E. Howard, "Dignity, Community, and Human Rights," in Abdullahi Ahmed An-Na'im, ed., *Human Rights in Cross-Cultural Perspectives: A Quest for Consensus* (Philadelphia: University of Pennsylvania Press, 1992), 83.

111. Afshari, "An Essay on Islamic Cultural Relativism," 248; Donnelly, *Universal Human Rights in Theory and Practice*, 64.

112. See generally Martin E. Marty, "Religious Dimension of Human Rights," *Emory International Law Review*, vol. 10 (1996), 97–106; Harold J. Berman, *The Interaction of Law and Religion* (New York: Abingdon Press, 1974), 21, 107; and Harold J. Berman, *Faith and Order: The Reconciliation of Law and Religion* (Atlanta, GA: Scholars Press, 1993), 1–20.

113. See Jeanne Hersch, ed., *Le droit d'être un homme* (Geneva: UNESCO, 1968); Louis Henkin, *The Rights of Man Today* (Boulder, CO: Westview Press, 1978); Bielefeldt, "Muslim Voices," 589–90; An-Na'im, "Human Rights in the Muslim World," 47–48; and Walter Kasper, "Theological Foundations of Human Rights," 253–69.

114. The philosophy of law stipulates that historicity is a necessary dimension of any law even if one believes that laws should be linked to religious sources. Legal norms are, from this point of view, always conceived within a place and time-bound framework. Laws and regulations are rationally formed and executed according to the needs of society. See T.M. Knox, trans., *Hegel's Philosophy of Rights* (Oxford: Clarendon Press, 1965), 14–18; Ronald M. Dworkin, ed., *The Philosophy of Law* (New York: Oxford University Press, 1977), 1–2. Also generally Ronald M. Dworkin, "Islamic Law: A System of Rules?" in *The Philosophy of Law*, 38–65; Thomas Morawetz, *The Philosophy of Law: An Introduction* (New York: Macmillan, 1980), 5–10; and Immanuel Kant, *The Philosophy of Law: An Exposition of the Fundamental Principles of Jurisprudence as the Science of Right* (1887), trans. W. Hastle (Clifton, NJ: Augustus M. Kelley, 1974).

8

Islamic Peace Education

Changing Hearts and Minds

Asna Husin

T he core of Islamic education has been to school the hearts and minds of developing students spiritually, preparing them for religious leadership. Education has always been the cornerstone of Islamic civilization, for religious and nonreligious occupations. But theologically, education is connected to understanding the presence of the divine in all things, through the Qur'anic message of vertical God-human relations (*habl min allah*) and horizontal human-to-human connections (*habl min al-nas*).[1] These two forms of relations are inseparable: The former guides the latter and the latter reinforces the former. This implies that one's worthy relations with the Creator should be manifested in his or her positive personal experiences and gracious social dealings. Otherwise, vertical relations have no bearing on one's day-to-day reality, violating the purpose of Islamic education and the Muslim way of life. This concept of a wholeness of human experience has not always been properly displayed within the lives of Muslims, leading them to think and act compartmentally, as if their relations to God showed only in their sense of piety, and religiosity allowed them to bypass the obligation to maintain commendable human relations. Such compartmental thinking has led some individuals to commit unworthy acts in the name of Islam. This internal problem, coupled by a widespread external campaign associating Islam with violence, has provoked both frustration and a growing sense of awareness among some thinking Muslims who truly hold up Islam as a religion of peace.

The Peace Education Program—Program Pendidikan Damai, known by its Indonesian acronym of PPD—was founded in Aceh in 2000 in the face of such internal concern and external dissatisfaction.[2] Internally, Aceh

151

was ridden by violence and continuing bloodshed. It was a theater of communal conflict and severe human rights abuses, testing the principles of Islamic peace that Acehnese hold dear in their hearts. They were caught between the Free Aceh Movement (Gerakan Aceh Merdeka, or GAM), lawless gangs, and the various national police and military forces (TNI). Fledgling non-governmental organizations (NGOs) and civic organizations were struggling to create a space for themselves, while voices of moderation, reason, and peaceful resolution of conflict were being silenced by coercive or violent means, including assassination, torture, and extortion. Externally, the drive and efforts toward a peaceful resolution to Acehnese conflict initiated after the fall of Suharto and the emergence of democratic reform (*reformasi*) in Indonesia met with setbacks. It was under these difficult and uncertain circumstances that the PPD aimed to reclaim Islamic peacemaking, though its new initiative of institutionalizing peace education within the established provincial school system was received with enthusiasm by some and with reservation by others.

This chapter describes the PDD's contribution to educating Acehnese religious and nonreligious students. It explores the history of the PPD, lessons learned, and the intended and unintended effect of these efforts on youth, teachers, and the community of legal scholars (*ulama*). We first survey the history of the program and its projects, the ways the original idea was socialized, the particular projects developed, the challenges encountered, and financial and organizational help secured. Then we review the program's peace manuals, their contents and methodology, how they were developed, and the number of implementing institutions and target pupils. Our survey concludes by looking at the impact of the program and its manuals on students, teachers, the *ulama,* and the general public. This chapter explores the intended and unintended consequences of peace activities that have been recorded in schools and in *dayahs* (traditional religious schools) or *pesantren* (modern Islamic boarding schools) to assess its potential for further enlargement and mainstreaming.

Pendidikan Damai Program

The Peace Education Program was initiated to promote Islamic peacemaking and elevate indigenous mechanisms for solving conflicts.[3] This initiative involved the heads of the Provincial Office of National Education (Dinas Pendidikan)[4] and the Provincial Office for Religious Affairs (Kantor Wilayah Departemen Agama, or simply Kanwil Depag), as well as the head of the Consultative Council of the *Ulama* of Aceh (MPU) along with the rectors of the Ar-Raniry State Institute for Islamic Studies and Syiah

Kuala University. These five individuals were the most influential leaders in Aceh.[5] The first two are certainly the most crucial, since all public schools in Aceh were under their jurisdiction.

Though the leaders had some concerns and questions about foreign ideas and influence, especially since the funds would come from the United Nations Children's Fund (UNICEF) and the Australian Agency for International Development (AusAID), they all supported the peace program. They were convinced that the two international donors would not interfere in either the contents of the work or the selection of people who would be involved in the program. Both Dinas Pendidikan and Kanwil Depag promised to help implement peace education in their schools: Sekolah Menengah Atas (SMA, the regular high school) and Sekolah Menengah Kejuruan (SMK, the vocational high school) under the Dinas, as well as Madrasah Aliyah (MA, the Islamic high school) under the Kanwil Depag.[6]

With such a positive response from Acehnese educational leaders and administrators, the PPD returned to UNICEF for confirmation, and in December 2000, the PPD and UNICEF met to discuss the details of the initiative.[7] Shortly afterward, these five advisory leaders formed a curriculum team, also consisting of five members,[8] to produce the first manual—*Kurikulum Pendidikan Damai,* or *Peace Education Curriculum*—in approximately one hundred days. The PPD felt tremendous pressure not only to complete the task by the deadline, but also to fulfill its own desire to produce a quality manual on Islamic peacemaking. An added complication was that neither the staff nor the curriculum team had a clear idea of what peace education really entailed, nor did the scholars or teachers have any practical experience in the field of peace education. Each member conducted research and found some exciting resources of written materials on the Internet and at libraries. While ideas were gathered for the project, there was still a large gap in the understanding of peace education and Islamic nonviolent ideas (the author was founder and director of the program). However, the intention to create a sound manual, and the process of crafting it impelled us to become clear about our goal. The team and staff met two to three times a week to update each other and discuss progress in and obstacles to the project. It took us a month to agree on the idea behind our first peace education manual; the rest of the time was focused on the contents. A consultant from Nonviolence International (NI) and its director came to Aceh to assist, and a couple of resource materials provided by UNICEF helped progress the work. Finally, after three months and some days of working constantly, the manual was sent to the publisher in June 2001.[9]

Completing the manual allowed the PPD, the primary organization steering the efforts at educational reform, to conduct its first training for teachers and facilitators. Fifty teachers from twenty-five schools were instructed in peace education, and by July 16, 2001, they began teaching the manual to their students. Of the twenty-five schools, fifteen are under Dinas Pendidikan and ten under the jurisdiction of Kanwil Depag, spread out in five of Aceh's then ten districts. The success of this project in a short time led to the enlargement of the program to cover ninety-six schools in 2002. The revision of the manual, the training of 147 additional teachers-facilitators, and the translation of the first book into English were among PPD activities for this year. Revising *Kurikulum Pendidikan Damai* involved adding a number of new modules to improve its contents, enhancing its methodology and including more graphics and exercises in its activities. In addition, the PPD hired an independent, professional evaluator who assessed the strengths and challenges facing the program.[10] The staff and those who have been affiliated with the program were encouraged by the positive report, which stated explicitly that "peace education works."[11] In 2002, the PPD also developed a brochure and a primer to market the program better, but its real expansion occurred on the side of the implementing schools. In a short time, the number of schools using the educational material increased from twenty-five to ninety-six, expanding into twelve districts across Aceh,[12] supported by 197 teachers-facilitators, and reaching more than twenty-seven thousand pupils.

In 2003, the Islamic peace education course was implemented in one hundred schools reaching thirteen different districts, involving more than thirty-seven thousand young adults. The PPD did not add more than four schools that year because it was focusing on advocacy and mainstreaming, under which five workshops with government officers and policymakers were proposed. The first five months of these mainstreaming efforts went extremely well, as the PPD was able to conduct the first two of the five intended workshops with success. Students, teachers, and school principals, asked by the PPD to speak on its behalf, discussed the benefits of peace education and how it had changed their lives. Not a single pupil, teacher, or school principal who had studied or taught the manual spoke against its implementation. There were numerous suggestions that peace education should also be taught to the military, government officials, and general public.

The PPD strategy of mobilizing pupils and teachers worked extremely well, and government officers and policymakers involved were convinced that peace education was crucial to changing behavior and attitudes. Unfortunately, the security situation in Aceh deteriorated and the government responded by imposing martial law on May 19, 2003. This intense security measure put the PPD's peace education work in an awkward position and threatened its activities. A number of official degrees (*maklumats*) issued by the martial law authorities seemed to work against our activities. The PPD director was personally very concerned not only for her own safety, but for the well-being of her office, staff, the program, teachers, and pupils. As at other NGOs, the PPD's office and staff were very vulnerable. All international NGOs were forced to leave.[13] The PPD decided to keep a low profile: the staff came to the office only when necessary[14] and the organization canceled all its public meetings and workshops both inside and outside Banda Aceh, for the authorities allowed no gathering of any kind.

After two weeks of martial law, as the PPD had not violated any laws, threatened security, or caused unrest, the staff wanted to confront the government edicts limiting its educational activities. However, it was not an easy situation. The PPD director's mobile phone was under surveillance, and twice she went to an intelligence office to report this (she was able to clear up the situation because she was a member of the governor's advisory team at the time). For the first time in its three years of operation, PPD was negatively labeled as the work of an NGO, implying that we worked for our own benefit and self-interest. A number of leaders and educators who had praised us and our work before distanced themselves from the PPD out of concern for their own safety. All of us were afraid of *maob*—an Acehnese idiom referring to the darkness that may or may not have a hidden being that harms you. The PPD staff had to be aware of interference from militias, military, and the local city council. However, UNICEF insisted on delivering on PPD promises. Consequently, the PPD faced financial shortages, and its director had to borrow funds to maintain the office and support staff salaries. The martial law implicated not only staff security and activities, but their financial well-being as well.

Despite the difficulties, the staff never lost their faith in the project to help Aceh and its youth. There was a consensus that PPD work was laying the foundation for a prosperous future. The PPD did a number of things to reclaim its mission. First, the staff met with the head of the MPU and the advisory committee for the *Ulama* Program, seeking their advice for maintaining both the high school and the *ulama* projects. Second, the staff consulted with the heads of Dinas Pendidikan and Kanwil Departemen Agama to reemphasize their commitment to Aceh education and reconfirm their partnership. Third, they advised PPD teachers to keep a low profile and convinced them that peace education was a nonpolitical, neutral initiative. Fourth, the staff encouraged youth advocates to campaign for peace education in their respective schools. And finally, letters were written to martial law authorities acquiring time for consultation. After many inquiries, the PPD was at last informed that they could continue their educational peacemaking work because the authorities believed that the "[PPD] were helping the government."

The government confirmation strengthened PPD conviction and allowed the staff to reassess their mission of teaching peace education in schools. They conducted the remaining training and, by mid-July, the manual was implemented in one hundred schools. Since the PPD was one of the few organizations operating in peacemaking in Aceh at the time, it was common to have intelligence officers observe the PPD's activities. By late August, three-and-a-half months after the initiation of martial law, the situation had improved considerably, and the PPD could conduct the remaining three advocacy workshops, including that on budgets. The workshops recommended that peace education be integrated into the subject of Islamic ethics (*akhlaq*) and be taught for two semesters in the sophomore year of high school. The recommendation was accepted by the government and supported by the *ulama*. However, and regrettably, this positive development in Aceh coincided with the UNICEF Education Section officer's move to another country. This created a discontinuity between UNICEF and PPD collaboration when the PPD could not sustain itself financially, and it did not have the time or expertise to raise funds and approach other donors; none of the PPD staff had done fundraising before. As the PPD lost all its high school financial support, the high school program was cut off despite Acehnese enthusiasm for its enlargement. The program was only re-energized in September 2004, nine months after UNICEF support ended, when the British Embassy in Jakarta granted the PPD a year's budget of U.S. $199,000. These funds allowed the PPD to mainstream peace education through *akhlaq*. Before we surveyed the incorporation of peace education into the high-school subject of Islamic faith and ethics, we focused on the PPD's second project, known internally as the *Ulama* Program.

The *Ulama* Program was initiated in early 2003, mirroring the success of the PPD high school program.[15] It was designed with the full cooperation of the MPU for use by Islamic boarding schools—the *pesantren* or *dayah*—to enhance the capacity of future *ulama* and other religious leaders in Aceh to implement Islamic strategies for nonviolent management of violent conflict. Five key *ulama* leaders representing different religious organizations served as the advisory committee, presided over by the head of the MPU.[16] The involvement of these five *ulama* was extremely critical, for they were PPD's gates to the rest of the *ulama* leadership. The active engagement of the two *dayah ulama* as members of the curriculum team was also essential, as they increased the project's legitimacy. The *ulama* initiative, like the high school initiative, was received with enthusiasm by some and with reservation by others. Some may have liked to reject the program, but could not express it openly because the work had been supported by great leaders. The reluctance and reservation within some of the *ulama* toward the program had partly to do with the sources of funding and the motives of the donors. They questioned the intentions of Western donors in supporting this Muslim institution, while their governments continued to support Israeli bombardment of Palestinians and kill innocent Muslims in the Middle East. "They want us to be peaceful while they are terrorizing our women and children?" said one prominent *ulama* leader; "they want us to practice nonviolence so that we do not fight them back," said another.[17] These frustrations reflect the mistrust of Achenese *ulama*, perhaps most in Indonesia, of Western interest in supporting peacemaking efforts. The *ulama* are not naïve; they see hypocrisy, inconsistencies, and double-standards of Western powers in this region and choose not to associate themselves with such activities because they could be implicated by the community. The above statements emerged during a workshop to review the *ulama* manual, which functioned also as a teaching opportunity for both the PPD and the *ulama*: It was a forum for everyone to express their skepticism against and support for peace education in a dialogue, while understanding the complexities of one's presumptions.

An indication of growth was the *ulama*'s overwhelming support for PPD educational peacemaking programs with religious scholars and institutions at the end of the workshop. The head of the advisory committee reminded the reluctant party that "the donors might have had a hidden agenda but none of us was certain of it. Therefore, we have to be mindful of their motives and use their contribution to our advantage." He specified that benefit by saying that "Islam is a religion of peace and reclaiming its peaceful nature and presenting it to our youth is our religious duty."[18] Another important justification is stated in his remarks published at the beginning of the manual. Throughout the history of Aceh, he states, the *ulama* played an important role in education and character building of the community (*ummah*).[19] They were at the forefront in addressing the problems of the nation. This, according to Dr. Muslim, could be witnessed in the *ulama*'s continuing involvement in community religious, educational, and social activities. In the contemporary world, as science and information technology has advanced at a high speed, creating different community dynamics from previous eras, the *ulama* have to compete with media in promoting Islamic peacemaking principles to the larger community. As such, the capacity building of the *dayah* pupils and the *ulama* with contemporary discourse and new skills is necessary in order to address current existing problems of the *ummah*. Dr. Muslim emphasizes that the peace education curriculum "is an attempt to realize this noble objective."[20]

The project consisted of two phases: creating the manual and piloting it in selected *dayahs* or *pesantren*. The creation of the manual required tremendous energy and determination on the part of the *ulama* team and PPD staff. One challenge was that Acehnese *ulama* were used to verbal exhortation, and presenting their ideas in writing was not their common practice. Another concern was choosing a proper Indonesian language rooted in *pesantren*, for the *dayah* applies a form of the language that is not commonly used by the university community or the general public.[21] The language of the *pesantren* is more classic, unique, and original, while some of the curriculum team, staff, and editor were not very familiar with it. The selection of the contents was another challenge, as Islamic teachings are comprehensive, with a long and vast intellectual history, the principles of which are far-reaching and dynamic. Finally, some of the teaching methodology that was rather uncommon to the *dayah* community was also a concern. All challenges were resolved through teamwork, sensitivity, and a strong sense of purpose, and when the edited manual was presented to a group of thirty-four *ulama* leaders, who met for two days to review the book from cover to cover, it was received with praise and appreciation.[22]

This does not mean that the *ulama* accepted the manual without changes. A few phrases and a number of ideas and concepts were altered to meet *ulama* expectations and requirements. But overall, the changes were minor, for they did not require major revisions or additional research. That the advisory committee had fully endorsed the book before it was presented to the review team might have helped it pass the test. By July 2004, the creatively designed manual was sent to the printing house, and by October, two thousand copies of the manual arrived at the PPD office.[23] Sadly, the PPD had distributed only one hundred to two hundred copies of the manual, largely to donors and direct clients, when the tsunami in December badly damaged the office and swept away all copies of the manual, along with other resources and documents.

In the aftermath of the tsunami, the United States Institute of Peace commissioned the reprinting of the manual and reenergized its translation efforts into English and Arabic. The Canadian International Development Agency (CIDA) supported implementation activities, which started in July 2006, to last for nearly three years. The activities focused on the training of *dayah* and *pesantren* teachers, as well as the application of the *Kurikulum Pendidikan Damai: Perspektif Ulama Aceh* in twenty-five *dayahs* and *pesantren*[24] in different districts across Aceh.[25] The implementation phase concentrated on mainstreaming efforts, using a television outlet to feature one *ulama* each week through an interesting, creative program called a peace flash. Like a traditional news flash, the program was a two- to-three-minute message on peace issues presented by the *ulama* on prime time in a special communication style. The audience was encouraged to send feedback; their comments would be drawn every other week for a small cash reward. There were at least twenty weeks of peace flashes in the first year and fifty-two in the second.[26] In addition, the PPD used the provincial radio and local newspaper to socialize the program and attract a wider audience. All these activities aimed to empower the *ulama* and strengthen their capacity in peacebuilding. Two advanced mediation and negotiation trainings for twenty interested *ulama* were conducted in 2007 and 2008 to help them improve their capacities and skills and to give them new mechanisms for solving community conflicts that empowered the conflicting parties. The PPD brought to Aceh for these two trainings three internationally acclaimed mediation trainers: Dr. Jennifer Beer (adjunct professor at the University of Pennsylvania) for the first training and Dr. Mohammed Abu-Nimer of the American University, along with Dr. Mubarak Awad of NI, for the second training. Finally, a two-day Ulama Peace Conference was convened in April 2008, bringing together 204 *ulama* leaders and *dayah* teachers, males and females, young and old, to celebrate their peace initiative as well as to explore the future of peace education in Aceh and its role in maintaining peace in the province.

Peace Education Manuals

The Peace Education Program has developed four manuals on Islamic peace education in its nine years of operation.[27] The first three are successive versions of the high-school manual, the *Kurikulum Pendidikan Damai*. The first and the second editions carry this title, as the second is only an improvement of the first. However, the third edition is a transformation of the previous editions, in response to the policy of incorporating peace education into national Islamic faith and ethics (*aqidah* and *akhlaq*). *Aqidah akhlaq* is a required subject, instituted by the government, and pupils have to pass its exam to graduate; thus, integrating peace education into this subject is a perfect channel for its regular and structured implementation. The third manual bears the new title *Kurikulum Aqidah Akhlaq dalam Konteks Pendidikan Damai* (*Islamic Faith and Ethics Curriculum in the Context of Peace Education*), published in December 2005 for sophomores in high school. At 311 pages, it is much thicker than the previous two editions, which have fewer than 100 pages each. Despite this transformation, the book carries the old format with minor changes to meet the requirements of *aqidah* and *akhlaq*. All the manuals, including the *ulama* book, have the same format. Among important characteristics of the books is the featuring of a Qur'anic verse or a Prophetic tradition at the beginning of each module, followed by an Acehnese proverb (*hadih maja*). The Qur'anic verse or Prophetic tradition functions as an inspiration for the whole text and a starting point for further discussion. This Islamic text is to give a religious meaning to issues considered mundane in contemporary discourse, and by altering these attitudes, the manual demonstrates the importance of each module scripturally and ethically.

The stipulation of the *hadih maja* is intended to use local indigenous culture and language to validate the issue under discussion, in order to increase the Acehnese sense of ownership. Incorporating the Acehnese proverbs demonstrates that the Acehnese in the past were a community, with important intellectual centers, and religiously tolerant cultures, valuing knowledge and respecting rights and responsibilities.[28] Upholding the rights of women and children and embracing pluralism, democracy, and justice were all part of Achenese history, and should be very much elements of the Acehnese present and future outlooks as well. The statement of the *hadih maja* also aims at reclaiming the Acehnese religious and cultural heritage, so that it is not lost in the midst of cultural contestations among local, national, and international spheres, or between the central culture and that of the periphery. The use of religious text together with Acehnese linguistic cultural heritage distinguishes the format of the modules from any other works, which proved to be very useful not only in attracting the attention of pupils, teachers, and general readers, but also in promoting religious and indigenous recognitions in shaping communal and world peace.

The revision of the second-year *aqidah akhlaq* curriculum for high school students was a monumental task that took two years to crystallize. Combining *aqidah akhlaq* with peace education was not easy, especially since *aqidah* requires a type of conviction and indoctrination, while peace education is taught through exercises, discussion, and dialogue. The present form of the manual combines a comprehensive knowledge of the Islamic spiritual and intellectual heritage with insights drawn from the peace education field, so that the new presentation of *aqidah akhlaq* does not look too mundane, nor does peace education appear as indoctrination. This module, *Kurikulum Aqidah Akhlaq dalam Konteks Pendidikan Damai*, presents Islam in its genuinely peaceful character, curbing the radicalism and extremism rampant in some Muslim and non-Muslim communities around the world.[29] The new book was well received by the *ulama*, educators, academics, and Indonesian peace education experts.

The manual presents peace within the Islamic tradition as an integrated and comprehensive unity of peace, with God, within oneself, with one's fellow humans, and with nature, combined with an Islamic faith that

teaches sincere submission and obedience to God and genuine following of His prophets and revelations (i.e., *aqidah*). Such faith is marked
by one's noble character traits in dealing with the divine and one's fellow
humans (i.e., *akhlaq*). All these concepts and ideas are presented in a single
whole, avoiding any sense of duality between the *aqidah akhlaq* materials
and those of peace education. The presentation covers the Islamic intellectual past and modern contemporary ideas and thoughts, the issues of
prophets as role models, human rights and character traits, democracy and
good governance, the rule of law and economic justice, as well as gender
equality and the role of the media, employing Islamic terms and concepts
throughout. These ideas are packaged to strengthen pupils' personality and
integrity, broaden their intellectual horizons, increase their ability for critical thinking, and impart to them analytical experience and skills. This is
accomplished by treating pupils as subjects actively participating in the
learning process, utilizing eye-catching activities and methods that combine discussion and dialogue, personal reflection and teamwork, as well as
collective study and role playing.[30] The application of learning-by-doing
and playing-for-learning methods makes this book unique—culturally attractive yet conceptually serious. The approach has fulfilled the objectives
of peace education and strengthened the *aqidah akhlaq* subject that the
national educational curriculum requires.

As indicated above, in addition to the high school book, the PPD has
also developed an *ulama* manual for use in Islamic boarding schools. The
reprinting of *Kurikulum Pendidikan Damai: Perspektif Ulama Aceh* was
completed in April 2005. This 385-page combined resource and training
book presents peace education from an Islamic Acehnese perspective. As
does the high school manual, the *ulama* book promotes a positive and
comprehensive understanding of peace, encompassing peaceful relations
with God, oneself, one's fellow humans, and one's environment. The curriculum teaches communal peace in accordance with a positive Islamic
approach, namely the absence of war and discrimination, and stresses the
necessity of justice: Peace is neither subjugation to inequitable situations
nor a passive acceptance of injustice, discrimination, and war.[31] The manual
treats a wide spectrum of issues, ranging from human-divine vertical relations, such as one's responsibilities to God, to personal issues, such as
anger management and body language; it also ranges from the history of
the Muslim community, as exemplified in the Hudaybiyyah Agreement[32]
and the peaceful conquest of Mecca in the year 630, to the importance of
intellectual empowerment and spiritual exercise. Nevertheless, the scope
of presentation deals with human-to-human relations (*habl min al-nas*),
including the issues of rights and responsibilities, pluralism, conserving

natural resources, communication, democracy and justice, conflict prevention and transformation, and leadership and counseling. All these matters are treated in a manner combining Islamic views with universal principles common to humanity. Islam is a religion for humanity, and shared values are understood to have come from the same source: God.

The *ulama* manual also deals with the issue of gender equality, one of the unspoken goals of this peace education manual. The team and the staff consciously present women, along with men, as peacemakers and community builders, both in images (pictures and caricatures) and in deeds, by presenting cases involving women and men. The manual's specific discussion of gender under the module entitled Plurality of Human Beings is quite progressive. Prior to the Medan manual review in January 2004, there was real concern that this section might generate controversy. Such fears were unfounded, as the *ulama* were highly open to it and the section was well received for a number of reasons. First, the case of gender equity is presented in a dignified manner, using an Islamic vocabulary of gender (*jins* in Arabic; *jenis kelamin* in Indonesian) rather than the widely used Western term of *al-jandar*. Second, the issue of gender equality is explored through an Islamic lens by utilizing verses of the Qur'an, the Prophetic traditions, and the practice of the Companions. Third, the matter is treated by presenting women as partners of men, not rivals; together, women and men should strive together to fulfill their human responsibility as the *khalifah* (successor, shaper, and protector) of God's will on earth. Finally, the *ulama* embraced the manual's treatment of gender because the manual presented an issue close to their hearts; it struggles along with them regarding the lack of female *ulama* in the Acehnese community, its causes and implications, and the ways to resolve the situation. The *ulama* agreed with the way the matter was presented and found it very pertinent. All these factors helped make the gender issue part of an authentic Islamic discourse, transforming it into an *ulama* issue rather than merely one about women.

The manual is of high quality in both content and design. The finished version made everyone proud to be associated with our mission of *jihad al-'aql*, or empowering the mind (*pencerahan akal*), a mode of peaceful *jihad* taught in Islamic religious literature also termed *jihad al-'ilm* (e.g., by al-Jassas, *Ahkam al-Qur'an*). Plausibly, people associated with the PPD are among those who justly claim this Islamic intellectual and legal heritage and appropriate it for contemporary needs in a practical way. The book challenges *ulama* and religious leaders to use this peaceful struggle to revisit the vast ocean of Islam's intellectual and spiritual heritage to reclaim aspects of the Islamic legacy for self-critical, open-minded tolerance, responsible liberty, a high purpose of human values, and respect for differences and pluralism. Our *ulama* clearly appreciated how they were being challenged, not only because it was done with respect, dignity, and high hopes for their leadership, but also because the criticism was initiated from within their own culture and tradition. They saw the manual as empowering the *ulama*, the *dayah*, and the *pesantren*.

The design, illustration, and presentation of the manual materials are unique and unfamiliar to the *dayah* and *pesantren* world—they are colorful, rich, and vivid. The design helps convey the message easily and clearly, and the *ulama* appreciates our youthful way (*cara anak muda*) of communicating. *Cara anak muda* is an interesting phrase: In this context, it does not connote the sense of the negative, irresponsible way of *anak muda*, but rather the positive, prudent traits of youth. The *cara anak muda* also signifies a contemporary and modern technique of presenting ideas and thought. One of the *ulama* acclaims: "this *cara anak muda* is very beautiful and attractive."[33] Another participant in the Medan workshop declared that "the design and illustration of the manual says more about the contents of the book, and it is highly valuable. It speaks of its quality and the people behind it."[34] A woman participant suggested that "it is interesting that the *ulama's* ideas and Muslim activism are being presented in this way."[35] The *ulama* as a whole appreciated the design of our manual—though this should not be taken to imply that the manual was embraced by all. As mentioned earlier, a number of *ulama* remain reluctant to join the peace journey.

Another key reason for *ulama* endorsement of seemingly modern issues is that the concepts and practices are not foreign to Islam. The terms may be new, argued one *ulama* participant, but the concepts and principles of the ideas are very Islamic. "Take human rights, for example," he continued; "as presented in the book it is part of the Islamic concept of *haqq* [rights and responsibility]."[36] The *ulama* participants highlighted our presentation of rights and responsibilities in an Islamic approach as two sides of the same coin. Our articulation of rights and responsibilities were generated from the divine, the Islamic concept of the true and real (*al-Haqq*)—clarifying that rights and responsibilities are not secular concepts—which were essential ingredients to its approval. The manual's expression of modern ideas and thoughts through Islamic conceptions and terms made those values familiar to our leaders. Consequently, they learned to trust the PPD and value its work as a Muslim organization. PPD efforts to gain *ulama* trust were sincere and they knew it; also, its endeavor to present seemingly modern values through an Islamic approach was religiously sound, for the PPD believed in it and conducted research to prove it. To some extent, this reflects the integrity of the PPD's work and mission.

The issue of methodology is an important area for discussion for education peacemaking. The *ulama* book employs the same format and attractive methodology as the high school curriculum. It does not repeat what was written earlier, except to reiterate that what is true for the high school book is repeated in the *ulama* manual. However, what is appropriate for the high school book may not always be appreciated within the *dayah* community, and therefore the manual omits it. The presentation of a certain exercise or role-play activity, for example, might be highly valued in high schools, but seen as too childish in the *pesantren*. In such a case, the specific exercise is replaced by a more suitable one. Although the *ulama* manual also employs certain exercises as activities, the frequency of the exercises is less than it is in the high school manual. This means that the *ulama* manual conveys messages and implants skills more through discussion, dialogue, role-play, group study, and teamwork, as well as debate. So in addition to learning-by-doing and playing-as-learning methods, the *ulama* book exploits another important methodology, known as thinking for reviving (*berfikir untuk penyegaran*). This mode of teaching is a technique developed specifically for this book through trial and experiment. It is inspired by our strong conviction that empowering the mind (*jihad al-'aql*)—employing contemplation and intellectual effort in striving to refresh Islamic teachings and values as a response to contemporary problems—is a major responsibility of the *ulama*. In this context, *dayah* pupils are trained to familiarize themselves with thinking and contemplating, so that it becomes their habitual custom and character trait. Thus, unlike the high school manual, the *ulama* training book is filled with critical and difficult questions that require serious thinking presented on the margin of each page. The addition of these side questions is a new invention, and to some degree, it is imitated in the latest Islamic ethics manual. The activity of our *ulama* manual is specifically geared toward this thinking process, for the PPD is aware that it is one *ulama* trait that needs special attention and strengthening.

Impact of Peace Education

Some of the effects of the high school project and *ulama* peacemaking program were direct and intended; others were indirect and unintended. Peace education has been taught in schools across Aceh, though on and off, for the past nine years. It also often uses local media, especially television, to disseminate peace ideas. The teaching of peace education in schools and our media outreach has made peace concepts and skills part of the general discourse, especially among young adults. The PPD cannot claim to have directly contributed to the Aceh Peace Agreement, which ended thirty years of bloodshed between the government of Indonesia and the Free Aceh Movement[37] that caused severe human rights abuses and oppression. But the PPD can assert that, prior to the agreement, many Acehnese civil society groups—youth, women, academics, and the *ulama*—had repeatedly called for a peaceful solution to Aceh's violence, and a number of key individuals in those groups were and are associated with the PPD in one way or another. One group which, in addition to the politicians and the conflicting parties, was directly involved in the long process of peace negotiations was the *ulama*. It is also one of the first groups that repeated the call for a peaceful solution to Aceh's problems right after the tsunami,[38] and brought that collective desire to Jakarta to meet the vice president of Indonesia and the head of the national parliament (DPR) only a few weeks after the disaster.[39] Some movers behind the cry for peace are the head or members of our PPD Ulama Advisory Committee, including Dr. Muslim Ibrahim of MPU and Teungku Daud Zamzami of the Association of the Dayah Ulama of Insafuddin.

When the *ulama* program was first introduced, a number of key *ulama* leaders passionately held that direct elections were un-Islamic and voiced the need to maintain the status quo, that the president, governor, or other elective officials were to be chosen by the parliament. A number of these Acehnese leaders are members of different PPD teams, including our advisory committee and the team that thoroughly reviewed the *ulama* manual in Medan in January 2004. It is unclear whether their affiliation with the PPD or their understanding of peace education has influenced them or not, but the reality is that some of these leaders, along with those who had viewed direct elections as compatible with Islamic democracy from the beginning, were among the first to call for a direct election in North Aceh. Another group of *ulama* who earlier disagreed with direct elections have muted their voices, either because they felt there was no point in presenting dissenting opinion against the wishes of the masses or they actually had changed their views. When the author personally asked this question to one of them, the answer was diplomatic: "Elections are not the utmost important issue as far as our faith (*kepercayaan*) is concerned."[40] This response could mean that, because the election is a matter of human-to-human relations, it is open to differing views and interpretations, and thus no one can claim to possess a complete understanding of it. It may also be construed to mean that, because the election has nothing to do with one's faith, it is acceptable, even if it acts on a wrong understanding. In other words, even though direct elections may be interpreted as un-Islamic, it is acceptable that people practice it; it is not directly related to religious belief and conviction. Whatever his response means, it shows a sense of flexibility in his view.

Working with the *ulama* has created genuine mutual trust between them and the PPD. This allows PPD staff to discuss sensitive issues with the *ulama* that otherwise would not be possible. The *shari'ah* stipulation is a type of religious, political, and social concession for Aceh, granted originally by President Abdurrahman Wahid and reinstated in several bills, including the current one on the Aceh Government Law (*Undang-Undang Pemerintahan Aceh*) passed in August 2006.[41] It is political because the president then believed that giving the Acehnese the authority to administer *shari'ah* would silence them from demanding independence, which was later proven not to be the case. It is also social if one puts the implementation of *shari'ah* in its proper context. In the last ten years of conflict, Aceh became a theater of widespread prostitution, drugs, and alcohol abuse, unprecedented in anyone's living memory. Consequently, there was a real yearning among sections of the Acehnese population for some order (*penertiban*) and clean-up (*pembersihan*). When the *shari'ah* was accorded by Jakarta, it was interpreted by these people as the answer to their moral longing. This is probably one of the reasons why the *shari'ah* local codes (*qanun*) that have been passed are all related to these moral concerns, overlooking the important *shari'ah* issues of justice and protection.[42] The *shari'ah* implementation is also religious because there have always been some sections of the Acehnese population, among both the religious establishment and the masses, who desired implementation of *shari'ah* all along. When it was honored, it was seen like "a lost child who had returned."[43] A group of Acehnese continues to support the present implementation of *shari'ah*, even when they agree in principle that some changes in approach are necessary to make it a comprehensive force of peace and protection, rather than a selective act of law enforcement leading to injustice and abuses.[44] These individuals believe in the good nature of *shari'ah* and its necessity for Muslims, but recognize and admit negligence perpetuated in its name.

Two groups of Acehnese thus emerged, one advocating for *shari'ah* and the other opposing its implementation. In this polarized context, the PPD attempted to explore a middle way to reconcile the two sides. The PPD speaks directly to the *ulama,* and not to the media, to maintain the *ulama's* trust. The PPD often asks if it is possible to implement *shari'ah* peacefully; it became one of the themes of our 2007 peace flash and was delivered by the head of the Shari'ah Office (*Dinas Syariat Islam*). The television editorial argued that *shari'ah* could be implemented peacefully by focusing not on punishment, but on education, care for the poor, and protection of orphans. Within this theme of implementing *shari'ah* peacefully, the PPD has also talked with the *ulama* on the possibility of changing the emphasis of *shari'ah* from laws on morality to laws on the environment, and to working closely with the government. One of the proposals on the table is to rally the *shari'ah* police (the *wilayatul hisbah*) and the public to create clean restaurants and public toilets across Aceh, giving a large fine for those who violate this *shari'ah* code of cleanliness.[45] Another is to create green cities in Aceh by a call from the *Dinas Syariat Islam* to the public to participate in donating and planting trees and cleaning the trash. If this is the intent of *shari'ah*, the PPD argues, it will be supported by almost all Acehnese, generating the beautiful image of Islam that it truly deserves.[46] Although these are only proposals, a number of *ulama* leaders have requested that they be put in writing for further study and circulation. In response to this request, the PPD has said that unless there is a commitment to moving in that direction, the PPD will not waste its energy on such writing. The ball is now being rolled back, and the PPD is using different angles to promote the idea of peaceful *shari'ah*. It is clear that the PPD can speak openly with the *ulama* and work together on peace education. This is among the important benefits of the peace program, which the PPD did not initially anticipate, but is taking advantage of as new developments unfold.

Peace education has also positively affected *dayah* students' understanding of the world and the multiple ways they can contribute to it. During recent visits to different *pesantren* implementing peace education, the PPD learned that students are learning new skills from the curriculum. One pupil said she realized that, to develop good communication skills, she had to be a good and active listener and respect the views of others, even when those views differed from her own. She showed new knowledge by emphasizing that building trust between communicant and communicator is an important aspect of effective communication, and that "this skill is very useful for us in our study with teachers (*teungku*), in our day-to-day relations among friends, or in our future work in the community."[47] A male pupil from a *pesantren* in East Aceh speaks of his thrill upon learning of the richness of the Islamic intellectual heritage presented in the *ulama* manual. "It encourages us to think and find answers to our own problems," he said. Another student said that "the requirement of working in groups and to practice dialogue over our differences in order to find a compromise is an interesting characteristic of this book; this kind of approach is suitable for *dayah* culture."[48] One peace education *ulama* trainer from Aceh Besar was inspired by the rich graphic and computer animation used by the PPD during the training of trainers, leading him to learn advanced computer skills from one of our PPD staff, which he now uses in his own training and teaching outside the PPD.[49] These are some of the benefits of peace education for students and trainers, and the list can be lengthened.

Finally, the *ulama* project manual is now being utilized by *pesantren* teachers and students who are not specifically studying peace education. Most of the books given to *dayahs* are kept in the library or the office of the teachers, which are accessible to anyone interested in reading the book. Four *pesantren* teachers in Darul Munawwarah, Pidie, spoke of their consulting the book during a PPD visit to that *dayah* in February 2007. One teacher said: "I like to read this book to find ideas and themes for public speeches I often deliver in different villages around here. I learn a lot from this manual." Another expressed his pleasure at reading the book, not only because of its attractive language and pictures, but also because the manual presents cases and issues of daily concern that are easy to grasp. Usage of Acehnese proverbs and local names is another draw for these young teachers, along with the application of foreign terms, in both English and Arabic. These terms, said one of them, "enrich our vocabulary; although at times it looks difficult, the answer is found in the glossary." One teacher, after challenging whether the PPD had abused the *ulama* names on the cover of the manual—as others do without their permission—stated: "I like the book but I was bothered by the thought that the names of *ulama* have been used without their knowledge. However, after knowing that they were truly involved in developing this book, I like it even better." He continues by saying that the manual was full of good ideas to be appropriated by students and teachers as well as the general public: "It increases our sense of awareness of what is going on around us and in our world. The *ulama* are being challenged here, and I think that challenge can help us improve our capacity." The discussion with these four teachers ended with a statement by a person who seemed reluctant to express his view for or against the book. "I read the book and it is okay. Many of the ideas expressed here are found in other *kitabs* [books]." His unenthusiastic expression may mean that we did not need the new book because it does not bring new ideas or that the book is needed because it emphasizes messages found in the traditional *kitabs.* Either way, the PPD suggested to him that even if the content of the manual is not new, its format and presentations are unique, and that this is one of the strengths of the book. Quietly, he seemed to agree with this last point; the book has had a definite impact on individuals, even the subdued ones.

The high school program has more stories to share, since the project has been in operation for longer and is larger than the *ulama* program, but due to space constraints, this chapter shall only relate a few of them. One encouraging story is the experience of students in a PPD school in East Aceh district.[50] Unlike other areas of Aceh, this particular subdistrict has a mixed population of half Acehnese and half Javanese.[51] When daily violence exploded, some members of the two communities attacked one another, turning the region into a theater of ethnic conflict. This reality was manifested in the way the Acehnese and Javanese pupils at this school related to each other. When peace education was initiated in that school in July 2001, students in one of the classes were separated according to ethnic lines: The Javanese sat on one side of the classroom and the Acehnese on the other, with a huge empty space in between and no communication between the two. Both students and teachers later reported a real sense of tension in the class at the time. In the first two weeks of peace education class, the situation remained as it was and the teacher could not bring the two groups to work together in cross-ethnic teams. By the third week, however, the teacher began to notice changes. A number of Acehnese and Javanese were willing to sit together in one team, even though the majority of their class of about forty students remained in exclusive ethnic groups.

The breakthrough changed the situation of the class. Slowly the two ethnic groups of students began to work and dialogue together about the same issues of concern, starting with neutral issues, such as self-introspection, managing anger, and sincerity, then moving toward more controversial issues, such as conflict and violence in their community or ethnic differences and respect for pluralism. The teacher reported that the class became truly synthesized by the ninth week of peace education lessons, when they had a role-playing activity on ethnic diversity in which each working team was requested to represent an ethnic group other than their own, while projecting the characteristics of the identified ethnic group according to the positive self-description and outside negative stereotyping. This module changed the class further, manifested later in their common agreement to uphold unity and a sense of togetherness while in the class, even if they had to return to ethnic separation outside the school. PPD staff recorded this success story during the staff visit to the school a few months later, when they had a chance to speak to both teacher and students. At the time, the PPD asked students if they could carry their school sense of unity and togetherness to their respective communities to bridge the communal divide outside school. The students responded that they would try, though the PPD has not returned to the school since then to check on the students' efforts: Several months after that encouraging encounter, a new regime of martial law was implemented, during which travel to the area was almost impossible.[52]

The success of the PPD high school project is related to pupils' newfound right to education. A number of teachers from different schools reported the same experience of their students demanding the realization of this right.[53] Before the peace education course, teachers said that students were usually thrilled to find a canceled class, because they would use this extra free time to play around. However, the cancellation or even postponement of peace education brought students to the teacher's office. They called for the teacher to teach the class because they did not appreciate missing one. Students came in groups and demanded to be educated. In some cases, students enjoyed the peace education class due to its participatory learning approach, in which students were active subjects, enriched by games, discussion, and role playing. For these students, being in peace education class was both fun and educational. The reports also suggested, in some cases, that the students' newfound right to education was expressed only toward peace education because learning peace education "makes us think but also enjoy the class," as one student of MA 1 school in Banda Aceh stated. This means that the request for fulfillment of their right to education has not been extended to other subjects because of the way that other subjects are taught. However, in a few cases, students' demand to be educated had a broader implication. They complained over cancellations of any subject based on their right to education, and demanded an explanation if a cancellation occurred. This last case is a true impact of the peace education curriculum, though a wider point should be considered: If all subjects are taught in a participatory fashion, combining knowledge and skill as well as seriousness and fun, students will enjoy their studies—an approach that was very much lacking then in Indonesia, including Aceh.

The third issue on the record of peace education success relates to the current visit by the envoy of the Japanese Embassy and UNICEF to Darul Ulum school, Jambo Tape, Banda Aceh.[54] They came to speak to teachers and students about the impact of the *akhlaq* peace education manual on students' understanding of conflict, violence, and peace. They asked how interesting the book was and why it was attractive to them, inquiring as to whether the knowledge and skills that were learned were passed on to the people around them, including friends and family. The donor representatives also inquired about students' mediation skills and the benefits of those skills in their daily lives. Students' responses to their questions satisfied everyone concerning their understanding and capacity. The PPD staff who accompanied the envoy came back to our office reporting: "It was unbelievable and the students' ability superseded my expectation. It makes me really proud to be part of this program."[55] The Japanese and UNICEF personnel who had visited the school because they were interested in supporting the enlargement of our program passed a message to the PPD director. "We were pleased to see the impact of the program on students and are looking forward to receiving your proposal," wrote Maki Noda, a UNICEF representative. The Japanese diplomat Cameron Noble[56] stated that "we have seen the impact of the book on students. As far as the Japanese side is concerned, I am for it, though I can't promise anything until it is approved by Tokyo."[57] After presenting the PPD proposal to the Japanese donor committee and his justification for the needs to support the project, he reiterated his confirmation: "I can now inform you that Japan is almost certain to support peace education."[58] The combined UNICEF-EOJ support of US$200,000 for the PPD began in August 2007 to last until April 2008. Funders supported PPD activities because they believe that peace education has increased the capacity of Acehnese young adults.

The last lesson deals with the impact of peace education on teachers. As stated previously, peace education employs a participatory learning approach that makes students active subjects of the teaching learning process. In many cases, this approach requires the classroom to be arranged differently to allow students to sit in groups, on the floor, or outside the classroom in an open yard. While this is one of the requirements of our peace education manual, teachers who have received PPD training adopt our peace education methodology and approach when they teach other subjects as well. This was true of many teachers using the 2001 and 2002 peace education manuals and of teachers using the *akhlaq* peace education book. All teachers who have changed their style or method of teaching indicate that the peace education approach is more interesting and communicative. They also suggest that by making students more active in the classroom, these young adults learn a lot easier and internalize their subject better. In addition, the peace education approach to teaching forces teachers to prepare for their class better and encourages students to learn more. This way of teaching allows students to find solutions to their problems both individually or in teams. "All of these encourage me to apply the same methodology to my other subjects, for I truly enjoy the fun and challenges," said a teacher from a school in Pidie.[59] The PDD deputy director reported his surprise in his visit to MAN 2, a school in Banda Aceh,[60] when he saw a peace education teacher in that school had arranged her classroom as if she was about to teach peace education. She then said that "today I am not teaching peace education but I like to set the classroom in the peace education manner because it gives me and students a different spirit of the teaching-learning process." Her phrase—a "different spirit"— refers to all the interesting aspects of peace education methodology outlined above and illustrates that peace education has helped improve the quality of teachers.

The above description of both our *ulama* and high school projects demonstrates that Islamic peace education in Aceh has affected the hearts and minds of thousands of young adults and future *ulama* leaders of Islamic

boarding schools. If such an effort is further strengthened, Aceh's historically known Islamic intellectual position of the Gate of Mecca can be re-
discovered. Located on the northern tip of the island of Sumatra, Aceh is
recognized today to be among Indonesia's more religiously conservative
and observant provinces. The *ulama* have always been the principal ini-
tiators of religious, academic, and cultural life, which, in turn, has given
them a special place within Acehnese society. While they continue to play
a dominant role as guardians of faith and values, they are facing a serious
challenge in our fast-changing globalized world. Peace education facilitates the ability of the *ulama* to deal with change in a less confrontational
way. The institutionalization of the program in many high schools and
dayahs has also proved to be an outstanding benefit. It has changed the
attitude of students and teachers in solving their problems and engaging
in the world around them. Simply put, peace education helps Aceh sustain
its newly acquired peace.

Notes

1. See Qur'an (3:112).

2. The PPD was established in October 2000 and officially registered in January 2003
as an independent affiliate of Nonviolence International (NI), a Washington, DC-based
NGO founded by the Palestinian peace activist Dr. Mubarak Awad. Its office is in the
provincial capital Banda Aceh, though its activities cover the entire province.

3. Islamic peace was not a new activity for NI. Karim Douglas Crow (author of chapter 5
of this volume), who then led NI's Islamic Peace Forum and later became a consultant for
PPD, had worked on Islamic peace for several years. See his comprehensive bibliography
on Islam and peace on NI's website, http://nonviolenceinternational.net.

4. At the time, Dinas Pendidikan was called Kantor Wilayah Departemen Pendidikan
(the Provincial Office of Indonesia's Department of Education), known simply as Kanwil
Pendidikan.

5. These five assumed an informal advisorship during this initial formation of the PPD.

6. Both Dinas and Kanwil schools are public schools, supported by the government. The
difference between the two sets of schools is that Dinas schools teach a two-hour class of
religion each week, while Kanwil schools divide their teaching hours into 30 percent for
religion and Islamic sciences and 70 percent for nonreligious sciences. Among the religious
sciences are Arabic, Islamic ethics (*akhlaq*), faith (*aqidah*), jurisprudence (*fiqh*), and theology
(*tawhid*); among nonreligious sciences are biology, chemistry, history, and mathematics.

7. Mr. Michael Beer was the director of NI in Washington; he assisted in forming the
PPD. The PPD also recognizes the initial contribution of the chairman of NI, Dr. Mubarak Awad, to establishing the PPD. Asna Husin, founder and director of the PPD, met
with Rolf Carriere (UNICEF Country Representative in Indonesia) and Perseveranda So
(UNICEF Education Section) for the initial meeting to discuss the project.

8. The five team members represented five different institutions: the Dinas Pendidikan,
Kanwil Depag, Ar-Raniry State Institute, Syiah Kuala University, and civil society or

NGOs. The only group of the five not represented in the curriculum team was the *ulama* body of the MPU. This absence was acceptable because three of the five team members possess the qualifications (*kepakaran*) of the *ulama*: They are teachers and scholars rooted in Islamic sciences.

9. Some insightful stories at the time of the manual's completion may be appreciated. Two weeks before the completion of the task, the TPK and staff had to work day and night, while night curfew was being imposed on the entire province of Aceh, including in the city of Banda Aceh. With the PPD's driver, one of the scary tasks the staff performed was to escort some members of the curriculum team to their houses because they were afraid of violating the curfew alone. However, a couple members were brave and drove home on their own.

10. UNICEF hired Carolyne Ashton of George Mason University to independently evaluate the PPD and its implementation of peace education in schools.

11. Ashton's presentation report to Aceh's education administrators at the Kantor Wilayah Departemen Pendidikan in June 2002.

12. By this time, some new districts had emerged. Currently Aceh consists of twenty-three districts.

13. The ban on international NGOs and foreigners visiting Aceh was only lifted a few days after the great tragedy of the tsunami on December 26, 2004.

14. A number of NGO offices were targeted at the time, and the PPD also came under intense pressure.

15. This project was supported by the United States Institute of Peace (USIP) and the Canadian International Development Agency (CIDA), and managed by PPD with assistance from NI.

16. The five advisory members were Dr. Tgk. H. Muslim Ibrahim, MA; Prof. Dr. Yusny Saby, MA; Tgk. H.M. Ibrahim Berdan; Tgk. H.M. Daud Zamzami; and a woman scholar of Dr. Arbiyah Lubis, MA. Currently, the *ulama* advisory committee consists of six members.

17. The first statement was by Teungku H. Syamaun Risyad, Lc of Dayah Ulumuddin, Cunda, Lhokseumawe, and the second one by Teungku Asnawi Ramli of Dayah Budi, Lamno, Aceh Jaya, expressed during the first Medan Workshop of the Ulama convened in January 2004.

18. Dr. Muslim Ibrahim expressed his view during the first *ulama* meeting January 24–25, 2004, during which thirty-four *ulama* leaders from all over Aceh gathered to review the *ulama* peace education manual.

19. The *ulama* were also credited for their contribution to the development of Islamic spiritual scholarship and Indonesian-Malay civilization.

20. See Dr. Muslim's remarks in *Kurikulum Pendidikan Damai: Perspektif Ulama Aceh* (Banda Aceh: Program Pendidikan Damai, 2005), vi–viii.

21. Initially, *dayah* (from Arabic *zawiyah*, or religious lodge) was the name for an Islamic boarding school in Aceh, while *pesantren* is the name for the same or similar institutions in other parts of Indonesia, especially in Java and Kalimantan (Borneo). This form of education was the earliest educational institution in the country and was introduced as Islam penetrated the archipelago. However, since the mid-twentieth century, Acehnese communities have utilized the names of both *dayah* and *pesantren* to signify two different kinds of Islamic boarding schools: *Dayah* refers to a traditional educational form of institution, in which students study only Islamic sciences, and the *pesantren* to a modernist boarding

school, the system of which has incorporated modern, so-called secular subjects, in addition to teaching Islamic sciences. In the past fifteen or twenty years, the Muslim communities in the province have reemphasized the Acehnese initial name of *dayah* for both traditional and modernist Islamic boarding schools, marking that the two names are used interchangeably. The names of *dayah* and *pesantren* are utilized in the present chapter in this sense.

22. The review meeting took place in Medan on January 24–25, 2004.

23. Developing the *ulama* manual took longer than the PPD had planned. Among other challenges, the implementation of martial law on May 19 was a major setback. Though it was not as badly affected as the high school project—the *ulama* project focused its activity in Banda Aceh and involved only team members—the security measure curbed activities and slowed down the pace of development. For the curriculum team and the advisory committee, martial law led to some uncertainty and disorientation in their work; it also increased the load of their activities, as they all had to perform numerous additional tasks in response to personal, social, and communal security. This, in turn, limited their concentration on developing the *ulama* manual.

24. Even as twenty-five *dayahs* and *pesantrens* have used the curriculum with support from the project, five additional *dayahs* have implemented the manual without teachers being remunerated. The PPD trained these teachers and provided the manual and teaching instruments. In addition, the five *dayahs* are treated like the other twenty-five, receiving supervision and teacher coaching. When CIDA extended the *ulama* project an additional ten months in July 2008, the PPD added to its list fifteen more implementing *pesantrens* and trained thirty more teachers to support peace education enlargement into the *dayah* system.

25. Though the manual was officially implemented in March 2007, some of the *dayahs* had begun applying it in January 2007.

26. The second year's editorial show of fifty-two weekly sessions was later transformed into an hour-long peace show to improve its each reach, substance, and quality.

27. In December 2009, with the assistance of the European Union through the facilitation of UNDP and the Terre des Hommes Italia, the PPD published its fifth book, titled *Cerita Rakyat Aceh Bernuansa Damai* (*Tales of the People of Aceh with Peace Teachings*, shortened as *Acehnese Peace Tales*), putting together twenty-one peace stories from across Aceh into a single collection.

28. The *Acehnese Peace Tales* by the PPD alone are another indication supporting the Acehnese claim of their past Islamic cosmopolitan and encouraging cultures.

29. The manual was initially applied in all 157 Madrasah Aliyah high schools across Aceh, but in 2007–8, with the support of UNICEF and the Embassy of Japan (EOJ), the PPD enlarged the program to cover ninety additional schools under the jurisdiction of the Dinas Pendidikan. In 2009 USAID/Serasi supported the manual's implementation into twenty-five more schools under the Dinas. At the completion of the USAID/Serasi project by February of 2010, the PPD will have implemented peace education through *aqidah akhlaq* subjects in 272 high schools targeting over 50,000 young adults yearly.

30. Since its inception in 2000, the PPD has become one of the promoters of participatory learning processes aimed at strengthening pupils' character, critical thinking skills, and analytical abilities by acquiring specific skills and knowledge. All PPD manuals are geared toward fulfilling this objective.

31. For a brief theoretical approach to Islamic peace, see the introductory section, "Landasan Filosofis," in *Kurikulum Pendidikan Damai: Perspektif Ulama Aceh* (Banda Aceh:

Program Pendidikan Damai, 2005), 2–9, and *Kurikulum Aqidah Akhlaq dalam Konteks Pendidikan Damai* (Banda Aceh: Program Pendidikan Damai, 2005), 1–9.

32. The pact of mutual respect between the Muslims and Meccan Quraish was agreed upon in 628, or year six of the *hijrah,* the migration of the Prophet Muhammad and Muslims to Medina to avoid persecution by the Meccan oligarchy. For details on points of the agreement, see the *ulama* manual *Kurikulum Pendidikan Damai,* 39–42.

33. The Late Teungku Armia M. Ali, Lc of Dayah Darussa'adah, Teupin Raya, Pidie.

34. Teungku H. Razali Irsyad, BA, head of MPU of Aceh Tengah (Central Aceh).

35. Teungku Dra. Hj. Nurbaiti A. Gani of Dayah Darul Istiqamah, Bireuen.

36. Drs. Teungku H. Bukhari Husni of Pesantren Darul Iman, Banbel, Aceh Tenggara (Southeast Aceh).

37. The Indonesian government and GAM signed a peace treaty facilitated by former Finnish president Martti Ahtisaari on August 15, 2005, in Helsinki, ending thirty years of Aceh conflicts that, as Ahtisaari stated shortly after the signing ceremony, marks "the beginning of a new era for Aceh."

38. The *ulama* convened their first public meeting in mid-January 2005, attended by *ulama* representatives and scholars from all over Aceh, during which they repeated their call for a peaceful solution to the Aceh conflict and directly connected peace to the efforts at rehabilitating and reconstructing Aceh in the aftermath of the tsunami (the author was present at this gathering).

39. The *ulama* sent a score of representatives to Jakarta at the end of January 2005 to nationally repeat their call for peace and the reconstruction of Aceh (we were one of those representatives and acted as the *ulama* spokesperson to address the media after meeting the vice president of Indonesia).

40. The question was directed to Teungku Daud Zamzami during one of the PPD Advisory Committee meetings in November 2007.

41. This new law on Aceh autonomy is the law passed by the national parliament to accommodate many of the points stipulated in the Helsinki Peace Agreement between the government of Indonesia and GAM, which reemphasizes the role of *shari'ah.*

42. The head of the then *shari'ah* provincial office (Dinas Syariat Islam), Dr. Alyasa' Abubakar, said during a recent peace education training for *dayah* teachers that the concentration of *shari'ah* implementation is focused on *khalwat* (a man and woman alone in an unauthorized situation), *maysir* (gambling), and *khamar* (drug and alcohol abuses) because the people of Aceh wanted it that way. He further stated that this could be witnessed by reviewing voices of the Acehnese recorded in the local newspaper of *Serambi Indonesia* from 2001 to 2003, in which people requested the cleanup of those practices. It would be interesting to determine whether his assertion has some basis, but the author has not had a chance to personally survey the newspaper. Since then, a number of new *qanuns* have been enacted, including the newest one that led to controversies regarding the *hudud* punishments against illicit sexual acts.

43. Dra. Salmiah Jamil, one of the peace education high school teachers, during an informal discussion on safeguarding the *shari'ah* at the house of the head of Wanita Islam Organization, in January 2007.

44. Supporters of *shari'ah* often speak of its implementation in Aceh by comparing it to a child: "We know our child [implementation] is not perfect, but as a mother we love the child unconditionally," said one female teacher. She continued: "We recognize some

problems in the implementation of the *shari'ah* but we have to continue to support it and make positive changes along the way. We care for *shari'ah* the way we care for our child."

45. Many restaurants, especially those in the street and inexpensive popular food stalls, and public bathrooms are extremely filthy. Enforcing a law on cleanliness is probably the only way to tackle the issue.

46. One of the criticisms of *shari'ah* implementation is that the *ulama* have not concentrated on the corruption law (*qanun*), which would also receive massive support from the Acehnese. When asked about the lack of drive for the *qanun* among the *ulama*, he answered that "if this *qanun* is our starting point, the *shari'ah* will never be implemented, for the government would resist its implementation because such a *qanun* will make most government officers and their cronies into perpetrators." He continues: "We begin from an easy step and climb up to the most difficult one, including corruption." (Dr. Teungku H. Ismail Yacob, during a discussion on the challenges of implementing the *shari'ah* peacefully at the PPD office in February 2007). In the same manner, the PPD uses the argument of "starting from an easy step" to generate *ulama* support for the *shari'ah* environment code.

47. Interview with a female *dayah* student in Samalanga.

48. Discussion with peace education students during a visit to Dayah Asasul Islamiyah, Peureulak, Aceh Timur (East Aceh), in February 2007.

49. He is Teungku Bustami of Dayah Riadhus Salihin, Aceh Besar (Great Aceh).

50. The area has now become part of a new district called Aceh Tamiang, located at the border with North Sumatra.

51. Most of these Javanese young adults are second- or third-generation Javanese, whose parents or grandparents migrated to Aceh either on their own or through the Suharto immigration program begun in the 1970s. Supporters see this program of transporting poor Javanese farmers to different areas of Indonesia as government efforts to ease population concentration in the dense island of Java. Critics see the program as an attempt to Javanize Indonesia. The program has successfully integrated Javanese into the local population and culture in some areas and generated serious problems in other places. In Aceh, the program was regarded as one of the factors that triggered a larger vertical conflict between Aceh and Jakarta. When violent conflicts erupted, the already existing tension between Acehnese and Javanese reached a higher level: The Javanese were seen as representing Jakarta interests at the expense of the local Acehnese. Both the military and rebels manipulated this tension, turning the situation into communal abuses and killings, often against the innocent, poor populations from both camps.

52. The PPD recorded this success story in its list of lessons learned, but unfortunately, this document—along with many others in its former office—was swept away by the tsunami.

53. This record of success was also destroyed by the tsunami; the information provided is based on the recollection of the PPD staff.

54. The envoy visited the school on February 9, 2007, to observe the implementation of the *akhlaq* peace education manual in the school, as there was interest in supporting the program's enlargement to ninety high schools under the Dinas Pendidikan. As stated earlier, the PPD received its support to form a joint PPD-Japan-UNICEF partnership in 2007–8.

55. The PPD deputy director, Armia Abd Rahman, accompanied the envoy to this school.

56. Noble later moved to UNDP and helped secure EU support for the PPD's *Acehnese Peace Tales* collection that was published in 2009.

57. E-mail communications between PPD director and Noda as well as Noble in mid-February 2007.

58. Noble's email in May 2007.

59. Report of PPD staff visits to schools in Pidie in May 2007.

60. Armia visited the school in October 2006 to accompany a British embassy representative who had earlier funded the PPD high school project; the teacher in question is Dra. Sakdiah.

9

Muslim Women Peacemakers as Agents of Change

Ayse Kadayifci-Orellana and Meena Sharify-Funk

I n the past two decades, there has been increased recognition in the conflict resolution literature of the constructive role that religio-cultural
traditions can play in resolving conflicts.[1] A number of scholars have
sought to present the possible peaceful role that Muslim organizations,
individuals, and communities can assume in responding to internal and
external sources of conflicts.[2] Although these studies break new ground,
providing insights into the profound importance of religion and culture
in conflict resolution, they contain very little information about the role of
women in reconciliation processes. This absence of attention to the role of
women leaves provocative questions unanswered: To what extent do Muslim women participate in conflicts and their resolution? Do they in any
way influence outcomes? Does Islamic tradition provide scope for women's
full participation in social and political life and their contribution to peacemaking, or does it limit women's opportunities to contribute to the overall
peacebuilding process?

This essay discusses the role that Muslim women have played and are
playing in resolving conflicts and building sustainable peace in their communities. Because of the need for much more research on this topic, our
approach is exploratory in nature, and intended to frame the issue for future
investigations of diverse and creative ways in which Muslim women are
engaging their religious and cultural traditions to prevent violent conflict,
bridge deep divides, and establish the foundations of a peaceful society.

Women and Peace Building: Shared Challenges

Since the beginning of the twentieth century, there have been vibrant debates that aim to articulate the relationship between women and war, but women's active involvement in official peacemaking processes has been quite limited until recent decades. In most societies, women's access to intellectual and political institutions has clearly been restricted, reducing opportunities to participate fully in the social, moral, economic, political, and educational lives of their communities. As Elise Boulding, a leading scholar in the field of peace research, argues, women have long been on the "underside of history."[3] However much value cultures may have placed on women's roles in the private sphere, access to the public sphere—and to forums in which decisions are made about war and peace—has been circumscribed.

Time and again, women have been associated with the ethics of care, peace, pacifism, and beauty of soul, whereas men have been associated with war, bravery, justice, and reason.[4] Some pioneering feminist writers even endorsed such views. As Virginia Woolf, in *Three Guineas,* states, to "fight has always been the man's habit, not the woman's. . . . Scarcely a human being in the course of history has fallen to a woman's rifle. . . . It is difficult to judge what we do not share."[5] More recently Sarah Ruddick, in her discussion of a feminist ethics of care, argues that women's approach to war is based on positive moral principles of care and love, whereas existing political practices are based on a different approach to moral judgment.[6] According to Ruddick, maternal thinking not only rejects war, but actively embraces a politics of peace because "maternal attentive love, restrained and clear sighted, is ill adapted to intrusive, let alone murderous judgments of others' lives."[7] This view is also mirrored in Carol Gilligan's influential work *A Different Voice,* which similarly privileges an ethics of care.[8]

It may be true that more men are involved in the decision-making processes that lead to war, as well as in the active fighting itself, and that more women "tend to be victims of wartime rape [and] refugees, suffer[ing] displacement and deprivation."[9] However, this does not account for the diverse roles women play in conflict situations, becoming partisans as well as victims. Current events and historical records provide many examples of women who have been involved in waging and supporting wars, or even leading armies, like Jeanne D'Arc. At times, war and conflict may bring unique benefits to women by creating opportunities to assume new roles as providers, breadwinners, and, at times, political leaders.[10] As J. Ann Tickner notes,[11] narrowly associating women with peace and pacifism can reinforce the exclusion of women in politics and international relations, and reproduce a gender stereotype of women as passive victims of war.

Rather than reliance on traditional stereotypes, a more nuanced exploration of women's perspectives, experiences, and voices would appear more
conducive to strengthening the role of women in peacebuilding and peace
negotiations.

Although distinctions can be overdrawn, women and men do experience war and conflict differently; they have different needs and interests.
As Christine Chinkin notes, women must address tremendous problems
during and after conflicts,[12] including caring for traumatized children and
ex-combatant family members who are trying to reintegrate into normal
life. Women may face special burdens in dealing with the challenges of
resettlements and meeting the everyday needs of their families within
a transformed economic context. For peace to be sustainable, such specific needs and interests must be addressed and reflected in the process of
peacebuilding.

Treating gender stereotypes with caution while carefully attending to
the concrete realities of social life is especially important for those seeking
to support Muslim women's peacebuilding efforts. Too often, research on
Muslim women has reproduced the stereotype of faceless, voiceless victims
of structural violence in a patriarchal world—victims who are in dire need
of emancipation. This depiction of Muslim women, hidden behind a *burqa*,
hijab, or veil, creates an image that is exotic and mysterious, yet weak and
defenseless. Quite often Islam itself is seen as the root cause of discrimination, oppression, and violence against women. Such descriptions render
questions about active peacebuilding by Muslim women moot: If Muslim
women are necessarily oppressed by their religious culture and need to be
saved by secularization or modernization, how can one imagine anything
more than a passive role for women in a peacebuilding process?

Although the stereotype of the passive and repressed Muslim woman
may be true in some cases, it fails to convey the diverse and complex experiences of Muslim women over fourteen centuries across many conti-
nents. Since the inception of Islam as a religious tradition, women have
participated in social, political, economic, and intellectual life, as poets,
Islamic scholars, spiritual teachers, warriors, heads of state, and business-
women. Though Muslim society, like virtually all traditional agrarian societies, developed a clear patriarchal structure, women's experiences were
by no means monochromatic. Lady Mary Wortley Montagu, the wife of
the first British ambassador to the Sublime Porte in Istanbul, noted in
1711 "that she believed Turkish women to be the only free citizens of the
Ottoman Empire: They had money of their own and could travel about
inconspicuously to meet possible lovers, covered as they were by heavy
robes and veils."[13] While the capacity of contemporary Muslim women to

achieve prominence in the public sphere is less than that of many women in Western societies, sweeping historical generalizations are both unwarranted and problematic—unwarranted because they distort past realities and problematic because they foreclose new ways of imagining Muslim women's roles in peacebuilding.

In short, Muslim women's experiences during and after conflicts can be as diverse as those of other women in different cultures. On occasion, Muslim women have actively supported or even led armies, as did Hassiba Ben Bouali of Algeria during the Battle of Algiers in 1956–57.[14] At other times, Muslim women have become victims of rape, torture, or displacement during violent conflicts. There are also many current and historical instances in which Muslim women have been active in peacemaking and reconciliation in their communities.

Gendered Discourses in the Muslim World: Muslim Women's Rights in Islamic Contexts

The need to confront stereotypes about Muslim women should not be an excuse to ignore real barriers within contemporary Muslim cultures to recognizing and enhancing women's peace efforts. Deep-rooted and sustainable peace cannot be achieved in Muslim societies without addressing their severe discrimination against women—a form of structural violence. The status and public comportment of women is a highly charged symbolic topic in Islamic-Western relations and in the internal politics of Muslim nations. Kandiyoti describes the status of women as "hotly contested ideological terrain where women were used to symbolize the progressive aspirations of a secularist elite or a hankering for cultural authenticity expressed in Islamic terms."[15] Conservative Muslims have used and continue to use the Qur'an, the *hadith,* and examples from the lives of prominent women in the early period of Muslim history as sources to confirm the gender asymmetries in their societies.[16] As such, they reinforce and reproduce the difficult conditions in which many women live.

Many modern scholars, both Muslim and non-Muslim, react to challenges that women in the Muslim world face and attribute them to what they regard as an inherent backwardness in Islamic religious culture. As Kandiyoti notes, the first women's reformist movements in the Muslim world emerged from the ranks of an educated, nationalist male elite who viewed women's issues within the broader context of a modernist progressive agenda. These modernists focused mainly on expanding women's education and ending practices such as seclusion, veiling, and polygamy. Women's issues have become a key focus for secularist elites in the Muslim world, who, like the modernists in the West, have found Islamic religious culture—in particular, uncritical reliance on traditional religious sources—to be the main source for violation of women's rights and equality in their societies.

Where secular nationalists sought to address issues of women's rights within a framework of modernization and secularization, others have sought to steer a course between outright emulation of Western societies and reactive celebration of traditional norms. Responding to the cultural and economic interferences of Western values into Islamic society, they have concentrated on the compatibility between Islam and modernization. Such scholars and activists, basing their positions on the same sources, have argued that Islam calls for an equal treatment of men and women and empowers women to take proactive roles in their communities.

The conservative and progressive Muslims derive their legitimacy from the same Islamic texts and examples, and the diversity of interpretation of Islam points to the interplay between cultural, socioeconomic, and political contexts and their influence on how religious texts are understood to address contemporary issues. As Riffat Hassan has noted, "it is obvious that the position of women in a country cannot be isolated from the sociocultural, political, and economic frameworks within which they function."[17]

Historically, the culture of patriarchy has conditioned the interpretation of Islamic sources, and—in conjunction with other factors—affected the status of women in society. The Qur'an has been interpreted mainly by men, in ways that have reflected male experiences with the legal, social, and political issues that Muslims face. Where the priorities, perceptions, or interests of men and women appear to diverge, these interpretations and the resultant Islamic rulings tend to favor male perspectives on social, political, and cultural arrangements. While traditional authoritative tendencies cannot realistically be represented as monolithic, patterns exist which, when compared, give coherence to a general traditionalist perspective.[18] Generally speaking, traditionalist culture is strongly patriarchal—women were extremely rare among the ranks of religious interpreters—and contained an inherent preference for patriarchal authoritative rule. From this perspective, religious as well as political authority was a distinctly male prerogative. Such a gender-selective approach to authority has restricted women's access to intellectual, religious, and political institutions, limiting opportunities for women.

In their analysis of Qur'anic verses emphasizing equality between men and women, such as "I shall not lose sight of the labor of any of you who labors in My way, be it man or woman; each of you is equal to the other" (Qur'an 3:195), most contemporary traditionalists claim that this equality pertains first and foremost to the level of piety. They argue that there is no contradiction in affirming the spiritual equality of men and women while upholding separate gender roles. The Qur'anic norm affirms righteousness as the single most important standard for defining the dignity and worth of a person, yet essential differences between the sexes require different distributions of rights and responsibilities.

In other words, women are spiritually and morally equal, but they have separate roles in society, usually defined by their status within the family unit as mothers, wives, sisters, and daughters.[19] This "equal before God, unequal before man" interpretation leads to strong preferences for a gendered division of labor,[20] for several traditionalist reasons. First, such a division follows what, for traditionalists, is the natural, divinely revealed order of labor: As women are the nurturers and men are the providers, the genders should specialize in the forms of labor that fit their natural predispositions. Second, the moral weaknesses and inherent vulnerabilities of men require limited interface between genders. Reducing social interaction between men and women protects both from sexual temptation and shelters women from exploitation. Third, maintaining distinctive gender codes has the added virtue of preventing Islamic communities from succumbing to the norms of Western, unisex societies, in which distinctions between the proper roles and functions of women and men in society have been blurred, leading to immoral behavior patterns, the breakdown of family structures, and other social problems.[21]

Critiques notwithstanding, traditional patriarchal attitudes have demonstrated remarkable staying power. Despite the wave of secular reform in the mid-twentieth century, traditionalist and revivalist responses have preserved traditional certitudes and convictions.[22] Though women are increasingly acquiring access to higher education and entering into political activism, they are still subject to patriarchal structures that reinforce traditional cultural norms in the public and private spheres. In response, many scholars of women and Islam have argued that such approaches to the construction of social norms effectively silence the voices of women. Because knowledge systems and social ideologies have almost invariably been composed, interpreted, and applied by men, there is a tendency to overlook serious problems and contradictions. Amina Wadud describes these problems as follows:

> In the Islamic state as imagined in conventional thinking, women are second-class citizens enjoying no right to self-determination. In historical *shari'ah*, Muslim women are simply appendages to their men, first their fathers and brothers, later their husbands (and possibly, at the end of a long life, finally their sons). Within historical *shari'ah*, the situation is one where Muslim men exercise domination over women and enjoy a monopoly of political power and force .... [Historical *shari'ah*]

cannot now be appropriately implemented because of its inability to accommodate modern understandings of gender relations and the status of women. Because it is male biased, a new interpretation needs to be arrived at—which it readily can—through a new methodology of Qur'anic interpretation.[23]

This modern methodology of Qur'anic interpretation calls for reconciliation between the eternal and temporal dimensions of God's revelation. It also calls for an understanding of the process of interpretation itself and a rereading of Islamic history and sacred texts. Many of the Qur'anic verses and *hadiths* refer to particular historical events. Some *hadiths*, in particular, appear to be inconsistent but still are valuable sources for peacemaking analysis.

Due to high illiteracy rates, especially among women, Muslims in general have limited access to the Qur'an and to a wide range of religious interpretations of the text, which increases their dependence on clergy. Furthermore, religious sources are written in classical Arabic, which differs from the contemporary Arabic used by many Arabs today and poses additional problems for Muslims from non-Arabic speaking societies. Many Islamic educational institutions, such as *madrasas*, offer only basic religious education, with virtually no attention to critical thinking and citizenship skills.

The socioeconomic and political contexts of communities also significantly affect the way religious texts are interpreted. In many Muslim societies, experiences of colonization, imperialism, and underdevelopment strongly affected the way in which Islamic positions toward women have been understood and interpreted. Riffat Hassan, reflecting on the experience of women in Pakistan,[24] states:

> Despite the fact that Islam made a very comprehensive survey of the position of women in society and laid down a very detailed legal framework for their rights and privileges, any powerful crusade against ... their liberation met with considerable opposition due to various sociological, economic, and political reasons. The forces of custom, orthodoxy, and reaction joining hands at times with colonial rulers did much to water down the rights of equality granted by Islam.

In her analysis of the rise of fundamentalism in the Muslim world, Fatima Mernissi observes that fundamentalist movements in the Muslim world represent an attempt to affirm Muslim identity in the face of rapid social changes that threaten the traditional social organization of the society, as well as a reaction to the boundary problems created by intrusions of colonialism, new technology, consumerism, and economic dependency.[25] Due to these conditions, many Muslims are resentful toward the West and thus are easily influenced by aggressive and radical interpretations of Islamic beliefs and core values.

Women as Peacemakers in the Muslim World: Historical Precedents

Despite real challenges and social inequalities, countless Muslim women are working tirelessly to address conflicts and build peace in their communities. These women, like many others in the non-Muslim world, are doing extraordinary work against seemingly insurmountable challenges and not without success. Their peace efforts are inspired by and derived from their faith, history, culture, and intellectual heritage, and they have adapted to the cultural and traditional sensitivities of their unique communities.

Unfortunately, the many devoted Muslim women who are working strenuously to address conflicts and build peace in their communities are largely invisible in scholarship and journalism. The lack of thorough research analyzing the peacebuilding and conflict resolution approaches of these women is a shortcoming of the field of peace and conflict resolution, and an opportunity for future researchers. Granting visibility to women peacebuilders will help to correct the impression that there are no Muslim women addressing conflicts and building peace in their communities.

The invisibility of Muslim women peacebuilders is a function of many convergent factors, some unique to the status of Muslim women in their society, others a result of organizational differences between Western and Muslim understandings of civil society institutions in general and peacebuilding institutions in particular.[26] Because Islam influences all aspects of life in Muslim societies, it is usually impossible to separate the religious from the nonreligious. Thus, individuals who work to reduce violence and resolve conflicts may not feel the need to articulate or emphasize the role of Islam in their work. Islam nonetheless reinforces their motivation to work toward peace under Islamic principles of ethics as stated in the Qur'an and *hadiths*; these are among their key resources for being peacemakers. Furthermore, even though Muslim communities have long traditions of social services, community assistance, and charitable work, they do not typically have organized institutions devoted solely to peacebuilding. Peace work is regarded as a collective responsibility; the perception is that those who are aware of the tradition, such as elders and religious leaders, are the natural peacemakers. These individuals often work on an ad hoc basis, as their services are required; however, they fall short in establishing stable institutions focused on peacemaking, conflict resolution, and being tied to a larger network of peacebuilding.[27] With respect to the role of women, patriarchal norms tend to hinder women's participation in public decision-making and prevent the granting of recognition to women's participation when it occurs, often through informal channels and processes.

To expand the role of Muslim women in peacebuilding, it is helpful to appreciate the heterogeneity and diversity of experiences among Muslim women throughout the centuries. Though their contributions have often been neglected by traditional Muslim historiographers as well as modern feminist thinkers, Muslim women have played critical and diverse roles since the formative years of Islam: They have been transmitters of *hadith*, poets, judges, preachers, warriors, benefactors, scholars, orators, ambassadors, political advisers, politicians, economists, and queens. Famous women Companions of the Prophet, such as his beloved wife Khadijah (who was the first to embrace his message), his daughter Fatima, his youngest wife Ayesha, and the first Muslim martyr Sumeyya, who refused to concede to torture and abuse, have informed and inspired many of these roles.

Women have also been important in preserving and transmitting the customs of the Prophet and his family. Transmission of *hadith* is a serious endeavor for Muslims, as it is the second source of Islamic law and the foundation for other fields of knowledge. After the death of the Prophet Muhammad in 632, the guidance of his wives Hafsa, Umm Habiba, Maymuna, Umm Salama, and Ayesha were critical to understanding and practicing the life of the Prophet and maintaining it in the historical memory of the Islamic community (*ummah*). Ayesha, particularly in Sunni Islam, is a pivotal figure in preserving *hadiths*, as she is recognized as one of the earliest reporters of the largest number of them and as one of their most careful interpreters. Abu Misa al Ashar reports that "whenever we Companions of the Prophet encountered any difficulty in the matter of any *hadith* we referred it to Aisha and found that she had a definite knowledge about it."[28] Aisha received the title Mother of Muslims because she dedicated her life to educating Muslim children, particularly girls. She was also known as an excellent orator and public speaker.[29]

Women continued to be important in the *hadith* literature throughout Islamic history, and authoritative *hadith* collections, such as Sahih Bukhari, could not have been completed without the efforts and contributions of many women. Many other women played important public roles. Some women would become preachers. Umm Waraqa was instructed by the Prophet to lead the men and women of her home and her village in prayer. The people of Umm Waraqa's home, however, were so numerous that the Prophet appointed a *muezzin* (one who calls the prayer) for her. She was also one of the few to hand down the Qur'an before it was written.

Historically, Muslim women were also crucial to public policy in different capacities. Women have served as judges, advisers, and inspectors. The Prophet himself is understood to have based his treatment of women on kindness, respect, and love, and to have paid heed to his wives' opinions on critical issues. During the Al-Hudaybiya Treaty, the Prophet asked his wife Umm Salama for advice, which he later took, even though her advice contradicted the opinions of influential male companions.

During the early Islamic period, a woman named Ash Shifa bint Abdullah was recognized for her skill in medicine and in public administration. Like Samra bint Nuhayk al Asadiyya, she was appointed inspector of the markets at Medina by Umar ibn Al Khattab, the second caliph of Islam.[30] Ash Shifa was also granted responsibilities for public health and safety in Basra, Iraq.[31] Other women have served their communities in different capacities. Rufaidah bint Sa'ad, who lived at the time of the Prophet, is recognized as the first Muslim nurse and was active in various community services to help the poor and needy. Al Udar al-Karimah Shihaab ad-Din Salaah (d. 1360) was the vice-regent Queen of Yemen and has been remembered as the champion of the poor. She has been recognized for contributions to public security, administrative order, and justice and for being a builder of schools and mosques.

Women were active in wartime during the earliest years of Islamic history. Apart from carrying food and water and serving as nurses, they also fought or led armies. Nusaibah bint Ka'b al-Ansariya actively fought during the Battle of Uhud. The Prophet's wife Ayesha led armies into a battle against Ali, who was the son-in law of the Prophet and would become the fourth caliph, in what was known as the Battle of the Camel. Later, women also became queens and governors. Shajar ad-Durr, who controlled Egypt during the thirteenth century, led the resistance against Crusaders. A woman named Shagab became ruler of the Abbasid Empire for a time, and Radiyah Begum ruled Delhi and was famed for her sense of justice and fair dealing.

In addition to being actively involved in leading armies, fighting battles, serving as nurses to the wounded, caring for prisoners of war, and attending to orphans, Muslim women were prominent in peacemaking. Islamic history offers numerous examples of courageous Muslim women have stood up to the commanders of invading armies, mediated conflicts, and reconciled opponents. Ibn Qunfudh of Morocco recorded an incident in which one of the women he studied with, Lala Aziza of Seksawa, reconciled a conflict between two rival groups.[32] He also described an encounter between Aziza and al-Hintati, the governor of Marrakesh and a powerful general who was attempting to conquer south Morocco. Ibn Qunfudh tells her story:

> Aziza walked out of the safety of the foothills and onto the harsh Marrakesh plains and stood—alone—before the great general and his army. She confronted al-Hintati with her words and his own faith. She spoke of God's demands for justice, the pull of the good, the wrong of harming God's creation. Aziza talked the general out of his

conquest. She convinced him to leave the people of Seksawa unharmed. He marched his army back to Marrakesh, and she returned to the mountains. The story of a woman who dared to stand up to a general and his army, armed only with her faith. Down through the centuries people have sought refuge there, people fleeing the excesses of central power or local conflicts, people falsely accused of crimes, people who have done great harm.[33]

Aziza's tomb is a sanctuary and it is still used as a space for mediating conflicts. Even during the time of the independence war with France, her tomb was a safe haven where many people would seek peace and calm in the midst of the conflict. Another woman known for her unique gift of resolving conflicts is Ghazal Ahmad 'Alwan al-Magdashiyya of Yemen (b. 1860).[34] Reciting poetry has been an important component of Yemeni conflict resolution tradition for centuries. As Flagg Miller observes, "central to dispute-mediation, a persuasive *zamil* [a particular kind of poetry] can sometimes conclude negotiations to both sides' satisfaction before they officially begin."[35] Although she did not receive any formal education and did not know how to write or read, Ghazal Ahmad was recognized as a versatile poet and mediator, and as one of the region's powerful political voices.[36] She is recorded as having successfully resolved a number of conflicts. Her poetry reflected her mastery of tribal and regional laws as well as her capacity "to wield power in order to ease tensions in her community."[37] Her name was given to the main lecture hall at the Empirical Research and Women's Studies Center at the University of Sanaa. However, the center's activities were terminated in 1999 following conservative anger over certain presentations made at a September 1999 conference on challenges for women's studies in the twenty-first century. *Al-Sahwa*, the Yemeni Congregation for Reform's weekly newspaper, criticized the conference, the center's curriculum, and its staff[38] and denounced the concept of gender (*al-jandar*) as alien to Islam. The center was renamed and restructured to comply with the conservative agenda of these groups.[39]

Peace in Islamic Sources

> Verily for all men and women who have surrendered themselves unto God, and all believing men and believing women, and all truly devout men and truly devout women, and all men and women who are true to their word, and all men and women who are patient in adversity, and all men and women who humble themselves before God, and all men and women who give in charity . . . . for all of them has God readied forgiveness of sins and a mighty reward (Qur'an 33:35).

Just as historical interpretations of Islamic sources have often failed to realize the potential for readings that accentuate equality between men and women, so too has history bequeathed an ambivalent legacy of interpretations concerning war and peace. Islamic sources, however, are rich with content on matters of social justice and peace, and familiarity with this content can provide a basis for understanding women's actual as well as potential contributions to peacebuilding in Muslim societies. Religious sources have empowered women in past and present generations to challenge injustices and make moral appeals to aggrieved parties.

Although there is no singular Islamic tradition of peace and peacemaking traditions, certain fundamental ethical principles and moral values provide coherence to Muslim peacemaking across cultures and historical periods. These principles and values are derived from the Qur'an, *hadith*, and *sunnah* (the example of the Prophet). Although passages in the Qur'an and other Islamic sources legitimize war to defend a community or correct injustice, references to values such as peace (e.g., *salam, silm, sulh*), forgiveness, patience, compassion, and mercy are central to the discourse of Islam's sacred texts.

Qur'anic discourse on peace begins with God, as al-Salam (peace) is one of the most beautiful ninety-nine names of God in the Islamic tradition (Qur'an 59:23). The Qur'an refers to peace as the greeting, language, and condition of paradise (10:10, 14:23, 19:61–63, 36:58), and God calls believers to the "abode of peace" (10:25). These uses suggest that peace is a positive state of safety or security, which includes being at peace with oneself as well as with fellow human beings, nature, and God.[40] Based on these verses, peace in Islam is associated with a wide range of concepts. These concepts include, but are not limited to, justice and human development, wholeness, salvation, perfection, and harmony.[41] Thus, peace in Islam is much more than a mere absence of war and must be defined in positive conceptual terms—such as the presence of justice, apt conditions for human development, and security.[42]

Other peace-related values that are central to the Qur'an, and thus to Islam, include love, kindness, benevolence, wisdom, knowledge, service, social empowerment, universality, dignity, the sacredness of human life, equality, individual responsibility, accountability, patience, collaboration and solidarity, inclusion and participation, and unity in diversity, among others.[43] Although all these values are critical for the Islamic ethics of moral action and establishing a peaceful society, the Arabic terms for unity (*tawhid*), compassion (*rahmah*), mercy (*rahim*), sound nature (*fitrah*), justice (*adl*), forgiveness (*afu*), and stewardship (*khilafah*) provide keys to understanding Islamic approaches to developing a sustainable peace on earth.

Tawhid, the "principle of unity of God and all being," urges Muslims to recognize the connectedness of all beings, particularly all human communities, and calls to work toward establishing peace and harmony among them. *Tawhid* is the basis of Islamic universalism, tolerance, and inclusivity, as everything emanates from God and everything is part of His creation irrespective of species, race, nationality, creed, or gender.[44] Thus, the principle of *tawhid* recognizes the unity of all human beings irrespective of gender or religious, ethnic, or racial origin, and asks Muslims to establish harmony across all humankind—men and women—based on mutual understanding and cooperation.

Before they take any action, Muslims invoke *rahmah* (compassion) and *rahim* (mercy) by reciting "*bi ism-i- Allah al-rahman al-rahim*" ("we begin in the name of Allah Who is compassionate and merciful") as a reminder that actions must be dedicated to God, who is Himself merciful and compassionate. True Muslims, in turn, must also be merciful and compassionate toward all God's creations. The salience of these values in Islamic invocations would appear to imply that, to be a true Muslim, one cannot be insensitive to the suffering of other beings, whether physical, economic, psychological, or emotional, nor can one be cruel to any creature. Thus, torture, inflicting suffering, or willfully hurting another human being or another creature is unacceptable according to Islamic tradition.[45]

According to Islam, *fitrah*, or the original constitution of human beings, is good and sound in character.[46] *Fitrah* recognizes that each individual—women and men—is furnished with reason and can be good, choosing to work toward establishing harmony. Moreover, this principle recognizes the goodness that inheres in each and every human being at birth, regardless of different religious, ethnic, racial, or gender backgrounds (Qur'an 17:70, 95:4, 2:30–34, 33:72). As such, it is a safeguard against dehumanizing the other. The idea of *fitrah* rejects notions of innate sinfulness and recognizes that all humans are related and derived from the same origin (4:1, 6:98):

> O mankind! Revere your Guardian-Lord, Who created you from a single person, created, of like nature, his mate, and from them twain scattered (like seeds) countless men and women—fear Allah, through Whom you demand your mutual (rights), and (revere) the wombs (that bore you): for Allah ever watches over you (4:1).

Adl, or justice, is the key to establishing harmony and sustainable peace among God's creation; the Qur'anic conception of peace cannot be attained unless a just order is first established. The Qur'anic notion of justice is universal and valid for all human beings, as the following verse indicates:

> O ye who believe! Stand out firmly for Allah, as witnesses to fair dealing, and let not the hatred of others to you make you swerve to wrong and depart from justice. Be just: that is next to piety: and fear Allah. For Allah is well acquainted with all that ye do (5:8).

In principle, Islamic justice should transcend any consideration of gender, religion, animosity, race, or creed.[47] Therefore, all Muslims must work to establish justice for all, including social and economic justice (Qur'an 4:135, 57:25, 5:8, 2:178, 2:30, 16:90). This notion of justice extends to both men and women, Muslim and non-Muslim, and cannot be achieved without an actively, socially engaged community:

> The believers, men and women, are protectors, one of another: they enjoin what is just and forbid what is evil: they observe regular prayers, practice regular charity, and obey Allah and His Messenger. On them will Allah pour His Mercy: for Allah is Exalted in power, Wise (9:71).

As Said and Funk have noted, "ever since Muslims first assembled themselves in political communities they have believed that a society guided by inspired laws, wise leadership and extensive consultation is superior to a society governed by the arbitrary whims of a king, dictator or oligarchy."[48] In an Islamic context, justice need not be retributive, yet peace cannot be real unless founded upon principle.

Afu, or forgiveness, which is repeatedly emphasized in the Qur'an, urges Muslims to reconcile. The Qur'an stresses that forgiveness is a higher value than hatred, and believers are urged to forgive when they are angry (Qur'an 42:37). Said, Funk, and Kadayifci note that "there is a clearly articulated preference in Islam for nonviolence over violence, and for forgiveness over retribution."[49]

Khilafah (stewardship or vice-regency) is closely tied to the Islamic understanding of social responsibility and reminds all Muslims that they are responsible for order on earth; as they are God's vice-regents (2:30, 33:72), they should try to bring all creatures under the sway of equilibrium and harmony and live in peace with creation.[50]

Based on these principles, the Islamic understanding of peace can be defined as a process in which human beings establish foundations for interacting with each other and with nature in harmony, instituting just socioeconomic structures where human beings can flourish and fulfill their potentials. Consequently, tyranny, discrimination, and oppression that perpetuate injustice toward any group in Muslim society are viewed as being among the greatest threats to peace and harmony.

The local conflict resolution mechanisms and practices that were developed in different parts of the Muslim world over the past fourteen centuries give voice to the above values, even as they reflect social and geopolitical conditions that facilitate or impede their expression. Local realities have affected the evolution of the Islamic traditions of peace and peacemaking, resulting in various approaches to resolving conflicts in the Muslim world. The impact of past struggles and historical traumas also conditions Muslim thinking about Islam and peacemaking; experiences of civil war and invasion, in particular, have reinforced modes of religious thought that highlight insecurity and downplay the importance of tolerance and dialogue. Some have argued that many imams or religious leaders lack the proper training to critically engage with this historical legacy and revisit opportunities to give newly revitalized expression to sacred values. Moreover, in present Muslim-majority contexts, strong perceptions of injustice stemming from the colonial experience privilege more adversarial (and stereotypically male) readings of religious sources. All these factors contribute to a lack of preparation to actively apply Islamic peacemaking values in contemporary Muslim societies. Educational programs could dramatically affect this state of affairs by training religious leaders in Qur'anic sciences, distributing textbooks and handbooks on Islamic values for peacebuilding and tolerance, developing curricula highlighting Islamic sources of peace and tolerance in the *madrasa* as well as public educational systems, and developing radio programs that address Islamic values of peace and reconciliation.

More active participation of women in religious life and study—though not guaranteed to produce a different voice, as Western feminists suggest—necessarily brings more diverse human experiences into the reading of foundational texts, and could also redirect attention to Islamic peacemaking values. This can have the salutary effect of destabilizing forms of thought that have detracted from applying core peaceful Islamic values, creating space to reappropriate Islamic peace traditions for both women and men. To some extent, this work has already begun. Three cases below, from Afghanistan, Thailand, and Kenya, show the way forward.

Contemporary Illustrations of Muslim Women Peacemaking

Sakena Yacoobi and Afghan Institute for Learning

Sakena Yacoobi, founder and director of Afghan Institute of Learning (AIL), has been working to rebuild her country and incorporate Islamic traditions of peace and conflict resolution into her practice. Empowered by her faith, Yacoobi established AIL in Peshawar in 1995, the same year the Taliban came to power.[51] This period was particularly restrictive for Afghan women, as the Taliban practiced one of the most radically conservative understandings of *shari'ah* law in the Muslim world. AIL persisted, however, and developed programs focusing mainly on health and education of Afghan women and children. AIL supported eighty underground home schools for 3,000 girls in Afghanistan after the Taliban closed girls' schools in the 1990s, and continued to use grassroots strategies to meet social needs after the Taliban's defeat in 2001. AIL now serves 350,000 women and children each year through its educational learning centers,

schools, and clinics, in both Afghanistan and Pakistan.[52] AIL's work includes teacher training programs, preschool education, advanced classes
for children whose education was interrupted by war and violence, wom-
en's learning centers, and grassroots community-based organization support programs. AIL also established a university for women and publishes
a magazine.[53] Its human rights and leadership training is derived from the
Qur'an and is recognized as the first organization to offer such training
to Afghan women.[54] Collectively, the organization was nominated for the
Nobel Peace Prize in 2005.

As a result of strong cultural traditionalism and the effects of protracted
conflict on social structure, legitimacy and authority in Afghanistan are
based on a combination of religion (Islam), tribal codes, and custom. Born
and raised in Afghanistan, Yacoobi understands that the culture and traditions of Afghan society not only constrain efforts to improve the status
of women, but also provide possibilities for transformation—like another
Muslim peacemaker within the Pashtun tribe, Abdul Ghaffar Khan (1890–
1988), who established the world's first known nonviolent army by invoking
Islamic principles of patience, kindness, and love, as well as Pashtun traditions of honor, bravery, and commitment to oath. Ghaffar Khan was an
incredible nonviolent Muslim activist who mobilized the frontier province
of the Indian subcontinent during British colonialism to protest oppression
and occupation. Just like Ghaffar Khan, Yacoobi's programs account for cultural sensitivities:[55] "Although traditional Afghan village social structures,
gender roles, and religious beliefs often actively discourage the education
of women, Sakena harnesses these very institutions to establish interactive
programs in education, health, human rights, peace education, environmental awareness, democracy, and income generation."[56] Like Khan, she utilizes
Islam's emphasis on social welfare, justice, and service, interpreting the Islamic understanding of *jihad* in its broadest sense.[57] She views education as
a sacred duty, consistent with the Islamic emphasis on justice and protection
of the poor, weak, and needy. She also supports the needs of the oppressed
by dedicating herself to attitudinal change through education and working
on local developmental projects, promoting hygiene and sanitation.

By teaching women to analytically study the Qur'an, Yacoobi equips
her students with knowledge of the Qur'anic principles of equality between men and women and their rights derived from Islam. In addition
to teaching women their rights, her programs include training on how
to negotiate on the basis of shared values, such as diversity, equality, fair-
ness, and justice, among others.[58] By integrating religious values with her
educational priorities, she empowers women to become effective leaders in
their communities.

In addition to consulting the Qur'an and religious laws, Yacoobi's programs use logic and reason to articulate sound arguments that are relevant to the daily experience and lives of Afghan society. Understanding the close linkages between education and peace, Yacoobi incorporates peace education in her curriculum. As a result of learning the skills to negotiate and solve problems, many women have been able to bring these ideas to their families and their communities. When women were faced with opposition, they could challenge a husband—or, for that matter, any male counterpart—by referring to Qur'anic verses and saying, "you are a good Muslim, aren't you? Then look, the Qur'an says that husbands must be fair to their wives."[59] This has had a concrete result on many occasions, leading some men to change their behavior. Some men who initially opposed the education of women came to actively support the efforts of wives, daughters, and sisters to learn.[60]

The current situation in Afghanistan remains quite challenging and presents significant dangers to Sakena Yacoobi and her programs. The Taliban is still powerful in many parts of the country. But armed with love and a strong sense of responsibility derived from her faith, Yacoobi continues her work despite these dangers.

Soraya Jamjuree and Friends of Victimized Families

Soraya Jamjuree, an eminent activist in South Thailand who aspires to bring reconciliation between Muslims and Buddhists, has been working tirelessly to address the consequences of conflict. Though the present violence between Muslims and Buddhists is a relatively recent phenomenon—militants, mostly from outside Thailand, have been fighting to create a separate state since 2004—its origins can be traced to assimilationist and discriminatory policies initiated by ethnic Thai Buddhist governments in Bangkok at the beginning of the last century[61] and the extremely heavy-handed policies of then Prime Minister Thaksin Shinawatra in the 1960s. The violence in southern Thailand is complicated by the Marxist guerrillas, funded by outside forces, who wish to secede from Thailand. In response to the attacks, the central government has used the military forcefully to crack down on the separatists and imposed martial law in the southern province. As a result, both Buddhist and Muslim families have suffered tremendous losses. As Goodman relates, "more than 2,300 people have been killed in insurgent violence and government counter-attacks."[62]

Jamjuree, founder of Friends of Victimized Families and a lecturer at Prince Songklah University in Pattani province of South Thailand, leads Muslim university students to work with those caught up in the violence. Supported by the Canadian government, she works with traumatized families, both Muslim and Buddhist, who have lost members of their families—particularly husbands and fathers—and are struggling with their children. They focus on women and children particularly as they recognize that many men die during the violence and women whose husbands have died face significant difficulties in trying to care for their families alone. To address the needs of these women, Jamjuree and her student teams visit them at their homes, help them meet their basic necessities by bringing them small gifts, food, and job opportunities, and offer psychological and emotional support. The program now extends to fifty families in the region.

Started in 2005, the program aims to build a healthy relationship between visitors and victims to improve the families' coping skills and establish a database of victimized people. To avoid a vicious cycle of revenge and hate between the two communities, Jamjuree aims to bring together the women from both sides and reduce their pain. As she states:

> When violence happens, maybe the victim's family wants to take revenge if they know who killed their husband or their son. I think we can reduce their pain, reduce their sadness and stop them from taking revenge. If we have success in this way, maybe we can stop the violence. Not now, but in the future.[63]

Jamjuree also has a community radio where she promotes an understanding of the different languages and cultures in southern Thailand. Her contributions to peace in the region, as well as the enhancement of women's rights, was recognized with an award by the National Human Rights Commission of Thailand on March 8—Women's Day—in 2006.[64]

Jamjuree has served as a mediator in her community to resolve various disputes. She helped mediate between a group of protesters called Student Network for People's Protection who were demonstrating against the abuses by the security forces and Thai authorities at the Pattani Central Mosque demonstrations on May 31, 2007.[65] The protest lasted for five days. On the fifth day the government called in prominent Muslim civil society leaders to mediate the conflict, including Jamjuree. A committee, consisting of religious leaders, local non-government organizations (NGOs), police, and military officers, was formed to investigate the cases of police abuse.

Like Sakena Yacoobi, Soraya Jamjuree has been inspired by a strong sense of responsibility derived from the Islamic principles of vice-regency and justice. Having written her master's thesis on the content and role of the Friday sermon (*khutba*) in the community, she understands the role of religion and culture in shaping attitudes of believers toward social issues.[66] Refusing to allow militants to create hate between Muslims and Buddhists,[67] she invokes Islamic ideals of forgiveness, apology, and compassion. Jamjuree faces significant threats to her life; however, she too derives courage and motivation from her faith. She states that "we believe God will protect us, because we do good things to help the people."[68]

Dekha Ibrahim Abdi and Wajir Peace and Development Committee

Dekha Ibrahim Abdi is a Muslim peacemaker from the Wajir district of Kenya. In 2007 she received the Right Livelihood Award, also known as the alternative Nobel Prize, for her peace and conflict resolution work in Kenya, Somalia, Ethiopia, Sudan, Uganda, and other parts of the world.[69] She is the founding member of the Wajir Peace and Development Committee (WPDC), formed to address the violence that erupted after the 1992 drought stirred political upheavals in Kenya. She is also a founding member of other peace initiatives, such as the Coalition for Peace in Africa and ACTION for Conflict Transformation.

Frustrated by constant violence, arms smuggling, refugee migration, kidnappings, and mistrust among clans, Dekha Ibrahim and a group of women invited women from different social strata to discuss the situation. Soon the Wajir Peace Group was established with the main objective of restoring peace by involving all stakeholders, especially women and youth. The group was successful in reducing violence and promoting peace, and it established the Wajir Peace and Development Committee in 1994 to ensure sustainability. Dekha Ibrahim and her colleagues utilized a combination of approaches to address the conflict. The model developed in Wajir used interfaith dialogue to help resolve tensions and conflict between religions, including all warring factions in negotiations to create possibilities for ownership of the peace process.[70] Rapid-response teams were formed to lessen resentment and reduce retaliation after provocative incidents.

The approach in Wajir was also sensitive to the region's cultural values and derived methods from its faith traditions. Because traditional Wajir culture accords women only a minor role in the public sphere, the group was aware that a peace movement led by women might not be successful. Therefore, although women maintained direct influence, they took measures to ensure that male elders and young male leaders of the community were also represented in the leadership of their peace initiative. By doing so, the Women for Peace nonviolent movement was accepted as mainstream and legitimate.[71] In Dekha Ibrahim's words,

> We started with small initiatives that quickly launched into a highly organized movement. We knew that though this was not so simply a women's problem, we women could inspire positive change through nonviolence .... But if we said we could do it singlehandedly, solely as women, the community would have crushed us.

People would have been very critical. So instead, we said, "Let us incorporate them and let them lead."[72]

In the long run, however, by providing successful examples of reducing violence and conflict resolution and by involving religious leaders and elders, Wajir was able to challenge and change traditional perceptions of women's role in society in general and in peacemaking in particular.[73]

The Wajir approach to peacebuilding worked in conjunction with Somali law, which required an entire clan to be involved in resolving a conflict and sought justice mainly through material appeasement. Drawing on traditional precedents, Wajir convened peace festivals to publicly honor and financially reward major stakeholders and gave peace awards to police chiefs who had once incited violence. In this way, the group transformed the way in which some major players conceived of their power and legitimacy, encouraging them to regard themselves as the peacemakers. As one of the first men to join Wajir notes, "The chiefs think differently now . . . . They pull up their socks so they can keep getting presents!"[74]

Believing that all religious traditions can contribute to peacebuilding, Dekha has found, in her own faith of Islam, inspiration and a tool in her work as a peacemaker. The first peace festival, organized in 1995, had as its theme and title the Islamic understanding of peace as a collective responsibility. In workshops that bring together Muslims and Christians, Ibrahim encourages people to analyze themselves using verses from the Qur'an. Her work has also been an inspiration in different parts of the Muslim world. The peace *shura* of another peacemaker in Afghanistan, Mohamed Suleman, is based on the Wajir model.[75]

Strengths and Limitations of Muslim Women's Peacemaking Initiatives

Contrary to stereotypical assumptions, peacebuilding in historical and contemporary Muslim communities is by no means an exclusively male prerogative. Although women's roles in the public sphere have been—and are still—circumscribed by traditional practices and assumptions, many Muslim women have found and continue to find in Islam a set of values and norms that affirm and encourage their own efforts to resolve conflict and build social peace. Many contemporary Muslim women peacemakers are engaging in a process of rediscovery, finding new meanings within Islamic tradition and new ways of perceiving such historical, or archetypal, Muslim women figures, especially but not limited to such archetypes as Khadijah, Fatimah, and Aisha, all of whom have long embodied and personified certain nonviolent qualities that all Muslim women can aspire to. Additionally, scholars of Islam are discovering many unknown historical Muslim women scholars and activists, such as Lala Aziza of Seksawa, whose stories inspire courage in modern-day peacemakers.

By rereading and rediscovering religious texts and traditions and embarking on bold social initiatives, contemporary Muslim women, such as Sakena Yacoobi, Soraya Jamjuree, and Dekha Ibrahim, are attempting to redefine what it means to be a Muslim woman in a conflict situation. Rather than accepting the role of a passive victim or a person who must be defended or liberated by others, they are demonstrating that Muslim women can be and are vital in reconciliation processes. By invoking a mandate in Islam for gender equality and peacemaking, they are stepping beyond more discrete ways of influence behind the scenes, such as using informal networks to relay information or attempting to persuade male members of the household to support and join peacemaking efforts. In the process, they are drawing upon and extending the range of resources within Islam for peacemaking, adding new examples of empowered women to those provided in Muslim historiography.

Although the principles and cases explored here demonstrate the potential vitality of Muslim women's peacebuilding, much more research is needed to generate a richer understanding of the challenges and opportunities Muslim women face when seeking to advance peace on an Islamic basis. Because Muslim women's peacebuilding efforts have not been thoroughly researched, a number of avenues for further exploration are open. First, there is a need for field research on and analysis of the role of Muslim women in peacemaking efforts. Such research might focus on the diversity of contexts and strategies used by particular activists, intellectuals, and organizations. Second, no systematic effort has been made in peace studies or Islamic studies to understand how Muslim women peacemakers network at both the local as well as global levels. This research would entail a project of tracing transnational conversations and peacemaking activism. It also would allow the researcher to explore the negotiations of different identities and peacemaking processes.

The previous two recommendations lead to a third area of further research—to analyze the overall effect of Muslim women peacemakers on society, the nation-state, and the larger Muslim community. Such recommendations beg future researchers to answer several questions. How are Muslim women who are involved in peacemaking activities influencing peaceful reform? Are traditional patriarchal authoritative processes challenged or complemented by such activism? The extent of knowledge is limited, and the field is wide open for new insights and contributions. One point, however, seems powerfully clear: In traditional Islamic contexts, the chances of women exerting effective leverage for peace appear to rise dramatically when they are equipped with knowledge of relevant values and precedents within their religious and cultural traditions.

Notes

1. D.W. Augsburger, *Conflict Mediation across Cultures* (Louisville, KY: Westminster/John Knox Press, 1992); Mohammed Abu-Nimer, *Nonviolence and Peacebuilding in Islam* (Florida: University Press of Florida, 2003); Raymond Cohen, *Negotiating across Cultures: International Communication in an Interdependent World* (Washington, DC: United States Institute of Peace, 1997); K. Avruch, *Culture and Conflict Resolution* (Washington, DC: United States Institute of Peace, 1998); Douglas M. Johnston, "Religion and Conflict Resolution," Fletcher Forum of World Affairs (Winter/Spring 1996); Cynthia Sampson, "Religion and Peace Building," in W. Zartman and L. Rasmussen, eds., *Peacemaking in International Conflict: Methods and Techniques* (Washington, DC: United States Institute of Peace, 1997); David R. Smock, ed., *Interfaith Dialogue and Peacebuilding* (Washington, DC: United States Institute of Peace, 2002).

2. Amr Abdalla, "Principles of Islamic Interpersonal Conflict Intervention: A Search within Islam and Western Literature," *Journal of Law and Religion,* vol. 15, no. 1–2 (2000–1), 151–84; Mohammed Abu-Nimer, "Conflict Resolution Approaches: Western and Middle Eastern Lessons and Possibilities," *American Journal of Economics and Sociology,* vol. 55, no. 1 (January 1996), 35–52; William Chittick, "The Theological Roots of Peace and War According to Islam," *Islamic Quarterly,* vol. 34, no. 3 (1990), 145–63; Karim D. Crow, "Nonviolence in Islam," (Washington, DC: Nonviolence International, 1997); Ayse S. Kadayifci-Orellana, *Standing on an Isthmus: Islamic Narratives of War and Peace in Palestinian Territories* (Lanham, MD: Lexington, 2007); Ayse S. Kadayifci-Orellana, "Islamic Tradition of Nonviolence: A Hermeneutical Approach," in Daniel Rothbart and Karina Korostelina, eds., *Identity, Morality, and Threat: Towards a Theory of Identity-Based Conflict* (Lanham, MD: Lexington 2007); Abdul Aziz Said, Nathan C. Funk, and S. Ayse Kadayifci, eds., *Peace and Conflict Resolution in Islam: Precept and Practice* (New York: University Press of America, 2001); Abdul Aziz Said and Nathan Funk, "Peace in the Sufi Tradition: An Ecology of the Spirit," in *Peace and Conflict Resolution,* 247–62.

3. Elise Boulding, *Underside of History: A View of Women through Time,* revised ed. (Newbury Park, CA: Sage Publications, 1992).

4. Georgia Wayler, *Gender in Third World Politics* (Boulder, CO: Lynn Reinner, 1996), 7–8.

5. Virginia Woolf, *Three Guineas* (San Diego, CA: Harvest Books, 1963), 3.

6. Sarah Ruddick, *Maternal Thinking: Toward a Politics of Peace.* (London: Women's Press, 1990); Kimberly Hutchings, "Feminism, Universalism, and Ethics of International Politics," in V. Jabri and E. O'Gorman, eds., *Women, Culture, and International Relations* (Boulder: Lynne Rienner, 1999), 17–37.

7. Ruddick, *Maternal Thinking,* 150.

8. Carol Gilligan, *In a Different Voice: Psychological Theory and Women's Development* (Cambridge, MA: Harvard University Press, 1982).

9. Donna Ramsey Marshall, "Women in War and Peace: Grassroots Peacebuilding," *Peaceworks,* no. 34 (August 2000), 8–9.

10. Marshall, "Women in War and Peace."

11. J. Anne Tickner, "Why Women Cannot Run the World: International Politics According to Francis Fukuyama," *International Studies Review,* vol. 1, no. 3 (1999), 3–11.

12. Christine Chinkin, "Peace Agreements as Means for Promoting Gender Equality and Ensuring Participation of Women: A Framework for Model Provisions," United Nations Division for the Advancement of Women, Office of the Special Advisor on Gender Issues and Advancement of Women, Department of Political Affairs, EGM Peace Report, December 10, 2003, http://www.un.org/womenwatch/daw/egm/peace 2003/reports/Final report.PDF (accessed November 24, 2009).

13. Lady Mary Wortley Montagu, *The Selected Letters of Lady Mary Wortley Montagu* (New York: St. Martin's Press, 1971), cited in Ferashteh Nouraie-Simone, *On Shifting Ground: Muslim Women in the Global Era* (New York: Feminist Press at CUNY, 2005).

14. Susan Sylyomovics, "Hassiba Ben Bouali, If You Could See Our Algeria," *Middle East Report* (January–February 1995), 8–13.

15. Kandiyoti Women, *Islam and the State* (Philadelphia, PA: Temple University Press, 1991), 3.

16. Deniz Kandiyoti, "Women, Islam and the State" *Middle East Report,* Gender and Politics, no. 173 (November–December 1991), 9.

17. Riffat Hassan, "The Role of Women as Agents of Change and Development in Pakistan," *Human Rights Quarterly,* vol. 3, no. 3 (August 1981), 68–75.

18. It is important to recognize the diversity and complexity of not only Muslims, but also the traditionalists, known as *mutaqlidun.* There have been and are many traditionalists who have upheld more reformist or moderate beliefs. For a good comparative analysis of contemporary traditionalists, see Muhammad Qasim Zaman, *The Ulama in Contemporary Islam* (Princeton, NJ: Princeton University Press, 2002).

19. Barbara Freyer Stowasser, *Women in the Qur'an: Traditions, and Interpretation* (Oxford: Oxford University Press, 1994).

20. See Norani Othman, "*Shari'a* and the Citizenship Rights of Women in a Modern Nation-State," Institut Kajian Malaysia dan Antarabangsa, Working Paper no. 10, Bangi, Malaysia, 1997.

21. For more about the problem of unisex societies according to Muslim traditionalists, see Lois Lamya al-Faruqi, "Women in a Qur'anic Society," *al-Tawhid,* vol. 1, http://www.al-islam.org/al-tawhid/women-society.htm (accessed November 24, 2009).

22. More scholars are distinguishing between premodern traditionalist characteristics and modern traditionalist characteristics by utilizing the labels of classical traditionalist and neotraditionalist. See Jon Armajani, "Differing Islamic Worldviews," in *Dynamic Islam: Liberal Muslim Perspectives in a Transnational Age* (University Press of America: Lanham MD, 2004), 11–12.

23. Amina Wadud, "Muslim Women as Citizens?" in Nissim Rejwan, ed., *The Many Faces of Islam: Perspectives on a Resurgent Civilization* (Gainesville, FL: University Press of Florida, 2000), 207.

24. Hassan, "The Role of Women as Agents of Change," 69.

25. Fatima Mernissi, "Muslim Women and Fundamentalism," *Middle East Report,* no. 153 (July–August 1988), 8–11.

26. Mohammed Abu-Nimer and S. Ayse Kadayifci-Orellana, *Muslim Peacebuilding Actors in Africa and the Balkans* (Washington, DC: Salam Institute, 2005).

27. See chapter 11 in this volume.

28. See Zakir Naik, "Women's Rights in Islam: Modernization or Outdated?" *Islamic Voice*, vol. 10–11, no. 129 (October 1997), http://www.islamicvoice.com/october.97/wome.htm (accessed November 24, 2009).

29. Amina Wadud, "Legacy of Aisha," *New Internationalists*, no. 345 (May 2002), http://findarticles.com/p/articles/mi_m0JQP/is_2002_May/ai_87424387 (accessed November 24, 2009).

30. See *Imam Zaid Malik Islamic Center Newsletter*, vol. 10, no. 3 (March 15, 2004), www.icnef.org/newsletters/2004/Mar2004.pdf (accessed November 24, 2009).

31. Hassna'a Mokhtar, Laura Bashraheel, and Somayya Jabarti, "Al-Angari Blames Ignorance of Rights for Women's Plight," *Arab News,* May 19, 2008.

32. Elaine M. Comb-Schilling, "Sacred Refuge: The Power of a Muslim Female Saint," *Fellowship: Islam, Peace, and Nonviolence,* vol. 60, no. 5–6 (May–June 1994), 17.

33. Comb-Schilling, "Sacred Refuge," 17.

34. W. Flagg Miller, "Public Words and Body Politics: Reflections on the Strategies of Women Poets in Rural Yemen," *Journal of Women's History,* vol. 14, no. 1 (Spring 2002), 94–122.

35. Ibid., 97.

36. Ibid., 96.

37. Ibid., 97.

38. Human Rights Watch, *Human Rights Watch World Report 2001: Yemen: Human Rights Developments,* http://www.hrw.org/wr2k1/mideast/yemen.html (accessed November 24, 2009).

39. Miller, "Public Words and Body Politics."

40. Ibid.

41. As commented by Yusuf Ali about Surah 19, verse 62 (note 2512): "*Salam,* translated 'Peace,' has a much wider signification. It includes (1) a sense of security and permanence, which is unknown to this life; (2) soundness, freedom from defects, perfection as in the word *salim*; (3) preservation, salvation, deliverance, as in the word *sallama*; (4) salutation, accord with those around us; (5) resignation, in the sense we are satisfied and not discontented; besides (6) the ordinary meaning of peace, i.e., freedom from any jarring element. All these shades of meaning are implied in the word *Islam.*" *The Holy Qur'an,* trans. Yusuf Ali (Medina, Saudi Arabia: The Custodian of the Two Holy Mosques King Fahd Complex, 1413 A.H.).

42. See Said and Funk "The Role of Faith in Cross-Cultural Conflict Resolution," *Peace and Conflict Studies,* vol. 9, no. 1 (May 2002), 37–50. See also Kadayifci-Orellana "Religion, Violence and the Islamic Tradition of Nonviolence," in *Turkish Yearbook of International Relations,* no. 34, Ankara University, 2003.

43. Abu-Nimer, *Nonviolence and Peacebuilding.*

44. Abu-Nimer and Kadayifci-Orellana, *Muslim Peacebuilding Actors.*

45. For more information on these, see Ralph H. Salmi, Cesar Adib Majul, and George K. Tanham, *Islam and Conflict Resolution: Theories and Practices* (Lanham, MD: University Press of America, 1998); and Majid Khadduri, *Islamic Law of Nations: Shaybani's Siyar* (Baltimore, MD: Johns Hopkins University Press, 1966).

46. Abdul Aziz Said, and Nathan C. Funk, "The Role of Faith in Cross-Cultural Conflict Resolution," *Peace and Conflict Studies,* vol. 9, no. 1 (May 2002), 37–50.

47. Kadayifci-Orellana, *Standing on an Isthmus*, 102.

48. Said and Funk, "The Role of Faith in Cross-Cultural Conflict Resolution," 42.

49. Said, Funk, and Kadayifci, *Peace and Conflict Resolution,* 8.

50. Chittick, "Theological Roots," 156.

51. David Little, *Peacemakers in Action: Profiles of Religion in Conflict Resolution* (New York: Cambridge University Press, 2006), 391.

52. Creating Hope International (CHI), http://www.creatinghope.org/sakenayacoo bibiography (accessed May 26, 2008).

53. See Afghan Institute of Learning, http://afghaninstituteoflearning.org/imports/ AIL_Programs.pdf, p. 6 (accessed December 2009).

54. Creating Hope International (CHI).

55. Social Innovation Conversations (SIC), Design for Change: Interview with Sakena Yacoobi http://cdn.conversationsnetwork.org/SI.DFC-SakenaYacoobi-2008.01.11.mp3 (accessed May 26, 2008).

56. See Ashoka: Innovators for Public, "Sakena Yacoobi," http://www.ashoka.org/node/3916 (accessed November 24, 2009).

57. Kadayifci-Orellana, *Standing on an Isthmus.*

58. Little, *Peacemakers in Action,* 392.

59. Ibid.

60. Ibid.

61. International Crisis Group, "Southern Thailand: Insurgency, Not Jihad," *Asia Report,* no. 98, May 18, 2005.

62. Aaron Goodman, "Thailand: Women for Peace Offering Solace to Victims of Conflict," *Frontline* (August 9, 2007), http://www.pbs.org/frontlineworld/rough/2007/08/thailand_women.html# (accessed May 8, 2008).

63. Ibid.

64. Asia Pacific Forum on Women Law and Development, *Forum News,* vol. 19, no. 1 (January–April 2006), http://www.apwld.org/vol191-03.htm (accessed May 15, 2008).

65. International Crisis Group, "Southern Thailand: Problem with Paramilitaries," *Asia Report,* no. 140, October 23, 2007, fn 89.

66. Jamjuree's 2000 study of the content and role of Friday *khutbah* in the community appears as a thesis in the library of Chulalongkorn University, Bangkok.

67. Goodman, *Frontline,* August 9, 2007.

68. Ibid.

69. USAID, "East Africa," http://eastafrica.usaid.gov/en/Article.1117.aspx (accessed May 28, 2008).

70. USAID, "Alternative Nobel Prize Goes to Kenyan Peacemaker," Aid in Action, December 2, 2007, http://eastafrica.usaid.gov/en/Article.1117.aspx (accessed November 24, 2009).

71. Emma Dorothy Reinhardt, "Kenyan Women Lead Peace Effort," *National Catholic Reporter Online: Paths to Peace,* April 26, 2002, http://www.natcath.com/NCR_Online/archives/042602/042602p.htm (accessed November 24, 2009).

72. Ibid.

73. Abu-Nimer and Kadayifci-Orellana, *Muslim Peacebuilding Actors,* 29.

74. Reinhardt, "Kenyan Women."

75. Right Livelihood Award, "Interview with Dekha Ibrahim," http://www.rightlivelihood.org/dekha_ibrahim_abdi_interview.html (accessed November 24, 2009).

10

Enhancing Skills and Capacity Building in Islamic Peacemaking

Qamar-ul Huda

In late August 2000, more than one thousand representatives of various religious traditions gathered at the United Nations in New York City for the Millennium Summit of World Religious Leaders.[1] It recognized, among other things, that religious peacebuilding is an important factor in contemporary affairs. As religious leaders acknowledged their dutiful roles in mediation, conflict resolution, and peacebuilding, the United Nations recognized the need to develop a strategic multilayered approach that included religious leaders in global peacebuilding efforts,[2] appreciating how religious leaders contributed to civil society and public life and underscoring their potential work in creating stable healthy societies. The Millennium Summit of World Religious Leaders raised critical questions about how religious actors participate in the public sphere, especially when, in many societies, separating the religious and secular is a fundamental value. To what extent can religious leaders and their institutions be involved in conflict prevention and peace stability without the fear that their work is an invisible form of proselytization? This chapter examines the theories and practices of Islamic peacemaking, focusing on specific areas of skills transmission for Muslim peacemakers to move beyond the strictly religious realm and into the larger realm of peacemaking and peacebuilding. It builds on the fields of both religious peacemaking and Islamic conflict resolution literature in an attempt to integrate religious leaders into a larger framework of peacemaking.

Islamic Religious Peacemaking

Religious peacemaking can be something like an isolated island, operating strictly within religious institutions and communities. More should be done to integrate it into international peacemaking efforts and the work of international organizations in conflict prevention and transformation. Religious peacemaking has a role to play in promoting human rights, democracy, women's rights, and education; providing relief to refugees and victims of natural disaster; and working to reduce child labor, poverty, hunger, and disease.[3] These areas are already the purview of major UN institutions—the United Nations Educational, Scientific, and Cultural Organization (UNESCO), World Health Organization (WHO), United Nations Development Programme (UNDP), the UN Division for the Advancement of Women, and the United Nations Children's Fund (UNICEF)—but despite the incredible efforts of these organizations, it is unclear to what extent religious leaders, and Islamic religious leaders specifically, are familiar with the vast network of international organizations and non-governmental organizations dedicated to peacebuilding.[4] In addition to leading religious services in the mosque, imams are crucial players in daily mediation efforts between communities and individuals and between communities and state officials. In religious schools across the Muslim world, seminaries (*madrasas*) give children a free education and remove them, in some cases, from a cruel life of poverty, abandonment, and abuse. Teachers and administrators are psychological and spiritual counselors as well as a social, economic, and religious support system; in many cases, they are navigating the future of an entire family by encouraging the education of children. In addition, like imams, they can be mediators for the community in times of crisis and sometimes are the sole individuals deciding on interfaith dialogue programs or intrafaith-reconciliation peacemaking projects.[5]

Islamic approaches to conflict resolution and peacebuilding have been developed by many scholars, including Abdul Aziz Said,[6] Mohammed Abu-Nimer,[7] Ali Asghar Engineer,[8] Abdullahi An-Naim,[9] and Chaiwat Satha-Anand.[10] Like their counterparts in Jewish, Christian, Hindu, or Buddhist peacemaking scholarship, Muslims scholars must deal with how violence is associated with the faith tradition and how contemporary politics shapes the debate about Islam. These scholars, and others like them, have returned to scripture, historical texts, and other narratives to demonstrate that at the heart of Islam is a message of nonviolence, tolerance, and respect for all creatures. Though the academic study of Islamic peacemaking is rooted in Western studies of conflict resolution and international relations, some Muslim scholars have challenged the appropriateness of

Western approaches to conflict resolution in a Muslim context. They argue that Islamic peacebuilding and conflict resolution methods are intrinsically different from Western models of peacebuilding, especially in their attention to culture and history, their use of indigenous practices of conflict resolution, and their reliance on religious traditions.[11] According to this line of thought, Islamic peacebuilding is built upon spiritual and theological models, whereas Western models stem from the rational secular field of conflict resolution. Western scholars have failed to consider fully the possibilities for religious peacemaking, and when it is recognized, it is usually examined through a few examples of Christianity or Judaism. As a result, Western studies of Muslim religious peacemaking are unbalanced and flawed by the foundational assumptions and theories of conflict resolution.

An often-cited example is the obsessive concentration in the Western conflict resolution literature on the political nature of Islam and the inability to separate religion from public affairs. In that literature, the inseparability of Islam from public life and governance is the source of spreading religious radicalism, intolerance of other faiths, and the move toward theocracy.[12] This, unfortunately, narrows the conversation about Islamic peacemaking into a discussion of how extremists co-opted the faith and how the faith's identity is now associated with radical extremism. It then becomes mired in the history of extremism, extremist ideology, tactics of extremists, neutralizing extremists, and finding the real moderate Muslim to rescue the tradition.[13] Peacebuilding in Islam thus focuses on simply defeating extremism: As one public official stated, "Islamic extremism and terrorism needs to be treated like the issue of slavery in the mid-19th century, it is evil and has to be eliminated."[14] Muslim critiques have pointed out that this analysis lays too much emphasis on Islamist parties and exaggerates their influence on religious identity and on the religious practices of everyday Muslims. To connect the imposition of *shari'ah* or the activities of extremists or Islamist parties to Islamic peacemaking is hardly insightful or realistic. To put it simply, the politicization of the image of the religion of Islam makes it even more complex to discuss the very topic of peacemaking without a reference to contemporary politics. That is to say that the contemporary politics of Islamist parties, the war between Western forces and al-Qaeda, and the rhetoric of radicalism often diminishes the profound work of peacemaking activities around the Islamic world. Why is it there is a predisposition to fixate on conflict-driven news items and not peacemaking efforts in Muslim communities?

Recent scholarship on Islamic peacemaking and peacebuilding has included significant historical, theological, scriptural, and contemporary case studies of Muslims involved in both. This approach can be called the proper information approach, built on the assumption that historical accuracy and a greater understanding of the past can counteract extremist ideology; it is hopeful that, once the interpretation is disseminated, Muslim extremists can be convinced of its validity and converted to peacemaking. In a sense, however, the approach is using selective historical studies to undermine radical interpretations of Islam. On one hand, the use of proper information fleshes out a historical context for the debate about peacemaking and conflict resolution in Islam and demonstrates a wide range of divergent views within this discourse. On the other hand, from the perspective of radicals, the approach is flawed because the opinions of past thinkers are viewed as illegitimate and unauthoritative. One of the qualities of reactionary fundamentalists and radicals is their belief in the absolute nature of their understanding of Islam, and this absolutism constructs a world vision that ties the self to the sacred.[15]

However, the proper information approach is just one accepted method in the Islamic peacemaking literature. The most dominant approach is to underscore the validity of violence, yet limit its use, to pursue justice and create peaceful societies. This group of scholars interprets the works of classical and late-middle period of legal scholars, from Malik ibn Anas (d. 795) and al-Shafi'i (d. 974), to al-Jawzi (d. 1200) and Ibn Taymiyyah (d. 1328), to examine how prominent Muslim legal scholars argued for and against the use of violence. This approach assumes an inherent relationship between Islam and violence because legal scholars (*fuqaha*) themselves sanctioned its limited use. However, they essentially miss the fundamental point that the classical Muslim legal scholars, either as a group or individuals, were acting in accordance with an intellectual field of jurisprudence dealing with war and peace; legal scholars, in any religious tradition, are not representatives of Islam.[16] In addition, this approach ignores or refuses to acknowledge any peaceful means of resolving conflicts in the Islamic tradition because the legal texts do not develop arguments on this subject, nor did *fuqara'* find evidence in the sacred texts. An example of this approach is commonly used by Harvard University trained political scientist Sohail Hashmi, who states that "the Islamic discourse on war and peace begins from the a priori assumption that some types of war are permissible—indeed required by God—and that all other forms of violence are, therefore forbidden."[17] Hashmi and others in the validity of violence approach completely miss the intellectual context and primary function of the classical *fuqara'*. Contemporary scholars have identified texts, medieval scholars, and specific trends amongst the *fuqara'* to justify their assumption that legalized violence was an essential component of the religion, which is erroneous and intellectually dishonest.

These approaches to Islamic conflict resolution and peacemaking studies are part of a wide range of scholarship. Some focus on textual, historical, theological, and scriptural examination; others on the Prophetic narratives. Some explore legal and just-war theories as well as rules of engagement in an Islamic context; others elaborate on themes of mercy, justice, compassion, tolerance, pluralism, and dialogue. Still others contextualize Islam within comparative studies in ethics, international relations, theology, postcolonialism, or secular humanist studies of human rights. Finally, there are those who examine specific conflicts to analyze examples of Islamic peacemaking. The scholars work across the academic disciplines, and their method of interpreting Islamic peacemaking reflects their intellectual framework. Specific methods in analyzing Islamic peacemaking include retrieving original sources for historical accuracy; returning to textualism (Qur'an, *hadith*, *sunnah*, legal texts) for the original intent of the texts; identifying key historical moments in the Prophet's life or his Companions to justify a particular interpretation; using specific major historical and theological studies; contesting authority with questionable statements; devaluing the authenticity of texts or selection of texts; identifying key figures of the past to demonstrate the legitimacy of peacebuilding; emphasizing *fiqh* and *shari'ah* from the classical or late-middle period to determine present questions on conflict; returning to classical just war theories and rules for engagement in Islam as a source for international relations, peacemaking, and conflict resolution; emphasizing the pluralistic and inclusive nature of scholarly opinions; identifying key themes, such as justice, love, compassion, sacrifice, interfaith relationships, mercy, and forgiveness; using sacred symbolism and rituals as examples of mediation; incorporating secular humanist theories to apply to Islamic principles; using empirical evidence to quantify the level of peace or conflict in Muslim societies; identifying Christian theological trends, such as liberation theology, to apply to Islamic peacemaking; applying comparative ethics of political theory and war; applying religious, nonreligious, Western, and Islamic principles of mediation; stressing asymmetric power relations between Western and Muslim societies; applying a postcolonial, less-developed nation, political-economy approach; and identifying key conflicts—such as those in Iraq, Palestine-Israel, or Kashmir—as a point of reference for Islamic peacebuilding.

Scholars and activists have modeled their thinking on Islamic peacebuilding and conflict resolution based on the above categories. In some cases, Islam is juxtaposed with current intellectual trends. In other approaches, some core values and principles are identified as essential and serve as the foundation for Islamic peacebuilding and conflict resolution.

Some Muslim scholars with theological or religious studies training commonly begin with the Qur'an and examples from the Prophet's life to justify a point as authentically Islamic. In other cases, Islamic peacebuilding is not restricted to an established precedence or religious text; rather, ideas are tied to particular moments in human experience, in cultural contexts, or in contexts of multiple histories or political and theological debates. But taken together, they emphasize an appreciation of multiple cultures within Islam and the fact that Islamic culture is not homogenous, either across the world or in any particular community.

Cultural anthropologists argue that cultural habits consist of inherited experiences from previous generations, but are, in turn, organized and interpreted by individuals in the present generation.[18] Culture is a discourse, a way for individuals or communities to express religious, psychological, social, political, and economic experiences—including through violence. John Burton argues that the root causes of violence in any culture or civilization lie in unmet human needs of security, identity, shelter, basic resources, and acceptance of others.[19] And Black, Scimecca, Avruch, and others stress that cultural considerations matter a great deal in conflict resolution; individuals in conflict zones need to alter their own perceptions as well as the attitudes of the parties involved to ensure that they cognitively understand their power in mediation and the process of transforming the conflict.[20]

The variety of approaches exemplifies the diversity of thought and practice by scholars who accept multiple approaches in peacebuilding and conflict resolution. For some, textual and legal evidence is needed in all parts of living. Others feel that key Qur'anic themes of justice, mercy, accountability, and reconciliation are enough of a foundation for their particular work. This multiplicity of approaches is reflected in Islam itself: Without a central body of religious authority, Muslims have had to rely on their own individual and larger authorities. This constitutes a serious challenge—and also window of opportunity—for those engaging in Muslim peacemaking. Which Islamic peacemaking approach is best to ease the pain of a victim of a twenty-five-year civil war who lost all his family? How do European Muslim peacemakers confront racism and rising Islamophobia? Should they turn to theology, historical accuracy, selective Qur'anic themes, key Islamic values and principles, revered historical figures of the past, or should they employ an interfaith approach? The heart of deciding which approach works for an individual or a community must consider the cultural, political, economic, and conflict context. However, who makes the decision is as important as what is decided. Too often, religious leaders in Muslim communities are heavily influenced by internal politics, international or local

Islamist movements, national interests, or the pressure of certain governments. All these pressures limit their independence in planning the most
effective strategy for peacebuilding efforts. Rarely do Muslim religious
leaders meet to discuss peacebuilding skills, and it is even more rare that
they are exposed to prominent non-Muslim non-governmental organizations (NGOs) that have the capacity-building skills to be critical players in
peacebuilding and conflict mediation.

The Content and Context of Peacemaking Skills

Peacemakers in Muslim communities need to consider how the state tends
to respond to domestic social and political conflicts, both historically and in
the present. A religious peacemaking program in Egypt cannot ignore the
state's arrest of thousands of Muslim Brotherhood members and *Jama'at
Islami* members in the past two decades. Following President Anwar Sadat's assassination in 1981, there has been a direct relationship between
the state's use of brute force against civilians and the radicalization of the
two major Islamist parties. This radicalization threatens domestic stability,
foreign investment, and the health of the national psyche, and it limits the
space for non-Islamist Muslims to participate in the public sphere. Muslim religious leaders have strong and emotional recollections of communities persecuted by the state. Whether it is the Kurds and Shi'ites in Iraq,
Sunnis of Hama in Syria, Moro Muslims in Philippines, or Shi'ites and
Sufis in Pakistan, the state-civilian relationship often is one of mistrust
and exploitation, which continues today in leaders' daily experiences. If
the primary objective for peacebuilding activities is to transform the current reality, it is crucial to understand these challenges to peacebuilding in
Muslim communities, which arise at several levels.

At the individual level, a peacemaking program relies on its ability to
change participants' perception of the conflict at hand, as well as their understanding of their role to the specific conflict and to the larger society.
There is a general agreement among facilitators that peacemakers' skills
should consist of conflict analysis, negotiation, mediation, dialogue, reconciliation, nonviolent mobilization techniques, and ability to work toward
finding common interests for the good of society.[21] For religious leaders,
these skills are central to religious peacemaking and include religious ethics, theology, scriptural reasoning, principles and practices of forgiveness,
compassion, justice, love, dignity, reflection, patience, solidarity, service,
tolerance, and reconciliation.[22] Essentially, however, all peacemaking activities, for religious leaders and nonreligious participants, aim to create
a process of self-examination and healthy self-criticism for individuals to

realize that they have the power to transform themselves and their communities. Regardless of their circumstances, they can be agents of change.[23]

However, the social, political, and economic realities of Muslim communities are a major challenge to peacemaking activities. In some communities, there may not be an active conflict, but neighboring states are interfering heavily in domestic affairs. The majority of Muslim communities are postcolonial societies built on bureaucracies, technocrats, and inherited systems of governance. An acute problem of political and economic stagnation fosters a culture of little imagination, creativity, or ability to take risks or challenge superiors.[24] Professional bureaucrats appoint subordinates who are loyal to them and will not challenge them. Those with competent skills, intelligence, qualifications, and merit tend not to be hired or promoted; the code for success is to be quiet and not draw attention to oneself. Such conditions breed inefficiency, corruption, frustration, alienation, and resistance to change.[25] State involvement or control over religious affairs in patriarchal societies is another important contextual issue that affects whether one can even conduct peacebuilding work. Many Muslim societies lack basic freedoms of speech and association, to say nothing of the freedom to question authority, work in a particular industry, or gain access to public office.[26] These markers are daily reminders of how power is asserted at the micro level (e.g., family, tribe, workplace, school, marketplace, community) and macro level (e.g., state, institutions, bureaucracies, military, media). Such reminders strongly reinforce the powers associated with hierarchies; at a deep conscious and subconscious level, citizens understand their place in society and the limitations they face.

In trying to organize basic meetings, workshops, or conferences on religious peacemaking, religious leaders fall somewhere in the hierarchical pyramid. Some need to seek approval from their superiors, ministries of religion and foreign affairs, office managers, family members, and mosque leadership. In some cases, they must also provide for the presence of intelligence services. Afghan intelligence attended the several religious peacemaking workshops the author conducted in Afghanistan, and most of the religious leaders had to obtain permission from their local superiors to attend. By factoring in the content and contextual challenges, one can appreciate why many Muslim religious leaders generally are skeptical about peacebuilding efforts. This skepticism is tied to five common trends in thought among Muslim religious leaders regarding participating in and implementing peacemaking activities.[27]

First, defining peace and measuring the success of peacebuilding work is a constant struggle. Participants agree that true peace involves equality, justice, freedom, and compensation to victims. Anything less involves compromise with those who are more powerful. That said, peace is also often viewed as a top-down process, created and implemented by ruling elites—the officials who have the power to make peace. Participants in religious peacemaking workshops commonly have asserted that they feel ineffective because they do not possess the power to make change.

Second, religious leaders often voice their sense that their societies are not truly governed by their people, or even by their own ruling elites; rather, Western powers dominate Muslim societies by controlling the elites' decisions. They identify Western powers as having created unstable societies, oppressive regimes, and chaos.

Third, many religious leaders view conflict as an inevitable component of life, beginning with their use of the creation story as an example of conflict between the divine and the angels. In the Islamic version of creation, God created Adam out of clay (earthly material) and asked the angels to bow down to the new creation. One angel, Iblis, refused to bow down, believing that man was a lesser form of creation.[28] Religious leaders refer to this narrative to argue that conflict has always existed and it is impossible to create societies without it; the best we can do is to minimize the amount of conflict that arises in life.

Fourth, any peacemaking that does not bring justice to both victims and oppressors is a worthless effort. Justice, according to some leaders, is the primary issue to be addressed in resolving conflict. Unless conflicting parties take part in resolving the problem and, simultaneously, receive justice from the appropriate authoritative institutions, conflict can be expected to continue eternally. In Islamic thought, the concept and practice of justice is synonymous with peacemaking. To ignore this crucial connection is to alienate a Muslim audience.

Finally, since the peacemaking and conflict resolution field is relatively new to Muslim religious leaders, there are common beliefs that these Western approaches are foreign to Muslim cultures and maybe contrary to their values. Embedded in the criticism are two important perceptions: first, that the approaches are secular in nature and do not account for religious components; and second, that the religious peacemaking models that are presented—nonviolence, reconciliation, dialogue—are based on Christian beliefs and practices.

Unresolved political, social, economic, and provincial disputes do not force religious leaders to trust peacemaking activities or seek ways to collaborate together. It is common to hear repeatedly from religious leaders that peacemaking training was initially a wonderful experience, but they had to rely on models and methodologies in interfaith activities that were not indigenous to their culture. Also, there are not enough trained facilitators specialized in religious peacemaking activities, a condition usually attributed to lack of funding, lack of experts trained in the field, and failure to institutionalize the work itself on the ground. However, these deficiencies are only chronic problems of supporting Muslim religious leaders' peacemaking efforts. Some religious leaders feel the training is limited because, after the workshops are completed, leaders return to a community suffering from conflict fatigue. Meanwhile, true interfaith dialogue workshops for Christian-Muslim religious leaders are infrequent and completely dependent on political and social circumstances that allow them to operate freely. Moreover, only a few international organizations supply these skills to the leaders, and too often, Western organizations rely on the same individuals and organizations to put together the meetings.[29] In any case, Muslim religious leaders complain that interfaith dialogue, while valuable, is not among their priorities or those of their community. They appreciate engagement with Christian religious leaders—probably their first dialogic experience—but view interfaith dialogue as secondary work to their obligations in serving their congregations.[30] In addition, there are issues of setting concise goals and objectives, conducting self-evaluations, and following up on peacemaking activities. This does not necessarily suggest a lack of interest or organizational skills, but it demonstrates the numerous internal and external unresolved problems that affect performance. With insufficient material guides and literature available in the local language, peacemaking activities do not have consistent reading packets or information to use.

Muslim religious leaders operate in a culture with a worldview of the other, a term that is obviously not restricted solely to Muslim societies. In general, the other is viewed in deeply suspicious terms. Especially when peacemaking workshops are organized, participants view the dialogue as a debate. This mentality suggests that the dialogue is an opportunity for one side to persuade the other of its incorrect faith tradition.[31] The emotional and psychological scars from conflict do not entirely heal with peacemaking activities, and in most situations, the internal animosity is invisible even as societies are being rebuilt.

Confronting Change and Theory of Change

Given the complex webs of social, religious, political, and economic issues involved in training Muslim religious leaders in peacemaking, the idea of change needs some attention. For peace practitioners, change is an accepted way to assuage conflict, and any positive step toward altering human behavior to prevent, mediate, and resolve conflict should be acted upon.[32] Change is an accepted way of thinking and practice for peace practitioners in the field, as trainers are familiar with numerous theories of change and strategic ways in altering human behavior to prevent, mediate, and resolve conflict. If changing attitudes, values, and behaviors is crucial to peacebuilding activities, then it is necessary to elaborate on particular challenges and methods that are associated with change.

In Western societies, changing oneself exemplifies growth, maturity, insight, wisdom, progress, independence—essentially, all things tied to individual prosperity. To change oneself is to acknowledge a better way of thinking and doing something, even if some core values and beliefs still prevail.[33] As the idea of change within a tradition is quite accepted in Western societies, peace practitioners are perplexed by the extent to which Muslim religious leaders debate, resist, and sometimes openly confront the idea of change. Muslim religious leaders (as well as some other religious leaders) often find the presumption of change a threat to their identity, religious ideas, practices, beliefs, tradition, and well-being of their community. In their historical legacy of reform, change and compromising fundamental core religious beliefs has resulted in political and social disruption. We can understand the concerns of religious leaders if we examine how the Arabic word for change (*badala*) or the verb to change oneself (*tabdil*) is used in the Qur'an and in Islamic theology: Both are used to express negative and positive consequences, in the former case, reflecting God's opprobrium toward individuals who rejected monotheism or specific groups who changed the original sacred texts. For example, in response to all believers who wish to change sacred words of scripture, it states, "The word of your Lord does find its fulfillment in truth and in justice: None can change His words: for He is the one who hears and knows all" (Qur'an 6:115). *La mubaddila li-kalimatihi*—"None can change His words"—clearly refers to changing God's revealed messages, but this repeated verse throughout the Qur'an is a reminder that changing any aspect of revelation is blasphemous.[34]

In the Qur'an, polytheists and opponents to the Prophet Muhammad are vigorously reprimanded after they audaciously request certain verses of the Qur'an to be changed. For instance, it states,

> But when our clear signs are recited to, those who rest not their hope on their meeting with us, say: "Bring us a different Qur'an or make amendments to this one," say: "It is not for me, of my own accord, to change it: I follow only what is revealed to me: if I were to disobey my Lord, I should myself fear the penalty of a Great Day [to come]" (10:15).

Religious leaders are trained in Qur'anic history, ethics, theology, logic, jurisprudence, grammar, syntax, and the larger field of exegesis. The one theme that is repeated and memorized is how God's wrath falls on communities that purposefully disobey, mislead, or spread discontent. As the Qur'an (5:13) states,

> But because of their breach of their covenant, We cursed them, and made their hearts grow hard; they change the words from their [right] places and forget a good part of the message that was sent them, nor wilt thou cease to find them—barring a few—ever bent on [new] deceits: but forgive them, and overlook [their misdeeds]: for Allah loves those who are kind.

Changing words in scripture is not taken lightly, since it changes the essence, interpretation, and ultimate meaning of the passages.

However, the Qur'an does use the word for change in the context of improving situations and helping communities, and as an opportunity for believers to prove themselves worthy of the divine. As an example to changing from suffering to prosperity, it states, "Then We changed their evil into prosperity, until they grew and multiplied, and began to say: 'Our fathers [too] were touched by suffering and affluence'... Behold! We called them to account of a sudden, while they realized not [their peril]" (7:95). *Thuma baddalna makana assayyi-atial hasanata* speaks of moving from a state of suffering to a changed state of goodness, prosperity, or well-being. The Qur'an uses change as a way to transform oneself positively toward following the divine and its message; it emphasizes using reason to make the proper choices, "because Allah will never change the grace which He has bestowed on a people until they change what is in their [own] souls: and verily Allah is He Who hears and knows [all things]" (8:53). In other sections, it states, "Unless he repents, believes, and works righteous deeds, for Allah will change the evil of such persons into good, and Allah is All Forgiving, Most Merciful" (25:70).

The Qur'an is clear that change is permissible and definitely encouraged when it is used to be more righteous, more pious, and more devout toward the one God, and when actions are congruent with revelations. Change is celebrated when it involves transforming oneself from a disobedient and immoral life to a virtuous life. The Qur'an praises those who commit themselves to be virtuous and righteous; the term *al-muhsineen* comes from *ihsan* or virtuous. For example, it states, "and Allah gave them a reward in this world, and the excellent reward of the Hereafter. For Allah loves those who do good" (3:148). "God loves those who do good"—*Allahu yuhibbu al-muhsineen*—is an awesome confirmation that good change encourages love from God. The phrase "we reward those who do good"—*inna kathalika najzee al-muhsineen*—from the Qur'an (37:110) is connected to receiving blessings from the divine. Changing from disobedience to a more righteous life brings both love and blessings to the believer.[35]

The multiple use of the word *change* in the Qur'an is associated with disobedience and wrongdoing as well, however, and religious leaders are aware of these various theological interpretations of change in the Qur'an and the additional multiple interpretations connected to it. Due to many social, political, historical, and economic influences on religious leaders, peace trainers need to be aware of how easy it is to be defensive on this topic. The fear of allegations of being part of negative change could tremendously affect peacemakers' legitimacy and authority in the Muslim community. Islamist groups such as the Jama'at 'Ulana Islami (JUI) in South Asia or the Muslim Brotherhood in Egypt view Western-supported peacemaking workshops as another opportunity for Western interests to penetrate their institutions. Generally, the residual resentment of Western colonialism and its policies against religious institutions are still very much alive within religious circles. Peace trainers need to be aware of these particular readings of Islam when constructing peacemaking activities.

Constructive Change

Peacemaking trainers assume that an exposure to diverse views will change the thinking of religious participants and thereby affect their constituents. It is common to read in manuals and peace workshop programs that they aim to "help different religious groups examine and better understand their beliefs" or "support religious leaders seeking ways to deal with extremism" or "open channels for more effective dialogue and cooperation." In highlighting the value of dialogue and bringing religious figures together who ordinarily do not meet, peace trainers aspire to make a connection between parties who do not understand each other. They strive to break down polarized thinking, form a network of leaders who can cooperate together on a number of projects, and cultivate an ethos of marginalizing extremists.[36]

The most effective strategy with Muslim religious leaders is to confront the very idea of change in the beginning of any peacebuilding program. There should be constructive strategies in conflict prevention, an explication of the underlying assumptions about how change comes about and what it means within the Islamic tradition. Peace trainers need to be sensitive to participants' appreciation—or lack of appreciation—of diversity, change, dialogue, interfaith relations, mediation and negotiation skills, and definitions of peace and peacebuilding. For many religious leaders the author has worked with in Pakistan, Afghanistan, Iran, Egypt, Jordan, and Syria, the very idea of change or dialogue can simply mean to be a less practicing Muslim. In workshops, high-ranking Muslim scholars have stated that "they want us to be moderate Muslims—we're not moderate Muslims, we practice all the time." In discussing extremism, peace trainers must be careful about the words they use, with the aim of separating devotion to Islam from the violence that is too often committed in its name.

Assessing religious participants' thorough understanding of peacebuilding and conflict resolution is vital, as it reveals their level of knowledge and the terms in which they understand the conflict resolution field. If these basic conversations are ignored, religious participants may deem that peacebuilding is a foreign venture. The sooner the audience is engaged in theories of how to achieve peace and why it is important for religious leaders to be active in this field, the more willingly they will be engaged. Peace trainers should not underestimate religious participants' ability to engage in a conversation on specific cognitive, social, political, or religious obstacles to peacebuilding, but such activities can only be carried out by a collective effort, with specific ideas and goals for what they hope to achieve. These decisions are based on assumptions, skills, and whether these combined factors are feasible. To bring peace through change, peace trainers must select methods, approaches, and tactics that are rooted in a range of theories about how peace can be achieved in an Islamic context. Trainers need to state that they believe that by doing a certain action successfully, they will produce movement toward peace, but then ask participants if the same is true for their community. If so, how is it true? If not, how can trainers and participants teach each other to identify the obstacles? What sources prevent both trainers and participants from moving forward on this action? Trainers must be prepared for responses that are solely macro-based. In the author's experience, participants often responded that Western policies were meant to dominate them, or that Western forces encouraged conflict so that they would never be united. Peace trainers should use these typical responses as moments to engage religious participants by further deconstructing the arguments and revealing the missing dimensions of civil society in peacebuilding activities. By opening the door for a collective conversation about this basic question on the first day of the training, one can raise reflection, inquiry, doubt, skepticism, understanding, and other forms of intellectual engagement. Bringing in religious leaders to form their definitions from their own traditions, as well as from the larger field of conflict resolution, can demonstrate that peacebuilding activity is their own project, not one imposed from external organizations or societies.

It is very common for peacebuilding activities to use more than one approach in changing the minds of participants. Some focus on who needs to change and which individuals and groups in society should receive more attention. Some focus on specific relationships that need to change, while others focus on institutions; policy; social norms; cultural practices; the role of media, natural resources, and foreign influences; or the way historical memories function in society. Religious leaders are well aware of the various dynamics at play in their societies and often insightfully analyze these issues. Peace trainers need to reinforce the point of individual accountability in peacebuilding as often as possible, since religious participants belong to hierarchical and nonindividualistic structures. While focusing on the micro issues, peace trainers cannot neglect the larger conflict context—that is, whether there are national political dialogues or reconciliatory programs in effect. Programmatic theories of change target institutions to release them from stagnation or create new institutions. Some peacebuilding activities actively promote establishing community-based peace councils as a creative and brilliant response to political stagnation. New community-level mechanisms can handle a range of disputes, improve communication between conflicting parties, and increase access for the disenfranchised. Community peace councils (CPCs) create a new generation of leaders to prevent and transform conflicts, and these leaders feel empowered to act, as they are no longer waiting for a response from a distant dysfunctional government institution. There are similar CPC initiatives for religious leaders who have been empowered by interfaith dialogue and interethnic peace councils in Kosovo and Bosnia after the Balkan War. The theory of change holds that religious leaders need to break their isolation and have social contact to construct dialogues on identity, religious beliefs, and promoting mutual understanding. In the Balkans, Nigeria, and South Africa, religious leaders were involved with land use, refugee compensation, reintegration of displaced persons, the reopening of schools, reassessing bias in religious texts, and strengthening community relations. Constructing change for Muslim religious leaders requires well-defined goals, objectives, assessment, and a series of follow-up peacebuilding activities to ensure that participants are accountable to their duties. By recognizing that Muslim religious leaders are already aware of a host of obstacles and challenges that confront them, it is more constructive to collaboratively construct short-term and long-term peacebuilding activities. Intrafaith and interfaith dialogues are a natural area for skills training; however, if it is not peace trainers' priority—or if they can design a more effective dialogical peacebuilding program—then they must be flexible for this to occur. Constructive change programs with religious leaders need to factor in their theological sensibilities and real-life limitations. Setting the bar too high can dampen anyone's peacebuilding spirits, yet it is important to remember that religious leaders play an exceptional role in the life of a community.

Refining Skills Transmission

Peace theories of change involve individuals, relationships, governance, social justice, economies, public attitudes, media, community reintegration, grassroots mobilization—all areas in which a culture of peace can be developed. Fostering a culture of peace means being critical of cultural and societal norms, values, and behaviors in using violence as a means to resolve disputes. Promoting negotiation and dialogue and addressing fundamental causes of conflict can develop long-term conditions of peace. Training workshops and conferences are built on the idea that knowledge and skills are a tool to nurture an awareness of conflict and peace indicators. Workshops for religious leaders usually discuss open communication, interfaith dialogue, religious pluralism, tolerating other opinions, and the basics of conflict resolution, but rarely do these workshops entail skills transmission and enhancement. It would benefit Muslim religious leaders—and all religious leaders generally—if peace trainers moved from these basic themes to include more sophisticated skills. Understanding when a conflict arises involves a knowledge-based approach, but applying certain skills to de-escalate conflict and ensure stability is as, if not more, important.

To develop effective peacebuilding skills for Muslim religious leaders, it is necessary to expand more practical models to implement peacebuilding work. Religious leaders in conflict zones require skills that allow them, first, to evaluate, negotiate, and mediate the conflict, and second, structurally change their situation. To make structural and institutional changes in times of conflict means religious leaders were previously prepared with skills and comprehend how to apply the appropriate skills. It is obvious to build upon their knowledge of Islam or theoretical knowledge of conflict resolution; however, what is vitally important is their capability to learn practical skills to transform their moment of conflict in sustainable ways. Critical skills in negotiating through a conflict are essential tools in peacemaking, but equally important is whether religious leaders are able to retain and apply the skills in challenging conflict scenarios.

Seven major areas for skills transmission are needed for Muslim religious leaders engaging in peacebuilding: organization management, understanding the source of the conflict, mediation and negotiation, strategic planning for intervention and transformation, acquiring knowledge of all parties involved, understanding the art of engagement, and training in the complexities of building sustainable peace. When religious leaders are involved in conflict prevention, mediation, negotiations, conflict management, conflict resolution, and postconflict stability, their effectiveness depends on their ability to function in that conflict. Muslim religious leaders need to expand their skills and capacity building in these areas while ensuring they are not co-opted by the political agendas of national and international organizations. A skills-enhancement approach will enrich their knowledge of peacebuilding and position them in the wider field of peacebuilding efforts. Essentially, their roles do not have to be restricted to a specific religious institution, nor should they be limited to one community.

Skills in organization management emphasize administering a staff, fiscal responsibility, project planning, project execution, project evaluation, fundraising, grantmaking, strategic communications with media and public awareness campaigns, managing and controlling information effectively, and generally professional practices in managing a nonprofit organization.

Understanding the root causes of conflict involves training in conflict assessment and management as well as apprehending the major turning points in conflict, patterns of conflict, and factors that contribute to intractability. This could include models on how to influence perceptions, pressure decision makers, and maximize techniques to pressure parties' assessment of conflict costs.

Direct skills in negotiation and mediation should emphasize best practices and lessons learned from other conflicts. Peacemakers should teach skills that encourage religious leaders to think strategically about intervention, the possible consequences of intervention, and the risks associated with various scenarios. This involves examining creative ways to attract parties to a reinvigorated process of negotiation and designing exercises to balance power between and within parties.

Strategic planning for conflict intervention and transformation includes training in advance conflict intervention, management, and transformation; examining sources of leverage, the role of third-party mediators, use of neutral space, and international resources for support; and establishing guarantees, assurances, and specific conditions with a time table. Peacemakers should study mechanisms that assist parties in coordinating efforts in conflict reduction, limiting the influence of spoilers, and using accessible experts for working groups or as consultants to maintain communication.

Acquiring knowledge of all parties includes training participants in understanding how to identify all local, national, and international parties and their respective interests in the conflict. Leaders can also be trained in consulting with parties; ascertaining who gains from the conflict and who gains from its end; and identifying forms of power involved with the parties, be they military, diplomatic, intellectual, religious, financial, international, tribal, or political. Workshops can also offer guidance on enhancing understanding of when to cultivate partners and when to mediate with various parties; knowing how to broaden the base of mediation; and knowing the effects of not including certain parties in weakening mediation efforts.

Training in the art of engagement in conflict transformation requires technical and organizational skills. Trainers need to emphasize how to advocate for educational reform on all levels, including religious education programs; how to understand the value of ongoing teaching enhancement programs; how to grasp majority versus minority rights; and how to work with refugees to reintegrate internally displaced persons. Comprehending ways to mobilize grassroots groups to advocate for positive action, ways to use the media, and other methods in raising awareness is also part of engagement skills.

Finally, advance training in postconflict reconstruction and providing technical knowledge in establishing a national truth-reconciliation program, public forgiveness forums, public truth-telling, and a memorialization of the conflict is a fitting and essential cap to training in peacebuilding. Guidance regarding the importance of creating national centers for interfaith or intrafaith dialogue and committing to dialogue on all levels can make dialogic efforts a priority. This includes examining best practices for recovery and healing programs, as well as eradicating biases in education, religious instruction, political, and legal institutions.

When Muslim religious leaders recognize the global picture in conflict prevention and conflict resolution, they acknowledge the critical importance of expanding their role to be active. One of the best ways Muslim religious leaders have contributed to conflict prevention is to set a good example for their communities. By being models of tolerance and inclusivity, they have literally saved thousands of lives in Nigeria, Sudan, Kashmir, Afghanistan, and Iraq. Building on this model, religious leaders can accept greater roles in constitutional processes, truth and reconciliation commissions, refugee repatriation, human rights investigations, women's empowerment and inclusion, education reform, strengthening rule of law and transitional justice, and establishing interfaith or intrafaith dialogue centers. All this, however, must include specific training skills and the willingness of Muslim religious leaders to expand their current responsibilities. Muslim religious leaders, just like their partners in other faiths, find the power of coalition building in times of crisis, and they use local, national, regional, and international coalitions as leverage to reduce violence. Coalition building is just one effective way of conflict prevention or reduction. Muslim religious leaders generally acknowledge their potential in civil society activities, and they see the benefit of serving the wider community. An increased interaction between religious leaders and nonreligious actors only furthers greater cooperation, stability, and peacebuilding activities.

Notes

1.   For the statement on their commitment to global peace, see the World Council of Religious Leaders, "About the Summit," www.millenniumpeacesummit.com/mwps_about.html (accessed November 24, 2009).

2. The UN summit was to lead to developing an advisory board of religious leaders; this has not happened yet.

3. See Jimmy Carter's speech on religious peacebuilding delivered to the Parliament of the World's Religions on December 3, 2009, http://cartercenter.org/news/editorials_speeches/parliament-world-religions-120309.html (accessed December 3, 2009).

4. The author has in mind Muslim religious leaders in, e.g., rural Nigeria, Liberia, southern Thailand, Mindano, rural Southeast Asia, where religious leaders serve in many authoritative capacities.

5. For a good example of religious actors in the former Yugoslavia, see Paul Mojzes, ed., *Religion and the War in Bosnia* (Atlanta: Scholars Press, 1998), and Sabrina Petra Ramet, "Nationalism and the Idiocy of the Countryside: The Case of Serbia," *Ethnic and Racial Studies,* vol. 19, no. 1 (January 1996), 70–88.

6. Abdul Aziz Said, Nathan C. Funk, and Ayse Kadayifici, eds., *Peace and Conflict Resolution in Islam: Precept and Practice* (Lanham, MD: University Press of America, 2001); Abdul Aziz Said and Meena Sharify-Funk, eds., *Cultural Diversity and Islam* (Lanham, MD: University Press of America, 2003).

7. Mohammed Abu-Nimer, "Conflict Resolution in an Islamic Context," *Peace and Change,* vol. 21, no. 1 (1996), 22–40; *Islam and Nonviolence* (Gainesville, FL: University Press of Florida, 2002).

8. Ali Asghar Engineer, "Sources of Nonviolence in Islam," in M. Kumar, ed., *Nonviolence: Contemporary Issues and Challenges* (New Delhi: Gandhi Peace Foundation, 1994).

9. Abdullahi An-Na'im, *Toward an Islamic Reformation: Civil Liberties, Human Rights, and International Law* (Syracuse: Syracuse University Press, 1996), and "The Islamic Counter-Reformation," *New Perspectives Quarterly,* vol. 19 (2002), 29–35.

10. Glenn D. Paige, Sarah Gilliatt, and Chaiwat Satha-Anand, eds., *Islam and Nonviolence* (Honolulu: University of Hawaii, 1993).

11. Ronald Fisher, *Interactive Conflict Resolution* (Syracuse: Syracuse University Press, 1997); Abu-Nimer, *Nonviolence and Peacebuilding;* and Khalid Kishtainy, "Violent and Nonviolent Struggle in Arab History," in Ralph Crow, Philip Grant, and Saad Ibrahim, eds., *Arab Nonviolent Political Struggle in the Middle East* (Boulder, CO: Lynne Rienner, 1990).

12. See Paul Marshall, *Radical Islam's Rules: The Worldwide Spread of Extreme Shari'a Law* (New York: Rowman & Littlefield, 2005); Gilles Kepel, *The Roots of Radical Islam* (London: Saqi Books, 2005); Richard Booker, *Radical Islam's War Against Israel, Christianity, and the West* (Shippensburg, PA: Destiny Image, 2008); and Brian Farmer, *Understanding Radical Islam: Medieval Ideology in the Twenty-First Century* (New York: Peter Lang Publishing, 2006). See also Jochen Hippler, ed., *The Next Threat: Western Perceptions of Islam* (London: Pluto Press, 1995); John Esposito, *The Islamic Threat* (New York: Oxford University Press, 1992); Daniel Norman, *Islam and the West: The Making of an Image* (Oxford: Oneworld Publications, 1993).

13. Martin Kramer, "Islam vs. Democracy" *Commentary,* vol. 95, no. 1 (1993) 35–44; Bernard Lewis, "Islam and Liberal Democracy," *Atlantic Monthly,* vol. 271, no. 2 (1993), 89–98; Judith Miller, "The Challenge of Radical Islam," *Foreign Affairs,* vol. 72, no. 2 (1993), 43–56; Emmanuel Sivan, *Radical Islam: Medieval Theology and Modern Politics* (New Haven, CT: Yale University Press, 1990); John Voll and John Esposito, "Islam's Democratic Essence," *Middle East Quarterly,* vol. 1, no. 3 (1994), 3–19; David Garnham and Mark Tessler, ed., *Democracy, War, and Peace in the Middle East* (Bloomington, IN: Indiana University Press, 1995).

14. Remarks by United States Undersecretary for Public Diplomacy Karen Hughes at the Faith and Service Conference, Washington, DC, May 22, 2006.

15. Scott Appleby, *The Ambivalence of the Sacred: Religion, Violence, and Reconciliation* (Lanham, MD: Rowman & Littlefield, 2000); William Shawcross, *Deliver Us From Evil: Peacekeepers, Warlords, and a World of Endless Conflict* (Uppsala, Sweden: Life and Peace Institute, 1995); Martin Marty and Scott Appleby, *The Glory and the Power: The Fundamentalist Challenge to the Modern World* (Boston: Beacon Press, 1992).

16. John Kelsay, *Islam and War: A Study in Comparative Ethics* (Louisville, KY: John Knox Press, 1993); Fred Donner, "The Sources of Islamic Conception of War," in John Kelsay and James Turner Johnson, eds., *Just War and Jihad: Historical and Theoretical Perspectives on War and Peace in Western and Islamic Traditions* (New York: Greenwood Press, 1991), 31–69; Sohail Hashmi, "Interpreting the Islamic Ethics of War and Peace," in Terry Nardin, ed., *The Ethics of War and Peace: Religions and Secular Perspectives* (Princeton, NJ: Princeton University Press, 1996); Majid Khadduri, *The Islamic Conception of Justice* (Baltimore, MD: Johns Hopkins University Press, 1984); Abdulaziz Sachedina, "The Justification for Violence in Islam," in J. Patout Burns, ed., *War and Its Discontents: Pacifism and Quietism in the Abrahamic Traditions* (Washington, DC: Georgetown University Press, 1996).

17. Sohail Hashmi, "Interpreting the Islamic Ethics of War and Peace," in *The Ethics of War and Peace*, 151.

18. Kevin Avruch, *Culture and Conflict Resolution* (Washington, DC: United States Institute of Peace Press, 1998); Peter Black, Joseph Scimecca, and Kevin Avruch, *Conflict Resolution: Cross-Cultural Perspectives* (New York: Greenwood Press, 1991).

19. John Burton, *Conflict: Resolution and Prevention* (New York: St. Martin's Press, 1990).

20. Roger Fisher and William Ury, *Getting to Yes: Negotiating Agreement without Giving In* (Boston: Houghton Mifflin, 1981); Dean Pruitt and Jeffrey Rubin, *Social Conflict: Escalation, Stalemate, and Settlement* (New York: McGraw-Hill, 1986); Herbert Kelman, "Interactive Problem-Solving: A Social-Psychological Approach to Conflict Resolution," in John Burton and Frank Dukes, ed., *Conflict: Readings in Management and Resolution* (New York: St. Martin's Press, 1990).

21. For examples of good practical manuals, see Barbara Hartford, Claudia Liebler, Susanna McIlwaine, Mohammed Abu-Nimer, and Cynthia Sampson, *Interfaith Peacebuilding Guide* (San Francisco, CA: United Religions Initiative, 2004); Susan L. Carpenter, *A Repertoire of Peacemaking Skills* (Fairfax, VA: Consortium on Peace Research, Education, and Development, 1977); and *Transforming Struggle: Strategy and the Global Experience of Nonviolent Direct Action* (Cambridge, MA: Program on Nonviolent Sanctions in Conflict and Defense Center for International Affairs, Harvard University, 1992).

22. See *Peacebuilding: A Caritas Training Manual* (Vatican City: Caritas Internationalis, 2002).

23. Burton, *Conflict*; John Paul Lederach, *Building Peace: Sustainable Reconciliation in Divided Societies* (Washington, DC: United States Institute of Peace, 1997); Ronald Fisher, *Interactive Conflict Resolution*; and John W. McDonald and Diane Bendahamane, eds, *Conflict Resolution: Track Two Diplomacy* (Washington, DC: Institute for Multi-Track Diplomacy, 1987).

24. Robert Johansen, "Radical Islam and Nonviolence: A Case Study of Religious Empowerment and Constraint among Pashtuns," *Journal of Peace Research*, vol. 34, no. 1 (1997), 53–71.

25. Cynthia Sampson, "Religion and Peacemaking," in William Zartman and Lewis Rasmussen, eds., *Peacemaking in International Conflict* (Washington, DC: United States Institute of Peace, 1997), 275–78.

26. Bahgat Korany, Rex Brynen, and Paul Noble, eds. *Political Liberalization and Democratization in the Arab World*, vol. 2 (Boulder, CO: Lynne Rienner, 1998).

27. These thoughts are based on fieldwork experience and personal interviews. They are common and general sentiments in peacebuilding activities.

28. See Qur'an (2:34): "Remember, when We asked the angels to bow in homage to Adam, they all bowed but *Iblis*, who disdained and turned insolent, and so became a believer." Iblis responds in Qur'an (7:12): "I am better than him [Adam], You created me from fire, and him You created from clay."

29. For more on problems with American organizations supporting peacemaking workshops for Muslim leaders, see Mohammed Abu-Nimer, *Nonviolence and Peace Building in Islam: Theory and Practice* (Gainesville, FL: University Press of Florida, 2003), 126–27.

30. For more on the views of interfaith dialogues in various Muslim communities, see Mohammed Abu-Nimer, Amal Khoury, and Emily Welty, *Unity in Diversity: Interfaith Dialogue in the Middle East* (Washington, DC: United States Institute of Peace, 2007), 15–39.

31. For more on the varieties of interfaith dialogue and changing the attitude of the so-called other to us, see Raimon Panikkar, *The Intra-Religious Dialogue* (New York: Paulist Press, 1999).

32. For a review of change theories, see Collaborative Learning Projects, "Reflecting on Peace Practice Case Studies," http://www.cdainc.com/cdawww/project_profile.php?pid=RPP&pname=Reflecting%20Peace%20Practice (accessed November 24, 2008).

33. These arguments are similar to most faith traditions; the tensions between traditional interpretations and practices versus modernist interpretations reveal themselves in peacemaking workshops.

34. See also Qur'an (18:27): "And recite [and teach] what has been revealed to thee of the Book of thy Lord: none can change His Words, and none wilt thou find as a refuge other than Him."

35. For more verses containing *Inna kathalika najzee al-muhsineen*, see Qur'an (28:14; 37:80, 121, 131; 39:34; 77:44).

36. Marginalizing extremism is a particularly difficult task for peace activities directed at Muslim religious leaders. Peace trainers have to work through another layer of mistrust with Muslim religious leaders because they understand the subtext of being selected to combat religious extremism.

Conclusion

Building on established principles of Islamic peacebuilding, best practices in the emerging field of Islamic peacemaking must be defined and refined. There is a real need to increase peacemaking activities through civil society organizations, tackle political stagnation, address historical memories of injustice, and find solutions to economic and political asymmetries and powerlessness in order to positively change Muslim communities. With the multiplicity of problems, however, is also a multiplicity of opportunities: The diversity of traditions, cultures, opinions, and civilizations within Islam greatly enhances and enriches the possibilities for peacebuilding. This volume has explored a range of methods and processes that Muslim peacemaking actors use to manage, resolve, and prevent conflict. Across the chapters, the authors have analyzed Islamic peacebuilding through various theoretical lenses of conflict transformation, ranging from theology and history to economics and gender concerns.

Conflict resolution and peacebuilding in Islamic thought has evolved tremendously since the seminal works of Sufyan al-Thawri (d. 778), al-Awza'i (d. 773), al-Shafi'i (d. 820), and Muhammad Jarir al-Tabari (d. 923). Even among the classical scholars, there were enormously divergent views on the subjects of *jihad*, martyrdom, war, and peacemaking, as noted in Asma Afsaruddin's analysis of al-Tabari's *Ikhtilaf al-fuqaha'* (*The Differences of the Jurists*; see chapter 2). The rich diversity of scholarly interpretations, however, created intellectual and political tensions, captured in the art of hermeneutics of the Qur'an, *hadiths,* and legal texts, where multiple interpretations in any context can justify peaceful or violent activities. Waleed El-Ansary's essay (chapter 3) reflects this tension among current scholars, practitioners, and juridical authorities in Islam. Today, the Grand Mufti of Egypt and other senior ranking religious leaders find their condemnations, debates, and pronouncements insufficient to control the spread of extremism, as radicals abuse and misappropriate the hortatory literary genre called *fada'il al-jihad* (The Excellences of Jihad), which was developed and often exploited by dynastic leaders to defend their territories. Just as the prominent scholar al-Shafi'i (d. 820) was the first jurist to permit *jihad* to be launched against non-Muslims as offensive warfare—though he qualified non-Muslims as referring only to the idol-worshipping Arabs—the juridical debate over qualifying *jihad* as warfare enabled modern-day jihadists to use these sources to justify their own violent actions.

Zeki Saritoprak (chapter 5) and Reza Eslami-Somea (chapter 7) offer insights into how Muslims have attempted to resolve the complex tensions within their faith and turn them toward peacemaking work. On one hand, reformers have focused on reconciling religious knowledge and practice with modernity. On the other hand, devout pacifists such as Bediüzzaman Said Nursi fundamentally interpreted faith in purely nonviolent terms. Modern reformers, such as Abdolkarim Soroush, Abdullahi An-Na'im, and Fazlur Rahman, have likewise struggled with the tensions of ideals and realities, evolving postmodern identities and tradition, and the serious challenges in creating a just society through democratic principles or with traditional interpretations of *shari'ah*. Islamic conflict resolution and peacebuilding efforts, too, are interwoven with these tensions, but the field has developed significantly from the *jus ad bellum* mantra of "to be at peace, prepare for war." Ayse Kadayifci-Orellana and Meena Sharify-Funk (chapter 9) show that Muslim women are significant peacemakers in conflict zones, as they mobilize, organize, and lead their communities toward creative solutions in fighting against illiteracy, tribal violence, child abuse, gender inequality, and other areas of injustice.

Current trends in the Arab and Muslim world demonstrate creative ways to negotiate the tensions within Islamic peacemaking by expressing points of view through new technologies and social-networking Web sites. Egyptian Muslim television preacher Amr Khaled launched a reality show, *Mujadidoun*, to portray a reformist approach to faith and life, and online Web sites, blogs, and social networking sites, such as Twitter, are being used to express dissent within organizations and communities, to organize nonviolent civil disobedience in Egypt, Iran, Lebanon, Pakistan, Bangladesh, and elsewhere, and to create new virtual communities that transcend conventional boundaries. It is common to obtain online *fatwas* for immediate answers to religious questions as well as to seek out guidance from an online imam regarding religious and nonreligious matters. The relative lack of freedoms in many predominantly Muslim states—especially relating to speech and the press—and the failure to produce liberal democratic institutions have not prevented civil society from utilizing new technology to have lively debates and discover alternative patterns of thinking.

Recommendations

The authors of this volume acknowledge that there is profound cause for concern about the weak linkages of Islamic peacemaking to the general enterprise of peacebuilding in the Muslim world. We have highlighted the problems of the historical legacies of debates over just-war theories and their unsavory consequences for contemporary religious leaders, scholars, and practitioners. There are serious challenges in advocating for Islamic principles of nonviolence and peacebuilding, as well as traditional methods of conflict resolution, in the midst of rising extremist movements seeking radical societal changes. There are contradictions in reformist movements that strive toward a more inclusive liberal democratic society, yet fall short of achieving their goals because of their fixations on making religious traditions the source of their reforms or neglecting religion altogether. Simultaneously, however, programs in many Muslim communities, such as Indonesia, Afghanistan, Thailand, and Kenya, have promoted innovative, low-cost, community-based development projects under conditions of protracted violence. Senior religious leaders in Muslim communities are critical peacebuilding agents, though their operations tend to work in isolation, disconnected from concurrent peacebuilding efforts.

Given that Arab and Muslim societies vary with distinct needs and features, however, we think it is important to list several broad and strategic recommendations to develop institutional capacity in order to prevent violent conflict from emerging and promote sustainable peace.

Economic Development

Among scholars in the conflict resolution field, there is a broad consensus on the inverse relationship between the level of economic development and propensity for armed conflict—that is, the poorer the society, the greater the likelihood that it will experience violence. Fragile Muslim states experiencing war or emerging from conflict are at risk of going bankrupt, as their governments face mounting fiscal and trade deficits as well as double-digit inflation rates. The world's financial crisis of 2008–09 has prevented the international community from investing in fragile states, and an economy in crisis triggers rising food prices, a shortage in food subsidies, limited domestic agricultural production, increased poverty rates, and decreased gross domestic product. International financial organizations, such as the International Monetary Fund (IMF), need to coordinate with fragile governments to avoid their defaulting on foreign debt. The international community should create regional development strategies to enhance trade links in neighboring countries, aggressively coordinate the removal of trade barriers on exports while increasing the competitiveness of export goods, and explore the possibility of duty-free access to U.S. and European markets for certain types of goods. In addition, there needs to be a comprehensive development strategy with the international community that reduces the management burden on government and non-governmental organization (NGO) partners. Microcredit programs should be supported to foster entrepreneurship and job creation, and foreign aid must be accompanied by accountability, transparency, and effective metrics for measuring progress or regression. A secure socioeconomic development program for rural and urban centers, with an emphasis on peacebuilding, could anchor effective conflict prevention.

Human Development

For the past twenty-five years it has been an accepted belief that democratic governance is the most important component to peacebuilding. However, autocratic, militaristic, and fragile states do not transform themselves into democracies, nor can it be expected that international pressure emphasizing elections and human rights will coerce states into becoming democratic. Security and stability in any nation heavily rests on human capital; ignoring the problems associated with human development and human security neglects the core drivers of instability. Developing and improving water, sanitation networks, and agricultural irrigation systems can alleviate water shortages. Peacebuilding efforts must be tied to serious international community efforts in investing in infrastructure development in public works, electrical and alternative-energy plants, roads, bridges, commercial centers, transportation systems, and existing educational institutions. Promoting high-quality and affordable health care prevents the spread of infectious diseases, improves maternal and child health, and increases life expectancy. Investing in the human development sector advances public services, stimulates economic ties, strengthens good governance, and promotes social well-being.

Mitigating Violence and Fostering a Culture of Peace

Conflict resolution in the twenty-first century is a nonexclusive process, as it involves Track II practitioners, NGOs, civil society groups, international advocacy groups, and individuals with a stake in the process. Current approaches to conflict resolution are more focused on human security than on state sovereignty. It is vital to identify methods and approaches and implement programs that will bring about a lasting settlement and sustainable peace. Mitigating violence in Muslim communities needs to be integrated with Islamic peacebuilding activities within the larger enterprises of cultivating a culture of peacemaking, in which the principles and values of peacemaking are affirmed publicly and privately. A culture of peace consists of instilling the skills and attitudes needed to recognize and defuse potential conflicts on personal, interpersonal, communal, regional, national, and international levels. In October 1999 the UN General Assembly passed Resolution 53/243 declaring a culture of peace, defined as a set of values, attitudes, traditions, and modes of behavior and ways of life based on respect for life, ending violence, and promoting nonviolence through education, dialogue, and cooperation.[1] It is critically important to foster a culture of peace through education; sustainable economic and social development; respect for all human rights; equality for women and men; democratic participation; and understanding, tolerance, and solidarity.[2] Fostering a culture of peace in Muslim communities will require the involvement of Islamic peacemakers, who will need to be trained in peace education, sustainable development, human rights, and peacebuilding skills—all of which, in turn, need an action plan of implementation.

Synchronized Multidimensional Peacebuilding

Peacebuilding is a multidimensional, highly complex process that involves the coordination of numerous actors—not only religious actors—simultaneously working at different levels and in different areas of society. No single organization is capable of owning all peacebuilding tasks. Peacebuilding efforts promote human security in conflict societies and strengthen the capacity of societies generally to manage conflict without violence. In Muslim communities, peacebuilders need to concentrate on both negative and positive peace; that is, the absence of physical, verbal, and psychological violence as well as the presence of structural, cultural, political, economic, and legal conditions that allow individuals to realize their potential. Concurrently, there is a need to promote cooperative conflict resolution, whereby conflict parties or individuals are encouraged to collaborate in developing a solution that supports all involved, rather than creating competition or threats. Muslim peacebuilders also need to critically assess, understand, and respond to the root causes of violent conflict, including structural inequities. Without this approach, participants rightfully question the real purpose of the activity. As mentioned above, organizations sponsoring peacebuilding strategies need religious leaders trained in the field of peacebuilding, and these organizations themselves need to recognize a long-term commitment to a comprehensive approach that focuses on local community while engaging the middle and top levels of leadership.

Conflict Resolution and Peacebuilding Training for Religious Leaders

Workshops for religious leaders are extremely useful to increase capacity and knowledge in the fields of peacemaking and conflict resolution. A focused strategy aimed at religious leaders and institutions should consist of a clear vision and methodology to build relationships, conflict prevention practices, postconflict healing, and social well-being. Religious leaders have firsthand knowledge of local issues, can gain local cooperation easily, and have direct access to disputants. There should be an emphasis on breaking the patterns of revenge, violence, and discrimination that are built on fear, insecurities, and historical memories of injustice. It is common for conflict resolution programs to recommend producing vibrant civil societies, with active organizations involved in promoting peacemaking attitudes, behavior, and values. Islamic peacebuilding efforts need to be developed with specific training manuals for particular cultural, political, and social contexts. However, this must be supplemented by an international network of trainers capable of imparting techniques and skills proven to have strategically transformed social structures on micro and macro levels. If participants regularly attend workshops and conferences on peacebuilding, but then return to the harsh reality of stagnation, corruption, and active conflict, then hopes for positive transformation are lost in pessimism, cognitive dissonance, disempowerment, and shattered hopes. In dealing with these realities, Islamic peacemaking experts, both practitioners and scholars, need to collaborate with international specialists of conflict resolution to genuinely debate, develop, and foster ways to be effective peacemakers in light of conflict and living in closed authoritarian systems.

Civil Society and NGO Support

NGOs such as the Acholi Religious Leaders' Peace Initiative in Uganda, the Inter-Faith Mediation Centre in Nigeria, the Jordanian Interfaith Coexistence Research Center, and the Inter-Religious Council of Sierra Leone work with religious leaders to change negative attitudes, modify behavior, and eliminate deep-rooted stereotypes of the other. For all the importance of their work, however, these organizations are struggling financially and need to be supported, encouraged to expand their base, and, if possible, integrated into the wider field of peacebuilding activities in their respective societies. The Edhi Foundation, the Wahid Institute, the Asian Muslim Action Network (AMAN), and the Arab Group for Christian-Muslim Dialogue also would benefit immensely from being involved in an international network of peacebuilding organizations. These and many more need to be supported and trained, and their work expanded in the areas of conflict prevention; mediation; violence reduction; and providing emotional, psychological, and spiritual support to victims of war. Enhancing these organizations needs to be coordinated with local governments to effectively change domestic policies that are harmful and overbearing on NGOs and to support structural changes, such as instituting peace modules in school curricula.

Self-Critical Problem-Solving Skills

Islamic peacemaking efforts need to recenter attention on providing real problem-solving skills to religious leaders and constituents who can analyze their problems, identify reasons for violent conflicts, formulate solutions to complex problems, and use practical mediation skills to facilitate change in their communities. Practitioners need to devise a comprehensive understanding of the context in which they implement programs; an only partial analysis—or an only intuitive understanding of the situation—could lead to negative consequences or costly mistakes. Islamic peacemakers need to ask crucial and fundamental questions to examine what a conflict is about; what needs to be done to prevent further harm; and what local, regional, and international forces are involved. The answers to these questions will assist practitioners in using peacemaking tools, frameworks, and models in their specific contexts. Since Islamic peacemakers are usually unfamiliar with the analytical tools for conflict prevention, mediation, transformation, and peacemaking, it is good to distinguish between program effectiveness and the effectiveness of peacebuilding. Meeting specific program goals is important, but it should be linked to the bigger picture and its ultimate effect on society. Goals must be outlined with criteria to ensure that specific ends are linked to the large and long-term goal of peacebuilding. Peacemakers must measure their effect on their communities in order for them to quantify, or at least map, the progress or relapse of their work. Specific analytical tools are desperately needed to strategically characterize the situation, create taxonomies, and define new ways to assess and evaluate the problem in order to understand peacemaking activities.

Reducing Ideological Support for Radicalism

Engaging Muslim civil society through a broader conflict resolution framework, and not solely a counterterrorism agenda, will reduce the ideology of radicalism. Terrorism is neither an ideology nor a discrete form of conflict; rather, it is a strategy or tactic of political violence used by actors in a wider context of conflict to achieve political goals. Policymakers and Muslim peacemakers should treat terrorism as a symptom, and not the sole cause, of any conflict. Focusing exclusively on acts of terrorism limits the analysis and understanding of the broader range of issues at work in any given situation. Using a conflict resolution framework, one can comprehend the broader set of issues, actors, and behaviors involved, as well as the history of a conflict and the grievances that terrorism is tied to—grievances that need long-term political, social, cultural, and economic solutions. To counter ideological support for terrorism, fellow actors within the ideological community must be supported to speak out against radicalism and have continual messages to counteract extremist propaganda. There is a need to focus on citizen-messengers, or those who can affect opinion and attitudes from the bottom up. Opinion makers, scholars, activists, journalists, teachers, parliamentarians, religious leaders, youth leaders, television personalities, entertainers, sports figures, intellectuals, business leaders, philanthropists, and other such citizen-messengers must be employed to spread positive ideas to neutralize extremist ideologies and resist violence.

Peace Education and Curriculum Reform

It is time for a comprehensive Islamic peace education curriculum founded on nonviolence—a nonbiased, human rights–based education. Private and public secondary schools, technical colleges and universities, and seminaries need to institute peace and conflict-resolution studies programs, where students can acquire essential conceptual and theoretical conflict-resolution knowledge. A vigorous peace education curriculum will allow students to study and also practice the art of applying conflict resolution theory to their own lives and communities.

Truth Commissions and Transitional Justice

Transitional justice aims for sustainable peace by seeking to establish the rule of law, democracy, and a culture of rights through a wide range of judicial and nonjudicial mechanisms designed to resolve past atrocities.[3] Generally, transitional justice is tied to truth commissions, retributive and corrective justice, prosecuting perpetrators of human rights violations, revealing the truth about past crimes through public truth-gathering forums, providing victims with reparations, scrutinizing governmental failures, and recommending and implementing reconciliation programs.[4] Transitional justice and truth commissions need to be supported in predominantly Muslim societies to address structural violence—that is, the entrenched socioeconomic conditions that cause poverty, exclusion, inequality, and deep divisions in society. Truth commissions must comprehensively address civil and political rights violations, but also economic, social, and cultural rights. Such commissions along with transitional justice mechanisms have the dual purpose of being forward and backward looking: The work seeks to illuminate, expose, and come to terms with a violent and repressive past, as well as identify practical strategies to promote peace and democracy in the future.

No doubt, much peacebuilding work is needed in predominantly Muslim communities. In addition to expanding the network of peacebuilding work on the ground, we underscore the importance of research by analysts and practitioners and the need to support their efforts to disseminate their work to appropriate policymakers, international peacebuilding organizations, and students of Islamic peacemaking and conflict resolution.

Notes

1. For the complete document, see UN General Assembly, "United Nations Declaration on a Culture of Peace," http://cpnn-world.org/resolutions/resA-53-243A.html (accessed March 4, 2010).

2. See United Nations Educational, Scientific, and Cultural Organization, "2009 Report on the International Decade for a Culture of Peace and Non-Violence for the Children of the World, 2001–2010," http://portal.unesco.org/en/ev.php-URL_ID=46796&URL_DO=DO_TOPIC&URL_SECTION=201.html (accessed March 4, 2010).

3. See Paul Farmer, *Pathologies of Power: Health, Human Rights and the New War on the Poor* (Berkeley: University of California Press, 2003), and Naomi Roht-Arriaza and Javier Mariezcurrena, ed., *Transitional Justice in the Twenty-first Century: Beyond Truth versus Justice* (Cambridge: Cambridge University Press, 2006).

4. See Martha Minow, *Between Vengeance and Forgiveness: Facing History after Genocide and Mass Violence* (Boston: Beacon Press, 1998); Ruti G. Teitel, *Transitional Justice* (Oxford: Oxford University Press, 2002); and Dinah Shelton, ed., *The Encyclopedia of Genocide and Crimes against Humanity* (Detroit: Macmillan Reference, 2004).

Glossary of Selected Conflict Resolution Terms

Arabic Terms

adl: justice (*adalah*); wisdom or acting justly.

afdal: meritorious or of high honor.

afu: forgiveness; one of the highest virtues to be followed.

ahkam: legal injunctions.

ahsan: the most grand, e.g., divine power or beauty.

ahsan al-nizam: the best of all systems.

ahsan taqwim: the most beautiful (see Qur'an 95:4).

akhlaq: individual ethics; the way a person lives according to the principles of ethics.

al-birr: the struggle of the human soul to do good and transcend its subliminal desires.

al-faraj wa l-batin: literally, "genitalia and stomach"; referring to the famous sayings that human beings often surrender themselves to the flesh.

al-Faridah al-Ghai'bah: The Neglected Duty, a book written by extremist 'Abd al-Salam Fara to justify assassinations.

al-fasad: corruption and the decline of goodness.

al-ghayah al-khayriyyah: the ultimate good.

al-jandar: gender.

al-jihad fi sabil Allah: literally, "in the struggle for God."

al-muhaddithun: scholars who are specialists in the sayings and customs of the Prophet.

al-'ulum al-naqliyyah: the transmitted religious sciences.

amal: the actions of an individual or group; service.

aman: giving safe conduct.

amanah: the responsibility that comes with trust.

aml-e-salih: good deeds; good actions of a person.

aqidah: basic creeds and doctrines of the faith.

aql: the use of reasoning and rational discourse.

asbab al-nuzul: the specific "occasion of the revelation"; the context of a revealed verse to the Prophet.

ausul-ad-din: principles of religion.

da'irat al-wujud: the great chain of being.

dar al-'ahd: the Ottoman Empire's relationship with its Christian tributary states.

dar al-harb: the abode of war.

dar al-Islam: the land of Islam.

dar al-salam: the abode of peace.

dar al-sulh: the land of agreed peace.

da'wah: the sharing of faith via missionary activities.

dayah: traditional religious school in Indonesia.

dhimmi: legal status of non-Muslim minorities, especially members of the Jewish and Christian communities.

fada'il al-jihad: "the virtues of armed combat"; a genre of literature defending the use of violence.

fada'il al-sabr: "the excellences or virtues of patience"; a genre of literature expanding on virtues of patience and nonviolence.

fadilah: practices of virtues.

faqr: spiritual poverty; the mystical notion of complete dependence on the divine.

fard 'ayni: legal concepts denoting individual obligations, e.g., prayer, fasting, charity.

fard kifa'i: the legal concept of community obligations to support orphanages, hospitals, schools, etc.

fatwa: legal decision rendered by an Islamic legal scholar; a qualified jurist who can make decisions of a general religious nature.

fiqh: area within Islamic law that deals with jurisprudence, directly dependent on the Qur'an and *sunnah*, and rulings evolved with jurist decisions.

fi sabil Allah: literally, "in the cause of God" or "in the path of God."

fitna: referring to schism, deep differences, and secessionist ideas that may cause anarchy or chaos.

fitrah: innate human nature, instinct, primordial nature, insight. Islamic theology argues that human beings are born with an innate knowledge of *tawhid* (oneness of the divine) to use with other attributes, such as virtues and intelligence.

fujur: wickedness; debauchery.

fuqaha (sing. *faqih*): experts in Islamic jurisprudence.

habl min allah: God-to-human relations.

habl min al-nas: human-to-human relations.

hadd (pl. *hudud*): offenses and their punishments specifically defined in the Qur'an, e.g., drinking of wine, theft, robbery, impropriety.

hadith: collected sayings of the Prophet Muhammad; the Prophet's sayings, actions, and tacit approvals. The collection of *hadith* is the second most important source for Islamic teachings, after the Qur'an.

hawa: individual passions; impulsiveness to satisfy egotistical desires.

hikmah: wisdom stemming from mastering philosophy, theology, mysticism, and the religious sciences.

hirabah: to become angry and enraged.

harb: war or enemy.

hubb (*muhabbah*): pure love.

hudna: a truce or ceasefire, usually temporary, in conflict.

ihsan: doing beautifully or making beautiful; benevolence. Faithful Muslims believe their deeds should be done in as if the divine is present.

ikhtilaf: agreement to allow differing opinions on any given subject.

ilm: field of knowledge, research, developing and acquiring knowledge; usually associated with higher insight.

iman: faith or belief; creedal statements of belief are in the one divine, the angels, the revealed books, the prophets, and the hereafter, all fundamental to Islamic theology.

irjaf: to bring commotion to society by violence and chaos; see also *rajafa, rajafat al-ard*

rajafa: to quake or tremble.

rajafat al-ard: the shaking of the earth.

islah: reform.

istihsan: juristic preference. Jurists may use this option to express their preference for a particular judgment in Islamic law over other possibilities. *Istihsan* is one of the principles of legal thought underlying personal interpretation methods.

jahada: one who is striving or in the act of the effort.

jalal: the awe-inspiring majesty of the divine.

jamal: the beauty of the divine.

jihad: exerting efforts according to the essential ethical principles of Islamic teachings.

jihad al-'aql: the use of intellectual efforts to bring forth a higher understanding of a subject.

jizya: originally, a poll tax on non-Muslim minorities.

kalam: field of Islamic theology based on dialectical theology and rational investigation.

kalam al-awa'il: attributing or invoking the opinions and views of previous scholars.

kamal: perfection of the divine.

khalifat Allah fi'l-ard (khilafah): man as God's vice-regent on earth.

khayr: to do good acts.

khayr mahd: pure goodness.

khutbah: the sermon of a preacher.

kufr: ungrateful or covering of truth; general term applied to unbelief or infidelity.

la dhanb lahu: one without sin; stated of someone who has passed away.

ma'rifah: knowledge; insight into divine essence.

madhab: a school of jurisprudence. There are four schools of jurisprudence in Sunni Islam: Hanafi, Hanbali, Malaki, and Shafii. The majority of Shi'ite Muslims follow the Jafari school of law.

mahabbah: spiritual love encountered in divine majesty.

maklumats: official decrees, issued by military authorities in Indonesia.

ma siwa' Allah: all that is other than God; parsing the theological distinction between divine and nondivine.

maslaha: the common good, a key principal objective in *shari'ah.*

masqasid al-shari'ah: the overall teachings and aims of Islamic law, as established by the classical jurists.

mihnah: a general reference to an inquisition.

mudarat: peaceful and calm manner in dealing with others.

muezzin: person who recites the call for prayer.

mufassirin: Qur'anic commentators.

muhabat: love.

muhsin: one who does good deeds, which makes something appear beautiful.

mujahid (pl. *mujahidun*): literally, "one who exerts himself"; those who participate in *jihad*, as both an inward and outward struggle for the realization of religious goals.

munkar: something disliked, clearly wrong and incorrect.

murjifun: to make a commotion toward someone else.

muruwwat: to act generously toward others.

musta'min: those who are providing safe shelter and protection to refugees or displaced persons.

nafs: the self or soul; has many interpretations, but usually accepted as the human self that lies between the spirit (*ruh*) and the body (*jism*); the element of the human being that needs constant attention and reform.

naskh: abrogation of certain verses in the Qur'an.

pencerahan akal: Indonesian for "empowering the mind," "being a critical thinker."

pesantren: modern Islamic boarding schools in Indonesia.

qanun: laws promulgated by Muslim sovereigns, e.g., Persian Qajar rulers or Ottoman rulers.

qat' al-tariq: literally, "breaking the road"; Qur'anic reference to individuals who brutally murdered innocent travelers during the time of the Prophet.

qudrah: omnipotence.

rahiba: "fear of God"; associated with inner wisdom.

rahmah: mercy of the divine; compassion; sprit (*ruh*), referring to the divine breath blown into Adam's body to take human form. The part of the human body not part of this world, but connecting the human to the divine.

sabr: patience.

sadaqah: voluntary charity, a category within almsgiving.

salah: prescribed ritualistic prayers; also, a term for goodness.

salam: peace.

shahada: testimonial creed of a Muslim believer.

shahid: martyr; honorific title for not only those who pass away in a struggle, but also those who die prematurely or in terrible circumstances.

shahwa: human passions and desires.

sharr: the discourse on evil; theodicy.

shari'ah: Islamic law.

shura: process of consulting others or seeking advice from others.

sirat el mustaqim: the right path.

sulh: peace, peacemaking, and reconciliation.

sulha: process of reconciliation between conflicting parties.

sun': the creations of individuals; what man makes.

sunnah: the general customs of the Prophet Muhammad that Muslims incorporate into their lives.

tafsir: commentary on the Qur'an.

tahkim: use of arbitration to resolve differences.

tajdid: renewal or reformist efforts within religious thought.

takfir: In Islamic law, the act of calling other Muslims nonbelievers or apostates because of violatons of the principles of faith.

tanzih: transcendence toward divine grace.

taqwa: consciousness of the divine in the moment.

tashbih: closeness of the divine to all creation.

taslim: surrendering the self to the will of the divine.

tawhid: pure monotheism; the oneness of the divine.

ta'wil: inner meanings and interpretations of the Qur'an.

thawab: rewards or blessings to be received in the hereafter.

ulama: trained religious scholars in the field of Islamic theology, law, philosophy, history, and related fields.

ulum al-awa'il: generally, the ancient wisdom and intellectual work of Greek philosophy.

ulum 'aqliyyah: pursuit of intellect studies.

ulum naqliyyah: scholars heavily trained in the texts of Islam, who then transmit their knowledge based on this training.

ummah: community of believers; originally, all those who believed in a monotheistic tradition, but transformed by Muslim jurists to mean the larger Islamic community.

ummah wasatah: the midde community, referring to Qur'anic and *hadith* sources that a balanced and middle path is the best way.

uswah hasanah: the Prophet as the perfect example to follow.

waqi: formulating an opinion according to the appropriate context of a group.

wasatah: process of mediation for conflicting parties.

yakeen: faith.

yawm al-mithaq: dignity of a human being.

zakat: obligatory alms for the poor, one of the five pillars of Islam.

zamil: a type of poetry.

zulm: oppression and clear injustice to a person, group, or society.

English Terms

capacity building: a process whereby people, organizations, and society as a whole are enabled to strengthen, create, improve, adapt, and maintain their abilities to manage their affairs, through training, mentoring, networks, technology, infrastructure, and organizational structure.

civil society: collective term for non-governmental, mostly nonprofit groups that help their society while working to advance their own or others' well-being. It may include educational, trade, labor, civic, charitable, religious, media, cultural, recreational, and advocacy groups.

conciliation: the process by which a third party or parties attempt to help disputants define the facts of a dispute and to reach agreement on the trade-offs needed to resolve it.

conflict: an inevitable aspect of human interaction, often understood when two or more individuals or groups pursue mutually incompatible goals. Conflicts can be waged violently or nonviolently.

conflict analysis: the systematic study of conflict; provides a structured inquiry into the causes and possible outcomes of a conflict to better understand how to address it.

conflict management: efforts to limit and contain conflicts, particularly violent ones, while building up the capacities of all parties involved to undertake peacebuilding.

conflict prevention: measures taken to keep disputes from escalating into violence or to limit the spread of violence if it occurs.

conflict resolution: efforts to address the underlying causes of a conflict by finding common interests and grander goals. These include fostering trust through reconciliation initiatives and strengthening institutions and processes through which the parties engage one another.

conflict transformation: emphasis on addressing structural roots of conflict by changing existing patterns of behavior and fostering a culture of nonviolent approaches.

dialogue: an exchange of ideas or conversation that seeks mutual understanding through the sharing of perspectives; requires mutual listening, but allows insight into another group's beliefs, feelings, interests, history, and needs.

evaluation: systematic collection and analysis of data on a project to understand the project's process and effect.

human rights: basic rights and freedoms to which all humans are entitled. Established by several international conventions and treatises, such as the UN Universal Declaration of Human Rights in 1948, rights include the right to life, liberty, education, equality before the law, association, belief, free speech, and religion.

jus ad bellum: Latin, justice to war; the set of criteria used before engaging in war or determining the factors to justify a war.

jus in bello: Latin, law of war; setting the limits of acceptable wartime conduct.

just-war theory: belief the use of force is acceptable only if it meets certain standards: right authority, just cause, right intention, last resort, proportional means, and reasonable prospects of success.

mediation: mode of negotiation in which a mutually acceptable third party helps the parties to a conflict find a solution that they cannot find by themselves.

negotiation: process of communication and bargaining between parties seeking to arrive at a mutually accepted outcome on issues shared.

nonviolent action: action usually used by a group of people to persuade someone else to change their behavior or thinking. Examples are strikes, boycotts, marches, and hunger strikes.

peacebuilding: originally used in reference to postconflict recovery efforts, now more broadly includes providing humanitarian relief, protecting human rights, ensuring security, fostering nonviolent modes of resolving conflicts, fostering reconciliation, providing economic reconstruction, resettling refugees or internally displaced persons, and providing trauma healing services.

peacemaking: activities to halt ongoing conflicts and bring hostile parties to an agreement or find common ground to suspend violent conflict.

problem-solving workshop: informal, usually confidential workshop that brings together adversaries to reevaluate their attitudes and think creatively about joint solutions.

reconciliation: the long-term process by which the parties to a violent conflict build trust, learn to live cooperatively, and create stable peace; may include judicial processes, dialogue, admissions of guilt, or truth commissions.

reframing: to view a problem from a new perspective in order to find ways to reduce tensions or break a deadlock. It is a process to redefine a situation or a conflict in a new way, based on input from other people.

training: processes of helping practitioners acquire and improve skills to be more effective in their roles. Usually within the context of a conflict, training may be a form of indirect third-party intervention; it tends to be short term and to focus on specific skills.

Appendix 1

The Amman Message

In the Name of God,
the Compassionate, the Merciful

(1) Whosoever is an adherent to one of the four *Sunni* schools (*Mathahib*) of Islamic jurisprudence (*Hanafi, Maliki, Shafi'i*, and *Hanbali*), the two *Shi'i* schools of Islamic jurisprudence (*Ja'fari* and *Zaydi*), the *Ibadi* school of Islamic jurisprudence, and the *Thahiri* school of Islamic jurisprudence is a Muslim. Declaring that person an apostate is impossible and impermissible. Verily his (or her) blood, honour, and property are inviolable. Moreover, in accordance with the Shaykh Al-Azhar's *fatwa*, it is neither possible nor permissible to declare whosoever subscribes to the *Ash'ari* creed or whoever practices real *Tasawwuf* (Sufism) an apostate. Likewise, it is neither possible nor permissible to declare whosoever subscribes to true *Salafi* thought an apostate. Equally, it is neither possible nor permissible to declare as apostates any group of Muslims who believes in God, Glorified and Exalted be He, and His Messenger (may peace and blessings be upon him) and the pillars of faith, and acknowledges the five pillars of Islam, and does not deny any necessarily self-evident tenet of religion.

(2) There exists more in common among the various schools of Islamic jurisprudence than there is difference between them. The adherents to the eight schools of Islamic jurisprudence are in agreement as regards the basic principles of Islam. All believe in Allah (God), Glorified and Exalted be He, the One and the Unique; that the Noble Qur'an is the Revealed Word of God; and that our master Muhammad, may blessings and peace be upon him, is a Prophet and Messenger unto all mankind. All are in agreement about the five pillars of Islam: the two testaments of faith

---

See this document at http://www.ammanmessage.com.

(*shahadatayn*); the ritual prayer (*salat*); almsgiving (*zakat*); fasting the month of Ramadan (*sawm*), and the *Hajj* to the sacred house of God (in Mecca). All are also in agreement about the foundations of belief: belief in Allah (God), His angels, His scriptures, His messengers, and in the Day of Judgment, in Divine Providence in good and in evil. Disagreements between the *ulama* (scholars) of the eight schools of Islamic jurisprudence are only with respect to the ancillary branches of religion (*furu'*) and not as regards the principles and fundamentals (*usul*) [of the religion of Islam]. Disagreement with respect to the ancillary branches of religion (*furu'*) is a mercy. Long ago it was said that variance in opinion among the *ulama* (scholars) "is a good affair."

(3) Acknowledgment of the schools of Islamic jurisprudence (*Mathahib*) within Islam means adhering to a fundamental methodology in the issuance of *fatwas:* no one may issue a *fatwa* without the requisite personal qualifications which each school of Islamic jurisprudence determines [for its own adherents]. No one may issue a *fatwa* without adhering to the methodology of the schools of Islamic jurisprudence. No one may claim to do unlimited *ijtihad* and create a new school of Islamic jurisprudence or to issue unacceptable *fatwas* that take Muslims out of the principles and certainties of the *shari'ah* and what has been established in respect of its schools of jurisprudence.

The Second International Conference of the Assembly for Moderate Islamic Thought and Culture—

"The Practical Role of Moderates in Reform and the Revival of the Ummah"

In the Name of God, the Compassionate, the Merciful

The Moderation Assembly for Thought and Culture held its second international conference, titled "The Practical Role of the Moderate Current in Reform and the Revival of the Ummah" in Amman in the Hashemite Kingdom of Jordan on 24–26 April 2006/24-25 I Rabi' 1427 with the attendance of leading scholars, thinkers, and leaders for Islamic action who adhere to the moderation programme.

After the conference participants deliberated the state of the Ummah and the role of the moderation programme in the reform and the revival of the Ummah in the shadow of the attacks on the Islamic world from outside and extremism and fanaticism from within. They agreed on the necessity of sincere and active persons in the Ummah to pool their energies to advance Islamic action from the theoretical to the practical frameworks,

See this document online at http://ammanmessage.com/index.php?option=com_content&task=view&id=30&itemid=34.

and cultivate strategies, working plans and programs that strengthen communication between the entities which comprise this program, upon which it relies, in order to extricate the Ummah from its [present] crisis and missteps. The conference participants also reviewed the decisions of the International Islamic Conference which was held in Amman on 4–6 July 2005 and which pertained to the adherents of true Islam of the eight schools of Islamic jurisprudence; recognizing them; respecting them and the inviolability of their blood, honour, and property; and repudiating those who are bold enough to undertake declaring Muslims as apostates and issuing *fativas* without possessing the necessary qualifications, and repudiating disagreement among Muslims and unifying their speech, and strengthening the fraternal ties which bind them and not leaving any room for internal discord among them.

And in view of the importance of the results of the conference, its decisions, and its role in deepening the understanding of moderation, the conference participants decided to adopt these decisions as part of the decisions and recommendations of the conference: "The Practical Role of the Moderate Current in Reform and the Revival of the Ummah" and for the *ulama* to be signatories to them as an affirmation of their adoption, adhering to them, and calling others to them. In the light of that and after reviewing the researches and the working papers presented at the conference and listening to the discussions and dialogue which revolved around them, the conference participants issued the following recommendations and decisions:

1. The conference participants present their sincerest thanks and appreciation to His Hashemite Majesty King Abdullah II Bin Al-Hussein for his patronage of this conference and they also value the support which the Jordanian government presented in order to make this conference a success.

2. Affirming that Islamic culture is the Ummah's fortress, the address of its civilizational identity and the locus of its uniquely defining characteristics and that the ministries and institutions which have a relationship to its objective take up supporting, preserving, and strengthening it, and emphasizing the way of moderation in carrying out its objectives in the Arab and Islamic world.

3. Reaffirming the principle and the means of connecting the constituent components of the moderation programme: *ulama*, parties, institutions, that is through the following means:
   (a) Supporting the idea of an international global forum after reviewing its basic organization and beginning with foundational working steps.

(b) Reaffirming the idea of an annual "encounters workshop" of the moderation movement and selecting a single point of conversation for research for every meeting, investigating it, and revealing the means to implement it.

(c) Employing the Web site of the Moderation Assembly for Thought and Culture as a core means for disseminating moderate thinking and the moderation programme until such time a new site is adopted and in addition to the other already accredited Web sites.

(d) Formation of a follow-up committee which meets periodically to follow up the implementation of the conference recommendations.

(e) Formation of a financial committee in order to guarantee the funding for implementation of the programmes and plans of moderation. Its mission will be to coordinate with the executive committee and the International Assembly in order to surmount the obstacles which may prevent implementation of these decisions.

(f) Casting in final form a final statement of the Moderation Movement or the International Moderation Assembly which shall be sent to Arab and Muslim leaders and to the Arab League and the Organization of the Islamic Conference for the purpose of accrediting the International Moderation Assembly as one of the civil institutions with which cooperation is facilitated through the Arab League and the Organization of the Islamic Conference, and charging the executive committee with casting this final statement.

(g) Formation of an academic committee whose mission is to assemble all of the literatures and researches about moderation that have been presented at different conferences and selecting from them that which may be published in different languages, and adopting a plan for distributing these publications to the various international Islamic communities so that they may benefit from them, according to the principles followed.

4. Launching an internal campaign of dialogue between the different Islamic movements and their constituents in order to reach common ground through understanding the intellectual frameworks and coordination of Islamic action against the threats which Islam and Muslims face in the Islamic world by follow-up through the International Moderation Assembly to the extent possible.

5. The Conference recommends that the International Moderation Assembly works to coordinate between all the institutions and the

Islamic agencies which adhere to the moderation programme, and proceeds to coordinate amongst them and to cooperate in proposing common Islamic initiatives in order to broaden the framework for proposing the Islamic Moderation Programme in the remaining arenas and on all levels, popular and elite.

6. Proceeding to strengthen the dissemination of the Islamic Moderation Programme through satellite channels, particularly those which declared themselves as having an Islamic orientation, along with the possibility of establishing a satellite channel which presents the Moderation Programme as practiced by the Assembly, provided the reasons and financial and technical capabilities and specifications are ample for doing so.

7. Confronting the erroneous understanding of Islam as disseminated by teaching programmes and intellectual, broadcast, and cultural means in the west and coordinating with individuals and agencies which are experienced in this regard and studying previous undertakings to correct the stereotypical images which emerge from that erroneous understanding, pursuing the appropriate means to participate in these undertakings, such as international conferences, and supporting appropriate research centers and cooperating with influential agencies, especially the Islamic Educational, Scientific and Cultural Organization (ISESCO) and the Arab Organization for Education, Culture, and Science.

8. Cooperating with individuals and Islamic bodies which possess a moderate orientation, in order to cast the strategy for the moderation movement and working plans in order to carry them out, and urging governments, official and civil organizations, and institutions to adopt and support them.

9. Continuing to emphasize the necessity of continuing dialogue and coordination between the schools of Islamic jurisprudence for the purpose of greater proximity and understanding.

10. Corresponding with Arab and Islamic heads of government and the league of Arab universities in order to accredit a special course in universities for studying the culture of moderation along with scholars participating in the International Moderation Assembly to prepare an academic programme book toward this objective and to present it as a proposal ready for implementation.

11. Affirming the Amman Message and calling for its broad adoption through media, educational and guidance agencies and likewise to affirm the decisions of the Moderation Conference which was held in Amman in 2004 and those of the Kuwaiti, Saudi, Bahraini,

and other conferences within the literatures of the moderation movement and disseminating them.

12. Confirming the results and recommendations which arose from the International Islamic Conference, which was held in Amman in 2005 and which emphasized the necessity of strengthening Islamic unity, respecting the schools of Islamic jurisprudence and forbidding Muslims from declaring their Muslim brethren as apostates, and mutual recognition of the eight schools of Islamic jurisprudence.

13. Affirming a committee on dialogue with leading western thinkers and politicians such that dialogue is initiated via a group which represents the Moderation Movement and not a single or regional dialogue since that is more responsive to transmitting the desired thinking to others and to the continuance of coordination with respect to it.

14. Nominating a number of non-Muslim personalities from the west and east in consultation with relevant centres, those who are regarded as fostering mutual understanding, moderation, and acceptance of the other, and inviting them to the upcoming conference within a plan which aims to broaden the circle of moderation from its Arab and Islamic framework to an international one.

15. Cooperating with university bodies specialized in the Islamic lands in order to coordinate with western universities and engage in dialogue with them concerning the fields of Islamic studies they offer and to actively engage in correcting the potentially negative and erroneous images with the readiness to cooperate in involving Muslim specialists in those fields in accordance with the principles of mutual exchange and cooperation among universities.

16. The Conference recommends encouraging the endeavors of Arab and Muslim artists and writing to artists' unions in the Arab and Islamic world to turn toward producing series and films which serve the way of Islamic moderation on the level of local consumption and which are in accordance with world marketing, and supporting this marketing in accordance with the principles followed between the cinematic and television sectors operating in the Islamic countries and the west.

17. The conference participants emphasize the lack of addressing the security situation in confronting all forms of extremism and fanaticism and the necessity of dealing with them through confronting their causes, including the policies of some of the ruling elite in the west and arresting the climate of hostility in their interaction

with Islamic issues and Muslims more generally, also in confronting the weakness displayed by Arab and Islamic governments in displaying a more complete picture of Islamic issues and Muslims. The conference participants believe in the necessity of directing correspondences and detailed studies in this regard at the decision makers and the research and study centers that are able to influence doing so.

18. The Moderation Movement emphasizes that its goal is to serve Islam through its middle-ground vision and that there is no reliance of any sort in the plans of its parties, symbols, and movement on violence in implementing its programme and that its relationship with rulers is advisory and consultative.

19. The economic resources of the Ummah is a trust placed with governments which requires dedicating a portion thereof in the service of the "religion of the Ummah," not only in the Arab and Islamic arena, but also in the universal and international arena.

20. The battle of concepts and terms is truly one of the battles which the Umma wages in order to establish its identity. In this regard the Moderation Movement emphasizes precise articulation of all these concepts and terms, such as "terrorism," "extremism," and "resistance." Moreover, it emphasizes the right of the Ummah to legitimate resistance of all sorts of occupation in the Arab and Islamic world, as the conference condemns the acts of self-destruction and random killing which the people of Iraq are exposed to and likewise the practices of the occupying forces in Iraq and Palestine and requests that they leave Iraqi, Palestinian, and Afghani lands.

21. [Given that] the Muslim woman established her capacity for intellectual and political participation, the Conference recommends supporting this role and broadening the intellectual submission that is in harmony with the firm bases of Islam with respect to the issue of women, emphasizing her just due in the framework of integration with her brethren in religion, and not within the framework of collision and conflict. The Conference recommends that a number of Muslim women be among the members of the International Moderation Assembly.

22. The conference emphasizes the need for action to eliminate the gap between those who are described as the elite in the Islamic world in intellectual, cultural, and other fields and ordinary Muslims. The conference emphasizes the necessity of action to intensify contact with young adults and youth, deemed as they are the

starting point for spreading the moderate Islamic discourse, and
supports their participation in the different executive plans, programmes, initiatives, and proposals.

23. The Conference affirms the importance of action to develop school
curricula in such a manner that strengthens the upbringing of the
new generation early on and which [enables] comprehending Islam and its moderation and the completeness of its different aspects and develops the independent self-reliant Islamic personality
that is able to discern and to avoid the different impaired images
of some of the dimensions of Islam in the school curricula that are
under the influence of a global assault in its different guises.

24. The Conference affirms that the spread of the Moderation Movement and support for it and confronting what internally and internationally contradicts it, necessitates action to annul emergency
and extraordinary laws and to realize a complete national reconciliation which affirms what the Islamic religion established of the
principles of freedom, justice, equal participation, internal questioning, and the primacy of the rule of law which are in themselves
democratic principles which realize a basis for national mutual
consensus between governments and peoples.

25. The conference participants decided to form a preparatory committee, to whom is entrusted the task of following-up on the measures to establish a Global Forum for Moderation, formed of the
following individuals:

- Imam Al-Sadiq al-Mahdi (Sudan)
- Dr. Mustafa Uthman Ibrahim (Sudan)
- Mr. Buqira Al-Sultani (Sudan)
- Dr. Isam Al-Bashir (Sudan)
- Dr. Saadeddine Othmani (Morocco)
- Hajj Mustafa Al-Sisi (Senegal)
- Dr. Ahmad Al-Kubaisi (Iraq)
- Dr. Wahba Al-Zuhayli (Syria)
- Dr. Umar Abd Al-Kafi (Egypt)
- Mr. Muntasir Al-Zayyat (Egypt)
- Dr. Abd Al-Wahhab Al-Masiri (Egypt)
- Dr. Muhammad Habash (Syria)
- Dr. Muhammad Amin Al-Rakala (Morocco)
- Dr. Abd Al-Halim Uways (Egypt)
- Mr. Muhammad Al-Tullabi (Morocco)
- Mr. Hani Al-Fahs (Lebanon)

- Eng. Marwan Faouri (Jordan)*
- Dr. Fayiz Al-Rabi' (Jordan)
- Dr. Muhammad Al-Khatib (Jordan)
- Dr. Hayil Abd Al-Hafiz Dawud (Jordan)
- Dr. Muhammad Al-Qudat (Jordan)

---

*   Eng. Marwan Faouri was confirmed as general coordinator for the International Moderation Assembly.

Appendix 3

A Common Word

In the Name of God,
the Compassionate, the Merciful

A Common Word between Us and You
(Summary and Abridgement)

Muslims and Christians together make up well over half of the world's population. Without peace and justice between these two religious communities, there can be no meaningful peace in the world. The future of the world depends on peace between Muslims and Christians.

The basis for this peace and understanding already exists. It is part of the very foundational principles of both faiths: love of the One God and love of the neighbour. These principles are found over and over again in the sacred texts of Islam and Christianity. The Unity of God, the necessity of love for Him, and the necessity of love of the neighbour is thus the common ground between Islam and Christianity. The following are only a few examples:

Of God's Unity, God says in the Holy Qur'an: *Say: He is God, the One! / God, the Self-Sufficient Besought of all!* (*Al-Ikhlas*, 112:1–2). Of the necessity of love for God, God says in the Holy Qur'an: *So invoke the Name of thy Lord and devote thyself to Him with a complete devotion* (*Al-Muzzammil*, 73:8). Of the necessity of love for the neighbour, the Prophet Muhammad said: "*None of you has faith until you love for your neighbour what you love for yourself.*"

In the New Testament, Jesus Christ said: *'Hear, O Israel, the Lord our God, the Lord is One. / And you shall love the Lord your God with all your heart,*

See this document online at http://www.acommonword.com/index.php?lang=en&page=option1

with all your soul, with all your mind, and with all your strength.' This is the first commandment. / And the second, like it, is this: 'You shall love your neighbour as yourself.' There is no other commandment greater than these" (Mark 12:29–31).

In the Holy Qur'an, God Most High enjoins Muslims to issue the following call to Christians (and Jews—the *People of the Scripture*):

> *Say: O People of the Scripture! Come to a common word between us and you: that we shall worship none but God, and that we shall ascribe no partner unto Him, and that none of us shall take others for lords beside God. And if they turn away, then say: Bear witness that we are they who have surrendered [unto Him]* (Aal 'Imran 3:64).

The words: *we shall ascribe no partner unto Him*, relate to the Unity of God, and the words: *worship none but God*, relate to being totally devoted to God. Hence they all relate to the *First and Greatest Commandment*. According to one of the oldest and most authoritative commentaries on the Holy Qur'an, the words: *that none of us shall take others for lords beside God*, mean 'that none of us should obey the other in disobedience to what God has commanded'. This relates to the Second Commandment because justice and freedom of religion are a crucial part of love of the neighbour. Thus in obedience to the Holy Qur'an, we as Muslims invite Christians to come together with us on the basis of what is common to us, which is also what is most essential to our faith and practice: the *Two Commandments* of love.

In the Name of God, the Compassionate, the Merciful, And may peace and blessings be upon the Prophet Muhammad.

A COMMON WORD BETWEEN US AND YOU

In the Name of God, the Compassionate, the Merciful,
Call unto the way of thy Lord with wisdom and fair exhortation, and contend with them in the fairest way. Lo! thy Lord is Best Aware of him who strayeth from His way, and He is Best Aware of those who go aright.
(The Holy Qur'an, *Al-Nahl*, 16:125)

(I) LOVE OF GOD

LOVE OF GOD IN ISLAM

The Testimonies of Faith

The central creed of Islam consists of the two testimonies of faith, or *Shahadahs*[i], which state that: *There is no god but God, Muhammad is the messenger of God*. These Two Testimonies are the sine qua non of Islam. He or she who testifies to them is a Muslim; he or she who denies them is not a

Muslim. Moreover, the Prophet Muhammad said: *The best remembrance is:* *'There is no god but God'....* [ii]

The Best That All the Prophets Have Said

Expanding on *the best remembrance*, the Prophet Muhammad also said: *The best that I have said—myself, and the prophets that came before me—is: 'There is no god but God, He Alone, He hath no associate, His is the sovereignty and His is the praise and He hath power over all things'* [iii]. The phrases which follow the First Testimony of faith are all from the Holy Qur'an; each describe a mode of love of God, and devotion to Him.

The words: *He Alone*, remind Muslims that their hearts [iv] must be devoted to God Alone, since God says in the Holy Qur'an: *God hath not assigned unto any man two hearts within his body* (*Al-Ahzab*, 33:4). God is Absolute and therefore devotion to Him must be totally sincere.

The words: *He hath no associate*, remind Muslims that they must love God uniquely, without rivals within their souls, since God says in the Holy Qur'an: *Yet there are men who take rivals unto God: they love them as they should love God. But those of faith are more intense in their love for God ...* (*Al-Baqarah*, 2:165). Indeed, *[T]heir flesh and their hearts soften unto the remembrance of God ....* (*Al-Zumar*, 39:23).

The words: *His is the sovereignty*, remind Muslims that their minds or their understandings must be totally devoted to God, for *the sovereignty* is precisely everything in creation or existence and everything that the mind can know. And all is in God's Hand, since God says in the Holy Qur'an: *Blessed is He in Whose Hand is the sovereignty, and, He is Able to do all things* (*Al-Mulk*, 67:1).

The words: *His is the praise*, remind Muslims that they must be grateful to God and trust Him with all their sentiments and emotions. God says in the Holy Qur'an:

> *And if thou wert to ask them: Who created the heavens and the earth, and constrained the sun and the moon [to their appointed work]? they would say: God. How then are they turned away? / God maketh the provision wide for whom He will of His servants, and straiteneth it for whom [He will]. Lo! God is Aware of all things. / And if thou wert to ask them: Who causeth water to come down from the sky, and therewith reviveth the earth after its death ? they verily would say: God. Say: Praise be to God! But most of them have no sense* (*Al-'Ankabut*, 29:61–63). [v]

For all these bounties and more, human beings must always be truly grateful:

> *God is He Who created the heavens and the earth, and causeth water to descend from the sky, thereby producing fruits as food for you, and maketh the ships to be of service unto you,*

that they may run upon the sea at His command, and hath made of service unto you the rivers; / And maketh the sun and the moon, constant in their courses, to be of service unto you, and hath made of service unto you the night and the day. / And He giveth you of all ye ask of Him, and if ye would count the graces of God ye cannot reckon them. Lo! Man is verily a wrong-doer, an ingrate (Ibrahim, 14:32–34).[vi]

Indeed, the *Fatihah*—which is the *greatest chapter in the Holy Qur'an*[vii]—starts with praise to God:

> *In the Name of God, the Infinitely Good, the All-Merciful. /*
> *Praise be to God, the Lord of the worlds. /*
> *The Infinitely Good, the All-Merciful. /*
> *Owner of the Day of Judgement. /*
> *Thee we worship, and Thee we ask for help. /*
> *Guide us upon the straight path. /*
> *The path of those on whom is Thy Grace, not those who deserve anger nor those who are astray (Al-Fatihah, 1:1–7).*

The *Fatihah*, recited at least seventeen times daily by Muslims in the canonical prayers, reminds us of the praise and gratitude due to God for His Attributes of Infinite Goodness and All-Mercifulness, not merely for His Goodness and Mercy to us in this life but ultimately, on the Day of Judgement[viii] when it matters the most and when we hope to be forgiven for our sins. It thus ends with prayers for grace and guidance, so that we might attain—through what begins with praise and gratitude—salvation and *love*, for God says in the Holy Qur'an: *Lo! Those who believe and do good works, the Infinitely Good will appoint for them love (Maryam, 19:96).*

The words: *and He hath power over all things*, remind Muslims that they must be mindful of God's Omnipotence and thus fear God[ix]. God says in the Holy Qur'an:

> *. . . [A]nd fear God, and know that God is with the God-fearing. / Spend your wealth for the cause of God, and be not cast by your own hands to ruin; and do good. Lo! God loveth the virtuous. / . . . (Al-Baqarah, 2:194–5) . . . .*
> *[A]nd fear God, and know that God is severe in punishment (Al-Baqarah, 2:196).*

Through fear of God, the actions, might and strength of Muslims should be totally devoted to God. God says in the Holy Qur'an:

> *. . . [A]nd know that God is with those who fear Him (Al-Tawbah, 9:36) . . . .*
> *O ye who believe! What aileth you that when it is said unto you: Go forth in the way of God, ye are bowed down to the ground with heaviness. Take ye pleasure in the life of the world rather than in the Hereafter? The comfort of the life of the world is but little in the Hereafter. / If ye go not forth He will afflict you with a painful doom, and will choose instead of you a folk other than you. Ye cannot harm Him at all. God is Able to do all things (Al-Tawbah, 9:38–39).*

The words: *His is the sovereignty and His is the praise and He hath power over all things*, when taken all together, remind Muslims that just as everything in creation glorifies God, everything that is in their souls must be devoted to God:

> All that is in the heavens and all that is in the earth glorifieth God; His is the sovereignty and His is the praise and He hath power over all things (Al-Taghabun, 64:1).

For indeed, all that is in people's souls is known, and accountable, to God:

> He knoweth all that is in the heavens and the earth, and He knoweth what ye conceal and what ye publish. And God is Aware of what is in the breasts [of men] (Al-Taghabun, 64:4).

As we can see from all the passages quoted above, souls are depicted in the Holy Qur'an as having three main faculties: the mind or the intelligence, which is made for comprehending the truth; the will which is made for freedom of choice, and sentiment which is made for loving the good and the beautiful[x]. Put in another way, we could say that man's soul knows through *understanding* the truth, through *willing* the good, and through virtuous emotions and *feeling* love for God. Continuing in the same chapter of the Holy Qur'an (as that quoted above), God orders people to fear Him as much as possible, and to listen (and thus to understand the truth); to obey (and thus to will the good), and to spend (and thus to exercise love and virtue), which, He says, is better for our souls. By engaging *everything* in our souls—the faculties of knowledge, will, and love—we may come to be purified and attain ultimate success:

> So fear God as best ye can, and listen, and obey, and spend; that is better for your souls. And those who are saved from the pettiness of their own souls, such are the successful (Al-Taghabun, 64:16).

In summary then, when the entire phrase *He Alone, He hath no associate, His is the sovereignty and His is the praise and He hath power over all things* is added to the testimony of faith—*There is no god but God*—it reminds Muslims that their hearts, their individual souls, and all the faculties and powers of their souls (or simply their *entire* hearts and souls) must be totally devoted and attached to God. Thus God says to the Prophet Muhammad in the Holy Qur'an:

> Say: Lo! my worship and my sacrifice and my living and my dying are for God, Lord of the Worlds. / He hath no partner. This am I commanded, and I am first of those who surrender [unto Him]. / Say: Shall I seek another than God for Lord, when He is Lord of all things? Each soul earneth only on its own account, nor doth any laden bear another's load .... (Al-An'am, 6:162–64).

These verses epitomize the Prophet Muhammad's complete and utter devotion to God. Thus in the Holy Qur'an God enjoins Muslims who truly love God to follow this example,[xi] in order in turn to be loved[xii] by God:

> Say, [O Muhammad, to mankind]: If ye love God, follow me; God will love you and for-give you your sins. God is Forgiving, Merciful (Aal 'Imran, 3:31).

Love of God in Islam is thus part of complete and total devotion to God; it is not a mere fleeting, partial emotion. As seen above, God commands in the Holy Qur'an: *Say: Lo! my worship and my sacrifice and my living and my dying are for God, Lord of the Worlds. / He hath no partner.* The call to be totally devoted and attached to God heart and soul, far from being a call for a mere emotion or for a mood, is in fact an injunction requiring all-embracing, constant and active love of God. It demands a love in which the innermost spiritual heart and the whole of the soul—with its intelligence, will and feeling—participate through devotion.

None Comes with Anything Better

We have seen how the blessed phrase: *There is no god but God, He Alone, He hath no associate, His is the sovereignty and His is the praise and He hath power over all things*—which is the best that all the prophets have said—makes explicit what is implicit in *the best remembrance (There is no god but God)* by showing what it requires and entails, by way of devotion. It remains to be said that this blessed formula is also in itself a sacred invocation—a kind of extension of the First Testimony of faith (*There is no god but God*)—the ritual repetition of which can bring about, through God's grace, some of the devotional attitudes it demands, namely, loving and being devoted to God with all one's heart, all one's soul, all one's mind, all one's will or strength, and all one's sentiment. Hence the Prophet Muhammad commended this remembrance by saying:

> He who says: 'There is no god but God, He Alone, He hath no associate, His is the sover-eignty and His is the praise and He hath power over all things' one hundred times in a day, it is for them equal to setting ten slaves free, and one hundred good deeds are written for them and one hundred bad deeds are effaced, and it is for them a protection from the devil for that day until the evening. And none offers anything better than that, save one who does more than that.[xiii]

In other words, the blessed remembrance, *There is no god but God, He Alone, He hath no associate, His is the sovereignty and His is the praise and He hath power over all things*, not only requires and implies that Muslims must be totally devoted to God and love Him with their whole hearts and their whole souls and all that is in them, but provides a way, like its beginning (the testimony of faith)—through its frequent repetition[xiv]—for them to realize this love with everything they are. God says in one of the very first revelations in the Holy Qur'an: *So invoke the Name of thy Lord and devote thyself to Him with a complete devotion* (*Al-Muzzammil*, 73:8).

LOVE OF GOD AS THE *FIRST AND GREATEST COMMANDMENT* IN THE BIBLE

The *Shema* in the Book of Deuteronomy (6:4–5), a centrepiece of the Old Testament and of Jewish liturgy, says: *Hear, O Israel: The LORD our God, the LORD is one! / You shall love the LORD your God with all your heart, and with all your soul, and with all your strength.*[xv]

Likewise, in the New Testament, when Jesus Christ, the Messiah, is asked about the Greatest Commandment, he answers:

> *But when the Pharisees heard that he had silenced the Sadducees, they gathered together. / Then one of them, a lawyer, asked Him a question, testing Him, and saying, / "Teacher, which is the great commandment in the law?" / Jesus said to him, "'You shall love the LORD your God with all your heart, with all your soul, and with all your mind.' / This is the first and greatest commandment. / And the second is like it: 'You shall love your neighbour as yourself.' / On these two commandments hang all the Law and the Prophets"* (Matthew 22:34–40).

And also:

> *Then one of the scribes came, and having heard them reasoning together, perceiving that he had answered them well, asked him, "Which is the first commandment of all?" / Jesus answered him, "The first of all the commandments is: 'Hear, O Israel, the LORD our God, the LORD is one. / And you shall love the LORD your God with all your heart, with all your soul, with all your mind, and with all your strength.' This is the first commandment. / And the second, like it, is this: 'You shall love your neighbour as yourself.' There is no other commandment greater than these"* (Mark 12:28–31).

The commandment to love God fully is thus the *First and Greatest Commandment* of the Bible. Indeed, it is to be found in a number of other places throughout the Bible, including Deuteronomy 4:29, 10:12, 11:13 (also part of the *Shema*), 13:3, 26:16, 30:2, 30:6, 30:10; Joshua 22:5; Mark 12:32–33; and Luke 10:27–28.

However, in various places throughout the Bible, it occurs in slightly different forms and versions. For instance, in Matthew 22:37 (*You shall love the LORD your God with all your heart, with all your soul, and with all your mind*), the Greek word for "heart" is *kardia*, the word for "soul" is *psyche*, and the word for "mind" is *dianoia*. In the version from Mark 12:30 (*And you shall love the LORD your God with all your heart, with all your soul, with all your mind, and with all your strength*) the word "strength" is added to the aforementioned three, translating the Greek word *ischus*. The words of the lawyer in Luke 10:27 (which are confirmed by Jesus Christ in Luke 10:28) contain the same four terms as Mark 12:30. The words of the scribe in Mark 12:32 (which are approved of by Jesus Christ in Mark 12:34) contain the three terms *kardia* ("heart"), *dianoia* ("mind"), and *ischus* ("strength"). In the *Shema* of Deuteronomy 6:4–5 (*Hear, O Israel: The LORD our God, the LORD is one! / You shall love the LORD your God with all your heart, and with all your soul, and with all your strength*). In Hebrew the word for "heart" is *lev*, the word for "soul" is *nefesh*, and the word for "strength" is *me'od*. In Joshua 22:5, the Israelites are commanded by Joshua to love God and be devoted to Him as follows:

> "*But take careful heed to do the commandment and the law which Moses the servant of the LORD commanded you, to love the LORD your God, to walk in all His ways, to keep His commandments, to hold fast to Him, and to serve Him with all your heart and with all your soul*" (Joshua 22:5).

What all these versions thus have in common—despite the language differences between the Hebrew Old Testament, the original words of Jesus Christ in Aramaic, and the actual transmitted Greek of the New Testament—is the command to love God fully with one's heart and soul and to be fully devoted to Him. This is the First and Greatest Commandment for human beings.

In the light of what we have seen to be necessarily implied and evoked by the Prophet Muhammad's blessed saying: '*The best that I have said— myself, and the prophets that came before me—is: 'There is no god but God, He Alone, He hath no associate, His is the sovereignty and His is the praise and He hath power over all things'*, [xvi] we can now perhaps understand the words '*The best that I have said—myself, and the prophets that came before me*' as equating the blessed formula '*There is no god but God, He Alone, He hath no associate, His is the sovereignty and His is the praise and He hath power over all things*' precisely with the 'First and Greatest Commandment' to love God, with all one's heart and soul, as found in various places in the Bible. That is to say, in other words, that the Prophet Muhammad was perhaps, through inspiration, restating and alluding to the Bible's First Commandment. God knows best, but certainly we have seen their effective similarity in meaning. Moreover, we also do know (as can be seen in the endnotes), that both formulas have another remarkable parallel: the way they arise in a number of slightly differing versions and forms in different contexts, all of which, nevertheless, emphasize the primacy of total love and devotion to God. [xvii]

(II) LOVE OF THE NEIGHBOUR

LOVE OF THE NEIGHBOUR IN ISLAM

There are numerous injunctions in Islam about the necessity and paramount importance of love for—and mercy towards—the neighbour. Love of the neighbour is an essential and integral part of faith in God and love of God because in Islam without love of the neighbour there is no true faith in God and no righteousness. The Prophet Muhammad said: "*None of you has faith until you love for your brother what you love for yourself.*" [xviii] And: "*None of you has faith until you love for your neighbour what you love for yourself.*" [xix]

However, empathy and sympathy for the neighbour—and even formal prayers—are not enough. They must be accompanied by generosity and self-sacrifice. God says in the Holy Qur'an:

> *It is not righteousness that ye turn your faces[xx] to the East and the West; but righteous is he who believeth in God and the Last Day and the angels and the Scripture and the prophets; and giveth wealth, for love of Him, to kinsfolk and to orphans and the needy and the wayfarer and to those who ask, and to set slaves free; and observeth proper worship and payeth the poor-due. And those who keep their treaty when they make one, and the patient in tribulation and adversity and time of stress. Such are they who are sincere. Such are the pious (Al-Baqarah 2:177).*

And also:

> *Ye will not attain unto righteousness until ye expend of that which ye love. And whatsoever ye expend, God is Aware thereof (Aal 'Imran, 3:92).*

Without giving the neighbour what we ourselves love, we do not truly love God or the neighbour.

LOVE OF THE NEIGHBOUR IN THE BIBLE

We have already cited the words of the Messiah, Jesus Christ, about the paramount importance, second only to the love of God, of the love of the neighbour:

> *This is the first and greatest commandment. / And the second is like it: 'You shall love your neighbour as yourself.' / On these two commandments hang all the Law and the Prophets* (Matthew 22:38–40).

And:

> *And the second, like it, is this: 'You shall love your neighbour as yourself.' There is no other commandment greater than these"* (Mark 12:31).

It remains only to be noted that this commandment is also to be found in the Old Testament:

You shall not hate your brother in your heart. You shall surely rebuke your neighbour, and not bear sin because of him. / You shall not take vengeance, nor bear any grudge against the children of your people, but you shall love your neighbour as yourself: I am the LORD (Leviticus 19:17–18).

Thus the Second Commandment, like the First Commandment, demands generosity and self-sacrifice, and *On these two commandments hang all the Law and the Prophets.*

(III) *COME TO A COMMON WORD BETWEEN US AND YOU*

A Common Word

Whilst Islam and Christianity are obviously different religions—and whilst there is no minimising some of their formal differences—it is clear that the *Two Greatest Commandments* are an area of common ground and a link among the Qur'an, the Torah, and the New Testament. What prefaces the Two Commandments in the Torah and the New Testament, and what they arise out of, is the Unity of God—that there is only one God. For the *Shema* in the Torah, starts: (Deuteronomy 6:4) *Hear, O Israel: The LORD our God, the LORD is one!* Likewise, Jesus said: (Mark 12:29) *'The first of all the commandments is: Hear, O Israel, the LORD our God, the LORD is one.'* Likewise, God says in the Holy Qur'an: *Say: He, God, is One. / God, the Self-Sufficient Besought of all* (*Al-Ikhlas*, 112:1–2). Thus the Unity of God, love of Him, and love of the neighbour form a common ground upon which Islam and Christianity (and Judaism) are founded. This could not be otherwise since Jesus said: (Matthew 22:40) *'On these two commandments hang all the Law and the Prophets.'* Moreover, God confirms in the Holy Qur'an that the Prophet Muhammad brought nothing fundamentally or essentially new: *Naught is said to thee [Muhammad] but what already was said to the messengers before thee* (*Fussilat* 41:43). And: *Say [Muhammad]: I am no new thing among the messengers [of God], nor know I what will be done with me or with you. I do but follow that which is Revealed to me, and I am but a plain warner* (*Al-Ahqaf*, 46:9). Thus also God in the Holy Qur'an confirms that the same eternal truths of the Unity of God, of the necessity for total love and devotion to God (and thus shunning false gods), and of the necessity for love of fellow human beings (and thus justice), underlie all true religion:

And verily We have raised in every nation a messenger, [proclaiming]: Worship God and shun false gods. Then some of them [there were] whom God guided, and some of them [there were] upon whom error had just hold. Do but travel in the land and see the nature of the consequence for the deniers! (*Al-Nahl*, 16:36).
We verily sent Our messengers with clear proofs, and revealed with them the Scripture and the Balance, that mankind may stand forth in justice . . . (*Al-Hadid*, 57:25).

Come to a Common Word!

In the Holy Qur'an, God Most High tells Muslims to issue the following call to Christians (and Jews—the *People of the Scripture*):

> *Say: O People of the Scripture! Come to a common word between us and you: that we shall worship none but God, and that we shall ascribe no partner unto Him, and that none of us shall take others for lords beside God. And if they turn away, then say: Bear witness that we are they who have surrendered [unto Him] (Aal 'Imran 3:64).*

Clearly, the blessed words: *we shall ascribe no partner unto Him,* relate to the Unity of God. Clearly also, worshipping *none but God,* relates to being totally devoted to God and hence to the *First and Greatest Commandment.* According to one of the oldest and most authoritative commentaries (*tafsir*) on the Holy Qur'an—the *Jami' Al-Bayan fi Ta'wil Al-Qur'an* of Abu Ja'far Muhammad bin Jarir Al-Tabari (d. 310 A.H. /923 C.E.)—*that none of us shall take others for lords beside God,* means 'that none of us should obey in disobedience to what God has commanded, nor glorify them by prostrating to them in the same way as they prostrate to God'. In other words, that Muslims, Christians and Jews should be free to each follow what God commanded them, and not have 'to prostrate before kings and the like;'[xxi] for God says elsewhere in the Holy Qur'an: *Let there be no compulsion in religion. . . (Al-Baqarah,* 2:256). This clearly relates to the Second Commandment and to love of the neighbour of which justice[xxii] and freedom of religion are a crucial part. God says in the Holy Qur'an:

> *'God forbiddeth you not those who warred not against you on account of religion and drove you not out from your homes, that ye should show them kindness and deal justly with them. Lo! God loveth the just dealers (Al-Mumtahinah,* 60:8.

We thus as Muslims invite Christians to remember Jesus's words in the Gospel (Mark 12:29–31):

> *'. . . the LORD our God, the LORD is one. / And you shall love the LORD your God with all your heart, with all your soul, with all your mind, and with all your strength.' This is the first commandment. / And the second, like it, is this: 'You shall love your neighbour as yourself.' There is no other commandment greater than these.*

As Muslims, we say to Christians that we are not against them and that Islam is not against them—so long as they do not wage war against Muslims on account of their religion, oppress them and drive them out of their homes (in accordance with the verse of the Holy Qur'an [*Al-Mumtahinah,* 60:8] quoted above). Moreover, God says in the Holy Qur'an:

> *They are not all alike. Of the People of the Scripture there is a staunch community who recite the revelations of God in the night season, falling prostrate [before Him]. / They believe in God and the Last Day, and enjoin right conduct and forbid indecency, and vie one with*

another in good works. These are of the righteous. / And whatever good they do, nothing will be rejected of them. God is Aware of those who ward off [evil] (*Aal-'Imran*, 3:113–15).

Is Christianity necessarily against Muslims? In the Gospel, Jesus Christ says:

He who is not with me is against me, and he who does not gather with me scatters abroad (Matthew 12:30).
For he who is not against us is on our side (Mark 9:40).
. . . for he who is not against us is on our side (Luke 9:50).

According to the *Blessed Theophylact's*[xxiii] *Explanation of the New Testament*, these statements are not contradictions because the first statement (in the actual Greek text of the New Testament) refers to demons, whereas the second and third statements refer to people who recognised Jesus, but were not Christians. Muslims recognize Jesus Christ as the Messiah, not in the same way Christians do (but Christians themselves anyway have never all agreed with each other on Jesus Christ's nature), but in the following way: *. . . . the Messiah, Jesus son of Mary, is a Messenger of God and His Word which he cast unto Mary and a Spirit from Him . . .* (*Al-Nisa'*, 4:171). We therefore invite Christians to consider Muslims *not against* and thus *with them*, in accordance with Jesus Christ's words here.

Finally, as Muslims, and in obedience to the Holy Qur'an, we ask Christians to come together with us on the common essentials of our two religions . . . *that we shall worship none but God, and that we shall ascribe no partner unto Him, and that none of us shall take others for lords beside God . . . (Aal 'Imran*, 3:64). Let this common ground be the basis of all future interfaith dialogue between us, for our common ground is that on which hangs *all the Law and the Prophets* (Matthew 22:40). God says in the Holy Qur'an:

Say [O Muslims]: We believe in God and that which is revealed unto us and that which was revealed unto Abraham, and Ishmael, and Isaac, and Jacob, and the tribes, and that which Moses and Jesus received, and that which the prophets received from their Lord. We make no distinction between any of them, and unto Him we have surrendered. / And if they believe in the like of that which ye believe, then are they rightly guided. But if they turn away, then are they in schism, and God will suffice thee against them. He is the Hearer, the Knower [Al-Baqarah, 2:136–37].

Between Us and You

Finding common ground between Muslims and Christians is not simply a matter for polite ecumenical dialogue between selected religious leaders. Christianity and Islam are the largest and second largest religions in the world and in history. Christians and Muslims reportedly make up over a third and over a fifth of humanity, respectively. Together they make up more than 55 percent of the world's population, making the relationship between these two religious communities the most important factor in contributing to meaningful peace around the world. If Muslims and Christians are not at peace, the world cannot be at peace. With the terrible weaponry of the modern world; with Muslims and Christians intertwined everywhere as never before, no side can unilaterally win a conflict between more than half of the world's inhabitants. Thus our common future is at stake. The very survival of the world itself is perhaps at stake. And to those who nevertheless relish conflict and destruction for their own sake or reckon that ultimately they stand to gain through them, we say that our very eternal souls are all also at stake if we fail to sincerely make every effort to make peace and come together in harmony. God says in the Holy Qur'an: *Lo! God enjoineth justice and kindness, and giving to kinsfolk, and forbiddeth lewdness and abomination and wickedness. He exhorteth you in order that ye may take heed* (*Al Nahl*, 16:90). Jesus Christ said: *Blessed are the peacemakers . . . .*(Matthew 5:9), and also: *For what profit is it to a man if he gains the whole world and loses his soul?* (Matthew 16:26).

So let our differences not cause hatred and strife between us. Let us vie with each other only in righteousness and good works. Let us respect each other, be fair, just, and kind to another and live in sincere peace, harmony, and mutual goodwill. God says in the Holy Qur'an:

> *And unto thee have We revealed the Scripture with the truth, confirming whatever Scripture was before it, and a watcher over it. So judge between them by that which God hath revealed, and follow not their desires away from the truth which hath come unto thee. For each We have appointed a law and a way. Had God willed He could have made you one community. But that He may try you by that which He hath given you [He hath made you as ye are]. So vie one with another in good works. Unto God ye will all return, and He will then inform you of that wherein ye differ* (*Al-Ma'idah*, 5:48).

Wal-Salaamu 'Alaykum, Pax Vobiscum

Notes

[i] In Arabic: *La illaha illa Allah Muhammad rasul Allah*. The two *Shahadah*s actually both occur (albeit separately) as phrases in the Holy Qur'an (in *Muhammad* 47:19, and *Al-Fath* 48:29, respectively).

[ii] *Sunan Al-Tirmidhi, Kitab Al-Da'awat*, 462/5, no. 3383; *Sunan Ibn Majah*, 1249/2.

[iii] *Sunan Al-Tirmidhi, Kitab Al-Da'awat, Bab al-Du'a fi Yawm 'Arafah, Hadith* no. 3934.

It is important to note that the additional phrases, *He Alone, He hath no associate, His is the sovereignty and His is the praise and He hath power over all things*, all come from the Holy Qur'an, in exactly those forms, albeit in different passages. *He Alone*—referring to God Y—is found at least six times in the Holy Qur'an (7:70; 14:40; 39:45; 40:12; 40:84 and 60:4). *He hath no associate*, is found in exactly that form at least once (*Al-An'am*, 6:173). *His is the sovereignty and His is the praise and He hath power over all things*, is found in exactly this form once in the Holy Qur'an (*Al-Taghabun*, 64:1), and parts of it are found a number of other times (for instance, the words, *He hath power over all things*, are found at least five times: 5:120; 11:4; 30:50; 42:9 and 57:2).

ⁱᵛ**The Heart**   In Islam the (spiritual, not physical) heart is the organ of perception of spiritual and metaphysical knowledge. Of one of the Prophet Muhammad's 鬱 greatest visions God says in the Holy Qur'an: *The inner heart lied not (in seeing) what it saw.* (*al-Najm*, 53:11) Indeed, elsewhere in the Holy Qur'an, God says: *[F]or indeed it is not the eyes that grow blind, but it is the hearts, which are within the bosoms, that grow blind. (Al-Hajj,* 22:46; see whole verse and also: 2:9-10; 2:74; 8:24; 26:88-89; 48:4; 83:14 et al.. There are in fact over a hundred mentions of the heart and its synonyms in the Holy Qur'an.)

Now there are different understandings amongst Muslims as regards the direct Vision of God (as opposed to spiritual realities as such) God, be it in this life or the next—God says in the Holy Qur'an (of the Day of Judgement):

> *That day will faces be resplendent, / Looking toward their Lord; (Al-Qiyamah,* 75:22-23) Yet God also says in the Holy Qur'an:
> *Such is God, your Lord. There is no God save Him, the Creator of all things, so worship Him. And He taketh care of all things. / Vision comprehendeth Him not, but He comprehendeth (all) vision. He is the Subtle, the Aware. / Proofs have come unto you from your Lord, so whoso seeth, it is for his own good, and whoso is blind is blind to his own hurt. And I am not a keeper over you. (Al-An'am,* 6:102-104)

Howbeit, it is evident that the Muslim conception of the (spiritual) heart is not very different from the Christian conception of the (spiritual) heart, as seen in Jesus's 鬱 words in the New Testament: *Blessed are the pure in heart, for they shall see God.* (Matthew 5:8); and Paul's words: *For now we see in a mirror, dimly, but then face to face. Now I know in part, but then I shall know just as I am known.* (1 Corinthians 13:12)

ᵛ See also: *Luqman*, 31:25.

ᵛⁱ See also: *Al-Nahl*, 16:3-18.

ᵛⁱⁱ *Sahih Bukhari, Kitab Tafsir Al-Qur'an, Bab ma Ja'a fi Fatihat Al-Kitab* (*Hadith* no.1); also: *Sahih Bukhari, Kitab Fada'il Al-Qur'an, Bab Fadl Fatihat Al-Kitab*, (*Hadith* no.9), no. 5006.

ᵛⁱⁱⁱ The Prophet Muhammad 鬱 said:

> *God has one hundred mercies. He has sent down one of them between genii and human beings and beasts and animals and because of it they feel with each other; and through it they have mercy on each other; and through it, the wild animal feels for its offspring. And God has delayed ninety-nine mercies through which he will have mercy on his servants on the Day of Judgement.* (*Sahih Muslim, Kitab Al-Tawbah*; 2109/4; no. 2752; see also *Sahih Bukhari, Kitab Al-Riqaq*, no. 6469).

ⁱˣ **Fear of God is the Beginning of Wisdom**

The Prophet Muhammad 鬱 is reported to have said: *The chief part of wisdom is fear of God—be He exalted* (*Musnad al-Shahab*, 100/1; Al-Dulaymi, *Musnad Al-Firdaws*, 270/2; Al-Tirmidhi, *Nawadir Al-Usul*; 84/3; Al-Bayhaqi, *Al-Dala'il* and Al-Bayhaqi, *Al-Shu'ab*; Ibn Lal, *Al-Makarim*; Al-Ash'ari, *Al-Amthal*, et al.) This evidently is similar to the Prophet Solomon 鬱 words in the Bible: The *fear of the LORD is the beginning of Wisdom* .... (Proverbs 9:10); and: *The fear of the LORD is the beginning of knowledge.* (Proverbs 1:7)

ˣ **The Intelligence, the Will and Sentiment in the Holy Qur'an**

Thus God in the Holy Qur'an tells human being to believe in Him and call on Him (thereby using the intelligence) with fear (which motivates the will) and with hope (and thus with sentiment):

Only those believe in Our revelations who, when they are reminded of them, fall down prostrate and hymn the praise of their Lord, and they are not scornful, / Who forsake their beds to cry unto their Lord in fear and hope, and spend of that We have bestowed on them. / No soul knoweth what is kept hid for them of joy, as a reward for what they used to do. (Al-Sajdah, 32:15-17)

(O mankind!) Call upon your Lord humbly and in secret. Lo! He loveth not aggressors. / Work not confusion in the earth after the fair ordering (thereof), and call on Him in fear and hope. Lo! the mercy of God is near unto the virtuous. (Al-A'raf, 7:55-56)

Likewise, the Prophet Muhammad ﷺ himself is described in terms which manifest knowledge (and hence the intelligence), eliciting hope (and hence sentiment) and instilling fear (and hence motivating the will):

O Prophet! Lo! We have sent thee as a witness and a bringer of good tidings and a warner. (Al-Ahzab, 33:45)

Lo! We have sent thee (O Muhammad) as a witness and a bearer of good tidings and a warner, (Al-Fath, 48:8)

[xi] *A Goodly Example*

The love and total devotion of the Prophet Muhammad r to God is for Muslims the model that they seek to imitate. God says in the Holy Qur'an:

Verily in the messenger of God ye have a goodly example for him who hopeth for God and the Last Day, and remembereth God much. (Al-Ahzab, 33:21)

The totality of this love excludes worldliness and egotism, and is itself beautiful and loveable to Muslims. Love of God is itself loveable to Muslims. God says in the Holy Qur'an:

And know that the messenger of God is among you. If he were to obey you in many matters, ye would surely fall into misfortune; but God hath made the faith loveable to you and hath beautified it in your hearts, and hath made disbelief and lewdness and rebellion hateful unto you. Such are they who are the rightly guided. (Al-Hujurat, 49:7)

[xii] This 'particular love' is in addition to God's universal Mercy *which embraceth all things (Al-A'raf, 7:156)*; but God knows best.

[xiii] *Sahih Al-Bukhari, Kitab Bad' al-Khalq, Bab Sifat Iblis wa Junudihi; Hadith no. 3329.*

Other Versions of the Blessed Saying

This blessed saying of the Prophet Muhammad's ﷺ , is found in dozens of *hadith* (sayings of the Prophet Muhammad ﷺ) in differing contexts in slightly varying versions.

The one we have quoted throughout in the text (*There is no god but God, He alone. He hath no associate. His is the sovereignty, and His is the praise, and He hath power over all things*) is in fact the shortest version. It is to be found in *Sahih al-Bukhari: Kitab al-Adhan* (no. 852); *Kitab al-Tahajjud* (no. 1163); *Kitab al-'Umrah* (no. 1825); *Kitab Bad' al-Khalq* (no. 3329); *Kitab al-Da'awat* (nos. 6404, 6458, 6477); *Kitab al-Riqaq* (no. 6551); *Kitab al-I'tisam bi'l-Kitab* (no. 7378); in *Sahih Muslim: Kitab al-Masajid* (nos. 1366, 1368, 1370, 1371, 1380); *Kitab al-Hajj* (nos. 3009, 3343); *Kitab al-Dhikr wa'l-Du'a'* (nos. 7018, 7020, 7082, 7084); in *Sunan Abu Dawud: Kitab al-Witr* (nos. 1506, 1507, 1508); *Kitab al-Jihad* (no. 2772); *Kitab al-Kharaj* (no. 2989); *Kitab al-Adab* (nos. 5062, 5073, 5079); in *Sunan al-Tirmidhi: Kitab al-Hajj* (no. 965); *Kitab al-Da'awat* (nos. 3718, 3743, 3984); in *Sunan al-Nasa'i: Kitab al-Sahw* (nos. 1347, 1348, 1349, 1350, 1351); *Kitab Manasik al-Hajj* (nos. 2985, 2997); *Kitab al-Iman wa'l-Nudhur* (no. 3793); in *Sunan Ibn Majah: Kitab al-Adab* (no.

3930); *Kitab al-Du'a'* (nos. 4000, 4011); and in *Muwatta' Malik: Kitab al-Qur'an* (nos. 492, 494); *Kitab al-Hajj* (no. 831).

A longer version including the words *yuhyi wa yumit*—(There is no god but God, He alone. He hath no associate. His is the sovereignty, and His is the praise. He giveth life, and He giveth death, and He hath power over all things.)—is to be found in *Sunan Abu Dawud: Kitab al-Manasik* (no. 1907); in *Sunan al-Tirmidhi: Kitab al-Salah* (no. 300); *Kitab al-Da'awat* (nos. 3804, 3811, 3877, 3901); and in *Sunan al-Nasa'i: Kitab Manasik al-Hajj* (nos. 2974, 2987, 2998); *Sunan Ibn Majah: Kitab al-Manasik* (no. 3190).

Another longer version including the words *bi yadihi al-khayr*—(There is no god but God, He alone. He hath no associate. His is the sovereignty, and His is the praise. In His Hand is the good, and He hath power over all things.)—is to be found in *Sunan Ibn Majah: Kitab al-Adab* (no. 3931); *Kitab al-Du'a'* (no. 3994).

The longest version, which includes the words *yuhyi wa yumit wa Huwa Hayyun la yamut bi yadihi al-khayr*—(There is no god but God, He alone. He hath no associate. His is the sovereignty, and His is the praise. He giveth life, and He giveth death. He is the Living, who dieth not. In His Hand is the good, and He hath power over all things.)—is to be found in *Sunan al-Tirmidhi: Kitab al-Da'awat* (no. 3756) and in *Sunan Ibn Majah: Kitab al-Tijarat* (no. 2320), with the difference that this latter *hadith* reads: *bi yadihi al-khayr kuluhu* (in His Hand is *all* good).

It is important to note, however, that the Prophet Muhammad ﷺ, only described the first (shortest) version as: *the best that I have said—myself, and the prophets that came before me,* and only of that version did the Prophet r say: *And none comes with anything better than that, save one who does more than that.*

(These citations refer to the numbering system of *The Sunna Project's Encyclopaedia of Hadith (Jam' Jawami' al-Ahadith wa'l-Asanid)*, prepared in cooperation with the scholars of al-Azhar, which includes *Sahih al-Bukhari, Sahih Muslim, Sunan Abu Dawud, Sunan al-Tirmidhi, Sunan al-Nasa'i, Sunan Ibn Majah,* and *Muwatta' Malik.*)

xiv Frequent Remembrance of God in the Holy Qur'an

The Holy Qur'an is full of injunctions to invoke or remember God frequently:

Remember the name of thy Lord at morn and evening. (Al-Insan, 76:25)

So remember God, standing, sitting and [lying] down on your sides (Al-Nisa, 4:103).

And do thou (O Muhammad) remember thy Lord within thyself humbly and with awe, below thy breath, at morn and evening. And be not thou of the neglectful (Al-'Araf, 7:205).

… Remember thy Lord much, and praise (Him) in the early hours of night and morning (Aal 'Imran, 3:41).

O ye who believe! Remember God with much remembrance. / And glorify Him early and late (Al-Ahzab, 33:41-42).

(See also: 2:198-200; 2:203; 2:238-239; 3:190-191; 6:91; 7:55; 7:180; 8:45; 17:110; 22:27-41; 24:35-38; 26:227; 62:9-10; 87:1-17, et al.)

Similarly, the Holy Qur'an is full of verses that emphasize the paramount importance of the Remembrance of God (see: 2:151-7; 5:4; 6:118; 7:201; 8:2-4; 13:26-28; 14:24-27; 20:14; 20:33-34; 24:1; 29:45; 33:35; 35:10; 39:9; 50:37; 51:55-58; and 33:2; 39:22-23 and 73:8-9 as already quoted, et al.), and the dire consequences of not practising it (see: 2:114; 4:142; 7:179-180; 18:28; 18:100-101; 20:99-101; 20:124-127; 25:18; 25:29; 43:36; 53:29; 58:19; 63:9; 72:17 et al.; see also 107:4-6). Hence God ultimately says in the Holy Qur'an:

Has not the time arrived for the believers that their hearts in all humility should engage in the remembrance of God … ? (Al-Hadid, 57:16);

…. [S]lacken not in remembrance of Me (Taha, 20:42),

and: *Remember your Lord whenever you forget (Al-Kahf, 18:24).*

xv Herein all Biblical Scripture is taken from the New King James Version. Copyright © 1982 by Thomas Nelson, Inc. Used by permission. All rights reserved.

xvi Sunan *Al-Tirmithi, Kitab Al-Da'wat, Bab al-Du'a fi Yawm 'Arafah, Hadith* no. 3934. *Op. cit.*

xvii ***In the Best Stature***

Christianity and Islam have comparable conceptions of man being created in the best stature and from God's own breath. The Book of Genesis says:

(Genesis, 1:27) *So God created man in His own image; in the image of God He created him; male and female He created them.*

And:

(Genesis, 2:7) *And the LORD God formed man of the dust of the ground, and breathed into his nostrils the breath of life; and man became a living being.*

And the Prophet Muhammad ﷺ said: *Verily God created Adam in His own image.* (Sahih Al-Bukhari, Kitab Al-Isti'than, 1; Sahih Muslim, Kitab Al-Birr 115; Musnad Ibn Hanbal, 2: 244, 251, 315, 323 etc. et al.)

And We created you, then fashioned you, then told the angels: Fall ye prostrate before Adam! And they fell prostrate, all save Iblis, who was not of those who make prostration. (Al-A'raf, 7:11)

By the fig and the olive / By Mount Sinai, / And by this land made safe / Surely We created man of the best stature / Then We reduced him to the lowest of the low, / Save those who believe and do good works, and theirs is a reward unfailing. / So who henceforth will give the lie to the about the judgment? / Is not God the wisest of all judges? (Al-Tin, 95:1-8)

God it is Who appointed for you the earth for a dwelling-place and the sky for a canopy, and fashioned you and perfected your shapes, and hath provided you with good things. Such is God, your Lord. Then blessed be God, the Lord of the Worlds! (Al-Ghafir, 40:64)

Nay, but those who do wrong follow their own lusts without knowledge. Who is able to guide him whom God hath sent astray ? For such there are no helpers. / So set thy purpose (O Muhammad) for religion as a man by nature upright - the nature (framed) of God, in which He hath created man. There is no altering (the laws of) God's creation. That is the right religion, but most men know not—/ (Al-Rum, 30:29-30)

And when I have fashioned him and breathed into him of My Spirit, then fall down before him prostrate, (Sad, 38:72)

And when thy Lord said unto the angels: Lo! I am about to place a viceroy in the earth, they said: Wilt thou place therein one who will do harm therein and will shed blood, while we, we hymn Thy praise and sanctify Thee ? He said: Surely I know that which ye know not. / And He taught Adam all the names, then showed them to the angels, saying: Inform Me of the names of these, if ye are truthful ./ They said: Be glorified! We have no knowledge saving that which Thou hast taught us. Lo! Thou, only Thou, art the Knower, the Wise. / He said: O Adam! Inform them of their names, and when he had informed them of their names, He said: Did I not tell you that I know the secret of the heavens and the earth ? And I know that which ye disclose and which ye hide. / And when We said unto the angels: Prostrate yourselves before Adam, they fell prostrate, all save Iblis. He demurred through pride, and so became a disbeliever… / And We said: O Adam! Dwell thou and thy wife in the Garden, and eat ye freely (of the fruits) thereof where ye will; but come not nigh this tree lest ye become wrong-doers. (Al-Baqarah, 2:30-35) [xviii] *Sahih Al-Bukhari, Kitab al-Iman, Hadith* no.13.

[xix] *Sahih Muslim , Kitab al-Iman, 67-1, Hadith* no.45.

[xx] The classical commentators on the Holy Qur'an (see: *Tafsir Ibn Kathir, Tafsir Al-Jalalayn*) generally agree that this is a reference to (the last movements of) the Muslim prayer.

[xxi] Abu Ja'far Muhammad Bin Jarir Al-Tabari, *Jami' al-Bayan fi Ta'wil al-Qur'an*, (*Dar al-Kutub al-'Ilmiyyah*, Beirut, Lebanon, 1ˢᵗ ed, 1992/1412,) *tafsir* of *Aal-'Imran*, 3:64; Volume 3, pp. 299-302.

[xxii] According to grammarians cited by Tabari (op cit.) the word 'common' (*sawa'*) in 'a common word between us' also means 'just', 'fair' (*adl*).

[xxiii] The Blessed Theophylact (1055-1108 C.E.) was the Orthodox Archbishop of Ochrid and Bulgaria (1090-1108 C.E.). His native language was the Greek of the New Testament. His *Commentary* is currently available in English from Chrysostom Press.

Appendix 4

Peace Education Curriculum
Perspective of Ulama of Aceh

How to Use This Manual
Purpose of This Manual
Philsophical Foundation

Chapter I Peace Symbols
Understanding Peace Symbols
Al-Jihad *al-Asghar* (The Minor Struggle)
Jihad *al-'Aql* (Empowering the Mind)
Al-Jihad *al-Akbar* (The Major Struggle)
The Hudaybiyyah Agreement (*Sulh al-Hudaybiyyah*)
The Conquest of Mecca (*Fath Makkah*)
Treasury of Aceh Tradition

Chapter II The Management of Emotion
Understanding Emotions
Facial Expression and Body Language
Managing Emotions
Anger and Its Management
Perceptions

Chapter III Rights and Responsibilities
Understanding Rights and Responsibilities
Claiming One's Rights and Responsibilities
Rights and Responsibilities Toward God

Bibliography

Abdul-Rauf, Muhammad. *A Muslim's Reflections on Democratic Capitalism.* Washington, DC: American Enterprise Institute, 1984.

Abrahamian, Ervand. *Iran Between Two Revolutions.* Princeton, NJ: Princeton University Press, 1982.

Abu-Nimer, Mohammed. "Conflict Resolution Approaches: Western and Middle Eastern Lessons and Possibilities." *The American Journal of Economics and Sociology,* vol. 55, no. 1 (1996), 35–52.

———. "Conflict Resolution in an Islamic Context." *Peace and Change,* vol. 21, no. 1 (1996), 22–40.

———. ed. *Reconciliation, Justice, and Coexistence: Theory and Practice.* Lanham, MD: Lexington Books, 2001.

———. *Islam and Non-violence.* Tallahassee: University of Florida Press, 2002.

Abu-Sahlieh, Aldeeb. "Introduction à la lecture juridique du Coran." *Revue de droit international et de droit compare,* vol. 65, no. 1–2 (1988), 76–104.

———. "Muslims and Human Rights: Challenges and Perspectives." In *Human Rights and Cultural Diversity,* ed. W. Schmale. Goldbach: Keip, 1993.

Adams, Charles C. *Islam and Modernism in Egypt.* New York: Russell & Russell, 1968.

Afshar, Haleh. "Islam and Feminism: An Analysis of Political Strategies." In *Feminism and Islam: Legal and Liberty Perspectives,* ed. Mai Yamani. London: Ithaca Press, 1996.

Ahmad, Aziz. *Islamic Modernism in India and Pakistan, 1857–1964.* Oxford: Oxford University Press, 1967.

Ahmed, Ishtiaq. *The Concept of an Islamic State: Analysis of the Ideological Controversy in Pakistan.* New York: St. Martin's Press, 1987.

———. "Abdullahi An-Na'im on Constitutional and Human Rights Issues." In *Islamic Law Reform and Human Rights,* ed. Tore Lindholm and Kari Vogt. The Hague: Nordic Human Rights Publications, 1992.

Akhavi, Shahrough. *Religion and Politics in Contemporary Iran.* Albany: State University of New York Press, 1980.

———. "Islam, Politics, and Society in the Thought of Ayatollah Khomeini, Ayatollah Taliqani, and Ali Shariati." *Middle Eastern Studies,* vol. 24 (1988), 404–31.

Al-Ashmawy, Muhammad Said. *L'islamisme contre l'Islam,* trans. Richard Jacquemond. Paris: Éditions la découverte, 1989.

Al-Basari, Al-Rabi' b. Habib. *Musnad al-Imam al-Rabi', Bab fi al-'Ilm wa talabih wa Fadlih.* Beirut: Mu'assasat 'Ulum al-Qur'an, 1988.

Al-Ghazzali, Abu Hamid. *Ihya' 'Ulum al-Din,* vol. 2. New Delhi: Kitab Bhavan, 1982.

Al-Jabarti. *Napoleon in Egypt: Al-Jabarti's Chronicle of the French Occupation,* trans. Shmuel Moreh. Princeton, NJ: Markus Wiener Publishers, 1997.

An-Na'im, Abdullahi Ahmed. "Islamic Law, International Relations, and Human Rights: Challenge and Response." *Cornell International Law Journal,* vol. 20, no. 2 (1987), 317–35.

———. *Toward an Islamic Reformation: Civil Liberties, Human Rights, and International Law.* Syracuse, NY: Syracuse University Press, 1996.

———. "The Islamic Counter-Reformation." *New Perspectives Quarterly,* vol. 19 (2002), 29–35.

Al-Andalusi, Sa'ib b. Ahmad. *Science in the Medieval World "Book of the Categories of Nations" (Tabaqat al-Umam),* trans. S.I. Salem and A. Kumar. Austin: The University of Texas Press, 1991.

Al-'Arabi, Muhyiddin Ibn. *Al-Futuhat al-Makkiyyah,* ed. M. 'Abd al-Rahman al-Mar'ashli. Beirut: Dar Ihya' al-Turath al-'Arabi, 1997.

Al-Ghazali, Shaykh Muhammad. *A Thematic Commentary on the Qur'an,* trans. A. Shamis. Herndon: International Institute of Islamic Thought, 2000.

Al-Jawziyyah, Ibn Qayyim. *Ahkam ahl al-Dhimmah,* ed. Subhi al-Salih. Beirut: Dar al-'Ilm li'l-Malayin, 1983.

Allard, Michel. *Le problème des attributs divins dans la doctrine d'al-As'ari et des ses premiers grands disciples.* Beyrouth: Editions del l'Impirimerie Catholique, 1965.

Al-Mahalli, Jalal al-Din, and Jalal al-Din al-Suyuti. *Tafsir al-Jalalayn.* Beirut: Mu'assasat al-Risalah, 1995.

Al-Qari, 'Ali b. Sultan Muhammad al-Harawi. *Al-Masnu' fi Ma'rifat al-hadith al-Mawdu'.* Al-Riyad: Maktabat al-Rushd, 1983.

Al-Qaysari, Dawud. *Risalah fi Ma'rifat al-Mahabbat al-haqiqiyyah.* In *al-Rasa'il,* ed. Mehmet Bayraktar. Kayseri: Kayseri Metropolitan Municipality, 1997.

Al-Razi, Fakhr al-Din. *Al-Arba'in fi Usul al-Din*. Cairo: Maktabat al-Kulliyat al-Azhariyyah, 1986.

Al-Raziq, Ali Abd. *Al-Islam wa Usul al-Hukumah* [Islam and the Foundations of Government]. Beirut: Dar Makhahat al-Haya, 1966.

Al-Sadr, Baqir. *Iqtisaduna*. Tehran: World Organization for Islamic Services, 1994.

Al-Sijistani, Abu Sulayman. *Muntakhab Siwan al-Hikmah*, ed. D.M. Dunlop. The Hague: Mouton Publishers, 1979.

Al-Suhrawardi, Shihab al-Din Yahya b. Habash. *Hikmat al-Ishraq* [The Philosophy of Illumination], ed. and trans. John Walbridge and Hossein Ziai. Utah: Brigham Young University Press, 1999.

Al-Taftazani, Sa'd al-Din. *Sharh al-Maqasid*. Beirut: 'Alam al-Kutub, 1989.

Al-Tahanawi, Muhammad 'Ali. *Kashshaf Istilahat al-Funun*. Beirut: Dar al-Kutub al-'Ilmiyyah, 1998.

Appleby, Scott. *The Ambivalence of the Sacred: Religion, Violence, and Reconciliation*. Lanham, MD: Rowman & Littlefield, 2000.

Arhaldez, R. "La loi musulmane à la lumière des sciences coraniques." *Archives de philosophie du droit*, vol. 38 (1993), 83–91.

Arjomand, Said Amir. *The Shadow of God and the Hidden Imam: Religion, Political Order, and Social Change in Shi'ite Iran from the Beginning to 1890*. Chicago: University of Chicago Press, 1984.

———. ed. *Authority and Political Culture in Shi'ism*. Albany: State University of New York Press, 1988.

———. *The Turban for the Crown*. Oxford: Oxford University Press, 1988.

Arkoun, Mohammed. *Pour une critique de la raison islamique*. Paris: Maisonneuve et Larose, 1984.

———. "The Concept of 'Islamic Reformism.'" In *Islamic Law Reform and Human Rights*, ed. Tore Lindholm and Kari Vogt. The Hague: Nordic Human Rights Publications, 1992.

———. *Rethinking Islam: Common Questions, Uncommon Answers*, trans. and ed. Robert D. Lee. Boulder, CO: Westview Press, 1994.

Arnold, T.W. *The Preaching of Islam*. Delhi: Renaissance Publishing House, 1984.

Asad, Muhammad. *Principles of State and Government in Islam*. Berkeley: University of California Press, 1961.

Augsburger, D.W. *Conflict Mediation Across Cultures*. Louisville, KY: Westminster/John Knox Press, 1992.

Avruch, Kevin. *Culture and Conflict Resolution*. Washington, DC: United States Institute of Peace, 1998.

Ayalon, Ami. *Language and Change in the Arab Middle East*. New York: Oxford University Press, 1987.

Aziz, Ahmad. *Studies in Islamic Culture in the Indian Environment.* Oxford: Oxford University Press, 1964.

Bacani, Benedicto. *The Mindanao Peace Talks: Another Opportunity to Resolve the Moro Conflict in the Philippines.* Washington, DC: United States Institute of Peace, 2005.

Baer, Gabriel. *Egyptian Guilds in Modern Times.* Jerusalem: Israel Oriental Society, 1964.

Baffoun, Alya. "Women and Social Change in the Muslim Arab World." In *Women and Islam,* ed. Azizah al-Hirbi. Oxford: Pergamon Press, 1982.

Baladhuri. *Futuh Al-Buldan.* Cairo: Maktabat al Tijariyyah al-Kubra, 1959.

Bannerman, Patrick. *Islam in Perspective: A Guide to Islamic Society, Politics and Law.* London: Routledge, 1988.

Bartoli, Andrea. "Mediating Peace in Mozambique." In *Herding Cats: Multiparty Mediation in a Complex World,* ed. Chester Crocker, Fen O. Hampson, and Pamela Aall. Washington, DC: United States Institute of Peace, 2000.

———. "Christianity and Peacebuilding." In *Religion and Peacemaking,* ed. Harold Coward and Gordon Smith. Albany: State University of New York Press, 2004.

Bartoli, Andrea, Edward Giradet, and Jeffrey Carmel, eds. *Somalia, Rwanda and Beyond.* Cambridge: Cambridge University Press, 1995.

Bayat-Philip, Mangol. "Tradition and Change in Iranian Socio-Religious Thought." In *Modern Iran: The Dialectics of Continuity and Change,* ed. Michael E. Bonine and Nikki R. Keddie. Albany: State University of New York Press, 1981.

Bazargan, Mahdi. *Bazgasht bi Qur'an* [Return to the Qur'an]. Tehran, n.p., 1984.

Beck, Lois, and Nikki Keddie, eds. *Women in the Muslim World.* Cambridge, MA: Harvard University Press, 1978.

Bennani, Boubker Jalal. *L'Islamisme et les droits de l'homme.* Lausanne: Édition de l'Aire, 1984.

Berman, Harold J. *The Interaction of Law and Religion.* New York: Abingdon Press, 1974.

———. *Faith and Order: The Reconciliation of Law and Religion.* Atlanta, GA: Scholars Press, 1993.

Binder, Leonard. *Islamic Liberalism: A Critique of Development Ideologies.* New York: Oxford University Press, 1994.

Boroujerdi, Mehrzad. "The Encounter of Post-Revolutionary Thought in Iran with Hegel, Heidegger, and Popper." In *Cultural Transitions in the Middle East,* ed. Serif Mardin. New York: E.J. Brill, 1994.

————. *The Iranian Intellectuals and the West: The Tormented Triumph of Nativism*. Syracuse: Syracuse University Press, 1996.

Boulding, Elise. *Underside of History: A View of Women Through Time*, rev. ed. Newbury Park, CA: Sage Publications, 1992.

————. ed. *Building Peace in the Middle East: Challenges for States and Civil Society*. Boulder, CO: Lynne Rienner Publishers, 1994.

Brown, Daniel. *Rethinking Tradition in Modern Islamic Thought*. Cambridge: Cambridge University Press, 1996.

Bulliet, Richard. "Conversion to Islam and the Emergence of a Muslim Society in Iran." In *Conversion to Islam*, ed. Nehemia Levtzion. New York: Holmes and Meier Publishers, 1979.

Butterworth, John. "Al-Farabi's Statecraft: War and the Well-Ordered Regime." In *Cross, Crescent, and Sword: The Justification and Limitation of War in Western and Islamic Tradition*, ed. James Turner Johnson and John Kelsay. New York: Greenwood Press, 1990.

Burgess, Heidi, and Guy Burgess. 1994. "Justice Without Violence: A Theoretical Framework." In *Justice Without Violence*, ed., Paul Wehr, Heidi Burgess, and Guy Burgess. Boulder: Lynne Reinner Publishers 1994.

Campbell, Richard, trans. and ed. *Society and Economics in Islam: Writings and Declarations of Ayatollah Sayyid Mahmud Taliqani*. Berkeley: Mizan Press, 1982.

Chehabi, H.E. *Iranian Politics and Religious Modernism: The Liberation Movement of Iran Under the Shah and Khomeini*. London: I.B. Tauris, 1990.

Chejne, Anwar. *Muslim Spain: Its History and Culture*. Minneapolis: University of Minnesota Press, 1974.

Chinkin, Christine. "Peace Agreements as Means for Promoting Gender Equality and Ensuring Participation of Women: A Framework for Model Provisions." United Nations Division for the Advancement of Women. Office of the Special Advisor on Gender Issues and Advancement of Women. Department of Political Affairs, December 10, 2003.

Chittick, William. *The Sufi Path of Knowledge*. Albany: State University of New York Press, 1989.

————. "The Theological Roots of Peace and War According to Islam." *The Islamic Quarterly*, vol. 34 no. 3 (1990), 145–63.

————. *The Self-Disclosure of God: Principles of Ibn al-'Arabi's Cosmology*. Albany: State University of New York Press, 1998.

————. "The Anthropocosmic Vision in Islamic Thought." In *God, Life, and the Cosmos*, ed. Ted Peters, Muzaffar Iqbal, and Syed Nomanul Haq. Aldershot: Ashgate, 2002.

Chittick, William, and Sachiko Murata. *The Vision of Islam*. Albany: The State University of New York Press, 1994.

Christelow, Allan. *Muslim Law Courts and the French Colonial State in Algeria.* Princeton, NJ: Princeton University Press, 1985.

Cohen, Raymond. *Negotiating Across Cultures: International Communication in an Interdependent World.* Washington, DC: United States Institute of Peace, 1997.

Collingwood, R.G. *The New Leviathan.* New York: Thomas Y. Crowell, 1971.

Combs-Schilling, Elaine M. "Etching Patriarchal Rule: Ritual Dye, Erotic Potency, and the Morrocan Monarchy." *Journal of the History of Sexuality,* vol. 1, no. 4 (1991), 658–81.

———. 1994. "Sacred Refuge: The Power of a Muslim Female Saint." *Fellowship: Islam, Peace and Nonviolence,* vol. 60, no. 5–6 (1994), 17.

Coomaraswamy, Ananda. *Transformation of Nature in Art.* New York: Dover, 1956.

Coomaraswamy, Rama. "Traditional Economics and Liberation Theology." In *In Quest of the Sacred,* ed. Seyyed Hossein Nasr. Oakton, VA: The Foundation for Traditional Studies, 1987.

Cooper, John. "The Limits of the Sacred: The Epistemology of Abdolkarim Soroush." In *Islam and Modernity: Muslim Intellectuals Respond,* ed. J. Cooper, Ronald L. Netter, and Mohamed Mahmoud. London: I.R. Tauris, 1998.

Coulson, Noel James. *A History of Islamic Law.* Edinburgh: Edinburgh University Press, 1964.

Cox, Gray. "The Light at the End of the Tunnel and the Light in Which We May Walk: Two Concepts of Peace." In *The Causes of Quarrel,* ed. Peter Caws. New York: Hougton Mifflin Company, 1989.

Crow, Karim D. *Nonviolence in Islam.* Washington, DC: Nonviolence International, 1997.

Dabashi, Hamid. *Theology of Discontent: The Ideological Foundation of the Islamic Revolution in Iran.* New York: New York University Press, 1993.

Danner, Victor. *The Islamic Tradition: An Introduction.* Amity, NY: Amity House, 1988.

Dozy, R. *Essai sur l'histoire de l'Islamisme.* Leiden: Brill, 1879.

Dumézil, Georges. *The Destiny of the Warrior,* trans. Alf Hiltebeitel. Chicago: The University of Chicago Press, 1969.

Dworkin, Ronald M. "Islamic Law, A System of Rules?" In *The Philosophy of Law,* ed. Ronald Dworkin. New York: Oxford University Press, 1977.

Dwyer, Kevin. *Arab Voices, The Human Rights Debate in the Middle East.* Berkeley, CA: University of California Press, 1991.

Eickelman, Dale. "Inside the Islamic Reformation." *Wilson Quarterly,* vol. 22 (1998), 80–89.

El Fadl, Khaled Abou. "*Ahkam al-Bughat*: Irregular Warfare and the Law of Rebellion Islam." In *Cross, Crescent, and Sword: The Justification and Limitation of War in Western and Islamic Tradition*, ed. James Turner Johnson and John Kelsay. Westport, CT: Greenwood Press. 1990.

―――. *Rebellion and Violence in Islamic Law*. Cambridge: Cambridge University Press, 2001.

Enayat, Hamid. *Modern Islamic Political Thought*. Austin: University of Texas Press, 1982.

Engineer, Ali Asghar. "Sources of Nonviolence in Islam." *Nonviolence: Contemporary Issues and Challenges*, ed. M. Kumar. New Delhi: Gandhi Peace Foundation, 1994.

El-Ansary, Waleed. "The Economics of Terrorism: How Bin Laden Is Changing the Rules of the Game." In *Islam, Fundamentalism, and the Betrayal of Tradition: Essays by Western Muslim Scholars*, ed. Joseph Lumbard. Bloomington, IN: World Wisdom Books, 2004.

Esack, Farid. *Liberation and Pluralism: An Islamic Perspective of Interreligious Solidarity Against Oppression*. Oxford: One World Publications, 1997.

Esposito, John L., ed. *Voices of Resurgent Islam*. New York: Oxford University Press, 1983.

―――. *Islam: The Straight Path*. New York: Oxford University Press, 1988.

―――. *Islam and Politics*, 2nd ed. Syracuse: Syracuse University Press, 1991.

―――. *The Islamic Threat: Myth or Reality?* New York: Oxford University Press, 1992.

Esposito, John L., and James Piscatori. "Democratization and Islam." *Middle East Journal*, vol. 45, no. 3 (1991), 427–40.

Fahmi, Hwadi. *Islam and Democracy*. Cairo: Cairo Center for Translation and Publication, 1993.

Fakhry, Majid. *A History of Islamic Philosophy*. New York: Columbia University Press, 1983.

Farrag, Ahmed. "Human Rights and Liberties in Islam." In *Human Rights in a Pluralist World: Individuals and Collectivities*, ed. Jan Berting, Peter R. Baehr, J. Herman Burgers, Cees Flinterman, Barbara de Klerk, Rob Kroes, Cornelis A. van Minnen, and Koo VanderWal. Westport, CT: Meckler, 1990.

Fatoohi, Louay. *Jihad in the Qur'an*. Kuala Lumpur: A.S. Noordeen, 2002.

Fischer, Michael, and Mehdi Abedi. *Debating Muslims: Cultural Dialogue in Post-Modernity and Tradition*. Madison: University of Wisconsin Press, 1990.

Friedmann, Yohanan. *Tolerance and Coercion in Islam: Interfaith Relations in the Muslim Tradition.* Cambridge: Cambridge University Press, 2003.

Fukuyama, Francis. *The End of History and the Last Man.* New York: Free Press, 2006.

Gibb, H.A.R. *Modern Trends in Islam.* Chicago: University of Chicago Press, 1947.

Glenn, Patrick. *Legal Traditions of the World: Sustainable Diversity in Law.* New York: Oxford University Press, 2007.

Gilligan, Carol. *In a Different Voice: Psychological Theory and Women's Development.* Cambridge, MA: Harvard University Press, 1982.

Girard, Rene. *Violence and the Sacred,* trans. Patrick Gregory. Baltimore: The Johns Hopkins University Press, 1979.

Goldziher, Ignaz. "The Attitude of Orthodox Islam Toward the 'Ancient Sciences.'" In *Studies on Islam,* trans. and ed. M.L. Swartz. New York: Oxford University Press, 1981.

Goma'a, Ali, ed. *Takshaf al-Turath al-Islam al-Iqtisadi* [Revealing the Islamic Economic Heritage]. Cairo: International Institute of Islamic Thought, 1997.

Gray, John. *Al Qaeda and What It Means to Be Modern.* New York: The New Press, 2003.

Guénon, René. "*Al-Faqr* or 'Spiritual Poverty.'" *Studies in Comparative Religion* (Winter 1973), 16–20.

―――. *The Reign of Quantity and the Signs of the Times.* Ghent, New York: Sophia Perennis et Universalis, 2001.

Gutas, Dimitri. *Greek Thought, Arabic Culture.* London: Routledge, 1998.

Ha'iri, Abdul-Hadi. *Shi'ism and Constitutionalism in Iran.* Leiden: E.J. Brill, 1977.

Hambly, Gavin R.G. *Women in the Medieval Islamic World: Power, Patronage, and Piety.* New York: Palgrave Macmillan, 1999.

Hamidullah, Muhammad. *Documents sur la Diplomatie a l'Epoque du Prophete et des Khalifes Orthodoxes.* Paris: G.P. Masionneuve, 1935.

―――. *The Muslim Conduct of State.* Lahore: S. Ashraf, 1961.

Hashmi, Sohail. "Interpreting the Islamic Ethics of War and Peace." In *The Ethics of War and Peace: Religious and Secular Perspectives,* ed. Terry Nardin. Princeton, NJ: Princeton University Press, 1996.

Hassan, Riffat. "The Role of Women as Agents of Change and Development in Pakistan." *Human Rights Quarterly,* vol. 3, no. 3 (1981), 68–75.

―――. "On Human Rights and the Qur'anic Perspective." In *Human Rights in Religious Traditions,* ed. Arlene Swidler. New York: Pilgrim Press, 1982.

Hayek, Friedrich von. "The Use of Knowledge in Society." *American Economic Review*, vol. 35, no. 4 (1945), 519–30.

Henkin, Louis. *The Rights of Man Today*. Boulder, CO: Westview Press, 1978.

Hersch, Jeanne, ed. *Le droit d'être un homme*. New York: UNESCO Publications, 1968.

Hirschman, Albert. *Rival Views of Market Society and Other Recent Essays*. New York: Viking Penguin, 1986.

Hitti, Philip K. *History of the Arabs*. New York: St. Martin's Press, 1970.

Hodgson, Marshall. *The Venture of Islam*. Chicago: The University of Chicago Press, 1974.

Holt, P.M., Ann K.S. Lambton, and Bernard Lewis, eds. *The Cambridge History of Islam, Islamic Society and Civilization*, vol. 2B. Cambridge: Cambridge University Press, 1982.

Hourani, Albert. *Arabic Thought in the Liberal Age, 1798–1939*, 2nd ed. New York: Cambridge University Press, 1983.

Huntington, Samuel. *The Clash of Civilizations and the Remaking of World Order*. New York: Touchstone, 1997.

Hutchings, Kimberly. "Feminism, Universalism, and Ethics of International Politics." In *Women, Culture, and International Relations*, ed. V. Jabri and E. O'Gorman. Boulder: Lynne Rienner Publishers, 1999.

Hyman, Arthur. "Jewish Philosophy in the Islamic World." In *History of Islamic Philosophy*, ed. S.H. Nasr and Oliver Leaman. London: Routledge, 1996.

Ibish, Yusuf. "Economic Institutions." In *The Islamic City: Selected Papers from the Colloquium Held at the Middle East Centre, Faculty of Oriental Studies in Cambridge, United Kingdom*, ed. R.B. Serjeant. Paris: UNESCO, 1980.

International Crisis Group. *Southern Thailand: Insurgency—Not Jihad*. Report no. 98 (May 18), Brussels, 2007.

International Crisis Group. *Southern Thailand: Problem with Paramilitaries in Asia*. Report no. 140 (October 23), Brussels, 2005.

Iqbal, Mohammed. *The Reconstruction of Religious Thought in Islam*. Lahore: Institute of Islamic Culture, 1986.

Jansen, Johannes J.G. *The Neglected Duty: The Creed of Sadat's Assassins and Islamic Resurgence in the Middle East*. New York: Macmillan Publishing Company, 1986.

Jayyusi, Salma Khadra, and Manuela Marin, eds. *The Legacy of Muslim Spain*. Leiden: E.J. Brill, 1992.

Johnston, Douglas, and Cynthia Sampson. *Religion: The Missing Dimension of Statecraft*. New York: Oxford University Press, 1994.

Juergensmeyer, Mark. *Terror in the Mind of God: The Global Rise of Religious Violence*. Berkeley, CA: University of California Press, 2000.

Kadayifci-Orellana, Ayse S. *Standing on an Isthmus: Islamic Narratives of War and Peace in Palestinian Territories*. Lanham, MD: Lexington Books, 2007.

Kalin, Ibrahim. "Roots of Misconception: Euro-American Perceptions of Islam Before and After 9/11." In *Islam, Fundamentalism, and the Betrayal of Tradition*, ed. Joseph Lumbard. Bloomington, IN: World Wisdom, 2004.

Kant, Immanuel. *The Philosophy of Law: An Exposition of the Fundamental Principles of Jurisprudence as the Science of Right*, trans. W. Hastle. Clifton, NJ: Augustus M. Kelley, 1974 [1887].

Keeble, Brian. *Art: For Whom and For What?* Ipswich, UK: Golgonooza Press, 1998.

Khan, Majid Ali. "A Comparative Study of the Universal Declaration of Human Rights and Declaration of Human Rights in Islam." *Islam and the Modern Age*, vol. 22, no. 3 (1991), 168–93.

Keddie, Nikki R. *Jamal al-Din al-Afghani: A Political Biography*. Berkeley, CA: University of California Press, 1972.

———. 1981. *Roots of Revolution*. New Haven, CT: Yale University Press.

Kelsay, John. *Islam and War: A Study in Comparative Ethics*. Louisville, KY: Westminster/John Knox Press, 1993.

Kerr, Malcolm. *Islamic Reform*. Oxford: Oxford University Press, 1966.

Khadduri, Majid. *The Islamic Law of Nations: Shaybani's Siyar*. Baltimore: The John Hopkins University Press, 1966.

———. *Political Trends in the Arab World*. Baltimore: The Johns Hopkins University Press, 1970.

Khan, Muhammad Zafrullah. *Islam and Human Rights*, 4th ed. UK: Islamic International Publications, 1989.

Kinross, Lord. *The Ottoman Centuries: The Rise and Fall of the Turkish Empire*. New York: Morrow Quill, 1977.

Kishtainy, Khalid. "A Violent and Nonviolent Struggle in Arab History." In *Arab Nonviolent Political Struggle in the Middle East*, ed. R.E. Crow, P. Grant, and S.E. Ibrahim. Boulder: Lynne Reinner Publishers, 1990.

Knox, T.M., trans. *Hegel's Philosophy of Rights*. Oxford: The Clarendon Press, 1965.

Kraemer, Joel L. "The *Jihad* of the *Falasifa*." *Jerusalem Studies in Arabic and Islam*, vol. 10 (1987), 293–312.

Kuran, Timur. *Islam and Mammon: The Economic Predicaments of Islamism*. Princeton, NJ: Princeton University Press, 2004.

Lahiji, Abdol-Karim. "Constitutionalism and Clerical Authority." In *Authority and Political Culture in Shi'ism*, ed. Amir Arjomand. Albany: State University of New York Press, 1988.

Larouni, Abdallah. *The Crisis of the Arab Intellectual: The Traditionalism or Historicism*, trans. Diamid Cammell. Berkeley, CA: University of California Press, 1976.

Layish, Aharon. "The Contribution of the Modernists to the Secularization of Islamic Law." *Middle Eastern Studies*, vol. 14, no. 3 (1978), 263–77.

LeBaron, Michelle. *Bridging Cultural Conflicts: A New Approach for a Changing World*. Hoboken, NJ: Jossey-Bass, 2003.

Lederach, J.P. *Preparing for Peace: Conflict Transformation across Cultures*. Syracuse: Syracuse University Press, 1995.

———. *Peacebuilding in Divided Societies*. Syracuse: Syracuse University Press, 1997.

Lewis, Bernard. "The Roots of Muslim Rage." *The Atlantic Monthly* (September 1990), 47–60.

———. "Islam and Liberal Democracy." *The Atlantic Monthly* (February 1993), 89.

Lee, Steven. "A Positive Concept of Peace." In *The Causes of Quarrel: Essays on Peace, War, and Thomas Hobbes*, ed. Peter Caws. Boston: Beacon Press, 1989.

Lindbom, Tage. *The Tares and the Good Grain*. Macon, GA: Mercer University Press, 1982.

Lindsey, Linda. *Gender Roles: A Sociological Perspective*, 4th ed. New York: Princeton Hall, 2004.

Lings, Martin. *Muhammad: His Life Based on the Earliest Sources*. Rochester, VT: Inner Traditions International, 1983.

Little, David. *Peacemakers in Action: Profiles of Religion in Conflict Resolution*. Cambridge: Cambridge University Press, 2006.

Little, David, and Scott Appleby. "A Moment of Opportunity." In *Religion and Peacemaking*, ed. Harold Coward and Gordon S. Smith. Albany: State University of New York Press, 2004.

Lutz, Mark, and Kenneth Lux. *The Challenge of Humanistic Economics*. Menlo Park, CA: The Benjamin/Cummings Publishing Company, 1979.

Maat, Bob. "Dhammayietra, Walk of Peace." *The Catholic Worker* (May 1995), 22.

Mack, Beverly B., and Jean Boyd. *One Woman's Jihad: Nana Asma'u, Scholar and Scribe*. Bloomington, IN: Indiana University Press, 2000.

Mahmasani, Subhi. "Adaptation of Islamic Jurisprudence to Modern Social Needs." In *Islam in Transition: Muslim Perspectives*, ed. John J.

Donohue and John L. Esposito. New York: Oxford University Press, 1982.

Mann, V.B., T.F. Glick, and J.D. Dodds, eds. *Convivencia: Jews, Muslims, and Christians in Medieval Spain.* New York: The Jewish Museum, 1992.

Mansur, Ibn. *Lisan al-'Arab.* Beirut: Dar al-Kutub al-'Ilmiyyah, 1993.

Martin, Richard. "The Religious Foundations of War, Peace, and Statecraft in Islam." In *Just War and Jihad: Historical and Theoretical Perspectives on War and Peace in Western and Islamic Traditions,* ed. John Kelsay and James Turner Johnson. New York: Greenwood Press, 1991.

Marty, Martin E. "Religious Dimensions of Human Rights." In *Religious Human Rights in Global Perspectives,* ed. John Witte and Johan D. van der Vyver. The Hague: Martinus Nijhoff, 1996.

Marty, Martin, and Scott Appleby. *The Glory and the Power: The Fundamentalist Challenge to the Modern World.* Boston: Beacon Press, 1992.

Mernissi, Fatima. "Education in the Traditional Arts and Crafts and the Cultural Heritage of Islam." In *Philosophy, Literature, and Fine Arts,* ed. Seyyed Hossein Nasr. Jeddah, Saudi Arabia: King Abdulaziz University, 1982.

———. "Muslim Women and Fundamentalism." *Middle East Report,* vol. 153 (1988), 8–11.

Midlarsky, Manus I. "Democracy and Islam: Implications for Civilizational Conflict and the Democratic Peace." *International Studies Quarterly,* vol. 42, no. 3 (1998), 485–511.

Millward, Willard G. "Aspects of Modernism in Shi'a Iran." *Studia Islamica,* vol. 37 (1973), 111–28.

Mishan, Edward. *Economic Myths and the Mythology of Economics.* Atlantic Highlands, NJ: Humanities Press International, 1986.

Mojzes, Paul, ed. *Religion and the War in Bosnia.* Atlanta, GA: Scholars Press, 1998.

Morawetz, Thomas. *The Philosophy of Law: An Introduction.* New York: Macmillan, 1980.

Mortimer, Edward. *Faith and Power: The Politics of Islam.* New York: Vintage Books, 1982.

Moyser, George, ed. *Politics and Religion in the Modern World.* London: Routledge, 1991.

Muhammad, Ghazi bin. *The Sacred Origin of Sports and Culture.* Louisville, KY: Fons Vitae, 1998.

Mujtabai, Fathullaj. *Hindu Muslim Cultural Relations.* New Delhi: National Book Bureau, 1978.

Naciri, Muhammad Makki. "Judicial Aspects of Religious Liberty in Morocco." *Conscience and Liberty* (1991), 73–75.

Najjar, Fauzi M. "Democracy in Islamic Political Philosophy." *Studia Islamica*, vol. 51 (1980), 107–22.

Nasr, Seyyed Hossein. "Review of *Ethics and Economics: An Islamic Synthesis*." *Hamdard Islamicus*, no. 2 (1982), 89–91.

———. "Present Tendencies, Future Trends." In *Islam: The Religious and Political Life of a World Community*, ed. Marjorie Kelly. New York: Praeger, 1984.

———. "Whither Islamic Economics?" *The Islamic Quarterly*, vol. 30, no. 4 (1986), 211–20.

———. *Traditional Islam in the Modern World*. London and New York: KPT, 1987.

———. "Islamization of Knowledge: A Critical Overview." International Institute of Islamic Thought Occasional Paper 17, Islamabad, Pakistan, 1992.

———. *Science and Civilization in Islam*. New York: Barnes and Noble Books, 1992.

———. *Religion and the Order of Nature*. Oxford: Oxford University Press, 1996.

———. *Islam and the Plight of Modern Man*. Chicago: Kazi Publications, 2001.

Nasr, Vali-Reza. "Religious Modernism in the Arab World, India, and Iran: The Perils and Prospects of a Discourse." *The Muslim World*, vol. 83, no. 1 (1993), 20–47.

Novak, Michael. *The Spirit of Democratic Capitalism*. New York: Simon and Schuster, 1982.

Nuwayhi, Muhammad. "A Revolution in Religious Thought." In *Islam in Transition: Muslim Perspectives*, ed. John Esposito and John Donohue. New York: Oxford University Press, 2006.

Ormsby, Eric L. *Theodicy in Islamic Thought: The Dispute over al-Ghazali's "Best of All Possible Worlds."* Princeton, NJ: Princeton University Press, 1984.

Ozdemir, M. Said. "Islam ve Siddet Risale-i Nur Perspektifi" [Islam and Violence: The Risale-i Nur Perspective]. In *Cok Kulturlu Bir Dunyada Imanli Anlamli ve Baris Icinde Yasama Pratigi: Risale-i Nur Yaklasimi* [Bringing Faith, Meaning and Peace to Life in a Multicultural World: The Risale-i Nur's Approach]. Istanbul: Nesil, 2004.

Paige, Glenn D., Sarah Gilliatt, and Chaiwat Satha-Anand, eds. *Islam and Nonviolence*. Honolulu: University of Hawaii, 1993.

Pagano, Ugo. *Work and Welfare in Economic Theory*. Oxford: Basil Blackwell, 1985.

Pagano, Ugo, and Waleed El-Ansary. "The Traditionalist Critique of Industrial Capitalism." *Sophia*, vol. 12, no. 1 (Summer 2006).

Perry, Whitall. *A Treasury of Traditional Wisdom*. Cambridge: Quinta Essentia. 1971.

Peters, Rudolph. *Islam and Colonialism: The Doctrine of Jihad in Modern History*. The Hague: Mouton Publishers, 1979.

Plantinga, Alvin. "The Free Will Defense." In *Philosophy in America*, ed. Max Black, reprinted in Baruch A. Broody, ed. *Readings in the Philosophy of Religion: An Analytical Approach*. Upper Saddle River, NJ: Prentice-Hall, 1974.

———. 1990. "God, Evil, and the Metaphysics of Freedom." In *The Problem of Evil*, ed. Marilyn M. Adams and Robert M. Adams. Oxford: Oxford University Press.

Postman, Neil. *Technopoly: The Surrender of Culture to Technology*. New York: Vintage Books, 1992.

Praamsma, L. *The Church in the Twentieth Century*. vol. 7. St. Catherine, Ontario: Paideia Press, 1981.

Putterman, Louis. *Division of Labor and Welfare: An Introduction to Economic Systems*. Oxford: Oxford University Press, 1990.

Rahman, Fazlur. "Islamic Modernism: Its Scope, Methods, and Alternatives." *International Journal of Middle East Studies*, vol. 1 (1970), 230–67.

———. *Islam*, 2nd ed. Chicago: University of Chicago Press, 1979.

———. *Islam and Modernity: Transformation of an Intellectual Tradition*. Chicago: University of Chicago Press, 1982.

———. "Status of Women in the Qur'an." In *Women and Revolution in Iran*, ed. Guity Nashat. Boulder, CO: Westview Press, 1983.

Rahnema, Ali. *Pioneers of Islamic Revival*. London: Zed, 1994.

Rajaee, Farhang. "Islam and Modernity: The Reconstruction of an Alternative Shi'ite Islamic Worldview in Iran." In *Fundamentalism and Society*, ed. Martin E. Marty and R. Scott Appleby. Chicago: University of Chicago Press, 1993.

Ramet, Sabrina Petra. "Nationalism and the Idiocy of the Countryside: The Case of Serbia." *Ethnic and Racial Studies*, vol. 19, no. 1 (1996), 70–87.

Rosenthal, Franz. *Knowledge Triumphant: The Concept of Knowledge in Medieval Islam*. Leiden: E.J. Brill, 1970.

———. *The Classical Heritage in Islam*. London: Routledge, 1975.

———. "Political Justice and the Just Ruler." In *Religion and Government in the World of Islam*, ed. Joel Kraemer and Ilai Alon. Tel-Aviv: Tel-Aviv University, 1983.

Ruddick, Sarah. *Maternal Thinking: Toward a Politics of Peace*. London: Women's Press, 1990.

Russett, Bruce M., John R. O'Neal, and Michaelene Cox. "Clash of Civilizations, or Realism and Liberalism Déjà Vu? Some Evidence." *Journal of Peace Research*, vol. 37, no. 5 (2000), 583.

Sachedina, Abdulaziz A. "The Development of Jihad in Islamic Revelation and History." In *Cross, Crescent, and Sword: The Justification and Limitation of War in Western and Islamic Tradition,* ed. James Turner Johnson and John Kelsay. New York: Greenwood Press, 1990.

———. "Justification for Violence in Islam." In *War and Its Discontents: Pacifism and Quietism in the Abrahamic Traditions,* ed. J.P. Burn. Washington, DC: Georgetown University Press, 1996.

———. *The Islamic Roots of Democratic Pluralism.* Oxford: Oxford University Press, 2007.

Sadra, Mulla. *Al-Hikmat al-Muta'aliyah fi 'l-Asfar al-'Aqliyyah al-Arba'ah.* Beirut: Dar Ihya' al-Turath al-'Arabi, 1981.

Sahas, Daniel J. *John of Damascus on Islam: The "Heresy of the Ishmaelites."* Leiden: E.J. Brill, 1972.

Said, Abdul Aziz, Nathan C. Funk, and Ayse Kadayifici, eds. *Peace and Conflict Resolution in Islam: Precept and Practice.* Lanham, MD: University Press of America, 2001.

Said, Abdul Aziz, Nathan C. Funk, Ayse Kadayifici, and Meena Sharify-Funk, eds. *Cultural Diversity and Islam.* Lanham, MD: University Press of America, 2003.

Said, Edward. *Covering Islam.* New York: Pantheon Books, 1981.

Saiyidain, K.G. *Islam, the Religion of Peace: Islam and Modern Age Society.* New Delhi: Leaders Press, 1976.

Sampson, Cynthia, and John Paul Ledrach, eds. *From the Ground Up: Mennonite Contributions to International Peacebuilding.* New York: Oxford University Press, 2000.

Saritoprak, Zeki. "An Islamic Approach to Peace and Nonviolence: A Turkish Experience." *The Muslim World*, vol. 95, no. 3 (2005), 413–27.

Satha-Anand, Chaiwat. "The Nonviolent Crescent: Eight Theses on Muslim Nonviolent Actions." In *Islam and Nonviolence,* ed. G. Paige, C. Satha-Anand, and S. Gilliat. Honolulu: University of Hawaii, 1993.

Sayeed, Khalid Bin. *Western Dominance and Political Islam: Challenge and Response.* New York: Oxford University Press, 1995.

Schacht, Joseph. *An Introduction to Islamic Law.* Oxford: Clarendon, 1964.

Schelling, Thomas C. *Micromotives and Macrobehavior.* New York: Norton, 1978.

Schimmel, Annemarie. *Islam in the Indian Subcontinent.* Leiden: E.J. Brill, 1980.

Schumacher, E.F. *Good Work*. New York: Harper & Row, 1979.

———. *Small is Beautiful: Economics as if People Mattered*. New York: Harper & Row, 1989.

———. *This I Believe and Other Essays*. Foxhole, Dartington: Green Books, 1997.

Schuon, Frithjof. *In the Face of the Absolute*. Bloomington, IN: World Wisdom Books, 1989.

———. *Castes and Races*. Middlesex: Perennial Books, 1982.

Shalaby, Ibrahim. "Islam and Peace." *Journal of Religious Thought*, no. 44 (1978), 42–49.

Shawcross, William. *Deliver Us From Evil: Peacekeepers, Warlords, and a World of Endless Conflict*. Uppsala, Sweden: Life and Peace Institute, 1995.

Shawkani, Imam. *Fath al-Qadir*, abridged by Sulayman 'Abd Allah al-Ashqar. Kuwait: Shirkat Dhat Salasil, 1988.

Shayegan, Daryush. *Qu'est-ce qu'une revolution religieuse*. Paris: Les presses d'aujourd'hui, 1982.

Shehadi, Fadlou. *Ghazali's Unique Unknowable God*. Leiden: E.J. Brill, 1964.

Siddiqi, Muhammad Nejatullah. *Muslim Economic Thinking: A Survey of Contemporary Literature*. Leicester: The Islamic Foundation, 1981.

Siddiqi, Muhammad Zubayr. *Hadith Literature: Its Origin, Development, and Special Features*. Cambridge: Islamic Texts Society, 1993.

Sina, Ibn. *Kitab al-Najat*, ed. Majid Fakhry. Beirut: Dar al-Ufuq al-Jadidah, 1985.

———. *Al-Mubahathat*, ed. Muhsin Bidarfar. Qom: Intisharat-i Bidar, 1994.

Smock, David. ed. *Religious Contributions to Peacemaking When Religion Brings Peace, Not War*. Washington, DC: United States Institute of Peace, 2006.

Smith, Wolfgang. "*Sophia Perennis* and Modern Science." In *The Philosophy of Seyyed Hossein Nasr (Library of Living Philosophers)*, ed. Randall Auxier, Lucian W. Stone, and Lewis Edwin Hahn. Chicago: Open Court Publishing, 2000.

———. *The Quantum Enigma: Finding the Hidden Key*. Ghent, NY: Sophia Perennis, 2005.

Soroush, Abdolkarim. 1990. *Qabz va Bast-i Tiorik-i Shari'at* [The Theory of Expansion and Contraction of Religious Knowledge]. Tehran: Serat, 1990.

———. *Reason, Freedom, and Democracy in Islam: The Essential Writings of Abdulkarim Soroush*, ed. Mahmoud Sadri and Ahmad Sadri. Oxford: Oxford University Press, 2000.

Stowasser, Barbara Freyer. "The Status of Women in Early Islam." In *Muslim Women*, ed. Freda Hussain. London: Croom Helm, 1984.

———. *Women in the Qur'an, Traditions, and Interpretation.* Oxford: Oxford University Press, 1994.

Sworder, Roger. "The Desacralization of Work." In *The Betrayal of Tradition: Essays on the Spiritual Crisis of Modernity,* ed. Harry Oldmeadow. Bloomington, IN: World Wisdom Books, 2005.

Sylyomovics, Susan. "'Hassiba Ben Bouali, If You Could See Our Algeria': Women and Public Space in Algeria." *Middle East Report,* no. 192 (January–February 1995), 8–13.

Talbi, Mohamed, and Maurice Bucaille. *Réflexions sur le Coran.* Paris: Seghers, 1989.

Taymiyya, Ibn. *Al-Siyasa al-Shar'iyya fi Islah al-Ra'iy wa al-Ra'iyya,* ed. Muhammad Mubarak, trans. Omar Farrukh as *Ibn Taimyya on Public and Private Law in Islam.* Beirut: Khayats, 1966.

Thompson, Henry. *World Religion in War and Peace.* Jefferson, NC: McFarland & Company, 1988.

Tibi, Bassam. "The Iranian Revolution and the Arabs: The Quest for Islamic Identity and Search for an Islamic System of Government." *Arab Studies Quarterly,* vol. 8, no. 1 (Winter 1986), 29–44.

———. *The Crisis of Modern Islam: A Pre-Industrial Culture in the Scientific-Technological Age,* trans. Judith von Sivers. Salt Lake City: University of Utah Press, 1988.

———. 1996. "War and Peace in Islam." In *The Ethics of War and Peace: Religious and Secular Perspectives,* ed. Terry Nardin. Princeton, NJ: Princeton University Press.

Tickner, J. Anne. "Why Women Cannot Run the World: International Politics According to Francis Fukuyama." *International Studies Review,* vol. 1, no. 3 (1999), 3–11.

Tritton, A.S. *The Caliphs and Their Non-Muslim Subjects.* London: Oxford University Press, 1930.

Tusi, Nasir al-Din. *The Nasirean Ethics,* trans. G.M. Wickens. London: G. Allen & Unwin, 1964.

Vakili, Valla. *Debating Religion and Politics in Iran: The Political Thought of Abdulkarim Soroush.* New York: Council on Foreign Relations, 1996.

Vincent, R.J. *Human Rights and International Relations.* Cambridge: Cambridge University Press, 1986.

Voll. John O. *Islam: Continuity and Change in the Modern World.* Boulder, CO: Westview Press, 1982.

Voll, John O., and John Esposito. "Islam's Democratic Essence." *Middle East Quarterly,* vol. 1, no. 3 (1994), 3–11.

Voll, John O., and John Esposito. "Renewal and Reform." In *The Oxford History of Islam,* ed. John Esposito. Oxford: Oxford University Press, 2000.

Waardenburg, Jacques. "World Religions as Seen in the Light of Islam." In *Islam Past Influence and Present Challenge,* ed. A.T. Welch and P. Cachia. Edinburgh: Edinburgh University Press, 1979.

———. "Islam as a Vehicle of Protest." In *Islamic Dilemmas: Reformers, Nationalists, and Industrialization,* ed. Ernest Gellner. Berlin: Mouton Publishers, 1985.

———. *Muslims and Others: Relations in Context.* New York: Walter de Gruyter, 2003.

Wadud, Amina. *Qur'an and Women: Rereading the Sacred Text from a Woman's Perspective.* New York: Oxford University Press, 1999.

Walzer, Michael. *The Revolution of Saints: A Study in the Origins of Radical Politics.* Cambridge, MA: Harvard University Press, 1965.

Watt, William M. *The Faith and Practice of al-Ghazali.* Chicago: Kazi, 1982.

———. *Islamic Philosophy and Theology.* Edinburgh: Edinburgh University Press, 1985.

Waylen, Georgina. *Gender in Third World Politics.* Berkshire, UK: McGraw-Hill, 1996.

Wheare, K.C. *Modern Constitutions.* London: Oxford University Press, 1966.

Wilson, Fred. *Psychological Analysis and the Philosophy of John Stuart Mill.* Toronto: University of Toronto Press, 1990.

Woolf, Virginia. *Three Guineas.* San Diego: Harvest Books, 1963.

Wortley Montagu, Lady Mary. *The Selected Letters of Lady Mary Wortley Montagu.* New York: St. Martin's Press, 1971, cited in Ferashteh Nouraie-Simone, *On Shifting Ground: Muslim Women in the Global Era,* New York: Feminist Press, 2005.

Zaideh, Farhat. *Lawyers, the Rule of Law, and Liberalism in Modern Egypt.* Stanford: Hoover Institution, 1968.

Zali, Munawir Sjad. *Islam and Governmental System: Teachings, History, and the Reflections.* Jakarta: INIS, 1991.

Zartman, William, and J. Lewis Rasmussen, eds. *Peacemaking in International Conflict: Methods and Techniques.* Washington, DC: United States Institute of Peace, 1997.

Zilfi, C. "*Vaizan* and *Ulema* in the Kadizadeli Era." Proceedings of the Tenth Congress of the Turkish Historical Society, Ankara, Turkey, 1994, 2493–2500.

Index

295

Contributors

Mohammed Abu-Nimer is an expert on Arab-Jewish dialogue and peace work in conflict zone areas. He has worked extensively in the Middle East, Sri Lanka, and Mindanao. His project captures the general and specific lessons, dynamics, and challenges associated with conducting evaluations of peacebuilding projects in conflict areas. He draws from the hundreds of training and dialogue workshops and the many evaluation teams he has led in a host of conflict areas across the globe. Abu-Nimer is the director of the Peacebuilding and Development Institute at American University. He is also the director and founder of Salam: Peacebuilding and Justice Institute and has been at American University's School of International Service since 1997. Abu-Nimer is a recipient of the 2005 Morton Deutsch Award from the Society for the Study of Peace, Conflict, and Violence and a co-founder of the Journal of Peacebuilding and Development. He holds a Ph.D. in conflict resolution from George Mason University.

Asma Afsaruddin is professor of Arabic and Islamic Studies at Indiana University. Her fields of specialization are the religious and political thought of Islam, Qur'an and hadith studies, Islamic intellectual history, and gender studies. She is the author of *The First Muslims: History and Memory, Excellence and Precedence: Medieval Islamic Discourse on Legitimate Leadership,* the editor of *Hermaneutics and Honor: Negotiation of Female "Public" Space in Islamic/ate Societies* and co-editor (with Mathias Zahniser) *of Humanism, Culture, and Language in the Near East : Essays in Honor of Georg Krotkoff.* She has also written over fifty research articles, book chapters, and encyclopedia entries on various aspects of Islamic thought and has lectured widely in this country and abroad. Afsaruddin is currently serving on the editorial boards of the *Routledge Encyclopedia of Medieval Islamic Civilization* and the *Bulletin of the Middle East Studies Association.* She was a visiting scholar at the Centre for Islamic Studies at the School for Oriental and African Studies, London, UK, and was previously a fellow at the American Research Center of Egypt in Cairo and the American Research Institute of Turkey in Istanbul.

Waleed El-Ansary is Assistant Professor of Islamic Studies, Department of Religious Studies at the University of South Carolina. He received his Ph.D. in the Human Sciences with concentration in Islamic Studies from George Washington University and his M.A. in Economics from the University of Maryland. He is an advisor to the Grand Mufti of Egypt as well as the Canadian Military Chaplains and is involved in interfaith dialog. His research focuses on the relationship between religion, science, and economics, and his publications include *The Economics of Terrorism: How bin Laden is Changing the Rules of the Game.*

Reza Eslami-Somea is an Associate Professor of Human Rights and International Law at Shahid Beheshti University's Faculty of Law in Tehran, Iran. He earned his first doctorate in Iran and his second from McGill University and Universite de Montreal, Canada, and has written on human rights, Islamic law, public freedoms and rights of women and minorities. He regularly attends conferences and seminars on democracy and peace education in the US, Europe and the Middle East, and organizes workshops for NGOs and community-based organizations in the region. He also teaches at United Nations University for Peace in Costa Rica, and is the UNDP consultant on human rights treaty reporting in Afghanistan. He is affiliated with the UNESCO Chair for Human Rights, Peace and Democracy at Shahid Beheshti University.

Qamar-ul Huda is trained in Islamic studies and Comparative Religion, and is the Senior Program Officer in the Religion and Peacemaking Program at the United States Institute of Peace. Dr. Huda's area of interest is in Islamic theology, intellectual history, ethics, and peacemaking. He examines comparative ethics, the language of violence, conflict resolution and non-violence in Islam. His research is on comparative Sunni-Shi'ite interpretations of social justice, ethics, dialogue, and the ways in which the notion of justice is appropriated. Dr. Huda has examined the production of religious knowledge, self-identity, the diversity of religious practices and peacemaking in *Striving for Divine Union: Spiritual Exercises for Suhrawardi Sufis* (RoutledgeCurzon). He has written on Islamic peacemaking, mystical treatises, inter-faith dialogue, and contemporary West and Islamic relations. He co-authored with David Smock a USIP Special Report entitled *Islamic Peacemaking Since 9/11.* He served as the Special Issue Editor of *The Muslim*

World on "Qawwali: Poetry, Performance and Politics." Dr. Huda earned his doctorate in Islamic intellectual history from University of California, Los Angeles, his Bachelor of Arts degree from Colgate University in International Relations and Comparative Religion, and studied in Islamic seminaries.

Asna Husin was born and raised in Aceh, Indonesia, and graduated in teaching Arabic from *Ar-Raniry State Institute for Islamic Studies* (IAIN). She received two Fulbright Scholarships for her MA in Middle Eastern studies from Harvard University (1992), and her PhD in religious studies from Columbia University (1998). After completing her doctorate, she was a visiting fellow at the *Center for the Study of Human Rights* at Columbia University. Dr. Husin directed the first Women's Program (1998–2000) for the World Conference on Religion and Peace (WCRP) in New York City. Dr. Husin returned to Aceh and established the *Peace Education Program* (*Program Pendidikan Damia* – PPD) as an independent affiliate of the NGO *Nonviolence International.* Now in its eighth year, PPD has developed curriculum for high schools throughout Aceh, currently reaching two hundred forty seven schools, and an Ulama Peace Manual being implemented in forty Islamic boarding schools. She also teaches at *Ar-Raniry State Institute for Islamic Studies,* serves on Aceh's *Provincial Commission on Education,* and has advised Aceh's Governor on educational and social issues. Asna has published articles on peace education, human rights and gender issues, and has presented papers at international conferences in Sidney, New Delhi, Oslo, Vancouver, Cologne and Rabat.

Ayse Kadayifci-Orellana is Assistant Professor at American University. She is the Associate Director and founding member of The Salam Institute for Peace and Justice, a non-profit organization for research, education, and practice in Washington, DC. The Salam Institute work on issues related to conflict resolution, nonviolence, and development with a focus on bridging differences between Muslim and non-Muslim communities. Dr. Kadayifci-Orellana is the author *Standing On an Isthmus: Islamic Narratives of War and Peace in the Palestinian Territories* and co-author of *Anthology on Islam and Peace and Conflict Resolution in Islam: Precept and Practice.* She has also written various book chapters and journal articles on mediation and peace building, religion and conflict resolution, Islamic approaches to war and peace, and Islam and nonviolence. She has facilitated dialogues and conflict resolution workshops between Israelis and Palestinians, conducted Islamic conflict resolution training workshops to imams and Muslim youth leaders in the US. She received her Ph.D. from American University and earned a Master's degree in Conflict Analysis from University of Kent in Canterbury, England.

Ibrahim Kalin received his Ph. D. from the George Washington University, Washington DC. As a broadly trained scholar of Islamic studies, he teaches a number of courses on Islamic history and culture at Georgetown University. His field of concentration is post-Avicennan Islamic philosophy with research interests in Ottoman intellectual history, interfaith relations, and comparative philosophy. Dr. Kalin has published widely on Islamic philosophy and the relations between Islam and the West. His book *Knowledge in Later Islamic Philosophy: Mulla Sadra on Existence, Intellect and Intuition* is forthcoming and being published by Oxford University Press. His book *Islam and the West* (published in Turkish) has won the 2007 Writers Association of Turkey award for best book. He has also co-authored a major study on the Turkish perceptions of the West. He has contributed to several encyclopedias including *MacMillan Encyclopedia of Philosophy 2nd Edition, Encyclopedia of Religion 2nd Edition, Biographical Encyclopedia of Islamic Philosophy* and the *Oxford Encyclopedia of the Islamic World*. He is a faculty member at Georgetown University and is the founding-director of the SETA Foundation for Political, Economic and Social Research based in Ankara, Turkey. Dr. Kalin is among the signatories of the *Common Word* (www.acommonword.com), a major initiative to improve Muslim-Christian relations.

Zeki Saritoprak is the Nursi Chair in Islamic Studies at John Carroll University. He holds a Ph.D. in Islamic Theology from the University of Marmara, Turkey. He earned his Master's degree in Islamic Theology and Philosophy, and his B.A. in Divinity from the same university. He studied Arabic language for several years in Cairo while doing research for his dissertation in Islamic Theology, entitled *The Antichrist (al-Dajjal)*. He is the Founder and former President of the Rumi Forum for Interfaith Dialogue in Washington, D.C. Dr. Saritoprak is the author of several books and academic articles in Turkish, English, and Arabic. He has served as guest editor for Special Issues of *The Muslim World* on Fethullah Gülen and *Islam and Christian-Muslim Relations* on Bediüzzaman Said Nursi. His next book, *Islam and the Eschatological Imagination: Jesus, the Mahdi and al-Dajjal*, is forthcoming from the University Press of Florida. He has courses at Harran University (Turkey), Georgetown University, the Catholic University of America, and Berry College in Rome, Georgia.

Meena Sharify-Funk received her doctorate from American University and is currently an Assistant Professor for the Religion and Culture Department at Wilfird Laurier University in Canada. Her area of expertise is in Islamic studies with a focus on contemporary Muslim thought and identity. She is interested in modern Muslim engagement with classical debates in Islamic intellectual history as well as with recent developments in Western thought and culture. Dr. Sharify-Funk has written and presented a number of articles and papers on women and Islam, Islamic hermeneutics, and the role of cultural and religious factors in peacemaking. She recently published *Encountering the Transnational: Women, Islam, and the Politics of Interpretation.* She has co-edited two books, *Cultural Diversity and Islam* and *Contemporary Islam: Dynamic, Not Static.*

United States
Institute of Peace Press

Since its inception, the United States Institute of Peace Press has published over 150 books on the prevention, management, and peaceful resolution of international conflicts—among them such venerable titles as Raymond Cohen's *Negotiating Across Cultures*; *Leashing the Dogs of War*, edited by Chester A. Crocker, Fen Osler Hampson, and Pamela Aall; I. William Zartman's *Peacemaking and International Conflict*; and *American Negotiating Behavior*, by Richard H. Solomon and Nigel Quinney. All our books arise from research and fieldwork sponsored by the Institute's many programs. In keeping with the best traditions of scholarly publishing, each volume undergoes thorough internal review and blind peer review by external subject experts to ensure that the research, scholarship, and conclusions are balanced, relevant, and sound. As the Institute prepares to move to its new headquarters on the National Mall in Washington, D.C., the Press is committed to extending the reach of the Institute's work by continuing to publish significant and sustainable works for practitioners, scholars, diplomats, and students.

Valerie Norville
Director

About the
United States Institute of Peace

The United States Institute of Peace is an independent, nonpartisan institution established and funded by Congress. The Institute provides analysis, training, and tools to help prevent, manage, and end violent international conflicts, promote stability, and professionalize the field of peacebuilding.

Chairman of the Board: J. Robinson West
Vice Chairman: George E. Moose
President: Richard H. Solomon
Executive Vice President: Tara Sonenshine
Chief Financial Officer: Michael Graham

Board of Directors

J. Robinson West (Chair), Chairman, PFC Energy, Washington, D.C.

George E. Moose (Vice Chairman), Adjunct Professor of Practice, The George Washington University

Anne H. Cahn, Former Scholar in Residence, American University

Chester A. Crocker, James R. Schlesinger Professor of Strategic Studies, School of Foreign Service, Georgetown University

Ikram U. Khan, President, Quality Care Consultants, LLC

Kerry Kennedy, Human Rights Activist

Stephen D. Krasner, Graham H. Stuart Professor of International Relations, Stanford University

Jeremy A. Rabkin, Professor, George Mason School of Law